Orality and Literacy in Early Christianity

Biblical Performance Criticism Series

Orality, Memory, Translation, Rhetoric, Discourse

The ancient societies of the Bible were overwhelmingly oral. People originally experienced the traditions now in the Bible as oral performances. Focusing on the ancient performance of biblical traditions enables us to shift academic work on the Bible from the mentality of a modern print culture to that of an oral/scribal culture. Conceived broadly, biblical performance criticism embraces many methods as means to reframe the biblical materials in the context of traditional oral cultures, construct scenarios of ancient performances, learn from contemporary performances of these materials, and reinterpret biblical writings accordingly. The result is a foundational paradigm shift that reconfigures traditional disciplines and employs fresh biblical methodologies such as theater studies, speech-act theory, and performance studies. The emerging research of many scholars in this field of study, the development of working groups in scholarly societies, and the appearance of conferences on orality and literacy make it timely to inaugurate this series. For further information on biblical performance criticism, go to www.biblicalperformancecriticism.org.

Books in the Series

Holly Hearon and Philip Ruge-Jones, editors
The Bible in Ancient and Modern Media: Story and Performance

James Maxey
From Orality to Orality: A New Paradigm for Contextual Translation of the Bible

Antoinette Clark Wire
The Case for Mark Composed in Performance

Robert D. Miller II, SFO
Oral Tradition in Ancient Israel

Pieter J. J. Botha
Orality and Literacy in Early Christianity

Forthcoming

David Rhoads
Biblical Performance Criticism: An Emerging Discipline in New Testament Studies

Joanna Dewey
Orality, Scribality, and the Gospel of Mark

Orality and Literacy in Early Christianity

PIETER J. J. BOTHA

CASCADE *Books* · Eugene, Oregon

ORALITY AND LITERACY IN EARLY CHRISTIANITY

Performance Biblical Criticism Series 5

Cascade Books
An Imprint of Wipf and Stock Publishers
199 W. 8th Ave., Suite 3
Eugene, OR 97401

www.wipfandstock.com

ISBN 13: 978-1-60608-898-2

Cataloging-in-Publication data:

Botha, Pieter J. J.

Orality and literacy in early Christianity / Pieter J. J. Botha.

Biblical Performance Criticism 5

xvi + 302 p.; 23 cm—Includes bibliographical references and index.

ISBN 13: 978-1-60608-898-2

1. Bible—N.T.—Criticism, interpretation, etc. 2. Bible. N.T.—Performance criticism. 3. Oral tradition. 4. Folklore in the Bible. I. Title. II. Series.

BS2555.5 B68 2012

Manufactured in the USA

To my father, in loving memory
Gert Botha
(12 July 1932—20 March 2012)

Contents

Acknowlegments

The author and the publisher gratefully acknowledge the permission to publish the following articles and essays in revised form.

"Mute Manuscripts: Analyzing a Neglected Aspect of Ancient Communication." *Theologia Evangelica* 23 (1990) 35–47.

"Mark's Story as Oral Traditional Literature: Rethinking the Transmission of Some Traditions about Jesus." *Hervormde Teologiese Studies* 47 (1991) 304–31.

"Greco-Roman Literacy as Setting for New Testament Writings." *Neotestamentica* 26 (1992) 195–215.

"Letter Writing and Oral Communication in Antiquity: Suggested Implications for the Interpretation of Paul's Letter to the Galatians." *Scriptura* 42 (1992) 17–34.

"Living Voice and Lifeless Letters: Reserve Towards Writing in the Graeco-Roman World." *Hervormde Teologiese Studies* 49 (1993) 742–59.

"The Social Dynamics of the Early Transmission of the Jesus Tradition." *Neotestamentica* 27 (1993) 205–31.

"The Verbal Art of the Pauline Letters: Rhetoric, Performance and Presence." In *Rhetoric and the New Testament: Essays from the 1992 Heidelberg Conference*, edited by Stanley E. Porter and Thomas H. Olbricht, 409–28. JSNT Supplements 90. Sheffield: Sheffield Academic, 1993.

"Paul and Gossip: A Social Mechanism in Early Christian Communities." *Neotestamentica* 32 (1998) 267–88.

"New Testament Texts in the Context of Reading Practices of the Roman Period: The Role of Memory and Performance." *Scriptura* 90 (2005) 621–40.

"'I Am Writing This with My Own Hand . . .': Writing in New Testament Times." *Verbum et Ecclesia* 30/2 (2009) 1–11.

"Authorship in Historical Perspective and Its Bearing on New Testament and Early Christian Texts and Contexts." *Scriptura* 102 (2009) 495–508.

Introduction

Today we are inundated with copies. It is not just books and articles that have proliferated in our worlds, but virtually everything we use. "We are so surrounded by facsimiles and reproductions that it is difficult for us to imagine a world with limited means of making copies."[1] Antiquity was such a world: one of endless variations, but almost never one of precise reproduction. It must have been a world with a continuing challenge to memory; access to originals (and especially textual ones) was rarely possible. Having to rely on memory, without copies, made antiquity an *oral* world to an extent difficult to appreciate today.

Antiquity did have a lot of writing. Yet, once more, circumspection is in order. Like all technologies, writing has distinct functions and implications depending on who is writing and when it occurs. In other words, it is an inappropriate assumption that because someone *wrote*, that activity is directly comparable to *our* writing today. It does not follow that differences can only lie in the content of writing. How, when, why, and what we write is determined by who we are, where we are, and what we believe ourselves to be.[2]

It is therefore better to see antiquity as a world with literacy *practices*.[3] In 1989 William Harris published an immensely learned and important study dealing with ancient literacy.[4] He focuses rather narrowly on the question of how *many* (what percentage of people) might have been able to read and write. He concluded, quite surprising at the time, not that many. Of course,

---

1. Small, "Visual Copies," 227.

2. Writing presents the intersection of culture, self-understanding and historical context; see Fishman, "Because This Is Who We Are."

3. Street, "Literacy Practices," 61: literacy practices refer to "both behaviour and conceptualisations related to the use of reading and/or writing." The term "literacy events" was coined by Heath, "No Bedtime Story," 50, to avoid an overly specific definition of literacy: "occasions in which written language is integral to the nature of the participants' interactions and their interpretive processes and strategies."

4. Harris, *Ancient Literacy*.

the underlying problem here is what we mean by *literacy*.[5] Statistical questions about Greco-Roman literacy, even if we could answer them, are not the most consequential ones to ask about ancient communicative practices.

Reading and writing, when considered as activities in and of themselves, will be misunderstood. Books are symbolic objects and they carry powerful social values. Reading and writing are events, and we need to analyze them in a wide and a deep context, searching for social and cultural qualities embedded in particular institutions and communities. They are processes involving the body in remarkable and context-specific ways. To discover them, it becomes necessary to do "thick" contextualization: to see orality and literacy in Greco-Roman antiquity as integrated aspects of a larger sociocultural whole.

It is with an eye on this that the complex and extensive research done on orality and literacy in other disciplines is emphasized in these studies. Bias brought about by *modern* literacy influences many of our current approaches. My hope is that these studies will contribute to a better understanding of communication in antiquity and thereby an improved understanding of the context of early Christianity—or at least that better questions will be asked about that context.[6]

These studies delve into what we can call, for lack of a more precise term, scribal culture. The scribal culture of antiquity exhibits a strong bias towards orality, with even literates often expressing little confidence in writing. There was a prevailing preference for the "living voice," and a strong belief that distinct bodies of knowledge which were never written down, and could not be written down, distinguished the insiders from the outsiders.

Perhaps there was a time when it could be claimed that orality–literacy research was of little relevance to historical understanding when it came to the texts of early Christianity,[7] but this is no longer feasible. In fact, denying the importance of multidisciplinary orality–literacy research would be to step neatly into the ethnocentric trap that Bruce Malina so often warns against.

Clearly, we have to work with a *particular* literacy, and even with literacies, taking into account their specific circumstances of acquisition and use.

---

5. Horsfall, "Statistics or States of Mind?" See also the valuable study of Hezser, *Jewish Literacy*.

6. My thanks to David Rhoads for encouragement and support to dust these articles off and putting them together here.

7. For example: "Much that has been written on orality and literacy in the first-century Mediterranean world is rather beside the point." See Malina, "Rhetorical Criticism," 98.

Approaching literacy as historically and culturally embedded is a perspective of immense importance. The relevance of these investigations to understanding some peculiar facets of Greco-Roman writings, and particularly the New Testament writings is obvious. Analysis of the orality of Hellenistic Roman culture can be a useful index to the world views and ways of thinking characteristic of inhabitants of that culture.

It is important to bear in mind that *even the "literates" were literate in a pre-print culture.* Cultural-anthropological characteristics of speech (oral, non-written communication) and the social effects of illiteracy permeate their written communication.[8]

Curiously, among New Testament scholars the concept of oral tradition tends to be applied only to pre-gospel Jesus traditions, while the rest of early Christian literature continues to be studied without an awareness of any need for applying the same concept. Even when leaving aside questions of cognition or the dissemination of religious traditions, with regard to Greco-Roman times the heavy oral aspect of writing events must be emphasized. A nagging problem here is the persistent assumption that oral traditions are inferior to literary traditions.

Fortunately, current research is moving away from such a prejudice. A most interesting new direction in oral tradition studies centres on the interaction of genre and occasions of performance.[9] In a world with living oral traditions, people are exposed to verbal art constantly, not just on specific entertainment occasions (which, incidentally, can happen every day in certain seasons). When they work, eat, drink, and do social group activities, myth, song, and saying are always woven into their talk. When they teach, learn, instruct, berate, and practice jurisprudence those living oral traditions will be there. We can describe the presence of living oral traditions as a sort of "bilingualism" among literates, a fluency in different modes of communication.[10]

There is a certain irony in our now relying upon mute textual or material documentation as our sole means of bringing the past to life. That is why I start off with a discussion based on anthropological research with a fairly wide sweep, to gain some perspective on our "mute manuscripts."

The Greco-Roman world exhibits a strong bias towards orality. There was a prevailing preference for the "living voice" (chapter 2), and a surprising

8. Botha, "Orality, Literacy and Worldview."

9. With regard to the NT texts, see esp. Rhoads, "Performance Criticism 1"; Rhoads, "Performance Criticism 2"; and Rhoads, "Performance Events."

10. See Martin, "Telemachus," 227.

widespread reticence towards writing, varying from mere indifference to active scepticism.

Of course, we actually do have to gain some sense of the details of Greco-Roman literacy as setting for New Testament writings. In chapter 3 aspects of ancient literacy events are discussed.

When the New Testament and early Christian writings are considered as situated, culturally mediated, and historically functional events, the issue is not a binary contrast between literacy and orality, but the physical and experiential aspects of ancient writing. Discussions of posture, education, costs, and time involved in physical writing in Greco-Roman times are discussed in chapter 4. Among others, I point to the disposition of subservience that surrounded the physical act of writing.

Writing, naturally, was done to have some people read. Study of New Testament documents is often subject to the inappropriate assumption that "reading" entails disembodied decoding of inherent meanings. Reading is a complex activity that is part of a cultural system, to be understood within pertinent technological parameters. Memory was heavily emphasized in communication practices of the Roman period, and a cultural-historical understanding of texts from that period should relate to such features (chapter 5).

Both writing and reading intersect in the concept "author." In chapter 6 I argue that authorship in Greco-Roman times must be understood as an interpretive, cultural construct. Writing activities were collective and participatory, and ranged, depending on the location and period, from government support to editorial, translation, and facilitation work to entertainment to legal practice to education, embedded in pre-print contexts without the judicial and social institution of copyright. Whatever it was that ancient authors did when they wrote down and diffused thought, "authorship" in antiquity must not be seen along the lines of modern, romanticist projections of the solitary, brilliant individual.

There are many intersections of oral communicative practices and writing. Literacy events were influenced by cognitive and interpersonal factors surrounding all writers and readers. In the last five chapters, facets of orality and literacy events are discussed in relation to a variety of individual, social, cultural, and economic concerns.

I begin this section with some of the social dynamics of the early transmission of the Jesus tradition (chapter 7). Despite several shortcomings, the informal, freely developing concept of tradition transmission still merits attention. To analyze the transmission process with a social-scientific model, rumor research is discussed and summarized. This model is then related to aspects of the development of the synoptic gospel traditions, and suggested as applicable to some Jesus stories.

When we turn to the Gospel of Mark (chapter 8), we find probably the best indications of a story whose origins lie in performance.[11] In an early attempt to understand Mark's story as oral traditional literature, I turned to the oral formulaic theory. The interpretation of Mark's gospel is inextricably linked to a conception of the gospel's genesis. By adopting a basic insight of the oral formulaic theory, it is argued that Mark provides ample evidence that allows it to be seen as an example of oral traditional composition. The immediate gain from the perspective of oral traditional composition is an alternative to the tradition/redaction cul-de-sac. The gospel of Mark does not merely contain oral traditions, but *is* oral composition. Instead of approaching the gospel either as a merging of various chronological, geographically influenced, and theological parts, identifiable by what is taken as narrative inconsistencies, linguistic usages, and historical infelicities, the gospel appears to be *part of* a traditional process.

In the last three chapters, some aspects of orality relating to Paul's letters are investigated. A self-evident terrain for such investigation is letter writing and oral communication in antiquity: by locating Pauline letter writing in the context of ancient communication makes the constraints of an orally based culture relevant to the understanding of his letters (chapter 9). The particular literacy practices prevailing in Greco-Roman times, letter writing in a scribal culture and the importance of oral performance are discussed. Paul's letter to the Galatians is briefly referred to in order to show how the letter establishes authority and verbal presence within an oral environment.

Paul and gossip (chapter 10) is a topic that one would not easily come across in conventional New Testament studies,[12] but gossip was a powerful and very present social mechanism in early Christian communities. Gossip played a considerable role in the tensions and misunderstandings surrounding the activities of Paul. Not only was Paul often a subject of gossip, but his dealing with this very potent form of social dynamic within the household context did little to abate the problems. I suggest that quite a few characteristics of Paul's written communication were generated by this phenomenon.

11. See the extensive argument recently developed by Wire, *Mark Composed in Performance*.

12. Happily, one can now point to some exceptions. Kartzow, "Female Gossipers"; Kartzow, *Gossip and Gender*; and Daniels, "Gossip in John."

Lastly, I analyze some aspects of the verbal art of the Pauline letters, how rhetoric, performance, and presence combine (chapter 11). Orality is not only an essential aspect of pre-modern communication but it is the ideal starting point for attempts to situate Pauline epistolography within the context of ancient literacy practices. To do this attention is firstly directed to the importance of recognising (and compensating for) our *visualism*, which is related to a modern, Western, literate bias. The constraints of an orally based culture necessarily bring the performative side of writing and reading letters to the fore. Hence, letter writing in antiquity cannot be separated from bodily presence, and so we have to consider phenomena such as "multi"-authorship, and the communal experience of letters reading.

Oral texts depended on writing for their survival, while written texts were deeply dependent on those oral aspects for their legitimacy. Both modes of communication were interwoven in the literacy of the ancient world. Often the one was basically the other.

PART 1

Setting

1

Mute Manuscripts

It is a truism to note that the world in which early Christianity came into being was a pre-technological world. What this observation implies, however,
is not always fully transparent. It is especially the issue of communication
technology that can easily be misunderstood. With this chapter, my aim is
to promote the relevance of research done on orality and literacy for the
interpretation and historical use of ancient texts, such as some early Christian documents. Even more importantly, I want to draw attention to an all-
pervading bias in many scholarly studies, a bias towards literate, visually
oriented thinking which is projected unto ancient texts.

To do this it is argued that from the realization that "the worlds in which
different societies live are distinct worlds, not merely the same world with
different labels attached,"[1] it follows that various ways of communicating
reflect historically determined, relative facets of human existence. Communication media not only *reflect* culture but also *influence* it fundamentally.
Writing is a socially determined phenomenon, like all human activities. The
immense complexities of these issues should be stressed. My approach is
somewhat generalizing; the idea is primarily to argue for the *importance* of
multidisciplinary investigations involving contemporary media research for
the understanding of certain texts from the Greco-Roman world, and *not* to
provide any final answers.

1. Sapir, "Status of Linguistics," 207.

Communication Media and Consciousness

Some Introductory Remarks

Every society can be seen as a "precariously put together fabric of meanings by which human beings seek to find guidance for their lives, to be consoled and inspired, in the face of finitude and death."[2] This "psychic unity of mankind" can, however, only be described substantially in terms of historical and cultural particularities.

Anthropology has taught us that there is a very broad range of differences among cultural groups in attitudes to, values about, and perceptions of the world and of themselves, as well as in ways of dealing with and experiencing associations and emotions. Cultural patterning extends to personality and interpersonal relationships. The diversity so obvious in human thought and the consequent differences between traditional and modern cultures have been mostly interpreted with an approach set within a binary framework. Terms used are "primitive" and "advanced," or the emergence of rationality from irrationality, or the contrast between logico-empirical versus mythopoeic thinking. A binary framework tends, however, to reduce human interaction and development to an unacceptably simple design.

We also find "the opposing tendency, adopted by many social scientists heavily committed to cultural relativism, which leads them to treat all societies as if their intellectual processes were essentially the same. Similar yes, the same no."[3] Goody notes that the specification of difference is not enough in itself; one needs to point to mechanisms, to causal factors.[4]

Awareness of the problems posed by cultural changes is a continuing feature of discussions in biblical scholarship.[5] Amongst biblical scholars cultural change is usually considered a relatively unimportant issue, and the adoption of cultural relativism is regarded with suspicion; as an interpretive approach cultural relativism is seen as opening up an unacceptable gap between interpreters and ancient texts. The point, however, is that to account for (at least some of) our difficulties in interpreting texts from a different culture (to the extent that one can meaningfully refer to something such as

2. Berger and Kellner, *Sociology Reinterpreted*, 76.

3. Goody, "Literacy," 226–27.

4. Ibid., 227.

5. E.g. Barr, *Bible in the Modern World*, 38–52; Nineham, *Use and Abuse of the Bible*, 1–39, 94–113; Barton, "Reflections"; Downing, "Our Access to Other Cultures"; Downing, "Interpretation and the 'Culture Gap.'"

"culture") we need to take cognizance of studies specifically attempting to grapple with these issues.

Scholars like Malina and Hollenbach have pointed out that terms such as wealth and poverty derive their meaning from the normative cultural values within which they occur.[6] Similarly, interpretation of New Testament texts that fails to take cultural differences seriously when it comes to concepts like *texts*, *tradition*, and even *writing* can only misrepresent those texts. This proposition can also be approached from a more sociological perspective, in that to understand the uniquely human manner of living, "great stress should be placed on the observation that culture is *learned*. Perhaps even more important is the fact that what is learned has first to be *discovered* or *invented* by someone and then *transmitted* to and shared by others. Every item in our cultural repertory is built on an initial act of innovation and then on a series of modifications in the course of time."[7] The alphabet, writing, and various communication technologies are innovative modifications, components of learned culture. Written texts and the phenomenon of writing are part of social worlds. Similar to institutions such as marriage, deeds such as lying, or customs like greeting-by-hand, writing exists as a society presumes it to be. Without cultural construction writing is nothing; it is created by "the social agreement that something counts as that condition."[8]

It follows that writing as such reflects and is interwoven with *specific* cultural phenomena, radically determined by and determining attitudes and experiences related to writing. Different communication media will have various far-reaching effects on human behavior, on the "fabrics of meaning" constituting human motivation and activities. "For some, at least, of the differences in intellectual processes that are indicated in a very general way by means of terms like 'open' and 'closed' can be related not so much to differences in 'mind' but to differences in systems of communication."[9]

The discussion up to now points to the realization that there are distinctive and important differences between modern contemporary notions of speech, language, and text and those of both oral and chirographic (or manuscript) cultures not conditioned as we are by extensive dependence upon visual material, such as the printed page. Our everyday contemporary relationship to words and books is historically unique. Our *way of communicating* has influenced our way of thinking. This has been noted and

6. See Malina, "Wealth and Poverty"; Hollenbach, "Defining Rich and Poor."

7. Bourguignon, *Psychological Anthropology*, 302.

8. D'Andrade, "Cultural Meaning Systems," 91.

9. Goody, "Literacy," 227.

elaborated upon explicitly or implicitly by a great many studies from various disciplines. And although no single study can possibly be seen as uncontroversial, the implication of contemporary media research is to call attention to the distance that exists between the epistemological worlds of modern and ancient experience of texts.[10]

Culture and Writing

"The general implications of introducing a means of recording speech are revolutionary, in its potentiality if not always in its actuality."[11] The development of writing was not a simple or irreversible advance in some march of progress and civilization, but it was a change of profound historical importance. Writing has transformed not merely communication but, more importantly, thought itself, altering "what we can do with our minds and what our minds can do with us."[12]

Goody's analyses are relevant because of the insight they provide into the cultural basis of the transformation of human cognition. His arguments point to the profound significance of the invention and development of non-biological means by which cognitive processes have been modified. Literacy is not just about phonetics or technical "skills" but about a whole approach to the use of one's own language and control over one's own life.[13]

It is important to note that Goody does *not* subscribe to the view that literacy is an autonomous causal agent. Neither do I. The consequences of literacy at all levels of human activity are contingent on the cultural circumstances in which they are embedded.[14] Some of these consequences are, importantly, cognitive. Cognitive functioning is related to cultural and historical contexts and connected to the use of a broad range of technologies. At least some of the differences among cultures and historical experiences can be related to how modes of communication conditioned modes of thought.

The introduction of different modes of communication, especially literacy and other forms of graphic representation (such as drawings, photographs, films, and television) brings about changes in interpersonal and intergroup relations.[15] Attitudes toward the past and, potentially, the future

10. See also Boomershine, "Peter's Denial," 47.

11. Goody, *Interface*, 54.

12. Goody, *Domestication*, 160.

13. Cf. Street, *Literacy in Theory and Practice*, 15; Scribner and Cole, *Psychology of Literacy*, 251.

14. See especially the discussion of Cole and Cole, "Rethinking the Goody Myth."

15. Ong, "Writing is a Technology."

are also modified. Consequently, altered conceptions concerning distances in space and time are brought about by the new means of communication. The existence or lack of literacy can be a major cultural factor in producing varying human attributes. This observation extends to both mental health and illness: "in other words, that literacy in a society, or the lack of it, plays an important part in shaping the minds of men and the patterns of their mental breakdown."[16]

Learning to write brings new possibilities to a culture. "Rather than devoting one's time to oral storage of knowledge organized in terms of the human life-world, one needed to face up to explicitly abstract questions."[17] Thus, writing creates an environment conducive to critical thinking. Contrasting oral and literate societies, Goody argues that "The *essential* difference . . . is . . . the accumulation (or reproduction) of skepticism. Members of oral . . . societies find it difficult to develop a line of skeptical thinking about, say, nature, or man's relationship to God simply because a continuing critical tradition can hardly exist when skeptical thoughts are *not* written down, *not* communicated across time and space, *not* made available for men to contemplate in privacy as well as to hear in performance."[18] Alluding to the influence of Aristotelian philosophy, Ong remarks that it "appears no accident that formal logic was invented in an alphabetic culture."[19] The very idea of interpretation "as an activity separate from other kinds of statement depends on the existence of writing."[20]

Writing affects concepts of justice. Goody suggests that the process of adopting writing is closely related to a sharpened concept of rules and norms.

> But where these remain implicit, at the level of "deep structure," they do not take the same shape, for the actor or for society, as when they are consciously formulated by the ruled or put up . . . by the rulers. First, they are not so "fixed"; they generally emerge in context (like proverbs), not in the "abstracted" way of a code. Secondly, they tend to be less generalized than literate formulae; or, rather, their generalizations tend to be embedded in situations. Thirdly, they are not formulated nor yet formalized into neat digests or *summae*. It is writing that enables one to pick out norms or decisions and set them out in the form of a guide, a handbook.

16. Carothers, "Culture," 307.
17. Ong, *Presence of the Word*, 34.
18. Goody, *Domestication*, 43.
19. Ong, *Presence of the Word*, 45.
20. Ong follows Olson, see Ong, "Before Textuality," 260.

> When this has been done, law[s] . . . distinguish themselves from "custom" within the total body of "rights," while the written is often given a higher truth value . . .[21]

The logic of writing extends to experienced reality on many levels. Religions familiar with writing "are clearly working on a more explicitly abstract (or generalized) base than those of purely oral societies (even centralized ones)."[22] Goody reviews the evidence for the "flexible" nature of orally oriented religions. He notes that traditional African systems of belief are open-ended in a meaningful way, encouraging the search after the truth and that "African religions are more . . . subject to change and absorption rather than to rejection and conversion."[23] This is an important hypothesis for understanding the diversity of Hellenistic religions as well as the scope of variety found in emergent Christianity. Various attitudes reflect different levels of involvement with writing.

A Revival of the "Great Divide" Theory?

From time to time the objection is raised that an interpretive approach accepting fundamental cultural differences leads to an unacceptable position: a so-called great divide that cannot be bridged. It is also claimed that this divisive approach is ethnocentric and leads to cross-cultural agnosticism[24] and forces one to adopt cultural relativism.

However, it is important to emphasize that cultural relativity in fact makes understanding *possible*. Without the analytical possibilities provided by historical *relationalism* one is ultimately faced with the unacceptable choice between either only one correct interpretation (one's own obviously), or that none is right (obviously only in so far as oneself is not affected). The ethnocentrist prejudice is as great a danger when not emphasizing uniqueness and discontinuities.[25]

21. Goody, *Logic of Writing*, 174–5.

22. Ibid., 15.

23. Ibid., 8.

24. Cf. Finnegan, *Literacy and Orality*, 59–85; Street, *Literacy in Theory and Practice*, 3–5, *passim*.

25. It is extremely difficult to formulate cultural relativity in clear, precise, and intelligible language; see Tilley, "Problem for Normative Cultural Relativism." Craffert has proposed *ontological pluralism* to conceptualize the problem: Craffert, "New Testament Interpretation"; Craffert, "Opposing World-Views"; Craffert, "Stuff World-Views Are Made Of"; Craffert, "'Seeing' a Body"; Craffert, "Multiple Realities"; Craffert, *Life*, 8–32. I discuss this problem in Botha, "Cultural-Anthropological History."

The many criticisms brought in against the "ugly broad ditch" (Lessing's *garstige Graben*) serves only to *complicate* matters. The immense differences between cultures and human experiences cannot possibly be ignored or minimized without gross disregard of the people involved. Pointing out ethnocentrist prejudice is highly relevant and important, but serves only to increase sensitivity to the vast and interrelated predicaments of cross-cultural communication. It does not solve the problems.

The challenge is to see the *intersection* of universalist *and* relativist claims of various viewpoints in the human sciences in their attempts at understanding and relating human behavior and nature. "To question the immutability of society is a revolutionary act; it implies that observations of alien ways of life may shed some light on our own. The differences between human groups are not so radical that we cannot recognize ourselves as we are, or as we might be, in others. Unless we draw this conclusion, we will find ourselves arguing that others are less than human, like the proponents of slavery who argued that Africans had no souls."[26] At the same time one must adopt a respect for differences and accept the irreducibility of human meanings in order to let others be themselves.

It is in this sense that Geertz provides us with a very significant guideline: our "accounts of other peoples' subjectivity" is to move back and forth between asking oneself "What is the general form of their life?" and "What exactly are the vehicles in which that form is embodied?" "Hopping back and forth between the whole conceived through the parts that actualize it and the parts conceived through the whole that motivates them, we seek to turn them, by a sort of intellectual perpetual motion, into explications of one another."[27] Whether ancient texts from which we construct imaginary people or modern contemporary speech, the point is that we should try our best to overcome our biases and listen to what *they are trying to say*.

As much rigor should be dedicated to the description and analysis of literacy as to other aspects usually focused on in our studies. When applied to contemporary studies of ancient texts, the implication of media criticism is that the (unspoken) conception of the medium in which we perceive and experience a text will inevitably influence our perception of its meaning. Therefore, to the degree that our goal is to understand these ancient documents in historical contexts, it is essential to understand the medium in which they originated. Historical interpretation requires an effort to experience the tradition in its intended medium.

26. Bourguignon, *Psychological Anthropology*, 79.
27. Geertz, *Local Knowledge*, 69–70.

The thesis of this chapter is that an unrecognized assumption underlies most exegetical activities, namely that writing implies a *constant* role and/ or function in communication. In other words an assumption which is a general statement on literacy as such, its impact and its uses— "imputing to literacy a set of supposedly inherent and unchanging qualities."[28] There is ample room, however, for doubt whether such a generalized assumption is possible or useful. These doubts have been argued in an exceptionally coherent way by Street.[29] Granted the important "connection" between various cultural experiences and the way knowledge is transmitted, the importance of applying comparative research becomes obvious.

Orality, Literacy, and Scribal Culture

When discussing these issues it is imperative to attempt some conceptual clarity. In what follows some characterizations as well as some descriptive examples are provided.

Orality

Orality is not necessarily spoken discourse as such. Clearly, spoken discourse is part of almost every imaginable facet of being human and transcends mentalities and cultures as a phenomenon. Many discussions about orality get bogged down when it is not clearly grasped that spoken discourse is not yet orality. There is quite a lot of evidence showing that highly literate persons can and do use oral strategies when communicating in certain circumstances,[30] or that whatever one can point to as possibly characteristically "oral" can be found in some literate tradition.[31]

Orality as a condition exists by virtue of communication that is not dependent on modern media processes and techniques. It is negatively formed by the lack of technology and positively created by specific forms of education and cultural activities. Therefore, it is not very useful to cite apparent oral strategies in literate situations (or vice versa) as an argument against orality as a culturally determinative factor. Orality refers to the experience of words (and speech) in the habitat of sound. "The word is something that

28. Baumann, "Introduction," in *The Written Word*, 12.

29. Street, *Literacy in Theory and Practice*.

30. Tannen, "Myth"; Tannen, *Spoken and Written Language*.

31. Akinasso, "On the Similarities"; Finnegan, *Oral Poetry*. Note, however, the cautions against uncritical selection and use of materials; see Foley, "Introduction," 64; Foley, "Oral Literature," 492.

happens, an event in the world of sound through which the mind is enabled to relate actuality to itself."[32] Verbalization, in the context of orality, cannot be an object in itself; the sheer ephemerality of speech prohibits this. By its nature it is part of the human life-world in which words exist as vocalization, as events.

Because an aural–oral culture necessarily has no records, it relates to time differently from the way we do. "In an oral–aural culture one can ask about something, but no one can look up anything. As a result, in an oral–aural culture there is no history in our modern sense of the term. The past is indeed present, as to a degree the past always is, but it is present in the speech and social institutions of the people, not in the more abstract forms in which modern history deals."[33]

The religious systems of societies without writing lack the *concept* of a religion, "partly because magico-religious activities form part of most social action, not being the attribute of a separate organization, partly because of the identification with a people, as in 'Asante religion.'"[34] It follows that a society with a heavy oral residue will lack the experience of "religious conversion." Whereas a written tradition articulates beliefs and interests in a semi-permanent form that can extend their influence independently of any particular political and cultural system, oral traditions are inextricably linked to their contexts, where one can only experience incorporation. "Conversion is a function of the boundaries the written word creates, or rather defines."[35]

The extensive use of repetition characterizes orality:

> In oral cultures virtually all conceptualization, including what will later be reshaped into abstract sciences, is thus kept close to the human life-world. Moreover, since public law and custom are of major importance for social survival but cannot be put on record, they must constantly be talked about, else they vanish from consciousness. Hence the figures around whom knowledge is made to cluster, those about whom stories are told or sung, must be made into conspicuous personages, foci of common attention, individuals embodying open public concern . . . Thus the epic hero, from one point of view, appears as an answer to the problem of knowledge storage and communication in oral–aural cultures (where indeed storage and communication are virtually the same thing).[36]

32. Ong, *Presence of the Word*, 22.
33. Ibid., 23.
34. Goody, *Logic of Writing*, 173.
35. Ibid., 10, 172.
36. Ong, *Presence of the Word*, 204–5.

An orally based society is constituted by a *collective memory*. To illustrate the concept we can turn to the study of Havelock in which Homer is portrayed as the educator of ancient Greece and the foe whom Plato realized he had to overcome.[37] Havelock explained the *Iliad* and *Odyssey* as encyclopedic storehouses of exemplary attitudes, ethics, politics, and so forth, the kind of information that a written culture can keep in a set of reference books, but which an oral culture must maintain mnemonically and mimetically through continual recreation of the poems in which this educative material is encoded.

Literacy

Literacy can only be defined within a context. More than familiarity with reading and writing, literacy is about an ideologically laden social activity which is part of a cultural system.[38] Not only should literacy be described at its various stages, but also in relation to various activities. "It is not even self-evident that 'literacy' is the most useful general term, or can be studied as one phenomenon."[39] For example "literacy" should probably refer to the ability to read—but does it also include the ability to write? Is a person capable of "writing" a few words but unable to read—a not unknown situation in antiquity—literate?[40] Does it refer to a person with a literary turn of mind? What kinds of texts would a person have to master to qualify as "literate"? Clearly, the answer depends on specific historical, cultural, and social circumstances.

The Printing Revolution

To illustrate what I have in mind when referring to literacy and a literate mentality a short discussion of the so-called printing revolution is in order.

Of the many movements that went into the making of modernity and the numerous factors facilitating its development, almost none can be fully understood without taking into account the influence the printing press has exerted upon them.[41] "The spatialization of sound initiated with the devel-

37. Havelock, *Preface to Plato*, 61–83.

38. De Castell, Luke, and MacLennan, "On Defining Literacy"; Graff, "Literacy"; Graff, "Legacies of Literacy"; Graff, *Labyrinths of Literacy*.

39. Baumann, "Introduction," in *The Written Word*, 2–3.

40. Youtie, "Βραδέως γράφων."

41. Eisenstein, "Some Conjectures"; Eisenstein, *Printing Revolution*; Ong, *Orality and*

opment of the alphabet was reinforced and intensified by the typographical developments in fifteenth-century Western Europe commonly referred to as the invention of printing."[42] The new print technology which developed in the sixteenth century made intellectual material much more abundant and allowed more efficient use of mental energies: developments with almost unimaginable consequences.

We habitually refer to the so-called Copernican revolution to characterize the shifts in Western experience that took place since the rise of modernity. But recent interpretations of Copernicus show that his work should rather be seen as conservative and not very concerned with emancipation from traditional modes of thought. When considering Copernicus's intellectual environment, changes wrought by printing deserve a more central place.[43]

The experience of Scripture and nature was transformed by the dissemination of knowledge provided by printing.[44] The functional differences between the manuscript book and the printed book helped to reorder the thought of *all* readers. Thus, "the changes wrought by printing provide the most plausible point of departure for explaining how confidence shifted from divine revelation to mathematical reasoning and man-made maps."[45]

Literate Experience of Communication

Naturally, one needs to bear in mind that the cultural metamorphosis produced by printing was really much more complicated than any single formula can possibly express. The point is, however, clear: we are post-printing revolution people. It was print, not writing, "that effectively reified the word, and, with it, noetic activity."[46]

The extent of the changes lying between our experience of writing and reading and those of oral or scribal cultures becomes visible when one tries to picture modern public life, or university studies without technology. That we are being flooded by texts is not simply a fact, but a *culturally significant* fact; reflecting and forming our society's perception of itself.[47]

Literacy, 117–18; Graham, *Beyond the Written Word*, 39–44.

42. Ong, *Presence of the Word*, 47.

43. Eisenstein, *Printing Revolution*, 253–59.

44. Ibid., 253–74.

45. Ibid., 271.

46. Ong, *Orality and Literacy*, 119; cf. Smith, "On Audio Visual Technologies," 193.

47. Baumann, "Introduction," in *The Written Word*, 9.

Scribal Culture

We need to discuss the situation where we are confronted with neither an oralist nor a loose connection between oral and literate, but a dynamic interaction between oral and written communication. That is, speaking broadly, scribal culture: culture familiar with writing but in essence still significantly, even predominantly, oral. In scribal culture reading is largely vocal and illiteracy the rule rather that the exception.

Some distinctions are in order, such as between high and popular culture. Havelock has delineated the developments regarding literacy in ancient Greece. With the advent of Hellenism a difference in Greek literature becomes visible. "High culture had become alphabetized or more correctly, alphabetization had become socialized. What was written was not worse but different."[48]

One must distinguish between knowledge of an alphabet and habitual book reading. By no means all who have mastered the written word have, down to the present, become members of a book-reading public. Learning *to read* is different, moreover, from learning *by reading*. The very fact that we have the social role of *scribes* in a society points to unique relationships with writing and reading. Scribality is characterized, among others, by the training of apprentices for writing, dictation, recitation, and special mnemonic devices for mastering letters. "At the most basic level . . . it is the reading process *per se*, in both its psychological and its physical aspects, that is today different from what it was in the West twenty-five hundred, and in considerable degree even 250 years ago."[49]

This can most clearly be seen in the role that memorization plays in scribal culture.

> These memory systems are intermediate between the oral and the chirographic-typographic, presupposing that knowledge is something necessarily to be memorized in full detail for instant recall (oral attitude) but also implementing memorization with a "scientific" systematization of data which is quite impossible without writing. They are part of rhetoric which as a reflectively organized technique is the product of a literate culture dealing with still urgent problems of oral performance.[50]

---

48. Havelock, *Literate Revolution*, 10.
49. Graham, *Beyond the Written Word*, 32.
50. Ong, *Presence of the Word*, 26

It must be accentuated that when it comes to the overlap and interaction of oral and written modes of communication many aspects still need to be researched.[51]

Some Implications

First-Century Mediterranean Societies as Fusions of Oral and Scribal Cultures

Though no one will deny that orality was part of the Greco-Roman world, we need to realize to what extent orality was the *norm*. Books and writing were elements of their societies, and even under certain circumstances extensively used, so that oral culture shared the stage with written culture. But a written text, at the time, "was something conceived as realizable only in the vocal act of reading aloud."[52] Written texts "would have been readable only with difficulty, unless one knew the text well."[53] A manuscript culture presupposes extensive memorization of written texts.[54]

The issue raised by these insights is that authors in antiquity were not authors or writers quite in the sense that would be understood today. For instance, they pursued and performed instructional functions for their community, fulfilling an essential role as agents and instruments of the oral tradition and cultural experience unfamiliar to the modern, individualistic and "objectivistic" sense of text production.

The description of first-century Mediterranean culture as an overlap between oral and manuscript culture yields the recognition that in "antiquity the most literate cultures remained committed to the spoken word to a degree which appears to our more visually organized sensibilities somewhat incredible or even perverse."[55] No one will deny the literary qualities of Plato's many writings, but it is significant to bear in mind that he protests that what is really essential to wisdom cannot be put into writing, for this is to falsify it.[56] He also states that writing serves mere recall, not memory or wisdom.[57]

51. Street, *Literacy in Theory and Practice*, 98–99, Goody, *Interface*; Finnegan, *Literacy and Orality*, 175–80.

52. Graham, *Beyond the Written Word*, 32.

53. Ibid., 34.

54. Ong, *Orality and Literacy*, 119.

55. Ong, *Presence of the Word*, 55.

56. *Ep.* 7, esp. 343.

57. *Phaedr.*, 274–77.

The Hellenistic era is often described as "a bookish age."[58] But we must be careful not to overestimate Hellenistic esteem for the written word.[59] The persistent exigency in a semiliterate context for oral use and transmission even of written texts made orality intrinsic to the culture. "Extensive memorization, the backbone of an oral-text orientation, remained an important part of the standard educational curriculum, and dictation, not writing by hand, was the author's standard method of 'written' composition."[60] Yates in particular has documented the extensive use of memory systems in use at the time, and then for works already existing in texts.[61] A corollary of oral composition and oral publication of written works[62] is the phenomenon of reading aloud[63] so that the dissemination of any text remained that of oral performance and recitation.

> These essential facts appear to have been obscured by the particular kind of literacy that we have developed in the modern West, especially since the industrial revolution . . . Consequently, we have constantly to question our assumptions about books, reading, and writing, not only when dealing with non-Western cultures that are often still highly oral, but also when studying our own culture prior to the nineteenth century. The original and basic orality of reading is the key to the fundamentally oral function of written texts outside of the special context in which we live today.[64]

Recognizing Literate Bias

> Many influential linguists of an earlier generation . . . and grammarians and educators deriving their practice from such theorists, assumed that there was little significant difference between speech and writing. The assumption that speech and writing were fulfilling the same functions and the inability to recognize their separate character made it possible to use one as the model for another.[65]

58. E.g., Pfeiffer, *History of Classical Scholarship*, 102.

59. Cf. Pfeiffer, ibid., 16–32; Kenyon, *Books and Readers*, 24–32; Boring, *Literacy in Ancient Sparta*, 62–63.

60. Graham, *Beyond the Written Word*, 35; Zumthor, "Impossible Closure," 27; Marrou, *A History of Education in Antiquity*, 150–57.

61. Yates, *Art of Memory*, 1–49.

62. Hadas, *Ancilla to Classical Reading*, 60–64; Kenyon, *Books and Readers*, 83–85.

63. Saenger, "Silent Reading," 370–73.

64. Graham, *Beyond the Written Word*, 33.

65. Street, *Literacy in Theory and Practice*, 7.

Much the same situation exists in New Testament scholarship. Due to ignorance of the fact that literacy is a social construction, uncritical and ethnocentrist concepts of the New Testament writings and traditions pervade our studies. A few, and much too briefly discussed, illustrations will have to suffice.

The quest for the historical Jesus has been dominated by efforts at identifying if not the *ipsissima verba* of Jesus, at least the reconstruction of his teaching by "discovering" authentic sayings of Jesus. Although the oral context of the transmission of Jesus stories is granted, the impact remains unrecognized: "The quest for an 'original' utterance in this real, oral setting is quixotic, for each utterance emerges not simply from an earlier utterance but from a whole new existential context."[66]

In the study of Paul's letters and also of other New Testament documents rhetorical criticism is very much in vogue nowadays. Noticeable, however, is the lack of attention to rhetoric in antiquity as orally constituted. Bäuml, in a discussion of medieval literacy and illiteracy, notes the very significant circumstance of a person's use of *another's* literacy and the crucial social functions of writing and reading implied by this.[67] Although it is well known that Paul also made use of another person's literacy (he dictated his letters), it is noteworthy that similar questions have not been asked about him.

The styles of various early Christian authors appear from time to time as subjects of scrutiny. Once again, it is interesting that linguistic features are continually described as literate phenomena, and little attention is given to the orally determined nature of linguistic phenomena that make up the New Testament materials. Even when referring to the "contexts" or "audiences" of many early Christian writings we tend to underestimate the transpersonal identification of reciter and group, the manifestation of collective values that the performance of a "text" articulates.[68]

Our very concept of the gospel authors as "redactors of tradition" reflects an anachronistic perception, even to the point of ignorance of the physical position adopted for writing.[69]

Entralgo has analyzed the origins of the dominant trait of Western medicine, namely its basic somatic orientation.[70] He creates an awareness of

66. Ong, "Text as Interpretation," 153.
67. Bäuml, "Varieties and Consequences," 242.
68. Cf. Foley, "Traditional Oral Audience."
69. Cf. Skeat, "Use of Dictation," 183–85.
70. Entralgo, *Therapy of the Word.*

the power of the word in the treatment of human illness. Not all medicine in antiquity was a *muta ars*,[71] especially not in popular culture. To understand phenomena such as exorcism in antiquity, or some of the healing stories, the role of a worldview determined by oral culture is clear. In fact, both the well known inability of modern interpreters to relate to these accounts, and explanations ignoring verbal power in oral experience graphically illustrate literate prejudices.

Suggestions for a Possible Agenda

Others, in various ways, have noticed this unsatisfactory gap in New Testament research. By briefly reiterating some of their research one can provide pointers for further research. What immediately comes to mind is the transmission of the gospel traditions, and Abel, Gager, and Kelber have accentuated the importance of research done on orality for this subject.[72] Among others, the dominant paradigm of linearity in most reconstructions of the traditions underlying the Gospels is mistaken, and we should find alternatives to conceptualizing the synoptic problem generally and specifically conventional ideas about criteria of reliability.[73]

In a neglected article, Lohr has drawn attention to the organic connection of the written gospels with the history of the gathering of the materials making up the gospels.[74] He analyzes the style of Matthew in the light of the techniques of oral composition and transmission and provides many insights into why the gospel appears such as it is.[75] Noteworthy is that Lohr still refers to Matthew's "adaptations and rearrangements" of Markan material: clearly literate thinking about the process.

The work of Kelber is well-known. His analysis of Mark has drawn extensive discussion but relatively limited reaction to his views on Paul.[76] Kelber tends to see orality and literacy as *alternatives* in his approach to the multifarious Jesus traditions.

71. Virgil, *Aeneid* 12.397.

72. Abel, "Psychology of Memory"; Gager, "Gospels and Jesus," 248–56; Kelber, "Mark and Oral Tradition."

73. See, especially, DeConick "Human Memory"; Kelber "Oral-Scribal-Memorial Arts." and Craffert, "Wie sê jy," 304; Craffert, "Shamanic Complex," 321 n1; Craffert, "Historical-Anthropological Research," 453–56.

74. Lohr, "Oral Techniques."

75. I have done something similar on the gospel of Mark, see Botha, *Die Dissipels*.

76. Kelber, *Oral and the Written Gospel*, 140–77.

An interesting contribution is by Corbett, who uses concepts such as literacy and its cognitive consequences to understand the influence of the Pharisees on early Judaism.[77] He discusses the "literate revolution" in Greece[78] and the spread of Cynicism in relation to developments in early Christianity.

Marshall has drawn attention to the importance of understanding Paul's invective and the issue of his "inconsistencies" in terms of Greek social and moral standards,[79] considering the social and cultural dimensions of these activities. Even more relevant would be to relate Paul's highly polemical stance and biting denunciations to the oral–aural mindset. In an orally oriented mentality the "very structure of knowledge had been largely polemic, for the old oral–aural anxieties of a world polarized around persons had been institutionalized by the centering of formal education around dialectic and rhetoric, both arts of verbal strife."[80] "Habits of auditory synthesis charged man's life-world with dynamism and threat . . . In such a view, polemic becomes a major constituent of actuality, an accepted element of existence of a magnitude no longer appealing to modern technological man."[81] Residual oralism reflects a reduction of irrelevant material to virtue–vice polarities. Even commonplace traditions were almost exclusively concerned with virtue and vice.[82] In fact, virtue and vice polarities are so deeply embedded in oral knowledge-storing systems[83] that it is little wonder we have difficulty in relating to Paul's reasoning. Paul's caustic remarks and self-boosting claims do not necessarily point to the existence of theological schools. It might even be that Paul's controversy with the "Jews" is simply an extension of this mentality "where individuals took for granted that their surroundings were swarming with active, enterprising foes."[84] The attempts at identification of the various opponents might be barking up the wrong tree. We might have attempts at in-group identity achieved by feeding on hostilities toward out-groups.[85]

77. Corbett, "Pharisaic Revolution."

78. He uses Havelock's *Literate Revolution*.

79. Marshall, "Invective," 360.

80. Ong, *Presence of the Word*, 236.

81. Ibid., 200.

82. Cf. ibid., 202.

83. Cf. Yates, *Art of Memory*, 20–21, 84–88.

84. Ong, *Presence of the Word*, 196.

85. Cf. ibid., 198.

The possibilities are numerous, and very interesting new questions can be formulated in connection with several aspects of understanding the people and events making up the history of early Christianity.

Concluding Remarks

Several contributions on Hellenistic culture, or on the so-called background to the New Testament, simply describe static components of ancient culture. Without minimizing the obvious relevance of these contributions, the value of interpretation, of relating various factors and facets to each other, must be stressed. Particularly, it is the insight that writing and speech are culturally embedded phenomena, similar to other social conventions, that we need to facilitate in a comprehensive approach to our texts. We need to avoid anachronistic terminology and conceptualizations and uncritical ethnocentrism when it comes to authorship, literacy, tradition, writings, and other aspects of ancient communication.

Thinking within (or conditioned by) an oral context and thinking within a literate context have distinct characteristics. But an approach that stresses oppositions is not very helpful.[86] Clearly, speech underlies most facets of human actions, as fountainhead of all human communication. We are confronted with the very difficult task, "that of specifying particular mechanisms"[87] when it comes to analysis of processes of communication.

In acknowledging the means and relations of communication, the intention is not to deny the relevance of many other forces that went into the making of the world of antiquity.[88] Selecting this topic reflects a perceived neglect, and following it through is no rejection of trying to trace all the large variety of relevant factors in a historical situation.

This task, however, though immense, is quite urgent.

---

86. Finnegan, *Literacy and Orality*, 175.

87. Goody, "Literacy," 241.

88. Cf. Cole and Scribner, *Culture and Thought*, 7.

2

Living Voice and Lifeless Letters

The Greeks of classical times considered writing to have been a factor in the development of their civilization. Aeschylus, in his play *Prometheus Bound*, describes Prometheus' boasts of the gifts he has given mankind:

> Listen to the sufferings of men—how at first they were witless and how then I gave them intelligence and reason . . . First of all, men looked with their eyes but saw nothing and with their ears listened but did not hear: as if dreaming they muddled through each moment of their long lives . . . They managed all without purpose until I revealed to them the patterns, hard to detect, of the rising and setting of the stars. The use of numbers, best of all knowledge, I invented for them and the composition of letters (γραμμάτων συνθέσεις), how to make them work as memory and mother of the arts . . . Such were the devices I invented for mankind.[1]

Technological achievements such as agriculture, building, astronomy, mathematics, navigation, medicine, and also writing represented cultural progress and social equilibrium in the Greek mind.

Although the Greek world knew writing during the second millennium BCE (archaeological evidence for 1600–1200, Linear B), for various reasons writing fell into disuse, so that by 1100 BCE, like most sections of the Mediterranean world, Greece was without writing. In the Eastern world, three systems of writing developed: Egyptian hieroglyphics, Mesopotamian cuneiform (Sumerian and Akkadian), and West Semitic alphabets. Due to economic contact, the Greeks learned their writing from the Phoenicians during the eighth century BCE.[2] Herodotus has this to say on the matter:

1. Aeschylus, *Prometheus vinctus*, 442–70.
2. Cf. Senner, "Theories and Myths," 13–14; Cross, "Invention."

"Now the Phoenicians . . . introduced into Greece upon their arrival a great variety of arts, of which the most important was writing, whereof the Greeks till then had, as I think, been ignorant. At first they shaped their letters exactly like all the other Phoenicians, but afterwards, in course of time, they changed their language, and together with it the shape of their letters."[3]

The practical and effective simplicity that the West Semitic systems provided over and against hieroglyphics and cuneiform helps to explain why they spread so far and were adapted to so many languages—that is, if the alphabet should be treated *not* as an unique invention (and there are good empirical and theoretical reasons for assuming that the alphabet was indeed such an invention).[4]

In contrast to other cultures, the Greek alphabet never became the exclusive property of a privileged few who gave it the aura of a sacred mystery, of an obscure and hidden code available only to those in power. Although often misrepresented in studies of the Classical and Hellenistic world, the role of writing was quite unique in this culture, forming a major factor in what can be identified as "Hellenism." Writing (the alphabet) also played a major role in the "unification" of cultural groups: "Dialects heard spoken can seem to be different languages; when seen written in a common alphabet they are revealed as variations of a shared possession."[5]

About the story of Roman literacy and the use of writing before Hellenistic times very little can be told: we simply know too little.[6] The Romans received the alphabet during the same developments that brought writing to Greece, probably during the eighth century BCE, by way of the Etruscans. Though there is little evidence for the use of writing over the following four centuries, we find from the third century onwards a process by which Greek models took over and shaped Roman literature and its language. With relative suddenness writing achieved a well-defined place and a sophisticated use in moulding the Latin language to Greek literary models. Extensive familiarity with books and reading, however, remained characteristic of a rather small group of people (mostly men), so that we must describe the relationship between writing and orality, and the role of writing within this still basically oral culture, carefully and with more attention to detail.

The Hellenistic age is often defined as a chronological phase in Western history, delimited by certain political developments, such as the conquests of

3. Herodotus, *Histories* 5.58.
4. See Goody, "Literacy and Achievement," 84–86.
5. Kitzinger, "Alphabets and Writing," 406.
6. Ibid., 416–18.

Alexander the Great and the start of the Roman empire. Clearly, a historical age is determined by much more than a few political events. The Hellenistic age should be characterized by, among many other things, the rise of a particular worldview, a widespread admiration for things Greek, and, pertinent to our discussion, a distinctive attitude towards writing and literacy.

In his famous study of oral tradition and transmission, Gerhardsson remarks that the writing down of the Gospels was really an emergency measure, which, among other reasons, was due to "a commonplace which we recognize from elsewhere in Antiquity: an attitude of scepticism towards the written word."[7] He refers to "the opposition to letters and writing which manifested itself in many cultures at the time when the art of writing was introduced and which lives on, in various ways and in various forms, long afterwards."[8] Similarly, Harvey, asking what kind of literary activity would have suggested itself to the authors of the gospels, in an aside describes the milieu in which the New Testament originated as "a culture which tended to frown upon the writing of books as such."[9] These remarks call for a more detailed examination of Hellenistic attitudes towards oral and written communication.

The Complex Interface between Oral and Literate Traditions

When we examine rhetoric, education, writing, reading, and recitation in various contexts in Greco-Roman antiquity the evidence indicates a society that is still largely oral with quite distinct (in comparison to modern notions) attitudes towards literacy. Hellenistic culture flourished at the same time that a complex relationship developed between oral and written modes of thought and communication.

The study by Lentz about orality and literacy in Hellenic Greece is an important contribution towards understanding the relationship between writing and speech. Lentz shows how the oral tradition of memory and performance interacted with the written tradition of verbatim preservation and abstract thought so that each reinforced the strengths of the other.[10] He considers this *symbiosis* as integral to the remarkable accomplishments of all aspects of Greek culture, from education to law, and from philosophy to literature. Hellenic society exemplifies the hypothesis that culture flourishes

---

7. Gerhardsson, *Memory and Manuscript*, 196–97.

8. Ibid., 157.

9. Harvey, "Review of M. D. Goulder," 189.

10. Lentz, *Orality and Literacy*.

when differing media are in competition for dominance. Hellenic literature and culture show the effects when differing media interact symbiotically, so that each supplements the strengths of the other.

Writing, however, while important to Greek culture, remained in many ways secondary to the memory and performance skills of the oral tradition. Also, *extensive* writing and familiarity with texts were the almost exclusive assets of a rather small section of society. This remains true for Hellenistic times, including the first two centuries of the Common Era. Memory dominated many aspects of the culture. Instruction in the schools remained largely oral, with students learning prescribed works by heart. Most students studied grammar for only a short time, many merely learning to recognize the letters that represented the sounds of the alphabet. The singers and reciters of literature remained a vital part of the culture and performed for purposes of both persuasion and entertainment.

Composition took place orally, and authors recited or dictated works to scribes who put them in writing to preserve them. The character of individuals vouched for the safety of written depositions in court, and the introduction of written evidence did not shorten the time allowed for oral presentations. The Greeks and Romans preferred to hear the witnesses' own testimony and to judge those individuals by the concrete details of their vocal and bodily action.

Writing never completely broke away from the sound of the human voice. Greeks and Romans seldom read written words without speaking them aloud. Silent reading was practiced, but the ancients never considered it necessary or desirable to separate compositions completely from their spoken form. Writing was the sign for the spoken word, not its replacement. The proposal by Lentz that one should refer to the *symbiosis* of the strengths of oral and literate traditions in Hellenism seems to offer an inadequate description of our evidence.

Eric Havelock's *Preface to Plato* predates Lentz's investigation. This book details the place of writing as the source of Plato's understanding of abstractions, and as a direct influence on the origin of philosophy. Havelock stresses the importance of literacy to the development of Greek philosophy through this awareness of abstractions as reasons for action in daily life. The date for the literate age is set by Havelock at about 450 BCE, [11] and he argues for a "dynamic tension" between the concrete worldview of orality and the abstract thought of literacy.[12]

11. Havelock, *Preface to Plato*.
12. Havelock, *Literate Revolution*; Havelock, *Muse Learns to Write*.

An interesting study (but not without some implausibilities) is Florence Dupont's *The Invention of Literature*, which has an important underlying thrust: a reminder that classical (Greco-Roman) literature has lost its proper contexts.[13] Ancient writing was very much a statement in quest of a speech act, so to speak. Undoubtedly, the Greco-Roman texts we possess today are, in many ways, either relics of or at least starting-blocks for performances, presentations, recitals, vocalizations, and such, and it requires some effort fully to recognize that fact.

The exploration offered here does not want to prove orality (or disprove the significance of literacy) for antiquity. "Orality" or "literacy" as such do not exist—except if one beforehand presumes writing/reading to be unchanging and fixed phenomena. What is needed is an extension of investigations concerning the complex interrelationship between orality and literacy during Greco-Roman times. Part of our struggle to come to terms with the peculiarities and subtleties of Hellenistic literature stems from our inability to correctly visualize ancient writing and text production. That failure follows from an inadequate historical perspective and disregard for context; when the "study of inscriptions is severed from the study of inscribing, the study of fixed meaning is severed from the study of the social processes that fix it. The result is a double narrowness. Not only is the extension of text analysis to non-written materials blocked, but so is the application of sociological analysis to written ones."[14] It is with a view on the repair of that split that this research is devoted, towards a more comprehensive understanding of Greco-Roman use of writing, and the contexts of text production.

The Limited Extent of Greco-Roman Literacy

A Pre-industrial, Predominantly Oral World

Various scholars have emphasized that society in ancient Greece and Rome was highly oral.[15] Whatever the expansion of literate consciousness after Aristotle, the fundamental form for the dissemination and transmission of

13. Dupont, *Invention of Literature*. She overstates the limitations of writing in antiquity (e.g., Dupont, *Invention of Literature*, 8, 14) and exaggerates the Romans' resistance to solitary reading (ibid., 243), among others. However, this is a passionate study of the gradual and inevitable shifts in the balance of literacy vs. orality from the sixth century BCE to the second century CE across Greco-Roman antiquity.

14. Geertz, *Local Knowledge*, 31.

15. Carney, *Shape of the Past*, 109–10; Havelock, *Literature Revolution*, 29; Hadas, *Ancilla*, 50–59; Kenyon, *Books and Readers*, 20–21.

written material remained that of oral reading and recitation.[16] A text was something to be vocalized, an aid to memory and a repository for the voice of an author.

To really grasp the limited extent of Greco-Roman literacy—and consequently the extent of indifference to things written—we should consider a variety of factors, such as technological developments (eye care, communication technology, industry), education (which was a very lengthy process, and so available to few), and social values. When one considers these factors,[17] one is forced to acknowledge the smallness of the section of these societies that can be called literate. Some could read, even less could read and write, and still less were fluent readers and writers.

Carney has provided us with a description of how we should picture aspects of ancient communication.

> A community at a low level of technology has rather low levels of information circulating within it, whereas a society which is highly developed technologically is inundated by communicators' messages. Specifically, traditional societies rely on oral communications and have none of our mass media. Most of their populations are illiterate, whereas industrialization requires mass literacy. Most of their communications are private and person to person, whereas most of the communications circulating in industrialized society are mass-produced and impersonal . . . In the societies under review . . . communications percolate out in irregular fashion. If one were close to an important person, he would know far more of what was going on than would another man who was closer to the scene of the action but not well connected.[18]

"Because They Do Not Know Letters"

This is the formula that was used by a hypographeus (or scribe) when he wrote a subscription for clients who were illiterate. Although a well-documented feature of Greco-Roman times, the use many people made of another person's ability to write, the extent and the diversity of contexts in which we find reference to persons being without letters (ἀγράμματοι) are often underestimated.

---

16. Finnegan, *Oral Poetry*, 166.

17. Cf. Graham, *Beyond the Written Word*, 30–35; Harris, *Ancient Literacy*.

18. Carney, *Shape of the Past*, 111–12.

My first example is a man about whom we know very little. Except for a waxed tablet from Pompeii, a document that was written in 40 CE,[19] we would not even have known about Annius Seleucus at all. This particular document was written *on behalf of* Seleucus by his slave Nardus because the former "said that he did not know letters." What is so striking is that a sum of 100,000 sesterces interest a month is discussed. Whether Seleucus himself possessed such very large amounts of money or only had access to such amounts we do not know. What is clear, however, is that a person in charge of incredibly large sums of money could fit into his society without being literate.

Although wealth is never a guarantee of literacy (and never has been), we have many instances of the Greco-Roman elite expressing regard for education and literary culture. We should surmise that education and literary culture probably had some connotations different to what we would expect, and, conversely, that illiteracy was, at the time, not that great a stumbling block we like to think it to be. "The illiterate person was able to function in a broad variety of occupations, to be recognized as a respectable member of his class, to attain financial success, to hold public office, to associate on equal terms with his literate neighbours."[20] Equally instructive is a document from a much later period,[21] the time of the persecution of the Christians under Diocletian.[22] The emperor's first anti-Christian edict of February 303 ordered the destruction of churches. In a declaration dated 5 February 304, Aurelius Ammonius, lector (reader, ἀναγνώστης) of a church in the village of Chysis, now abandoned, states under oath that the church contains nothing of value. At the end of the declaration a second hand wrote the following: "I, Aurelius Ammonius, swore the oath as aforesaid. I, Aurelius Serenus, wrote on his behalf because he does not know letters."

To modern sensibilities it seems strange that the former lector of a church is said to be illiterate.[23] But writing and reading in Greco-Roman

19. For the text, see Sbordone, "Preambolo," 145–48.

20. Youtie, "Ὑπογραφεύς," 201.

21. *Oxyrhynchus Papyrus* 33.2673.

22. Cf. Eusebius, *Ecclesiastical History* 8.2.4–5

23. Both Rea ("Declaration") and Youtie ("Ἀγράμματος," 163) suggest that Coptic Christians are involved here, and consequently that Ammonius could only read Coptic. But we do not know, and it remains remarkable that Ammonius knows Greek—he is simply ignorant of letters (μὴ εἰδότος γράμματα). Either way, a remark of Youtie ("Βραδέως Γράφων," 259) concerning the so-called 'slow writers' probably also applies here: "With these people we move through a vague area between literacy and illiteracy, a rough frontier obscured by contradictions and evasions." The (somewhat bizarre) notion

times functioned as subsets of an extensive oral environment: rather restricted crafts, carrying little of the association with wealth, power, status, and knowledge that writing eventually acquired. Indeed, we have some evidence indicating that, for some inhabitants of Egypt at least, should they "be deemed illiterate in Greek [it] held no significance for them, and for some the reputation of illiteracy in Greek, the language of the alien and worldly bureaucracy, may have become a point of pride."[24]

Plato

When we consider Plato, the only Greek philosopher to relate writing to an epistemology, we find him revealing himself to be in the midst of the interaction of oral and written communication media. Plato certainly displays a remarkable consciousness of abstraction; at the same time, he remains indebted to both memory and concrete examples in his discussions of epistemology. He attacks *both* the oral tradition (the poets) and writing. As a matter of principle, Socrates, Plato's teacher, never wrote a word because he believed in spoken dialogue as the only means of philosophical instruction. According to Plato, Socrates said,

> You know Phaedrus, that's the strange thing about writing which makes it truly analogous to painting. The painter's works stand before us as though they were alive, but, if you question them, they maintain a most majestic silence. It is the same with written words; they seem to talk to you as though they were intelligent, but if you ask them anything about what they say, from a desire to be instructed, they go on telling you just the same thing forever. And once a thing is put in writing, the composition, whatever it may be, drifts all over the place, getting into the hands not only of those who understand it, but equally of those who have no business with it; it doesn't know how to address the right people, and not address the wrong. And when it is ill-treated and unfairly abused it always needs its parent to come to its help, being unable to defend or help itself.[25]

---

of a church clerk being completely illiterate is not all that unique in late antiquity (see the discussion by Clarke, "An Illiterate Lector"). What we probably should surmise the situation to have been is that memorization played a major role in the transmission of traditions, even in what was considered to be "readings."

24. Youtie, "Because They Do Not Know Letters," 108.

25. Plato, *Phaedrus* 275d.

In fact, the most famous expression of hostility to writing in Greek literature is found in Plato's *Phaedrus*. Through Socrates' speech, Plato laments the invention of writing (by the Egyptian god Thoth). Socrates quotes Ammon: "this invention will produce forgetfulness in the minds of those who learn to use it, because they will not practise their memory."[26] Thus, Socrates goes on to argue, the true word is "written with intelligence in the mind of the learner, the living and breathing word of him who knows, of which the written may justly be called the image."[27]

Writing, Plato says, is an intrusion, something inhuman, pretending to establish outside the mind that which can only be in the mind. As an artificial contrivance, a manufactured thing, it destroys aspects of the very essence of being human: memory and internal resources. One will get tied up in what is non-living, and end up spurning real thinking. There is an uncanny insight in Plato's discussion: "If a book states an untruth, ten thousand printed refutations will do nothing to the printed text: the untruth is there for ever."[28]

These protests are set in the context of a debate about "written speeches," and as the dialogue develops it becomes clear that Plato's real concern is with the difference between oral and written *teaching*. The dialogue appears to have been triggered by the appearance of technical textbooks, such as Anaximenes's *Rhetoric against Alexander*. Plato also knows of medical textbooks[29] and of textbooks that claim to impart the rules for composition (speeches and tragedies). He argues that knowledge gained in this way is totally insufficient for the acquisition of the whole art of rhetoric and wisdom. What is gained is merely some knowledge that is a necessary preliminary.[30]

What Plato is rejecting is the belief that a book can be a passport to a kind of "instant" skill. He himself wrote not systematic treatises but dialogues, preserving the Socratic tradition of "inquiry." Books are deficient as teachers, fit only to be used as "reminders" of what is already known. "What you have discovered is a receipt for recollection, not for memory . . . it shows great folly . . . to suppose that one can transmit or acquire clear and certain knowledge of an art through the medium of writing, or that written words

26. Ibid., 275a2–4.
27. Ibid., 276a6–10.
28. Ong, "Writing is a Technology," 27.
29. Plato, *Phaedrus* 268a–b.
30. Ibid., 269.

can do more than remind the reader of what he already knows on any given subject."[31]

In the *Phaedrus* Plato disparages writing and its use as a substitute for "live," oral teaching. Yet Plato wrote extensively, and it is only because he did so that we know anything of Socratic or Platonic philosophy. He wrote in the form of dialogues, preserving to some degree the active, living relationship between teacher and student.

One of the basic tenets of Platonic philosophy, namely the theory of Forms, derives, consciously or unconsciously, from the perception of the relationship of written words to their referents. For Plato, the reality that we perceive is much too imperfect to be the really real; there must be a True Reality (the world of forms) of which what we experience is but a reflection. Accordingly, knowledge is always only a reflection, a memory, of the ultimate, unchanging Forms/Ideas, as good writing is a reflection of living speech. Writing provides Plato with a metaphor of something that can always and only be a reflection of something else and is thus incomplete.

The complexity of Plato's relationship to writing really comes to light in his *Seventh Letter*. Here we read first that Plato himself has never written anything and will not write anything on his true philosophy: "No writing by me concerning these matters exists or ever will exist. This knowledge is not something that can be put into words like other branches of learning; only after long partnership in a common life devoted to this very thing does truth flash upon the soul, like a flame kindled by a leaping spark, and once it is born there it nourishes itself thereafter."[32] The fixed nature of a written text makes it unsuitable for expressing the deepest perceptions of reality.[33]

> That is why any serious student of serious realities will shrink from making truth the helpless object of men's ill-will by committing it to writing. In a word, the conclusion to be drawn is this; when one sees a written composition, whether it be on law by a legislator or on any other subject, one can be sure, if the writer is a serious man, that his book does not represent his most serious thoughts; they remain stored up in the noblest region of his personality. If he is really serious in what he has set down in writing then surely not the gods but men "have robbed him of his wits."[34]

---

31. Ibid., 275.
32. Plato, *Ep.* 341c–d.
33. Ibid., 342–43.
34. Ibid., 344.

The *Seventh Letter* moves beyond a contempt for writing as an inferior substitute for teaching to a total rejection of writing as a medium of expression for serious philosophy. Plato sets up a firm divide between the few insiders and the many outsiders, in line with the intellectual exclusivism of his other writings.[35] Thus there is a firm divide between the mass of Plato's thought, which is publicly set out in the dialogues, and his "deepest thoughts," which are never written down. There is an "unwritten doctrine" that is distinct not only from Plato's other teaching but also from "all other sciences."

> The two attitudes evident in Plato is a fair representation of much of Hellenistic attitudes towards writing. There was a widespread preference for the "living voice" in education, and also a strong belief that distinct bodies of teaching which is never written down, and cannot be written down (which constitutes a body of secret lore different in content from what appears in writing) distinguishes the insiders (the true believers) from the outsiders. In a way we can say that since Socrates, orality was the favoured means of expression for those who called themselves "Platonic."[36]

This Platonic understanding that the living voice of the teacher is superior to any "inscription" of that voice, profoundly determined Greco-Roman advanced education.[37] Written works are important, but only so long as they are accompanied by dialogue. Even in the context of voluminous writing, an author may express reservations about the written word.[38]

Papias of Hierapolis

A well-known expression of prejudice in favor of the "living voice" is found in a remark of Papias's *Exposition of Sayings of the Lord* (as quoted by Eusebius): "For I did not imagine that things out of books would help me as much as the utterances of a living and abiding voice."[39]

35. Cf. Plato, *Seventh Letter* 312–14.

36. Cf. Marzillo, "Performing an Academic Talk," 184–86.

37. Graff, *Legacies of Literacy*, 24–30.

38. This emphasis in ancient education correlated with a conservative (and political) impulse. Plato's objection that the written text can get into the wrong hands and cannot explain itself, is an objection to the fact that the reader can freely interpret the text without the author ("authority") being able to indicate the correct "meaning." So, the Platonic influence is not just about the author to stand as a voice behind the text, but to enforce canonical interpretations. See Gee, "Legacies of Literacy."

39. Eusebius, *HE* 3.39.4.

Papias's words demand a context—the original literary and genetic context is irrecoverably lost—so we need to turn to the social and cultural context in which these words made sense.

A Common Proverb

Papias's phrase is closely echoed in a passage written by Galen, in the opening paragraph of his *Treatise on the Preparation of Medicine*: "There may well be truth in the idiom current among most craftsmen (τεχνιτῶν), that reading out of a book is not the same as, or even comparable to, learning from the living voice."[40] Not only is Galen using the exact phrase of Papias, "from the living voice" (παρὰ ζώσης φωνῆς) but he is pointing to the given nature of the phrase: a saying or proverb in current use. We have, in fact various allusions to the importance of the "living voice." Quintilian tells us "that the living voice, as the saying goes, provides more nourishment";[41] and Pliny writes that "the living voice, as the common saying has it, is much more effective."[42] Quintilian is referring to a rhetorical school, and the contrast is between giving pupils declamations to read and giving them a live performance from the teacher. Pliny is urging a friend to come and listen to an orator rather than reading at home out of books. In both cases the phrase is mentioned to be proverbial (*ut dicitur*). Written speeches do exist, but their use is deprecated. The stress is on the primacy of the live performance of a show declamation.

Galen's reference comes in the context of learning medicine, the practical problems of identifying herbs. Texts should not be used outside a teaching situation, but preferably, like other technical studies, teaching should be learned from a teacher and practical experience. In this sense the living voice is promoted: book learning cannot possibly be a match for it. Although conclusions must be tentative, we can detect a cultural assumption of the first and second centuries that the production of a book was not an inevitable, or even necessarily a desirable end in itself: books are secondary to oral teaching. You will gain more, however, from the living voice and from sharing someone's daily life than from any treatise.[43]

---

40. Galen, *De Compositione Medicamentorum Secundum Locum* 6.1.

41. Quintilian, *Inst. Orat.* 2.2.8.

42. Pliny, *Letters* 2.3.

43. See Seneca, *Letters* 6.5; advice given after a promise of sending books to Lucilius, *Letters* 6.4.

The Living and Remaining Word

Papias, as far as we can determine, was no philosopher. He had a few weird ideas, and he appears to have been a Christian teacher; but he was not necessarily an educated one, although he does display some rhetorical skill.[44]

He probably quotes current wisdom in his reference to the living voice. Papias's concern is with teaching and with the passing on and preservation of authentic tradition. He expresses scepticism about the efficacy and value of written traditions. Written texts are secondary and subordinate to oral instruction and traditions. The living voice of the teacher has priority, even when written material is available: "And I shall not hesitate to supplement (συγκατατάξαι) the traditions with what I learnt well from the elders, for of their truth I am confident . . . but if by chance someone should come who had actually learned from (παρηκολουθηκώς) the prominent leaders I examined their words (what Andrew, Peter, Philip . . . disciples of the Lord were saying). For I did not imagine that things out of books would help me as much as the utterances of a living and abiding voice."[45]

Clement of Alexandria

Clement of Alexandria is a philosopher, and he knows Platonic philosophy. He quotes not only the *Phaedrus* but also the *Second Letter*. He is the author of various writings, but at the beginning of his *Stromata* (Miscellanies of Christian Teachings) we find an elaborate defense for writing the book. "Now this treatise is not a carefully composed piece of writing for display, but just my notes stored up for old age, a remedy against forgetfulness, nothing but a rough image, a sketch of those clear and living words which I was thought worthy to hear, and of those blessed and truly worthy men."[46]

Although Clement felt no need to justify his other works, the particular exercise of forming and committing to writing the "Christian philosophy" of the *Stromata* caused him to explain his actions. In other words, we witness a sort of esoteric conception of teaching. Clement's chief concern is above all "the justification of teaching through writing."[47] The *Stromata* are a record of teaching aimed at the preservation of "true tradition." He tells us that the note he is writing is a kind of sketch of words and people. These people

44. Cf. Schoedel, *Apostolic Fathers,* 91.

45. Eusebius, *HE* 3.39.2–4.

46. Clement of Alexandria, *Strom.*1.11.1; cf. Eusebius, *HE* 5.11.3.

47. Osborn, "Teaching and Writing," 34.

maintained the true tradition of blessedness in their teaching, handed down from father to son, from Peter, James, John, and Paul. It is a touching picture of the intimacy of the early church.[48] But the revelation (of divine secrets) is to the few. The sacred secrets, like God, are entrusted to word (λόγος), not to writing (1.13.2). This is a clear assertion of the limitations of Scripture. It also indicates the importance of oral tradition in the Christian movement.

The stature of the oral tradition as the normal method of teaching (and transmitting) the Christian faith is beautifully illustrated by a remark of Justin: "Among us you can hear and learn these things from those who do not even know the letters of the alphabet—uneducated and barbarous in speech, but wise and faithful in mind—even from cripples and the blind."[49] Clement omits some matters for which his "readers" are not ready: "So that others won't think we are giving a sword to a child" (1.14.3). He himself is guided by special knowledge. Truth itself is veiled, and his *Miscellanies* so presents it; oral teaching is the only way of knowing the veil, and uncovering truth. Written words of necessity need help (1.14.4). Christianity, with "truly sacred mysteries," offers pure light and a vision of the one God.[50] This secret side of worship can by definition not be made known, but Clement does give away a lot of *other* mysterious religious practices: *symbola* and traditions that deserve our careful attention in order to understand the secret, oral traditions closely guarded by the ancients.

Clement is very much a man of his times. Greco-Roman culture was permeated with the concept of secrecy. At one end of the social scale in antiquity were the *arcana imperii*, the secrets of the imperial government known only to the emperor and his confidential advisors/supporters. At the other end were the secret societies of the slaves whose members made themselves known to each other by inconspicuous signs and passwords. Within the world of free men secrecy was omnipresent: in political activities, in business, in the crafts and professions.

Pagans described Jewish religious practices as mysteries,[51] and they themselves participated in innumerable mystery cults. Part of religion (or beyond religion) was magic, which was practiced by almost everyone. Philosophical schools, usually closed to outsiders, had their secret traditions taught and transmitted by means of speech. The disgust felt for making

---

48. Ferguson, *Clement of Alexandria*, 109.
49. Justin Martyr, *1 Apol.* 60.11.
50. Clement, *Exhortation to the Greeks*, 12.120.
51. E.g., Plutarch, *Moralia* 7.1–3.

public one's secrets through writing is nicely illustrated by the author(s) of
1 Enoch:

> After this judgment, they shall frighten them and make them
> scream because they have shown this (knowledge of secret things)
> to those who dwell on earth. Now behold, I am naming the names
> of those angels! These are their names: . . . The fourth is named
> Pinemʼe [Penemu], this one demonstrated to the children of the
> people the bitter and the sweet and revealed to them all the secrets
> of their wisdom. Furthermore he caused the people to penetrate
> (the secret of) writing and (the use of) ink and paper; on account
> of this matter, there are many who have erred from eternity to
> eternity, until this very day. For human beings are not created for
> such purposes to take up their beliefs with pen and ink . . . Death,
> which destroys everything, would have not touched them, had it
> not been through their knowledge by which they shall perish . . .[52]

Notable Exceptions?

When forming impressions of Greco-Roman cultural attitudes we should
beware of relying on a small literary elite. This is a point that MacMullen
often makes;[53] a perspective he describes as seeing all head and no body. It
is with this reminder that we should understand negative references to oral
tradition in antiquity.

Cicero, in one of his letters to Atticus, exclaims: "Where are those who
talk about the living voice? I got a much better idea from your letter than
from his talk about what was going on . . ."[54] The remark follows from comparison of a verbal report of some news to a letter referring to the same.
Cicero clearly affirms the fact that high regard for oral tradition was quite
widespread (*ubi sunt qui aiunt*, ζώσης φωνῆς), but that he felt himself—at
least in this one instance—at odds with this sentiment. But then Cicero was
indeed quite at odds with most of his fellow men and cultural times contemporaries. Not only was he a senior consular, but also highly educated:
a critical literate. However, and very interestingly, in the *same* letter Cicero
writes: "My curiosity is insatiable: but I have no complaint at your omitting
to write about the dinner. I would much rather hear it by word of mouth."[55]

---

52. *1 Enoch* 69:1–11; Isaac, "1 Enoch," 47–48.

53. E.g., MacMullen, *Paganism*; MacMullen, *Christianizing*.

54. Cicero, *Letters to Atticus* 2.12.

55. Ibid. Elsewhere Cicero expresses scepticism about the value of textbooks (*Against*

Seneca also expressed a reservation to oral tradition: "Why, after all, should I listen to what I can read for myself? 'The living voice,' it may be answered, 'counts for a great deal.' Not when it is just acting in a kind of secretarial capacity, making itself an instrument for what others have to say."[56]

Seneca is here arguing for a sophisticated attitude towards philosophy. Instead of merely memorizing Zeno or Cleanthes, one should be able to think and teach for oneself. "Assume authority yourself and utter something that may be handed down to posterity."[57] If the living voice is merely a means of passing on tradition, then a book can do as well: "Let's have some difference between you and the books!"[58]

Once again we see the general high regard for oral tradition, but also how a highly educated philosopher, explicitly claiming to be literate, realizes the limitations of oral teaching. Books are indeed of secondary importance, but making oral tradition into a vehicle for mere memorization and transmission would make it similar to writing: one would be "dependent on some original and constantly be looking to see what the master said."[59] Also, the uses of communication media are fluent and dynamic. The mere existence of written traditions influence and change attitudes. It is quite possible that both Papias and Clement reflect tensions within early Christianity. The Christian movement was entering a "scholastic" phase during the second century: the process of defining its canon of "prescribed texts" from which all future Christian teaching would be derived, and probably simultaneously engaged the process of suppressing the "living voice" of developing tradition (as exhibited in Montanist prophecy or in the Gnostic gospels).

An illustration of how the power of spoken words was associated with texts can be seen in the invocation of magic to deal with intellectual property in antiquity.[60] Literary property was often seen as bound up with magic, and clearly sometimes as secret information.[61] In antiquity an author had no rights to his or her book even *before* publication, no control over its fate after publication, and no prospect of being able to correct it after it was copied.

Caecilius 47), echoing Alcidamas's attack on Isocrates (Alcidamas, *Against the Sophists* 1–2, 9–16).

56. Seneca, *Letters* 33.9.

57. Ibid., 33.8.

58. Ibid., 33.9.

59. Ibid., 33.9.

60. An association pointed out by Wincor, *Ritual to Royalties*, 20–22.

61. Rev 22:18–19 and *1 Enoch* 104:11 are well-known examples. See Aune, *Revelation 17–22*, 1208–16, on these "integrity formulas" and "conditional curse formulas."

"Once a poem has left your hands, you resign all your rights; a speech when published is a free being," according to Symmachus, the fourth-century *rhetor* (*Ep.* 1.31; cf. Horace, *Ep.* 1.20; Martial 1.3).

Concluding Remarks

Discussions of orality and literacy in the Greco-Roman world must consist of both broad, theoretical issues and consideration of specific evidence. This study aims to contribute to the understanding of attitudes toward writing in antiquity by analyzing a few specific instances.

How the possibilities of writing is developed by a society depends on many factors, such as the social structure and values of the people employing the script. With regard to these factors we it seems that a preference for orally transmitted teaching was widespread in Hellenistic times and in the Roman Empire. This preference, as is well-known, is also common in the rabbinic academies, which shows to what extent early Judaism truly reflects its character as an instance of Greco-Roman culture—an example of the "great similarities between the methods, behavior, practices and notions prevalent among Jews and gentiles alike."[62]

This oral teaching tradition was recognized to have a higher authenticity-value than written texts, even though it was constantly updated and amended in the light of practice and changing circumstances. Oral tradition and oral mentality pervaded Greco-Roman culture. Writers could rely on the matrix of the teaching situation to expand and explain the text. The role of the teacher, the "living voice" was crucial.

In scribal culture we find a commitment to the give-and-take of small-group dialectic (interaction). To such a commitment written documents are closed systems, one-way discourses, which are totally inappropriate to teaching and transmission of life's traditions. Writing, though useful for certain things, is the antithesis of the movement and experience of life itself.

In the instances that we have looked at, we have found a general reticence towards writing, varying from mere indifference to active scepticism. The scribal culture of antiquity seems to exhibit a bias towards orality and little awareness of a *dichotomization* between the spoken and the written. The written was not set up over and against the spoken (as we moderns with our heavy literacy bias do), but the written was rather seen as an extension of speech. Even "literates" (people making extensive use of texts) often had little confidence in writing as a substitute for oral communication.

62. Liebermann, *Hellenism in Jewish Palestine*, 193.

Finally, a few brief remarks about some implications of this oral bias. Although the fact of oral tradition and its importance is generally acknowledged, both the extent and importance of the oral teaching tradition in antiquity are easily underestimated. We really need to re-learn how to "read" our texts explicitly with an awareness of the all-pervading presence of orality and oral traditions. One consequence of such an awareness is easy to spot. It leads to a different attitude to our manuscripts and textual criticism, and the whole concept of an "original" version needs re-evaluation.[63]

Another implication is, if history is of any importance to our religious reflection and theologizing, concepts of authority and of the use of Scripture need to be revised. In view of the above, I think that we should move from a doctrine of Scripture to a more comprehensive *theology of tradition*.

By realizing how impoverished our conventional perception of tradition has become we also become conscious of the plight of our infatuation with things written and learn to value the living and abiding voice of our fellow humans.

63. Botha, "Teks van die Nuwe Testament." In Homeric studies there are two approaches to the status of textual variants found in different written sources. On the one hand, the textual variants are seen as reflections of the process of recomposition in performance (characteristic of oral and orally-derived texts), with a fixed text evolving *after* a period of performances. Thus, variants represent the multiformity of transmission (see esp. Nagy, "Homeric Questions"; Nagy, *Poetry as Performance*). On the other hand is the proposal for an early fixed text through oral dictation, justifying attempts to recover the archetype text (with which to assess textual variants). See, e.g., Janko, "Homeric Poems."

3

Greco-Roman Literacy
and the New Testament Writings

Introduction

It has often been claimed that "Christianity emerged in a Mediterranean culture that was not illiterate. Education was widespread. Books were produced on a scale theretofore unknown. A large reading public consumed prose written with a rhetorical cast."[1] We find in this statement a perception of Greco-Roman communication that, on the face of it, seems unproblematic, and with which few seem to disagree. This perception is not without consequence, specifically as regards New Testament scholarship. Talbert uses the notion of widespread literacy in connection with the synoptic problem; assumptions concerning Greco-Roman literacy abound in New Testament research.

That large collections of books existed and that more people had contact with reading/writing (supposedly than in earlier times) are in themselves relatively meaningless statements; they gain value only when situated within a socio-cultural context. Talbert did not discuss literacy analytically, so we must assume that modern conceptions provide the framework within which his statement must be understood.

This is not an unimportant issue. The claim about first-century literacy is a general conclusion used to understand a specific instance: it helps to interpret the origins and dissemination of Christian writings. This is what this chapter is about: ancient literacy as part of the historical setting of the New Testament.

---

1. Talbert, "Oral and Independent," 101–2.

But there is a second, even more difficult aim. Recently, various scholars have asked for a reader-response perspective to be used as the basis for analysis of New Testament writings. This is an approach that describes the literary techniques by which an author shapes the reader's experience of a text.[2] In these proposals we once again clearly see certain assumptions about ancient books and reading at work. Not only the extent and levels of literacy need to be discussed, but the whole (and immensely complicated) issue of the social uses of writing in antiquity: why did people write and what were their attitudes towards written artifacts? Indeed, as will be made clear in this chapter, probably very few people actually read in a sophisticated manner.

Exploring Uncharted Areas

Bias and Prejudice

To an extent New Testament scholarship's problematic use of literacy arguments is simply a reflection of the failure of scholarship in general to adequately discuss these matters.

Tarn and Griffith, for instance, write of a small highly educated public and of another "larger one which had education enough to read greedily but not to read seriously," this being catered for by "popular literature."[3] This tells us something about Tarn's assumptions concerning popular culture and reflects some idealization of the Hellenistic world. Popular (written) literature did not exist in antiquity; the papyri conclusively show that the "literary" texts were copies of Homer and Euripides (almost exclusively). Other genres or writings were not intended for mass consumption. A supposed example of popular literature, such as the mimiambs of Herodas,[4] was not written in common everyday language. Reading did not feature in Greco-Roman popular culture.[5]

Another example is the claim by Fouquet-Plümacher that the Roman empire had, since the first century BCE, a thriving book trade ("ausserordentlich leistungsfähig"), but can only point to two booksellers: Atticus and Sosius.[6] At the time, "the phenomenon of publishing as a profession seems

2. E.g. Fowler, "Who Is 'the Reader,'" 5–23; Petersen, "Reader," 38–51; Combrink, "Readings," 189–203.

3. Tarn and Griffith, *Hellenistic Civilization*, 268.

4. See Beare and Eicholz, "Herodas," 507.

5. Harris, *Ancient Literacy*, 126.

6. Fouquet-Plümacher, "Buch/Buchwesen 3," 276.

not to have existed."[7] Having some book*sellers* is something quite different from having a publishing industry. In any case, the activities of a few (or even a few hundred) very wealthy men can hardly be used to characterize the Roman empire.

The belief that the success of Hellenism—the remarkable spread of Greek culture—is basically due to the easy availability of books, education, and scholarship, is fairly fashionable. But some research has shown that, considering relevant data, antiquity lacked an awareness of a diversity of literary texts. The implication of this lack has remained largely unnoticed, something that should probably be ascribed to modern scholars' idealization of classical antiquity and a disregard for classes other than the elite.[8] With regard to classical Athens, Thomas provides interesting illustrations of "how modern scholars tend to approach ancient documents from modern documentary usage and how this misconceives ancient written record."[9]

We need to take (at least) two specific steps in order to think realistically about ancient literacy. In the first place, we must realize that literacy is a technology *with a history*. It waxes and wanes according to intricate and involved historical processes.

Although the Greek world knew writing during the second millennium BCE, for various reasons writing fell into disuse, so that by 1100 BCE, like most sections of the Mediterranean world, Greece was without writing. Due to economic contact the Greeks learned their writing from the Phoenicians, during the eighth century BCE (as claimed by Herodotus 5.58). This adoption was a dramatic step that introduced writing to the Western world. From Greece writing probably spread through the western Mediterranean world, and its movement into Italy led to a form of writing that constitutes our own alphabet.[10] The Romans developed monumental writing into a fine art. As of the first century BCE, inscriptions of great precision, clarity, and beauty were carved on stone throughout the Roman empire, symbols of the power and authority of Rome. Thus began the spread of the Latin alphabet to the rest of Europe, where it was never to lose its hold.

Even so, writing never gained a strong enough hold in the West not to be threatened with extinction. In the Middle Ages, it fell almost exclusively

7. Easterling, "Books and Readers," 19–20.

8. Finley, *Ancient History*, 10; Wood and Wood, *Class Ideology*, 4–5, 246–59; Harris, *Ancient Literacy*, 11.

9. Thomas, *Oral Tradition*, 15–92, esp. 45.

10. For the history of Western writing, see Havelock, *Origins*, 22–50; Kitzinger, "Alphabets and Writing," 397–419.

into the care of the church. Writing once again became restricted to a rather small group of officials, a circumstance reminiscent of its exclusive use by ancient Egyptian and Mesopotamian scribes, and differing from its use in the Greco-Roman world of antiquity. Outside the church, people once again depended entirely on speech until literacy began to spread anew in the twelfth century.

To see ancient literacy in its proper context, we should, in the second place, free ourselves from our preference for and admiration of literacy. Clanchy writes: "Writing gives the historian his materials and it is consequently understandable that he has tended to see it as a measure of progress. Furthermore, literate techniques are so necessary to twentieth-century western society, and education in them is so fundamental a part of the modern individual's experience that it is difficult to avoid assuming that literacy is an essential mark of civilization."[11]

The technology of writing is a *cultural phenomenon* with social and communicative functions, a social product shaped by factors such as politics and ideology.[12] Literacy "has different effects according to circumstances and is not a civilizing force in itself, although there is a relationship between national minimal literacy averages and the mastery of modern industrial technology."[13] Writing cannot possibly be seen as a monolithic entity; the potentialities of writing depend on the many variables concerning technology, cultural attitudes, needs, beliefs, and so forth that can be found in any particular society.[14]

A notable attack on the unrealistic definitions of literacy, the little appreciation of conceptual complications presented by studies of literacy and the ignorance of sociohistorical context pervading literacy scholarship has been made by Graff.[15] "The meaning and contribution of literacy . . . cannot be *presumed*; they must in themselves be a distinct focus of research and criticism."[16]

11. Clanchy, *From Memory*, 7.
12. Cf. Street, *Literacy*, 96.
13. Clanchy, *From Memory*, 7.
14. Goody, *Domestication of the Savage Mind*; Stubbs, *Language and Literacy*.
15. Graff, *Legacies of Literacy*, 3; Graff, *Labyrinths of Literacy*; Graff, "Literacy."
16. Graff, *Legacies of Literacy*, 5.

Some Clarifications

Concepts of literacy and thus criteria for its achievement have altered significantly during the course of time, from place to place, and from group to group.[17] Any definition of literacy, besides the inevitable arbitrary elements in it, creates as many problems as it attempts to avoid.

The definitions used by various sociologists and historians for literacy differ significantly. The availability of signature evidence has influenced considerable research, which has been criticized for exactly this fact. In cultures in which signatures have been important, they have for some people been virtually the only writing accomplishment.[18]

Other historians have preferred to define literacy with reference to reading ability, which is usually more widespread than the ability to write. Clanchy argues that in medieval England reading ability and writing ability were quite independent of each other.[19] He emphasizes the difficulties of writing within a manuscript technology,[20] an observation of direct relevance to understanding first-century literacy. Reading in antiquity was *also* physically very demanding.[21]

The challenge here is to relate literacy in a comprehensive way to the contexts and communicative practices of people. Many studies tend to discuss literacy only in quantitative terms relating to reading and writing. The whole problem of understanding literacy is that activities such as reading/writing and speaking are inextricably part of a larger network of cultural activities, of symbolizing and symbolic effort.

Talk of orality and literacy must be very carefully controlled. There simply is no such thing as "orality" (only in an analytical, cultural-anthropological ideal sense); we can only describe aspects of *Greco-Roman* orality, or, as this study attempts, of *Greco-Roman* literacy. In studies broaching these issues we find allusion to the oral *and* the written[22] or the oral *against* the written.[23] Little attention seems to be directed at Greco-Roman communication,

17. Stubbs, *Language and Literacy*, 4–14; Botha, "Orality-Literacy Studies"; Heath, "Functions"; Harris, *Ancient Literacy*, 3–10.

18. Stone, *Literacy and Education*, 98–99, argues for the usefulness of the ability to sign marriage registers as an index to literacy in early modern England; Collinson, "Significance of Signatures," queries its usefulness as an index to literacy.

19. Clanchy, *From Memory*, 183.

20. Cf. ibid., 88–97.

21. Kenyon, *Books and Readers*, 67–70; Achtemeier, "*Omne Verbum Sonat*," 17.

22. Achtemeier, "*Omne Verbum Sonat*."

23. Kelber, *Oral and the Written Gospel*.

of which texts and speech and writing are instances, and which in themselves are functions of various societal and cultural activities. I am not denying the value of generalizing—it is of the utmost importance—but want to highlight the complexities at stake here and the importance of consistent historical interpretation when it comes to studying oral and written communication in antiquity.

Acknowledging that infinite gradations of literacy and reading ability can exist within any segment of a population is of course the basic starting point. Still, we do need some generalizing *in order to understand specifics better*. For this study, three broad categories will be distinguished (without claiming that sharp polarities existed, and expressly stating that these are types, inherently far simpler than reality). *Semi-literates* are persons who can write slowly or not at all, and who can read without being able to read complex or very lengthy texts. They are inevitably an amorphous group, and during the first century of the Common Era probably made up approximately ten (to fifteen) percent of Greco-Roman societies. Of these few capable of some reading/writing skills a small segment can be called literate: fluent readers and writers. Harris provides an extensive discussion of the probable statistics for Greco-Roman literacy: "Among the inhabitants of the Empire in general, though a few used writing heavily and though some knew how to use written texts without being literate, for most the written word remained inaccessible."[24]

Some Evidence

We shall obviously never know in a clear-cut numerical way how many people were literate in the Roman empire. In part, this is due to the fact that nobody at the time thought it expedient to collect data that can be used in a trustworthy sense by future generations of scholars (a point in itself against awareness of the importance of literacy).

It follows that one has to deduce literacy levels from various possible indications, which necessitates interpretation. Thus, the evidence, "though plentiful, is sporadic and not infrequently ambiguous."[25] Indirect evidence concerns elementary schooling (an aspect of antiquity that has not been investigated for purposes of establishing literacy achievement)[26] and indications for the need of literacy.

24. Harris, *Ancient Literacy*, 232.
25. Kenney, "Small Writing," 168; cf. Easterling, "Books and Readers," 16–17.
26. Harris, *Ancient Literacy*, 11.

It has been claimed that the number and character of the public inscriptions of the cities of the Mediterranean world (such as Ephesus or Athens) show that a high proportion of the citizens of the Roman empire were literate. Not everybody, however, needed to be able to read these documents to be impressed by them, which were, for the largest part, the main reason for them having been made.[27] Inscriptions had a strong symbolic meaning in antiquity (witness, for example, the many addressed to divine beings and the curse tablets), and despite saying what was meant (for the ancients) they are a poor reflection of common literacy. Thomas writes, "The stone documents of Greece cannot be interpreted adequately without appreciating the oral background to the ancient use of writing."[28]

The use to which people put their literacy is not the same thing as the level of literacy itself, according to MacMullen.[29] He argues that, especially concerning the epigraphic evidence from the Roman empire, publishing statements on stone was part of the package that we call Romanization: one of the ways of being Roman, an expression of being part of a special group. How misleading epigraphy concerning literacy levels can be is evident from the city inscriptions found in southeastern Syria, which are in Greek, while the procurators who were used to doing business in Greek still needed an interpreter.[30] The epigraphic "habit" was an expensive one, and reflects forces other than popular literacy.[31]

Graffiti can also be an index to literacy—but how reliable is this source of information? For instance, as is well known, Pompeii has quite a lot of graffiti. The quantity of these writings has impressed various scholars[32] to the extent that they claim widespread literacy that extended well beyond the elite.[33] Aside from the question how far graffiti at Pompeii can be an indication of literacy in the Roman empire (Pompeii being in many other respects quite unusual within the context of Greco-Roman cities), how many

27. Ibid., 90.

28. Thomas, *Oral Tradition*, 286.

29. MacMullen, "Epigraphic Habit," 237.

30. Jones, *Greek City*, 290.

31. Cf. MacMullen, "Epigraphic Habit," 245. Millar, "Epigraphy," 80–136, is a real eye-opener to the value of epigraphy for historical research and also for gaining a sense of one's overwhelming ignorance of major cultural phenomena in Greco-Roman civilization.

32. E.g., Pattison, *On Literacy*, 62.

33. Cf. Hopkins, "Economic Growth," 39.

wrote and for what purposes are simply not known.[34] Proper examination dissolves this evidence into very little; what can be deduced is "that some Pompeians wrote on walls a lot, a handful of them quoting literary texts but most of them much less ambitious."[35] And, incidentally, these records tell us quite curious things about the loves and erotic fantasies of Pompeians rather than about the general level of literacy. Harris's conclusion regarding literacy in Pompeii, a prosperous town with approximately 15,000 inhabitants,[36] is worth quoting in full:

> Several thousand of the Pompeians of 79 must have had some ac-
> quaintance with writing, but perhaps not more than two or three
> thousand; these will have included all the members of the curial
> class, some but not all of the artisans and tradesmen, a markedly
> lower proportion of the women in the families of these latter
> groups, very few of the really poor, but a substantial number of
> slaves (far more male than female) in the more prosperous house-
> holds. In the countryside around the town, the proportion of liter-
> ates will have been lower: there very few of the small farmers or
> of the farm slaves are likely to have been able to read and write.[37]

Finally, a comparative method is essential for any analysis of literacy and its uses. Harris writes:

> Investigation of the volume of literacy in other societies, and in
> particular of the growth of literacy in early-modern and modern
> Europe, has shown that writing ceases to be the arcane accomplish-
> ment of a small professional or religious or social elite *only* when
> certain preconditions are fulfilled and *only* when strong positive
> forces are present to bring the change about. Such forces may be
> economic, social or ideological or any combination of these things
> . . . But without these preconditions and without such positive
> forces, literacy remains a restricted possession—a state of affairs
> which may seem perfectly acceptable even in a culture which is
> in a sense penetrated through and through by the written word.[38]

---

34. See, also, the reservations of Kaimio, *Romans and the Greek Language*, 180, on the representativeness of graffiti at Pompeii.

35. Harris, "Literacy and Epigraphy," 104.

36. In 1979 Grant could confidently claim Pompeii's population to be 100,000 (*History*, 243–44); today estimates range from 12,000 to 30,000 inhabitants at the time of the city's destruction in 79 CE. See Gulletta and Kockel, "Pompeii."

37. Harris, "Literacy and Epigraphy," 110.

38. Harris, *Ancient Literacy*, 11–12; cf. Heath, "Functions," 16.

One of the ways in which a deficient education and illiteracy become apparent in a culture is the commonness of people's recorded ages to end in five or zero.[39] More than 40,000 extant inscriptions give the age at death of members of the Roman empire, and almost every sample of these figures shows a very large excess of ages divisible by five. The inference is difficult to avoid that this population, "like most modern populations where age-rounding is endemic, was probably characterized by widespread illiteracy."[40] Duncan-Jones's conclusion, after a careful statistical analysis, is that "it is very striking that in modern cases where rounding exceeds an index level of 30 (the Roman average by area is much higher, about 55), illiteracy of 70% or more is also found . . . it would appear that a substantial portion of those commemorated on Roman tombstones might have had difficulty in reading their epitaphs, or at least difficulty in writing their names."[41]

Ancient Literacy

Little Reading, Less Writing

Certain technical realities must be borne in mind when considering the probabilities for literacy in antiquity. Convenient writing materials were relatively expensive and in limited supply. One need only be reminded of the common use of potsherds as writing material. Furthermore, the simple fact that eye care was extremely rudimentary meant that those with poor eyesight were excluded from the written word.[42]

With regard to economy, once again certain structural conditions preclude the possibility of significant literacy. There was no printed advertising, no insurance, no timetables; and there was a constant supply of persons (slaves or freedmen) who could act as substitute writers and readers, or, more often, as messengers.[43] There were few incentives to learn to read.

In the Roman empire, outside the largest cities (in other words, areas like Asia Minor, Syria, and Palestine) the situation probably was very like Lévi-Strauss's description of the villages in eastern Pakistan. Although all the inhabitants were illiterate, "each village had its scribe who acted on behalf of the individuals or of the community as a whole. All the villagers know

---

39. See the comparative data cited by Duncan-Jones, "Age-rounding," 333–53.

40. Duncan-Jones, "Age-rounding," 335.

41. Ibid., 347.

42. Corbett, "Historical View," 40; Rosen, "Invention of Eyeglasses," 13–46, 183–218.

43. Harris, *Ancient Literacy*, 19.

about writing, and make use of it if the need arises, but they do so from the outside, as if it were a foreign mediatory agent that they communicate with by oral methods."[44]

To summarize this section: Most inhabitants of the Greco-Roman world (including bureaucratic Egypt) could get by without being able to read and/or write. Some might merely have been able to write their names; others, though not completely illiterate, might still have preferred to have letters or legal documents written for them. Getting a letter copied was quite costly; two drachmas during the reign of Claudius, according to a papyrus letter published by Youtie.[45] Two drachmas could hire you a skilled artisan such as a foreman or industrial worker for two to three days, at the time.[46]

The possibility of widespread literacy, and the probability of a literate culture cannot be very great with regard to Greco-Roman antiquity: as a society, the major factors creating literacy were absent, and many factors making it unlikely were fully present.

Education

It is self-evident that literacy is heavily dependent on schooling. Lockridge has shown how mass literacy is related not so much to urbanization, but to the proliferation of towns making schools possible and available.[47] In an agrarian society such as the Roman empire,[48] schooling must have been puny. Public funding and incentive for schooling presuppose sufficient interest, clearly lacking in the small villages making up the vast Roman empire. The cost of schooling cannot be overlooked,[49] although that differed considerably from place to place.

Greco-Roman education is a highly complex historical phenomenon.[50] As a topic, particularly elementary education, it is in need of serious reconsideration. For instance, the famous and almost ubiquitous notion of a

44. Lévi-Strauss, *Tristes Tropiques*, 298.

45. Youtie, "P. Mich. Inv. 855," 147–50.

46. Cf. Lewis, *Life in Egypt under Roman Rule*, 208.

47. Lockridge, "Literacy in Early America," 183–200.

48. Jones, *Greek City*, 259–69; Garnsey and Saller, *Early Principate*, 28–33; Saldarini, *Pharisees, Scribes and Sadducees*, 35–8; Stambaugh and Balch, *New Testament*, 65–69.

49. Jones, *Greek City*, 220–26.

50. For overviews of Greco-Roman schooling see, with various perspectives, Jackson, "Education and Entertainment," 4–30; Beck, "Education," 369–73; Marrou, "Education and Rhetoric," 185–201; Stowers, *Letter Writing*, 32–5; Veyne, "Roman Empire," 19–21; Harris, "Literacy and Epigraphy," 95–102; Harris, *Ancient Literacy*, 233–48.

fixed tripartite education system—three stages with each its own teacher and discreet curriculum—is quite problematic, if not misleading with regard to education in antiquity.[51] The terminology in our sources is more obscure than most discussions would have them.[52] Schools in the Roman empire were physically makeshift. Archaeological evidence for schools is particularly scarce—which is understandable as schools were normally in or practically in the street.[53] This was due to financial reasons, probably for publicity, and certainly also due to—interestingly—Greco-Roman public opinion that feared the sexual corruption of the boys.[54] And they were not at all very common. Pliny wrote to Cornelius Tacitus asking for help in appointing teachers at Comum, which had no school for boys[55]—and Comum cannot be regarded an unusual town. Pliny himself probably had tutors at home, a system he commends to his friends[56]—that is, the circle of the ruling elite.

Very relevant to this discussion is the contempt that Greeks and Romans often expressed for those who taught reading and writing.[57] Quintilian hints that men became teachers who had not themselves progressed much beyond the *primae litterae*.[58]

What about the role of slaves with regard to ancient education? Bonner in particular has made a case for the important role that literate slaves played in and their value to Roman society.[59] But the first thing to realize is that literate slaves *do not* point to widespread literacy. The very existence of a market for 'literate' slaves shows the general disregard for literacy current at the time. That these men were responsible for most of primary/elementary education[60] does not necessarily imply that schools taught effective literacy, nor is it an indication of the promotion of writing

51. Booth, "Elementary," 1–14; Kaster, "Notes," 323–46.

52. Harris, *Ancient Literacy*, 234.

53. Bonner, "Street-teacher," 509–28; Bonner, *Education in Ancient Rome*, 115–25.

54. Pliny, *Ep.* 3.3.3–4; Quintilian, *Inst. Orat.* 1.2.4–5; 1.3.17; Courtney, *Commentary*, 379, 476.

55. Pliny, *Ep.* 4.13.

56. Ibid., 2.18; 3.3

57. Cicero, *Tusculanae Disputationes* 3.12.27; Cicero, *Epistualae ad Familiares* 9.18.1; Plutarch, *Moralia* 830; Tacitus, *Annals* 3.66.3; Pliny, *Ep.* 4.11.1; Juvenal 7.198; Dio Chrysostom 7.114.

58. Quintilian, *Inst. Orat.* 1.1.8.

59. Bonner, *Education in Ancient Rome*, 37–38.

60. Ibid., 38.

What we probably should picture is a situation where some boys (mostly boys) attended elementary schools. It never turned into a large percentage, and numbers decreased sharply with corresponding progress in levels of education. The school-going public consisted of children from wealthier families and slaves (also from wealthy families). Education within the family played a major role. This fact, tied to the status of elementary schooling probably facilitated *craft literacy*: practical, very basic knowledge of letters and numbers. It is relevant to bear in mind that "young children will have particular difficulty in learning to read if they grow up in a home or cultural background with no tradition of literacy and hence no appreciation of the purposes of written language."[61] Seen within the broad context of Greco-Roman society, it is probably safe to conclude with the following: "Mass literacy is impossible without mass education; and there is no evidence, a handful of Hellenistic exceptions apart, that city fathers or central government were ever minded to lay out hard cash on educating the children of all citizens, let alone the populace at large. 'Higher' education was another matter: publicly-funded chairs of rhetoric . . . provided professional training for the ruling class and hence assisted political stability."[62]

"Popular" Literature and Book Publishing

When discussing the "popular" culture of Greco-Roman societies, the simple fact is that we are only beginning to understand something about popular culture and life outside the elite, ruler class. One reason for this is, you guessed it, the lack of documentary evidence. Fortunately, due to the extensive papyri finds, it is possible to describe some aspects of life in Egyptian towns and villages.

The Egypt that was part of the Roman empire was divided into some thirty administrative districts. Each such nome (νόμος, *praefectura*) had a capital, the metropolis, where its administration was centered. Population statistics are not available—and with current evidence scarcely calculable—but these capitals probably were quite large. From these towns we meet a class, the metropolites, the local or minor gentry, in Lewis's terms.[63] This class comprised presumably the descendants of the Greek settlers attracted to Egypt by the Ptolemies, but its boundaries are difficult to determine. Metropolites were allowed membership at the age of fourteen after a formal

---

61. Stubbs, *Language and Literacy*, 99.
62. Kenney, "Small Writing," 168, summarizing Harris.
63. Lewis, *Life in Egypt*, 36–64.

verification of status (viz. parents' membership), and were taxed at a reduced rate both for themselves and their slaves. The metropolites used their wealth in ways that combined conspicuous consumption with social prestige, and persisted in parading their ties, real or imagined, to Hellenism by modelling their lives and their physical surroundings as much as possible on those of the four Greek cities of Egypt (particularly Alexandria).

What do the masses of papyri from Egypt tell us about the level of literacy of metropolite society? Homer, it is clear, was by far the all-time favorite, both for adult consumption and in the schoolroom with regard to literary texts. The not infrequent use of papyrus for school exercises suggests a wealthy background. The various evidences of literary activity and receptivity evoke the picture of a section of society made up of people who, generally speaking, could read and write. Illiterate metropolite men were clearly exceptional.

This must probably be understood in a context where writing and reading functioned as an expression of being "Greek," and private libraries for ostentation (then as now). Literature was seen as an important facet of the life of an aristocrat. Reading Homer and (the very few) other famous Greek texts were "compulsory" for being part of a privileged class. Books were high-prestige items.[64]

This picture stands in sharp contrast to the situation among the "commoners" and in the peasant villages,[65] where illiteracy was very much the norm. The metropolites were, in terms of the society, rather small groups, leaving behind a disproportionate impression of their importance. I would think their very obvious wealth shows us that they must have been a rather small group.

A type of literature that seems to have enjoyed some dissemination in the Hellenistic age consisted of technical manuals. One would easily think that these were intended for widespread and individual reading. But the interesting thing about these books—about which a lot more should be learned—is that only a few of them had a practical purpose. "These treatises . . . are of a peculiar character. Some of them are either purely theoretical or refer exclusively to architecture and military industries . . . Others are more concerned with pseudo-philosophical questions, and their references to industry are connected with experiments bearing on the 'philosophical' tenets of their respective creeds."[66] So, instead of finding widely used practi-

64. Cf. Starr, "Used-book Trade," 156.

65. Lewis, *Life in Egypt*, 65–83.

66. Rostovtzeff, *Social and Economic History*, 1203.

cal texts, we discover a curious lack of practical writings, and the technical ones that got written being used for all sorts of purposes.

This is probably due, simply, to the fact that oral technologies "enhance the ability of societies to retain large quantities of information about not only heroic deeds of the past but also 'technical knowledge.'"[67] The existence of impressive technological advances within a culture does not necessitate dependence on written language.[68] Antiquity, it seems, placed an inordinate value on heroic and epic traditions, and preserved them in written form. Calendric, agricultural, and navigational knowledge remained within the "hands" of oral technologists.[69]

The only mass-produced texts of antiquity were coins. Not only the overwhelming variations in types, but that those types "play so constantly and (even to modern eyes) so skillfully with different concepts of imperial government that, in an age when news could not be propagated by newspaper and radio, their intention cannot be doubted. They were, in essence, organs of information."[70] Coins are iconographic texts, they do not reflect a literate world. "The imagination and mind's eye of the modern Westerner is affected quite differently from that of the ancient reader of Pausanias or Virgil. In a culture and civilization not undergirded by the dissemination of the printed page, visual language was part of the lingua franca in a way foreign to our present experience."[71]

It is a well-known fact that publication in antiquity consisted of an oral presentation of the particular text.[72] Despite this, we often find modern projections upon ancient book circulation. Texts in Greco-Roman societies "circulated in a series of widening concentric circles determined primarily by friendship, which might, of course, be influenced by literary interest, and by the forces of social status that regulated friendship."[73] Most readers depended largely, if not exclusively, on privately made copies of texts, without the substantial intervention of any commercial system of distribution.[74] Bear in mind, that this was a world where one had no guarantee that a work was even by its putative author.

---

67. Couch, "Oral Technologies," 593.

68. Ibid., 587–602.

69. Ibid., 593.

70. Sutherland, "Intelligibility," 54.

71. Oster, "Numismatic Windows," 200.

72. Hadas, *Ancilla to Classical Reading*, 60–64.

73. Starr, "Circulation," 213.

74. Ibid., 215–16.

Book dealers (which are totally different from book publishers), were, in Starr's words, the owners of small shops that dealt in luxury items, apparently only handling current literature and not selling older works.[75] The book trade seems to have become more important by the end of the first century—to judge by references in Pliny,[76] Martial,[77] and Quintilian.[78] Tenuous as such, it is doubtful to what extent, if any at all, this can be extrapolated to the world outside Rome. The salient fact is that literature was a symbol of social status (and conversely, a point of access to the upper class, a way of making contact with the elite), and remained the preserve of the aristocracy except in oratorical events and public performances.[79] Reference should also be made to the used-book trade in the Roman world, for which Starr can once again be cited: "At most, a used-book trade potentially affected only a comparatively small group: those lucky enough to have had a literary education but not wealthy enough (or inclined) to own or employ their own copyists or to buy many new books."[80]

The conclusion that reading books was not a popular recreation seems quite justified.[81]

So What?

The discussion so far brings us to the realization that literacy in the first century Mediterranean world was rather limited. Beyond such a basic conclusion one steps obviously with caution and trepidation, yet, one implication is quite clear: Greco-Roman literacy remained a kind of imitation talking. It functioned as a subset of a basically oral environment, and that means that, when we turn to interpreting the culture and communication of the time, we need to be continually reminded of its orality. It was a literacy that was formed, shaped, and conditioned by the oral world that it penetrated. At the time literacy was a rather restricted and a relatively unprestigious craft.

Ancient communication, including reading and writing, was an oral, collective activity and not the private, silent experience that we consider it to be (such as reading books, magazines, watching TV, and even listening

75. Ibid., 220.

76. Pliny, *Ep.* 4.7.2.

77. Martial, 1.117.1, 4.72.

78. Quintilian, *Inst. Orat.* praef. 3.

79. Starr, "Circulation," 223.

80. Starr, "Used-book Trade," 148.

81. Cf. also Havelock, *Origins of Western Literacy*, 68–73.

to the radio and lectures). Reading silently was unusual, reading in solitude even more so.[82] Greco-Roman communication was connected to the physical presence of people and to living speech to an extent that is consistently underestimated today.

Investigating the traditions of classical Athens, Thomas found that many of the sources are not valuable as evidence for the past events they record, being oral traditions. "But they provide valuable evidence of a different sort. Since oral traditions closely reflect contemporary ideals and beliefs, they can be very valuable in highlighting them."[83]

Understanding the nature of the ancient sources is essential, both for evaluating the sources and for appreciating the methods of using them.

Uses of Writing

The Functions of Literacy in the Greco-Roman World

We read for a variety of purposes: to pass time, to get information, and to gain aesthetic experiences. We also write for a variety of purposes: to transmit information, to control or limit the activities of others (bureaucratic writing), to aid one's memory (notes, lists), and so on. These purposes are often assumed to be self-evident, as they are to highly literate people. They are, however, not entirely natural functions of language; some of them are partly created by writing itself.[84] Like children learning to read, people whose contact with writing is marginal or nonexistent, are unsure about the functions of writing and even experience difficulty in understanding the purposes of writing.[85] Many of the supposed purposes of literacy are completely beyond their needs and practices.

It is doubtful whether most people in antiquity would have regarded writing as a superior technology (given the difficulties of ancient writing/ reading—among other reasons). "Oral technologists had command of a procedure that allowed them to retain any information they were interested in preserving . . . Contemporary oral specialists are singularly unimpressed with phonetic writing; they do not view literacy as an opportunity."[86]

---

82. Achtemeier, "*Omne Verbum Sonat*," 15–6; Botha, "Mute Manuscripts," 43. [X-ref]
83. Thomas, *Oral Tradition*, 283.
84. Goody, *Domestication*.
85. Stubbs, *Language and Literacy*, 98–99.
86. Couch, "Oral Technologies," 593.

The extent and diversity of the functions and uses of literacy are self-evident. A few will be discussed in a little more detail.

Politics and Hegemony

Lévi-Strauss has hypothesized that writing should be linked to exploitation: "My hypothesis, if correct, would oblige us to recognize the fact that the primary function of written communication is to facilitate slavery. The use of writing for disinterested purposes, and as a source of intellectual and aesthetic pleasure, is a secondary result, and more often than not it may even be turned into a means of strengthening, justifying or concealing the other."[87] This side of writing has also been stressed by Graff. Building on the work of Antonio Gramsci, Graff distinguishes between domination (or coercion, typically exercised through force) and hegemony (consensual formation, indoctrination, and maintenance of society). Clearly, literacy is important for hegemony: "For most of literacy's history, these functions have centered upon elite groups and their cohesion and power. For them, the uses of literacy have been diverse but have included common education, culture, and language (such as Latin); shared interests and activities; control of scarce commodities, such as wealth, power, and even literacy; and common symbols and badges, of which literacy could be one."[88]

The major user of writing in the Greco-Roman world was the imperial government. The emperor exercised power through extensive use of written correspondence.[89] The more or less centralized power of the emperors became possible when it became possible in organizational terms to control particularly the senatorial officials and the armies, which presupposes, to a large extent, letters and other documents. Naturally we should not generalize about the extent of literacy using the example of the emperor; a much better indication is Pliny's lack of surprise at want of written evidence concerning a sentence by earlier governors.[90]

It is clear that in the Roman empire there was no incentive to invest in basic literacy. On the contrary, it "should be obvious that in Greece and to an even greater extent in the Roman Empire the illiteracy of the masses

---

87. Lévi-Strauss, *Tristes Tropiques*, 299.
88. Graff, *Labyrinths of Literacy*, 12.
89. Cf. Millar, *Emperor*, 313–41.
90. Pliny, *Ep.* 10.58–60.

contributed to the stability of the political order, much as it has done, *mutatis mutandis*, in many other historical contexts."[91]

In the Greco-Roman city-states, political power was closely linked to cultural hegemony, which came to depend in part on a direct knowledge of texts. At the same time we should not underestimate the possibilities of even limited literacy. Literacy can help to create and defend the rights of at least some citizens. "Being able to read documents for oneself and being able to write one's own *libellus* did not guarantee anything, but it was better than being unable to do so."[92] In a famous statement, Euripides has king Theseus saying, "when the laws are written the weak man and the wealthy man have equal justice (δίκη)."[93]

Letter Writing

The writing of letters has infinite possible uses. With regard to antiquity the main point to grasp is that letters facilitated and served *oral communication*.[94] The concept of the letter was that of written conversation.[95] Letters create appearance in the experience of the recipient(s) by evoking the physical presence of the author(s).

By far most surviving letters were intended to cover a considerable distance; they seem not to have been used much for communicating with someone nearby. Usually letters were written due to the mere opportunity to communicate. Letters of invitation are rather few in number and usually self-contained (lack of names, etc.); messages were oral, and "an accompanying letter of invitation might be used to add a dash of style."[96] In fact, letters often served as a means of validating the bearer who would then deliver the message in person.[97]

---

91. Harris, *Ancient Literacy*, 333.

92. Ibid., 334.

93. Euripides, *Supplices* 433–37.

94. Botha, "Paul's Letter to the Galatians" see below, 193–211.

95. Ussher, "Letter Writing," 1574; Malherbe, "Ancient Epistolary Theorists," 15; White, *Light*, 190–92.

96. Harris, *Ancient Literacy*, 230.

97. White, *Light*, 204; Aune, *New Testament*, 166–67; cf. Street, *Literacy*, 119.

Religion

Most people had little need to write or even to read in order to express their religious feelings or find out about the divine world. Visiting a shrine or praying or looking after the household *lararium* and attending festivals did not require literacy. With regard to the unknown, many preferred to consult nonwritten "texts" such as entrails or the flight patterns of birds, or oracles and prophets.

However, written prophecies circulated (though, as Harris has noted, not copied in great numbers).[98] Dedications were inscribed, prayers were at times recited from book-rolls, magical spells circulated in written form, and some inscriptions informed those approaching a shrine what to do and what not to do. The imperial cult made heavy use of epigraphical texts, and shrines and temples some times accumulated written material.[99]

But more significantly, the written word itself exercised religious power: it was sometimes believed (or simply felt) to have some special and profound quality that caused or allowed people to bring about extraordinary results. One need only remember the Sibylline Books.[100] There are also the magical papyri and Jewish attitudes to writing the name of God. Age sanctified all writings, and poetry was divinely inspired.[101]

Some intellectuals, who, it is important to note, felt themselves at odds with "traditional" views, produced a considerable body of religious writings.[102] But the use of the written word to convey religious messages remained connected to the oral (this is so even for Paul). Philostratus tells about Appolonius's encounter with Elis, who, fancying himself quite an "evangelist" (ἐγκωμιαστικός τίς εἶναι σφόδρα) for Zeus, was at the point of giving a public reading of an oration praising Zeus that he has written, because that was the way you reached an audience (*Vit. Ap.* 4.30)—a description not irrelevant for understanding the dissemination of the gospels.

Reading and Writing as Cultural Activities

The relationship between author, written language, and "reader/reading public" is not at all self-evident. The concept of personal authorship probably

98. Harris, *Ancient Literacy*, 218.

99. MacMullen, *Paganism*, 11.

100. Cf. Pease, "Sibylla."

101. MacMullen, *Paganism*, 10.

102. Ibid., 9–18.

had little meaning in antiquity, where books were published without the name of the author or with another person's name. The inclination to invent an author for a text stands in stark contrast to our own age after "the demise of the author." Works were seen rather as a collective, cultural enterprise.

Reading is a "way of taking meaning from texts." "Ways of taking" from books are "as much a part of learned behaviour as are ways of eating, sitting, playing games and building houses."[103] Consequently the literacy events to which people are exposed and the meanings they "take" from them require a broad framework of socio-cultural analysis in order for ancient reading and writing to make sense.[104]

These insights provide us with a framework to reassess Paul's use of the Old Testament, for instance. What we can gather from instances where authors provide us with their "ways of taking" from the writings of others should be highly relevant to the interpretation of the New Testament.

When approaching literacy as historically and culturally embedded, the work of Piaget could provide yet another perspective. He has argued that a great deal of the language of children (without writing, obviously) is egocentric;[105] that is, it does not have the function of communicating with others, and further that young children do not appreciate what is involved in communicating with others and cannot adapt their language to their listeners. The relevance of these observations to understanding some peculiar facets of Greco-Roman writings, and particularly the New Testament writings, are obvious. Analysis of the oral aspects of Hellenistic Roman culture can be a useful index to the world views and ways of thinking characteristic of inhabitants of that culture.

Greco-Roman Literacy as a Setting for the New Testament

Early Christian writings must be seen in their historical environment. They did not originate like modern books and were not disseminated like modern texts. Questions such as the synoptic problem, the structure and style (and integrity) of the gospels and of Paul's letters should be reformulated with historical realia in mind.

Communal "reading" not only breeds communal discussion. Ong remarks that sizable prose narrative, "with a tidy structure . . . moving through closely controlled tensions to a climax, with reversal and denouement" is

103. Heath, "What No Bedtime," 49.

104. Ibid., 74.

105. Piaget, *Language and Thought*.

uncharacteristic of pre-modern literature, because of "the difficulty that narrators . . . had in feeling themselves as other than oral performers."[106] Nelson writes, "For works designed to be read aloud certain kinds of critical approach are therefore inappropriate. The attempt to discover unity and cohesion of plot in such compositions may lead only to the imposition of irrelevant structures and to distorted interpretation."[107]

Similarly, Lord writes, "Enamored of the meretricious virtues of art, we may fail to understand the real meaning of a traditional poem. That meaning cannot be brought to light by elaborate schematization, unless that schematization be based on the elements of oral tradition, on the still dynamic multiform patterns in the depths of primitive myth."[108]

A few other problem areas can briefly be iterated. Totally unexplored at this stage are the partly or largely symbolic functions of early Christian writings, as writings. Another interesting inquiry would be to return to the—currently neglected—question concerning the motives that gave rise to these texts, particularly the gospels. Our standard way of referring to the evangelists as authors is to picture them writing their gospels, and the dominant method used to interpret them, redaction criticism, needs the assumption that the gospel authors were, among other things, editors: consulting, reading, reworking other texts in their own writing activity. Many facets of the conventional conceptualization probably need readjustment.[109]

The "political" side of Paul's letters has received little attention: how he uses writing to control and influence others and to promote a (probably) minority viewpoint. Writing and social status, and reading and social status (two categories that do not necessarily overlap fully in the Greco-Roman world) are clearly very complex issues, but need to be related to our investigations into the social status of early Christianity, and the "new consensus" probably needs some adaption.[110] If early Christianity reflects a fair cross section of society, it would follow that a rather small percentage within those groups were literate. What is probably true in any case is that we have a completely disproportionate impression of an extremely small group of Christians.

A major aspect of the limited extent of Greco-Roman literacy in general is the fact that many of the inhabitants of the Roman empire spoke neither

106. Ong, "Writer's Audience," 17.

107. Nelson, "From 'Listen, Lordings,'" 120.

108. Lord, *Singer of Tales*, 221.

109. Cf. Botha, "Orality-Literacy Studies."

110. Cf. Malherbe, "Ancient Epistolary Theorists," 29–59.

Greek nor Latin.[111] It is therefore the more noteworthy that extremely few Christian writings or translations in languages other than Greek and Latin from the first three centuries have come down to us. Also, there are a strikingly small number of papyrus fragments dating from the second and third centuries. The written word probably was not important to early Christianity, and it is a (well liked) modern-day fiction that Christianity spread mainly by means of the written word.

The very smallness of the Christian movement probably contributed to the reasons why some turned to writing. Paul used writing to be present where he could not be. Possibly some gospel storytellers tried to achieve access to classes of status by getting their stories into writing. Literacy usually emerges in conjunction with novel social enterprises.[112] This suggests that Christian writing, in Greco-Roman culture, was used to preserve information connected to changing social enterprises or *different* socio-cultural activities.

Concluding Remarks

One reason for the necessity of this research is a recognition of the importance of rethinking assumptions about literacy and its impact during the first century. The need for reassessment stems from our initial inclination to assume a univocal meaning for the term *literate* and what such basic activities as reading and writing meant during Greco-Roman times.[113] Media criticism does indeed have *quite a lot* to say with a view to responsible reading of New Testament writings.[114]

This argument is consequently skeptical of the validity of the widespread separation of historical and literary criticism in New Testament scholarship. Also, in the spirit of critical historical understanding, this research can turn to self-awareness. We are indeed also different from our ancestors: "instead of growing better memories and better brains, we grow paper, pens, pencils, typewriters, dictaphones, the printing press and libraries."[115]

The formidable scholar, Elias Bickerman, once wrote that "without both ignorance and arrogance, who would dare to publish a historical work?"[116] I

---

111. MacMullen, Changes in the Roman Empire, 32–40; cf. Youtie, "Ἀγράμματος."
112. Couch, "Oral Technologies," 594.
113. Cf. Chaytor, *From Script to Print*, 1–9; Troll, "Illiterate Mode," 97–99.
114. Cf. Combrink, "Role of the Reader," 198.
115. Popper, *Objective Knowledge*, 239.
116. Bickerman, *Jews*, ix.

am acutely aware of the many shortcomings of this presentation. However, if interest in this topic can be kindled and relevant critical discussion generated, this chapter would have served its purpose.

4

Writing in the First Century

Introduction

It has become quite fashionable to emphasize the pitfalls of anachronism when attempting historical interpretation of texts, and rightly so. Proper contextualization is of immense importance to responsible analysis and understanding.

A seemingly innocuous question concerns the physical and material aspects of writing in antiquity. Yet the historical appropriateness of some proposals about how the oral tradition about Jesus became written texts, for instance, surely requires consideration of the concrete aspects of writing in the Roman Mediterranean world. What we perceive a text to be, and how we should go about understanding it, is influenced by what we think about how the text came into being.

In a nutshell, the following proposes that we will gain a better historical grasp on the early Christian texts when we study the realia of writing. In this study I focus on some of the physical constraints and characteristics of writing in antiquity.

Writing upon One's Knees

In her discussion of the "illiterate mode" of medieval written communication, Denise Troll notes, "the material and tools were so problematic that they affected the process of book production and the appearance of the books produced—which in turn affected the cost, availability, and the quality of books, and the medieval experience of reading and writing."[1]

---

1. Troll, "Illiterate Mode," 99.

The physical position of writing is part of the experience of writing, and consequently of importance to understanding some of the social, epistemological and psychological ramifications of writing. Interestingly enough, much about the posture of writing in antiquity is often assumed. For instance, recall Mack's description of the creation of the Gospel of Mark: "It was composed at a desk in a scholar's study lined with texts and open to discourse with other intellectuals."[2]

It is well known that the ancient Egyptian scribe did not use a table when writing: "When writing on a roll, the Egyptian always sat and this is the position displayed by statues of scribes . . . Egyptians sat either with the hind part of the body on the ground with the legs crossed in front or with the body resting on the crossed legs . . . In a squatting position the loin cloth of the scribe is tightly stretched so as to provide a firm support for the papyrus . . . He never uses a table of any kind."[3] Like the Egyptians, the Greeks and Romans did not use tables or writing desks, but it seems that they sometimes sat on a seat of some kind when writing. The papyrus roll was spread upon the lap or placed upon one knee or one thigh only.[4] A small tablet may have been used in support; Greco-Roman writing was done with a sharpened reed pen (and not a brush as used by classic Egyptian scribes).

"Writing on one's knees" is quite unlike a modern scholar's activities. In antiquity scribes were typically not accustomed to writing on tables or desks, as shown by a very wide range of artistic, archaeological, and literary evidence.[5] When a scribe was making relatively brief notes on a wax tablet or on a sheet of papyrus or parchment, he would usually stand and write while holding the writing material in his left hand. In the case of a more extensive task, such as the copying of a lengthy manuscript, a scribe would sit, occasionally on the ground but sometimes on a stool or bench, supporting the scroll or codex on his knees.[6] That is, scribes wrote their scrolls or sheets by holding, shifting, and balancing them on their thighs.[7]

An illustration of this is a colophon (scribe's mark, signature, or note) at the close of a papyrus scroll containing portions of the third and fourth books of the *Iliad* (third century), which mentions the cooperation of the

2. Mack, *Myth of Innocence*, 322–23.

3. Černý, *Paper and Books*, 13–14.

4. See Parássoglou, "A Roll."

5. Turner and Parsons, *Greek Manuscripts*, 5–6; Parássoglou, "Δεξιὰ χείρ."

6. Metzger, "When Did Scribes," 123.

7. Ibid., 125–26.

stylus, the right hand, and the knee in writing: κάλαμός μ᾽ ἔγραψε δεξιὰ χεὶρ καὶ γόνυ.[8]

Given that such a writing position—often without back support and crucially without forearm support[9]—is not only uncomfortable but also strenuous, the ongoing delegation of writing to servants, slaves, and hired crafts persons is particularly noteworthy. Consider also the demand of availability: the scribe was required to provide his writing skills in basically any conceivable situation, from the bathroom to the bedroom, from the banquet to the street corner, and often while traveling. Adding to the physical stress was the need to refresh the ink on the reed pen. The ink pot was either on the ground, or, as illustrated by a third-century relief, held by a slave.[10]

These physical constraints had an effect on the appearance of ancient writing. The width of columns on a scroll averages about six to nine centimeters, the width of a thigh. In some papyrus writings the successive columns are not exactly vertical; sometimes they incline to one side or the other, and the writing may have a tendency to be larger at the bottom than at the top of the column.[11]

It is only by the eighth century that artistic representations of persons writing on desks or tables begin to appear, and by "the end of the ninth century and throughout the tenth and eleventh centuries, examples of persons writing on desks, tables and stands multiply noticeably."[12]

Clearly, there was no desire, no *want*, no perceived need for desks in antiquity when it came to writing (and reading). Some reasons are conventionally suggested for persisting with the ancient custom of holding the scroll or loose pages on one's lap on which one was writing: "Writing in antiquity was, to a considerable extent, done by slaves. It is quite possible that the adoption of writing desks in early medieval times is connected with

8. The papyrus roll "declares": a reed, right hand, and knee wrote me. *P.Lond.*Lit. 11. See Turner and Parsons *Greek Manuscripts*, 5 n.13. Also *P.Oxy.* 2079.21–22.

9. Of course, ergonomic and physiotherapeutic studies of ancient scribes do not exist; it is, however, fairly easy to correlate possible body stress of scribal posture with problems studied by contemporary investigation of modern problems; such research show, for instance, how forearm support reduces the incidence of musculoskeletal discomfort and disorders. I consulted the following: Cook, Burgess-Limerick, and Papalia, "effect of upper extremity support"; Marcus et al., "A prospective study of computer users"; O'Sullivan, et al., "Lumbopelvic kinematics"; Rempel, et al., "A randomised controlled trial."

10. Cf. Parássoglou, "Δεξιὰ χεὶρ," 10, plate 2.

11. Turner and Parsons, *Greek Manuscripts*, 5; cf. Johnson, *Bookrolls and Scribes*, 92, 100.

12. Metzger, "When Did Scribes," 130.

the circumstance that 'ancient society, being little concerned with the comfort or efficiency of slaves, provided no artificial support for the professional scribe who was a slave; whereas the medieval scribe, usually a monk, was more likely to improve his means of writing.'"[13] The use of the codex became widespread only in late antiquity. Writing a codex makes different demands than writing a scroll, and the medieval desk probably solved some of these difficulties.[14] The growing popularity of large deluxe codices must also have contributed to the altering of the ancient customs of scribes.[15]

The posture of the ancient scribe at work was tied up with methods of instruction and the realities of ancient schooling: "At every level, teaching was geared to fit the condition of the ancient classroom, which, if it was provided with seats at all, contained only benches. Most of the time, ancient students had only their knees on which to rest a text . . ."[16]

Most of all, the posture reflects an attitude: writing was labor. Literariness, high education, though inextricably connected to writing, was not the same thing as writing. In antiquity a distinction between reading and writing was maintained in ways that seem strange (and problematic) to present perceptions of literacy. Writing and reading were not perceived as sides of an undifferentiated process, despite their obvious overlap.

"For He Writes Slowly"

The first-century Mediterranean world was not an "illiterate" world—of course; but the real issue is the meaning of terms such as "literate" and "illiterate." In the Roman period people of various backgrounds participated in elementary education, and some progressed to subsequent stages of learning. Yet the connections imparted by elementary education and the demands of daily life in ancient societies placed writing into particular "subsets" of social and institutional life. People could (and did) exploit the skills they had learned in schools by drafting messages, compiling daily lists and accounts, and by testifying to the authenticity of documents by adding subscriptions or signatures.

13. Ibid., 132, quoting Meyer.
14. Small, *Wax Tablets*, 155.
15. Metzger, "When Did Scribes," 133.
16. Cribiore, *Gymnastics*, 131.

We also know that significant percentages (in fact, the vast majority of all first-century Mediterranean societies) were ignorant of "letters," unable to read or write—even those who had to deal with "letters" quite often.

What we need to understand is that the degrees of literacy, the various possibilities along the spectrum of writing and/or reading skills, did not correlate directly with class, wealth, and status indicators. That is, *literary activities* and *literacy skills* did not correlate.

In the Greco-Roman world the lack of (proficient) writing skills did not engender stigma or disdain. Illiterate persons usually had recourse to a network of literates: the ubiquitous scribe, a relative, a friend, a slave in a nearby household.

The papyri from Roman Egypt inform us about the βραδέως γάφοντες, "those writing slowly" and the ὑπογραφεῖς, "substitute writers." In these papyri we glimpse a world where someone writes on behalf of another as that person either writes slowly or does not know letters.[17] We learn about illiterates and semi-literates manipulating the world of (Greek) writing quite effectively.

A remarkable illustration of this is Petaus, the κωμογραμματεύς (town clerk) of Ptolemais Hormou and associated villages towards the end of the second century CE. His signature is found on several documents, written in rigid, multi-stroke letters of varying size. However, we also have a sheet of papyrus on which Petaus practiced his signature, repeatedly. On this papyrus he writes, Πεταῦς κωμογρα(-μματεὺς) ἐπιδέδωκα (his name, title, and a verb "I have submitted"): the formula required to sign documents in his official capacity.[18] The papyrus shows that at the fifth attempt Petaus omitted the first vowel of the verb, and he continues to leave the vowel out while writing the formula another seven times. Obviously he could not reproduce the formula correctly by heart and needed a model to copy (i.e., the line immediately above). He clearly could not read with understanding his own writing. Yet Petaus knew where and how to sign and was quite capable of dealing with the demands of his office, in which he made use of professional scribes.[19]

Quite possibly Paul was one of these "slow writers" (Gal 6:11) and, we can safely assume, so were several other early Christian authors.

17. Youtie, "Ἀγράμματος"; Youtie, "Βραδέως Γράφων"; Youtie, "Because they"; Youtie, "Ὑπογραφεύς."

18. *P.Petaus* 121.

19. On Petaus: Youtie, "Βραδέως Γράφων," 239–43; Turner, *Papyrologist*, 36–47; Hanson, "Ancient Literacy," 171–74.

"By the Hand of a Scribe"

In the world of Greco–Roman writing another widespread and powerful force was at work. Even among the members of the elite and in scholarly circles who used writing with varying degrees of sophistication, practicing writing as such was mostly relegated to assistants, secretaries, and servants. Although they were undoubtedly educated, their background and education socialized them to have distinct attitudes towards physical writing.

Learning to write in the ancient school was not governed by the same rules that regulated the process of learning to read. As a consequence "defining the relationship between writing and reading in Greco-Roman pedagogy is not a straightforward endeavor."[20] Interaction between reading and writing was far less pronounced in Greco-Roman societies than it is among ourselves as "writing was a separate skill."[21]

This particular attitude towards learning writing skills reflects deepseated convictions about civilization and achievement: "Quintilian and all the theorists and schoolmasters who have followed suit are silent on the subject of the differentiated practices of reading and writing. There is only one education worth *writing* about and that is liberal education. Its early stages are usually beneath notice. What counts is training to be an orator."[22]

Although a limited ability in writing was central to early or initial education, advanced education was associated with discrete ideas about literacy. After elementary education, specialized writing skills were taken over by trades, crafts, and slave schools. By contrast, advanced, "liberal" education focused on a training in social distinction and in the linguistic skills suited for the fashioning of governors.[23] This bifurcation was profound. After the initial exposure to teaching, the privileged boy's companion group changed from the free and slave children (the *vernae*) of the household to the *liberi* of

20. See Cribiore, *Gymnastics*, 176. Our picture of Greco–Roman pedagogy is multifarious and incomplete at best. Recently scholars have started to reconsider and improve our understanding of primary and secondary education, see Booth, "Schooling"; Kaster, "Notes on 'primary.'" Noteworthy is that literate education was recognizably the same throughout the empire, whether in Latin or Greek speaking areas (cf. Morgan, *Literate Education*, 66–67). In some cases the first elements of reading and writing must have been taught at home (Harris, *Ancient Literacy*, 307). Bloomer writes, "Slaves were schooled in profitable literate trades. Poor boys picked up reading and writing in a portico or rented shop stall"; see Bloomer, "Schooling in Persona," 61–62.

21. Lane Fox, "Literacy and Power," 144; Cribiore, *Writing*, 176–78; Hanson, "Ancient Illiteracy," 179–183.

22. Bloomer, "Schooling in Persona," 62.

23. Morgan, *Literate Education*, 226–34.

the school.[24] His teachers changed from nurses, parents, freedmen, and the people from his father's household to professional teachers and the world of his peers. Going to school meant rehearsing the social and sexual segregation of going to court or to elections, practicing to speak in the forum (on behalf of others), becoming adept carriers of the emblems of Roman civic life.[25]

When we study the writing exercises of these young people at school (the *hermeneumata*),[26] we can see that they were learning to make distinctions; to categorize; to argue within a circumscribed field of characters, events, and solutions. They were learning not just how to speak, but who may speak and about what on whose behalf. Orally and in writing they were reproducing, and thereby positively identifying themselves with, "the cultural material and the ethical precepts" of their world, becoming active users of "a vital marker of social status and power."[27] They were learning about the inextricably connected social subordinations that constituted the Mediterranean world: where, in their perceptions and deliberations, to place various *personae* and what actions and sensibilities were appropriate to them. Their schooling did bring about linguistic and rhetorical expertise, but this expertise "came to distinguish them from those with a craft literacy or vernacular or spoken linguistic skills."[28]

The "liberal" education that Quintilian writes about concerned declamation, but the subjects of the declamatory speeches by the students were not neutral topics merely for the practice of technique. Declamation abounds with examples of those figures who prompt speech but will never be admitted to civil speech: freedmen, slaves, women. "At the least, like other childhood games, declamation taught competition, rule following, and inculcated habits of stratification and distinction."[29] In their actions as in their words, those boys were telling themselves and each other *this is what we do and this is how we do it because this is who we are.* Those who approved, their fathers, were affirming *you are one of us.*

---

24. Bloomer, "Schooling in Persona," 60–61.

25. Ibid., 61; Morgan, *Literate Education*, 234–39.

26. The *hermeneumata*, like the *progymnasmata*, are school texts (exercises) of the Roman period. See, among others, Webb, *Progymnasmata*; Morgan, *Literate Education*, 64–65; Bradley, *Slavery and Society*, 26; Dionisotti, "From Ausonius' schooldays?"; Bloomer, "Schooling in Persona."

27. Cf. Morgan, *Literate Education*, 198.

28. Bloomer, "Schooling in Persona," 62.

29. Ibid., 69.

These habits shaped literary practices that often did not entail writing for themselves. The simple fact is that Greco-Roman societies *insisted* on the "institution" of scribes (rather than mass education). Advanced education (to become part of civil society) and specialized training (to write long texts) were considered *distinct* and very unequal aspects of society.[30]

The remarkable thing about all of this is the teachers *who were not elite persons themselves* but often slaves and mostly freedmen. This fact reminds us that we should beware the numbers trap. "Literacy" is not merely about how many writing how much. Of course, individuals could (and did) write for themselves and on their own. But even when writing by oneself, the attitudes, the expectations, the bodiliness of hierarchy and status sensitivities were present; the "natural and right order of things" were implicated.[31]

To write, even by one's own hand, entailed *writing by the hand of a scribe*.

"For Best Writing . . . 25 Denarii"

Writing was a prized skill. The *Edictum Diocletiani de pretiis rerum venalium* was issued between 21 November and 31 December 301 in the name of the two *augusti* Diocletianus and Maximianus as well as the *caesares* Constantius and Maximianus. The term "edict" was derived from the expression *dicunt* in the *praefatio* (praef. 4), but in the text itself we find the terms *lex* (praef. 15) or *statutum* (praef. 15, 18, 19, 20). This "law" was published empire-wide as part of a comprehensive administrative and financial reform whose primary goal was to secure provisions for the Roman army.

The *praefatio* names the occasion and purpose of the *Edict*, namely to set maximum prices as a way to control the *avaritia* of merchants and traders, who sometimes demanded eight times the usual amount for goods. Soldiers were particularly vulnerable, as they often had to spend a significant share of their pay for purchases at marketplaces. For overcharging, for instances of illegal negotiations, or if goods were hoarded, the *Edict* threatened capital punishment.

The *Edict* then continues with a list of foods, goods, and services, indicating more than a thousand maximum prices in *denarii*. In column 7, lines 39–41, we find the tariffs set for scribal work: 40 *denarii* for the preparation

---

30. This began to change in the late empire and late antiquity, and most noticeably in the Christian empire, where we find scribal and secretarial special skills becoming important means of rising to power and gaining status.

31. Cf. Morgan, *Literate Education*, 268–270.

of a lot of four parchments, 25 *denarii* for 100 lines of best quality script, and 20 for the same number of lines of second-grade quality script.[32]

It is worth exploring the world of "payment for lines written" further, in order to gain some understanding of costs involved, and thereby learn something about values associated with writing.

It must be emphasized that the following are exercises in historical imagination; some speculations about what could have been involved for New Testament "authors" to have produced their documents and to have them copied. Precision and certainty are impossible. Any description today must rely on generalization, even though we know that the actual use of (writing) technology in different contexts was quite diverse. Technological application is continually re-imagined and re-deployed according to unique circumstances by creative human beings.

The limitations of our current documentation are severe. For instance, the *Edictum Diocletiani* does *not* specify what is meant by a "line" nor what is "best" writing (*scriptor in scriptura optima versus n. centum*). Putting together the following general picture is intended simply to contribute to a *background* for discussions of the contexts of early Christian writings.

Copyists charged by the number of lines (στίχοι), and books were priced this way.[33] In literary works, copyists maintained an average hexameter line, composed of sixteen syllables with a total of about 36 letters per line.[34] For the purposes of this exercise I assume that the copying of early Christian documents followed this standard, including Paul's letters (considering the exceptional length of his letters).[35]

It is not a simple matter to use the *Edictum Diocletiani* as a guide to actual prices (if it can be used at all). An interesting alternative is *Papyrus London* Inv. 2110: a fragmentary papyrus dating from the first half of the third

32. The *Edict* is accessible in Graser, "Edict of Diocletian." On the economic crisis that led to the *Edict* (and discussion of the problems interpreting it), see Drinkwater, "Maximinus to Diocletian"; Corbier, "Coinage"; Meissner, "Über Zweck."

33. Ohly, *Stichometrische Untersuchungen*, 86–125; Haines–Eitzen, *Guardians of Letters* 87–88.

34. Harris, "Stichometry," 137–45; Ohly, *Stichometrische Untersuchungen*, 22. It should be noted that Johnson found the average line length (a sort of "normal" range) "at roughly 13 to 24 letters per line" for prose texts among the Oxyrynchus bookrolls that he studied. See Johnson, *Bookrolls and Scribes*, 114. There was "no consistent correlation between width of column and letter counts." See ibid., 114.

35. The typical papyrus letter is about one page (averaging about a 100 words); even literary authors like Cicero and Seneca did not write letters as lengthy as Paul's. See Richards, *Secretary*, 213.

century CE. It is an account of the receipts of a professional scriptorium.[36] In this papyrus two prices are quoted, 47 *drachmai* for a book of 16,600 lines and 13 *drachmai* for a book of 6,300 lines. This gives us a range of price (for a long text and for a shorter text?) of 0.283 to 0.207 *drachmai* per 100 lines.

Copying the Gospel of Luke at these prices would entail 5.7 or 7.9 *drachmai*; if we take the average (0.245 *dr.* per 100 lines) the price would be 6¾ *drachmai* (see Table 1). The account from the scriptorium makes clear that the cost for the papyrus is not included in the price for copying.[37]

The cost of papyrus is a notorious problem.[38] Papyrus rolls were produced in lengths of about 6 meters (20 sheets of ±30 cm wide glued together) and a height of about 25 centimeters[39] (to fit comfortably on the 'knee') and sold in Egypt for about 4 *drachmai* a roll.[40] If we take the estimates of lines (Table 1) and use 30 lines per column, at an average width of 9 centimeters,[41] to which inter-column spacing should be added (2 cm.), New Testament writings set on rolls would entail:

36. The text is published by Ohly, *Stichometrische Untersuchungen*, 88–90, 126–129.

37. *P.Lond.*Inv. 2011, col. 1 line 9, indicate two prices for the same item (a scroll containing books), namely 41 *drachmai* and then for "the *stichoi* of these books (τῶν αὐτῶν βιβλίων στίχων)" 47 *drachmai*. The first price must be for something other than the cost of copying, namely the cost of the necessary papyrus. See Skeat, "Length," 67.

38. Which cannot be properly dealt with here. See the discussion by Skeat, "Was Papyrus Regarded."

39. The conventional estimate is 25 cm.; the Herculaneum papyri has a standard height of 19–24 cm. Johnson shows that early Roman period scrolls are 19–25 cm. high, in the later Roman era 25–33 cm. came to dominate. See Johnson, *Bookrolls and Scribes*, 141–43.

40. The price of 4 drachmai for an unused roll remained fairly constant during the first two centuries in Egypt. See Bagnall, *Reading Papyri*, 13; Drexhage, *Preise, Mieten/Pachten*, 384–89; Harris, *Ancient Literacy*, 195; Hedrick, *Ancient History*, 73; Lewis, *Papyrus*, 129–34.

41. Johnson has found that the typical column width among literary papyri from Oxyrhynchus is about 6 cm., averaging about 24 letters. For my calculation a line is 36 letters, hence a column width of 9 cm.

Table 1: Estimated Costs of Copying Some Early Christian Documents

	Στίχοι[38]	*Drachmai* ±225 CE	"labor days"[39]	*Edict Diocl.,* 301, *denarii*[40]	*Edict Diocl.,* Skilled labor days[41]
Matthew	2,560	5½–7½	4⅓	512–640	9
Luke	2,750	6–8	4⅔	550–688	9½
Acts	2,560	5½–7½	4⅓	512–640	9
John	2,020	4–6	3½	404–505	7
Mark	1,610	3½–4½	3	322–403	5½
Romans	980	2–3	1⅔	196–245	3⅓
1 Corinthians	910	2–2⅔	1½	182–228	3
2 Corinthians	610	1⅓–1⅔	1	122–153	2
Galatians	310	⅔–1	½	62–78	1
Ephesians	330	⅔–1	½	66–83	1
Revelation	1,350	2¾–3¾	2⅓	270–338	4⅔
Hermas	3,650	7½–11	6	730–913	12⅔
Ep. Barnabas	880	1¾–2½	1½	176–220	3
Hebrews	715	1½–2	1⅓	144–180	2½
1 Timothy	240	½–⅔	½	48–60	1
Gospel of Thomas	660	1½–1¾	1	132–165	2
Didache	300	⅔–¾	½	60–75	1

42. These estimates ignore all text-critical questions. There are of course arbitrary aspects in any such calculations, given the evidence. The line totals are rounded in multiples of 5 for easier calculation. The point is not absolute precision (which is impossible) but reasonable approximation. Statistics for NT στίχοι: Harris, "Stichometry. Part II," 313–30; Metzger, *Manuscripts*, 38–40; Metzger, *Canon*, 298–99; Murphy-O'Connor, *Paul the Letter-writer*, 120.

43. Calculated at five hours per day, writing two lines per minute.

44. At 20 and 25 den. per 100 lines respectively. Note that the information based on the *Edictum Diocletiani* is included for interest's sake only; in a way these are artificial prices. The *Edict* aims at providing *maximum* prices. It does *not* tell us what "a line" entails. There is also a problem with the "value" of Diocletian *denarii*. By the time of the *Edict*, the *denarius* was no longer in circulation.

45. The *Edict* sets the wage for an agricultural worker (*operarius rusticus*) at 25 *denarii, with keep (pastus)*. The scribe's wage *excludes* support. The *Edict* sets the wage for various skilled workers (e.g., *faber intestinarius, faber tignarius,* and *carpentarius*) at 50 *denarii* a day, including food (*pastus*). Scribal work probably fell in this category. For comparative purposes I include cost for daily support (taken at 12–15 *denarii*).

Table 2: Estimated Costs of Papyrus Scrolls

	Lines	Columns	Length, cm.	*drachmai*
Matthew	2,560	85	940	6½
Luke	2,750	92	1,010	7
Acts	2,560	85	940	6½
John	2,020	67	740	5
Mark	1,610	54	590	4
Romans	980	33	360	2½
Pauline letters	4,450	149	1,635	11
Revelation	1,350	45	495	3½

This can be compared with 𝔓45 (which is a codex) as a control. 𝔓45 has columns of writing of 16 x 19 centimeters (w x h, per page); if we include inter-columnar space of 2 cm the gospels set on rolls would entail:

Matthew (49 columns)   49 x 18 = 882 cm
Mark (32 columns)   32 x 18 = 576 cm
Luke (48 columns)   48 x 18 = 864 cm
John (38 columns)   38 x 18 = 684 cm
Four Gospels, single scroll = 3,006 cm

Using 𝔓46 as comparative basis, the Pauline Letters (including Hebrews) would transcribe onto a roll of 2,806 centimeters. These calculations correlate sufficiently with those in Table 2.

Thus, a copy of Matthew (in the second century) would probably have required handing over at least 12 *drachmai*, about 6 for the papyrus and 6 more for copying. Copies of Luke and Acts on a single scroll would be about 27 *drachmai*. Instead of a copy of Matthew, one could buy 72 loaves of bread or 18 liters of wine. A cheap tunic (χιτών) made by apprentices cost between 16–24 *drachmai*, a white shirt (for special occasions) about 40 *drachmai*, and a bath towel 3 *drachmai* 3 *oboloi*.[46]

16. These are all prices from the second half of the second century, in Egypt. See Drexhage, *Preise, Mieten/Pachten*. Szaivert and Wolters, *Löhne* includes detailed lists of prices; such compilations should be used circumspectly, especially for translation into

The price for copies of early Christian texts cannot be seen as particularly exorbitant. What is more revealing is that during the second century an "average" six-person household required *at least* a thousand *drachmai* a year for food, clothing, and housing *just to survive*.[47] By the middle of the second century the average wage for a day-laborer was about 1 *drachma* 1 *obol*, which increased with about 3–5 *oboloi* towards the third century.[48] (There are 6 *oboloi* to the *drachma*.)

When we turn to the origins of the New Testament writings the costs calculated in Table 1 are incomplete. *Papyrus London* 2110 indicates costs for *copying* an existing text; surely an *author* required more extensive assistance than just copying. Did a scribe contracted to perform secretarial work include the time spent on preparatory work in the cost of the final copy's number of *stichoi*? Probably not, when we consider the amounts in Table 1.

So what was involved in writing a New Testament document? We gather from the working methods of the two Plinys, Cicero, and others that for longer works, including letters, writing began with note-taking, which would be worked up into a draft copy, after which a proper version of the work was prepared to be sent off to its recipients.[49] Writing a rough draft could be completed quickly, while the refined version was written more carefully and typically on fine papyrus. The rough draft(s) would also entail composition, dictation, possible discussion, redirection and consultation of notebooks (e.g., notes kept by the author and/or the scribe).[50]

Dictation, it is important to keep in mind, often played a role in the various aspects of authoring.[51] Dictation probably was part of not only note-taking and composition, but of editing, compiling, and publication.

---

first-century values. We need to keep in mind that during the early empire, Egypt was mainly a closed currency area, and the tetradrachm was tariffed at 1 *denarius*, making the *drachma* equal to the *sestertius*. See Duncan-Jones, *Money and Government*, 90.

47. See Drexhage, *Preise*, 440–54.

48. Ibid., 405.

49. Dorandi, "Den Autoren"; Dorandi, "Zwischen Autographie und Diktat"; Botha, "Authorship."

50. Composition in memory—even for very long texts—is possible and was done; probably most Greco-Roman authors were quite practised at doing so. See Chapter 6, below. Yet we have many indications of authors deliberately seeking advice from friends and/or employing correctors. "Paul may have had a particularly retentive memory, but it would have been more in keeping with the ethos of his age to have noted, either personally or by a secretary, such items as he felt might be useful in his oral instruction and written communication" See Murphy-O'Connor, *Paul the Letter-Writer*, 36—a description probably valid for other New Testament authors as well.

51. In fact, one of the defining *characteristics* of Greco-Roman literacy is the

We do not know, but I imagine writings such as the Gospel of Mark, Luke-Acts, and letters such as 1 Corinthians or Romans being completed in at least three phases: note-taking and basic composition, rough draft, and copy for (initial) distribution. That is, they were written out, in various forms, at least three times.

By means of a few experiments I have established that I can copy a page of 30 lines (at about 36 letters per line), writing in capitals, in about ten minutes. A practiced, motivated professional would easily match or even improve on this, that is, writing at three lines (*stichoi*) per minute. However, as I write with modern materials using a quality ballpoint pen (therefore without the need for dipping the pen in ink nor for sharpening the point) I would submit three lines per minute as probably an upper limit for writing done quickly—handwriting which Turner describes as *informal round hand*.[52] The average over a period of time could be closer to two lines per minute.

Writing with precision and attempting calligraphic appearance was very difficult and almost impossible for me to do quickly. Even with considerable practice it was challenging to improve on one line per minute, though I think it safe to submit that an experienced professional could probably do about 1.5 lines per minute of *formal mixed hand*.[53] A long time ago Eduard Stange suggested a tempo of about 1.5 lines per minute for Paul's secretary.[54]

---

presence of dictation. Typically, authoring in antiquity entailed two different activities accomplished by (at least) two different individuals. Especially for literary texts, autograph manuscripts seem quite exceptional in antiquity (and the Middle Ages). Cribiore reminds us of the importance of "interior dictation." See Cribiore, *Writing*, 93 n. 172. On dictation in Greco-Roman times, see Dorandi, "Zwischen Autographie und Diktat"; Harris, *Ancient Literacy*, 336, 224 n. 247; Johnson, *Bookrolls and Scribes*, 39–40; Skeat, "Use of Dictation"; Small, *Wax Tablets*, 170–74.

52. Turner classified literary hands of the first four centuries CE into three main groups: (1) Informal round hands; (2) Formal round hands; (3) Formal mixed hands. Turner and Parsons write, "The class of informal round hands is large . . . It includes hands so quickly written as to be almost characterless—'nondescript.'" See Turner and Parsons, *Greek Manuscripts*, 21.

53. Turner's "formal mixed" is similar to the "severe" style of handwriting used in other papyrological handbooks (e.g., Kenyon, *Palaeography*, 75–6). The assumption is that New Testament authors did not publish in a "formal round" hand which is almost instantly recognisable (from the generous size of their letters and the use of serifs or decorated roundels). It is, of course, possible that the New Testament authors published in a calligraphic hand, in something similar to "biblical majuscule"—which is not confined to the writing of biblical texts (it is a terminological relic). "Of all styles of ancient handwriting this one attained the greatest fixity of form." See Turner and Parsons, *Greek Manuscripts*, 22. For my purposes here the calligraphic option is left out of the account.

54. Stange writes, "Rechnen wir für die flüchtige Abschrift einer Seite des Nestleschen

That would seem to be a useful guideline for neat writing—that is, writing out a proper version ready for circulation.[55]

I also noted that fast writing can keep up with *slow* dictation, but not for long periods.

To take down a speech absolutely requires some form of speedwriting or shorthand—as all secretaries and journalists working without modern recording devices know.[56] Though longhand writing was certainly used to compose some early Christian texts, the role of scribes capable of speedwriting and/or shorthand must be considered.

Speedwriting is more than twice as fast as longhand, due to using less letters and abbreviations. Speeds of up to 120 words a minute are possible for short periods of time, with speeds of 80 words a minute being regularly attained. Yet speedwriting is nowhere near as fast as symbolic shorthand systems.

Speedwriting and shorthand were well-known in antiquity. Using symbols for letters, syllables, words, and short phrases, σημειογράφοι (later called ταχυγράφοι), *notarii*, and *exceptores* could easily take down speeches.

According to Plutarch, the first speech recorded in this way was delivered by Cato on 5 December 63 BCE, demanding the death penalty for the Catilinarians. Plutarch adds that Cicero had scribes specially trained for this purpose.[57] Cicero's freedman and secretary, Tiro,[58] devised a system of

---

Testaments (ca. 30 Zeilen) bei Akzentloser Minuskelschrift mindestens 10 Minuten, für das paulinische Diktat derselben aber, das ja nicht onhe einzelne Wiederholungen und Stockungen abging, mindestens das Doppelte, also 20 Minuten, so ergibt das für das Diktat des Römerbriefes 11⅓ Stunde, des I.Korintherbriefes 10⅓, des Philipperbriefes 2½, aber auch noch für I.Thessalonicherbrief 2⅓ Stunde." See Stange, "Diktierpausen,"109.

55. Making use of the data collected by Dixon, Kurzman, and Friesen, "Handwriting performance," 360–70, it can be calculated that handwriting, on average, requires 0.465 seconds per letter (sentences in English, cursive script) or about 17 seconds for a 36 letter line; which equals about 3 *stichoi* per minute.

56. Generally, maximum possible writing rate is 40 words per minute and maximum possible speaking rate is considered to be 200 words per minute. See Gould and Boies, "Writing," 1146. Of course, the notion of the "speed" of speech is itself problematic. See Wainschenker, Doorn, and Castro, "Quantitative Values."

57. See Plutarch, *Cato Minor* 23. 3. Plutarch also reports that Julius Caesar kept a slave "who was accustomed to write from dictation" sitting next to him as he travelled. See Plutarch, *Caes.* 17.4–5.

58. Marcus Tullius Tiro, slave (born as a child of a war prisoner) and secretary of Cicero, who eventually manumitted him (in 53 BCE), was clearly a highly educated and gifted person who probably shaped Cicero's work and heritage to a remarkable extent. Yet, due to his status he will always remain a shadowy figure. McDermott doubts whether Tiro actually devised a shorthand system. See McDermott, "M Cicero and M Tiro," 272. Cf. Milne, *Greek Shorthand*, 1; Teitler, *Notarii and Exceptores*, 172–73.

signs (*notae*) for prepositions and other short words and then invented signs for endings (*declinationes*). These *notae Tironianae* were widely used in the imperial administration and later by the Church.

Martial mentions both the shorthand scribe (*notarius*, 14.208) and the shorthand teacher (10.62.4): "Quick as speech is, the hand is quicker; before the tongue stops, the hand has finished."[59] Quintilian notes the impact of the competent shorthand scribe:

> The condemnation which I have passed on such carelessness in writing will make it clear what my views are on the luxury of dictation, which is now so fashionable. For, when we write even quickly the hand cannot follow the rapidity of our thoughts so we have time to think, whereas the presence of our *amanuensis* hurries us on, and at times we feel ashamed to hesitate or pause, or make some alteration, as though we were afraid to display such weakness before a witness. As a result, our language tends not merely to be haphazard and formless, but in our desire to produce a continuous flow, we let slip positive improprieties of diction, which show neither the precision of the writer nor the impetuosity of the speaker.[60]

Seneca writes about the remarkable things invented by slaves: "What about signs for words with which a speech is copied in writing, however rapid, and the hand follows the speed of tongue."[61] About his uncle, Pliny the Younger reports: "In his journeys . . . he found leisure for this sole pursuit [continuing his studies]. A shorthand writer (*notarius*), with bookroll and tablets (*pugillaribus*), constantly attended him in his chariot, who, in winter, wore a particular sort of warm gloves, that the sharpness of the weather might not occasion any interruption to his studies; and for the same reason my uncle always used a sedan chair in Rome."[62]

From papyri and wax tablets found in Egypt we learn about Greek shorthand. From the second century onwards, examples of Greek shorthand and parts of manuals survive in large numbers. In these we find properly organized systems, made up with syllabaries and commentaries, groups of words, arranged in fours or occasionally eights, with a sign attached to each,

---

59. Martial, *Epigrams* 14.208.

60. Quintilian *Inst. Orat.* 10.3.19–20.

61. Seneca, *Ep.* 40. 25.

62. Pliny, *Ep.* 3.5

which had to be memorized.[63] Initially, this was practiced only by slaves and freedmen trained as scribes.[64]

Was tachygraphy (in Greek) common during the first century? All indications are that it was. Cicero (in a letter to Atticus, 45 BCE) explicitly uses the Greek phrase διὰ σημείων to refer to shorthand, indicating the existence of such systems.[65] Cicero's son writes (to Tiro)—to justify his less-than-sterling performance studying philosophy in Athens: "But I beg you to see that a copyist (*librarius*) is sent to me as quickly as possible, most preferably a Greek (*maxime quidem Graecus*), for that will relieve me of a lot of trouble in writing out lecture notes" (the assumption being that a competent scribe could be found in Rome).[66]

Oxyrhynchus Papyrus 4.724 (155 CE) is an apprenticeship contract with a shorthand teacher, the agreement entails a two-year training period.[67]

To visualize the kind of secretaries involved in the creation of the New Testament documents I would consider the following examples: In 108 the slaves Sabinus and Diadumenus, both *notarii* of "P. Dasumius Tuscus," were manumitted by testament in Rome (*CIL* 6.10229). Dating from the year 111, *P.Oxyrynchus* 44.3197 tells us that in Egypt the νοτάριοι Ammonas, Epaphrys, Agathys, Sarapas, and Eucaerus, together with a large number of other slaves, were distributed among the heirs of a certain Ti. Julius Theon.

As there was no organizing authority determining the "real" form of ancient shorthand writing, the modern debate about what should be and what should not be considered ancient shorthand and whether dictation was *syllabatim* or *viva voce* seems somewhat fruitless. Clearly both approaches were practiced as situation proscribed and possibilities were available.[68] In *P.Michigan* 2.121, dated to 42 CE the scribe uses "frequent phonetic spellings, and a great deal of abbreviation."[69] Scribes, we can be very certain, made use of various forms of speedwriting.

---

63. Milne, *Greek Shorthand*, 3–6.

64. Teitler, *"Notarii and Exceptores,"* 27–29, 31–34.

65. Cicero, *Ad Atticum* 13.32.

66. Cicero, *Ad Familiares* 16.21.8.

67. The earliest indication of Greek tachygraphy among the papyri dates from the late first century. See Giovè Marchioli and Menci, "Tachygraphie," 11.

68. Dictation *syllabitim* is self-evident. See, e.g. Seneca, *Epistulae* 40.10; Bahr, "Paul and Letter-writing," 470–71. Dictation *viva voce*: secretaries recorded speeches in the Senate (cf. Seneca, *Epistulae* 40.25; Suetonius, *Divus Titus* 3.2; Seneca, *Apocolocyntosis* 9.2).

69. See Turner and Parsons, *Greek Manuscripts*, 100.

Obviously, not all scribes were stenographers—but *notarii*/νοτάριοι often were both scribes and shorthand writers. What exactly distinguished them from other writers such as *librarii, scribae, scriptores, epistulares,* γραμματεῖς, γραφικοί, ὀρθόγραφοι, κωμογραμματεῖς, ὑπογραμματεῖς, and ὑπομνηματογράφοι (to name but *some* of these crafts/functions) we do not know, though they probably shared many of the same skills and training. One implication seems fairly certain: producing a literary text involved several people during the "authoring" process.

Very likely most early Christian authors employed a variety of secretarial skills for their writings. Some general considerations support this view. Scribal skills often included more than just writing. "The training of slaves in clerical skills to increase their value was common."[70] It is precisely such skills which made the difference for making use of scribes and not simply writing oneself. Knowing how to read and write did not make the specialist role of scribes superfluous. Also, the very speed with which early Christian *literature* spread through the Roman empire must have been due, in part at least, to the successful participation of competent scribes in the movement.

With all these considerations in mind, some possibilities about the investment of time for the New Testament writings can be calculated. (Note that the focus is on the *writing*, time spent on research, composition, and rethinking is left out of consideration.)

Performing the Gospel of Mark requires about seventy-five minutes, the Letter to the Romans about forty-five; it can be assumed that dictation at normal speech speed would require about the same time. However, composing, formulating, and consultation of notes inevitably intruded, so that note-taking at the first stage, even in shorthand, would have taken at least one-and-a-half times longer, though possibly twice or even three times as long.[71]

70. See Booth, "Schooling," 11. An aspect also emphasized by Mohler, "Slave Education"; and Forbes, "Education and Training." On the presence of slaves in Roman education, see Bloomer, "Schooling in Persona," 61–62. Opportunities for slaves with literate training: Joshel, *Work*, 46–91; and Treggiari, *Roman Freedmen*, 123.

71. The assumption is that there is some interaction between author and scribe(s). Composition by speaking is faster than composition by dictation which is faster than composition by writing (about 20% faster, if modern standards are any indication); see Gould and Boies, "Writing," 1146. Interestingly, involvement in language production (i.e., composition) affects the speed and legibility of handwriting, and conversely focus on speed (/legibility) impacts on understanding and recall. See Brown, Brown, and Carr, "Adapting to Processing"; Van Galen, "Handwriting," 179.

What must further be taken into account is the time needed by the scribe(s) to prepare the papyrus sheets, score the lines on the sheets, prepare the ink and pens, arrange notebooks, and other such activities.

How many hours should count as a working day? I would suggest a working day of five hours of actual writing. This is to realistically account for availability of daylight, weather conditions and all sorts of (inevitable) interruptions.[72] In Table 3 I have compiled some calculations with regard to time involved in writing basic versions of some early Christian literature.

To factor in the cost of papyrus at the time of writing these documents a price of 5 *denarii* per scroll can be used (transport costs increased the price of papyrus outside Egypt). If Mark wrote in Rome he kept a scribe or two busy for about seven days and consumed at least two rolls of papyrus (10 *denarii*). Luke would have used about three-and-a-half rolls (17 *denarii*) and kept a few scribes busy for twelve days.

It is doubtful whether early Christian authors actually paid for their papyrus and scribes. They probably had patrons supplying writing materials and scribes, or, as at least in the case of Paul, scribes probably gave their assistance voluntarily.

Whatever the case may have been, the creation of most early Christian documents reflects dedication and commitment. Though nothing wildly exorbitant, we are once again reminded of a fairly serious investment of resources.

More to the point, we are reminded of *the many hands* involved in the writing of the New Testament and early Christian literature. Producing literary texts was in many ways labor intensive. Also, we are reminded of the past as a different country. To take Paul as an example, an exercise like this serves "to remind the reader that everything took a lot longer in Paul's day. We need to slow down radically if we are to appreciate the rhythm of his life. We tend to imagine that travel and communications were just somewhat slower than today. In fact, there was a huge quantitative difference, which had a great impact on the quality of communication."[73]

---

72. Secretaries working in British parliamentary committees during the 1880s worked in pairs taking turns at shorthand notetaking and longhand text preparation. Apparently they maintained 2–3 hours of continuous shorthand writing; after a "turn" of fast writing was over, the longhand transcripts were prepared, again in bouts of about 2 hours with overall shifts of about 5 hours. Written (final) manuscripts were produced at about 47 words per minute (cf. "The Shorthand Congress," 195).

73. Murphy-O'Connor, *Paul: His Story*, viii; cf. Hartman, "On Reading," 138.

Table 3: The Time Needed to *Write* Some Early Christian Texts

	Στίχοι	Perform (minutes)[74]	Note-taking[75] (hours)	Draft copy[76] (hours)	Revised copy[77] (hours)	At least–probably[78]
Matthew	2,560	125	3	23	29	5–11 days
Luke	2,750	130	3	25	31	6–12 days
Acts	2,560	120	3	23	29	5–11 days
John	2,020	100	3	19	23	4–9 days
Mark	1,610	75	2	15	18	3–7 days
Romans	980	50	1½	9	11	2–5 days
1 Corinthians	910	50	1½	8	10	2–4 days
2 Corinthians	610	33	1	6	7	1–2½ days
Galatians	310	16	¾	3	4	½–1½ days
Ephesians	330	22	¾	3	4	½–1½ days
Revelation	1,350	60	1½	12	15	2½–6 days
Shepherd of Hermas	3,650	180	7	34	41	7–16 days
Epistle of Barnabas	880	50	1½	8	10	1½–4 days
Hebrews	715	35	1	7	8	1½–3 days
1 Timothy	240	15	½	2	3	⅓–1 day
Gospel Thomas	660	35	1	6	8	1½–3 days
Didache	300	16	¾	3	4	½–1½ days

74. My estimates, based on reading the Greek text aloud, and some experiments with performed NT texts.

75. Performance time × 1.5. That is, assuming shorthand taking down of the dictation (performing the text) plus half that period of time.

76. Writing at 2 lines per minute, and adding time for reading, consultation of notes and preparation of writing materials (estimated at equivalent to reading the complete text).

77. Writing at 1.5 lines per minute.

78. A text could hardly have been written out in usable format quicker than for a "draft" copy (column 5), hence that figure is the "at least" time required. Realistically, the text was taken down, written out and neatly rewritten, hence the "probably," which represents the sum of columns 4, 5 and 6.

Pupil and Freedman and Assistant in His Literary Work

This is how Aulus Gellius describes Marcus Tullius Tiro, ex-slave of Cicero: "the pupil and freedman and an *adiutor* in [Cicero's] literary studies."[79] Authors, we know, not only dictated their works to scribes but also made use of them for note-taking, editing, proofreading, correcting, reading, and research. Which raises an interesting question: who wrote what?

The scribe, the literate slave, could be used as a mere copyist, just a means to get words onto papyrus, but more often than not the scribe was secretary, research assistant, reader and messenger. He (or she)[80] could even be a co-author. Gellius had a high respect for Tiro—he mentions Tiro's "care and learning"[81]—though he sometimes missed little things: "Therefore I am not so much surprised that Marcus Tullius erred in that matter, as that it was not noticed later and corrected either by Cicero himself or by Tiro, his freedman, a most careful man, who gave great attention to his patron's books."[82]

Cicero refers to Tiro frequently in his letters, remarking on how useful he is to him for studies and literary work.[83] Tiro's duties included taking dictation, deciphering Cicero's handwriting, revising and rewriting as well as managing the copying of texts. He probably authored several books himself. Aulus Gellius says, "[Tiro] wrote several books on the usage and theory of the Latin language and on miscellaneous questions of various kinds"[84] and Plutarch cites him as a source for incidents in Cicero's life.[85]

Clearly, the scribe, the one wielding the pen, was more than just an instrument. We cannot know in how many steps an author's work progressed or to what extent further readings and additional research and/or

79. Gellius, *Noctes Atticae* 13.9.1.

80. We know less about the literacy education of girls than we would like to know—a telling fact in itself—but there is some evidence of female scribes. Teitler refers to the only two female stenographers known from antiquity. See Teitler, *Notarii and Exceptores*, 31–32. There were also female calligraphers. See Haines-Eitzen, "Girls trained." The best discussion of women and education I am aware of is Cribiore, *Gymnastics*, 74–101. Girls who attended schools probably "learned reading, writing, and perhaps reciting as a mimicry of male behavior." See Bloomer, "Schooling in Persona," 75.

81. Gellius, *Noct. att.* 1.7.1

82. Ibid., 15.6.1–2

83. Cicero writes, "I see that you are interested about Tiro. Though he is serviceable to me in a thousand ways, when he is well, in every department of my business and my studies, yet my anxiety for his recovery is founded on his own kindness and high character, rather than on my convenience." See Cicero, *Epistulae ad Atticum* 7.5.

84. Gellius, *Noct. At.* 13. 9.

85. Plutarch, *Cicero* 41, 49.

consultations resulted in actual reworkings of the text. We do know that material was noted in the margins of the previously collected parts or added to the verso of the scroll. Various supplementary notes, and linguistic or stylistic improvements found their place either on the margins and on the empty places of the recto or on the verso; insertions and additions not made by the author himself but written down by a scribe or the professional διορθωτής (corrector).

Often the secretary was entrusted with the responsibility of writing the text from incomplete notes. Authors regularly left considerable scope to their secretaries; either on purpose, or due to rapid dictation, or because often only an outline or draft was provided. The line between editing and co-authorship is impossible to draw: "If one writer excerpts or copies portions of another's work, but adds comments, supplements, appendices or insertions—or subtracts or epitomizes—then whether we regard the 'new' work thus produced as distinctively a different document in its own right, or as a 'new edition' or adaptation of the old, becomes a matter of degree only."[86]

The various roles assistants/scribes played in "writing" a text are, as an issue, not unknown in New Testament scholarship, and have drawn mostly the attention of Pauline scholarship. Usually, there is an insistence that there is a difference between a co-author and an *amanuensis*. But how would we know such a difference? Can we discover the different contributions of copying, editing, and re-writing? In cases of deliberate co-authorship various options present themselves.[87] The authors may have considered the substance of the letter individually, and then gone over the general plan of what they were to compose, or perhaps suggested the style and expression which they had separately chosen while thinking about the message before collaborating towards an agreed content and form.

Richards gives a useful overview of the use of a secretary in the Greco-Roman world.[88] He notes that secretarial assistance was common, but the role that a secretary played varied greatly, depending on the degree of control he had over the content, style, and/or form of a letter. Richards classifies the various roles of a secretary into four broad categories: (1) When the secretary functioned as a "recorder," he would write the letter exactly as it was dictated by the author. (2) When the secretary served as an "editor," he would take extensive notes of the author's dictation to be used later in the composition of a final draft. The secretary's personal contribution consisted

---

86. Hall, "Hirtius," 412–13.

87. Cf. Prior, "*Paul the Letter-writer*," 39–50.

88. Richards, *Secretary*, 15–67.

of relatively minor decisions about syntax, vocabulary, and style. (3) When the secretary worked as a "co-author," the same type of procedure would be followed as in an editorial role except that the secretary's contribution would be greater. (4) When the secretary functioned as a "composer," he would construct a letter on behalf of the author without receiving instructions about its specific contents. Secretary/scribes probably played similar roles in the writing of literary texts.

A related question is whether an author assumed full responsibility for the content and form of a book. The answer probably depended on circumstances, though "the scribe" must have been a handy excuse in cases of unpleasant and awkward communications. This is typical of slave societies: "Blaming the slave was a convenient way of avoiding embarrassment."[89]

As an approach to understanding the textual characteristics of the gospels and especially the synoptic problem, or Acts and Revelation, little attention to possible roles of secretarial assistants and scribal options has been paid. Given our evidence, answers to our questions would be almost impossible. Yet, most of the answers to our questions regarding gospel origins and the inscripturation of traditions simply ignore the material aspects of ancient literacy.

Recently Kim Haines-Eitzen[90] has shown the importance of scribes in the production, reproduction, and interpretation of early Christian texts. She argues that early Christian scribes were not only copyists but also the creators *and* users of texts who not only conserved texts but also modified them in accordance with their own theological knowledge and proclivities. Is it not possible that the very origins of Christian writings lie among such (small) groups of itinerant and marginal scribes? The very anonymity of most early Christian literary texts points in this direction.

Be that as it may, there is a fateful reason why we know so little about the contributions by scribes and secretaries to ancient works.

The Master's Voice

The key to understanding Greco-Roman literacy is often described as the "living voice." Can we be a bit more precise about that "voice"? In his *Rethinking Writing*, Roy Harris notes, "how literate people view writing is often colored by their opinions concerning literacy and their own status as literate

---

89. Fitzgerald, *Slavery*, 58.
90. Haines-Eitzen, *Guardians of Letters*.

members of the human race."[91] He wants us to rethink writing in broad socio-historical context. His concerns are with the limitations and problems with functional or utilitarian literacy, but his insight that what one thinks writing *is* as crucial to how one understands literacy, is important.[92]

When we look at ancient manuscripts and visualize the pen making the markings in ink and we consider the hand holding the pen: how do we see the body behind the hand? The hands that held the pens that wrote the texts were the hands of stooped bodies, sitting low down. These were bodies looked upon, looked down on by authors and patrons and even clients.

The hands that made those artifacts, handled them, wrote them, corrected them, took care of them, were the hands of subservient persons. We, today, look at these writings as instruments to get into "the minds" of authors. The "text" is a surrogate or extension of a "noble mind." I would like to prompt us to consider literacy not as a window and *not* to treat the artifacts of inscription separated from persons, settings, and communicative modalities.

Or, to adopt a more theoretical tone,[93] we should dare to visualize the *interplay* of structure and construction, of history and agency. What can and what should be said about the *institutional contexts* that gave *distinct* (i.e., Greco-Roman) significance to the literacy events we call the New Testament and early Christian texts?

Writing in Greco-Roman times was part of a system which was influenced by considerations such as the writing materials and the provision of technical support available in society. These aspects in turn were extended by cultural factors such as mores forbidding upper-class individuals from being physically lower than lower-class individuals. Scribal duties, which required at least some bending, were relegated to people low enough in class to stoop.

Seneca may be defending the virtues of the properly trained philosophical (Stoic) mind, but he affords us a glimpse on how writers (scribes) were seen. He describes several useful things that have been invented, among them: "our signs for whole words, which enable us to take down a speech, however rapidly uttered, matching speed of tongue by speed of hand. All this sort of thing has been devised by the lowest grade of slaves. Wisdom's seat is

91. Harris, *Rethinking Writing*, ix.

92. Cf. ibid., x.

93. The useful conceptual term in this regard is "practice," reflecting the legacy of thinkers such as Marshal Sahlins, Raymond Williams, Anthony Giddens, Michel Foucault, and Pierre Bourdieu.

higher; she trains not the hands, but is mistress of our minds." [94] It is not a matter of denying slaves and scribes intelligence or great skill—in fact, Seneca lists in detail many astounding achievements by lower-class people—yet he insists: "[although both the hammer and the tongs] . . . were invented by some man whose mind was nimble and keen, but not great or exalted. The same holds true of any other discovery which can only be made by means of a bent body and of a mind whose gaze is upon the ground."[95]

We like to think of education (specifically reading and writing) as forces of liberation and class-transcending powers. Education, however, can also be divisive and hierarchical. In the Greco-Roman world, "the highest level of linguistic and literary achievement came to those who completed the secondary stage of education and then studied with a teacher of rhetoric. Greco-Roman culture regarded the well-delivered and persuasive speech as the most characteristic feature of civilized life. In contrast to our own culture, linguistic skill focused on oral speech; the written word was secondary, derived from primary rhetoric."[96] In addition, in that world writing, in its wider sense, was considered *labor*: "The laborious is clearly not the noble. There are many things that are laborious, which you would deem not appropriate to boast of having done; unless, you actually thought it glorious to copy out stories and whole speeches in your own hand."[97]

The copyists and the literary scribes, the *amanuenses* and the *librarii*, the correctors and the calligraphers were all either slaves or freedmen. That the scribes who took down dictation, corrected and improved texts, and were responsible for copying and distributing books were from the slave and freed classes should not surprise us, and we should not forget the stigma attached to such labor. "No matter how indispensable these scribes were, they were not members of the upper classes."[98]

In the physical act of writing literary texts there was a social dynamic at work, and the (scribal) writer need not to have been a slave *de jure* to be caught up in the social, moral, and even aesthetic value judgments enacted by one being the dictator and the one "taking dictation." Mastery is more than a metaphor or some idealized hope or trope of the governing class. At stake is not so much a proscription of who may read and write (as physical activities) but an expectation of who reads and writes in what capacity:

94. Seneca the Younger, *Letters* 90.25–26.

95. Ibid., 90.10.

96. Stowers *Letter Writing*, 33–34.

97. *Rhetorica ad Herennium* 4.6.

98. Haines–Eitzen, *Guardians of Letters*, 31.

"the maintenance of subordinates was inextricably connected to practices of reading and writing, indeed to the development of upper-class speech."[99] A scribe was not just writing a text, but performing a code; an almost ceremonial act necessarily circumscribed by one being the superior and the other the inferior.

The creation of early Christian literature was due to the application of skills and practices typically used elsewhere, and by doing so the NT and other early Christian authors not only advanced the spread of the Jesus movement, but gave it a remarkable "scriptural" identity.

Yet we should be careful not to romanticize these subordinates using their skills to promote an alternative society. In their emulation of literary practices powerful distinctions were still at work. It could not have been otherwise. They may have criticized power and evoked alternatives to abuse of power, but their writings also reflect claims to power. Inevitably they engaged a process of organizing and negotiating and establishing power and control. As in the contact with the influential classes where elite and non-elite are to a degree complicit by maintaining society,[100] the early Christian scribes were inscribing who may speak and about what; who will be the "competent" speaker and who will be the "proper" listener.

Concluding Remarks

This discussion has as its aim the consideration of Greco-Roman writings as events, as situated "actions" where the issue is not a binary contrast between literacy and orality, not about people just decoding or encoding text, but rather as socially embedded and culturally mediated performances. The participants in these events were socialized into and enacting particular views of what writing might be. We need to look at ancient writing as structured practices where people took roles in these events, and were part of larger-purpose endeavors.

The argument is informed by what Barton emphasizes:

> literacy practices . . . need to be seen as part of social practices. People do things for a reason; people have purposes. Literacy serves other purposes. In general, people do not read in order to read, or write in order to write; rather, people read and write in order to do other things, in order to achieve other ends . . . The importance of viewing reading and writing in terms of social

99. Bloomer, "Schooling in Persona," 60.
100. Ibid., 76.

practices is that we see the purpose behind the activities; we also see how intertwined the written word is with other forms of communication, especially spoken language.[101]

The explorations in this chapter have been undertaken for illustrative purposes to gain some sense of values and implicit and explicit costs involved with making and distributing of early Christian literature. We have seen that physical writing was done sitting down with the papyrus roll or sheet resting on the lap, the knee used to support the writing. It has become clear that producing literary texts required several people, necessitating extensive material support and settings where the allocation of time could be made. Most of all, writing in Greco-Roman times reflected the enactment of socially established values and attitudes where servitude was all pervasive.

Woolf argues that "the study of Roman writing practices sheds new light on many aspects of early imperial society, economy, religion, and government, and suggests new connections between them,"[102] and this chapter is a small contribution in this regard.

101. Barton, "Social Nature," 8.
102. Woolf, "Literacy," 875.

5

Memory, Performance, and Reading Practices

Introduction

It is a familiar scene, often introduced by clear signals that privacy and silence are now required. One pulls the chair up to the desk and arranges some of the books and other papers already lying there. Then, glasses are picked up, cleaned with a tissue or the hem of the blouse or some piece of cloth, perched on the nose, and steadied behind the ears. Adjustment of the study-lamp and little shifts of the chair and arms to reduce the shadows on the book follow. One reaches for pencil or highlighter, and the soft sounds of scratching in the margins of book or notebook become audible. There may also be the *tip tap* of fingers on a keyboard. So, seated at a desk, surrounded by a distinct pool of light, enveloped by silence or soft, gentle music interspersed by adjustment to the position of the glasses, every once in a while lifting them off and rubbing the skin between the eyebrows, screwing the eyelids shut to soothe tired eye muscles: we all recognize the activity of "reading." These are the things we do when we read.

It is bewildering to imagine reading activities during the many centuries preceding our times. Silent studying is a rather recent phenomenon, as is our conception of working privately. In the Roman world, in that crowded daily life, people were never alone, sharing even their most intimate moments with servants, slaves, family, and friends. In the Greco-Roman world one would find an *auditorium* in the house of an educated man, and not a study. Obviously, until just a little more than a hundred years ago, no one could switch on a study lamp.

Imagine: before the invention of glasses, before the thirteenth century, readers squinting their way through nebulous outlines of a text. After all, a quarter of all humankind is myopic. In addition there are almost three hundred *other* conditions of impaired eyesight from which we may suffer. Even more bewildering is to imagine the long line of students before us who did not make use of desks. The desk, so characteristic of our trade, came in use with the development of the printing press. Imagine, if you can, research without underlining sentences and words.

In antiquity, writing was mostly done while sitting cross-legged—writing "on the knee" was the Greek phrase—and reading was often done standing.

Clearly, reading has a history.[1] This chapter has a very modest aim. I explore *some* aspects of reading practices in the first-century Roman world in order to suggest points for an agenda for researching New Testament documents informed by an ethnography of ancient communication.

Reading and Memory in Antiquity

Reading is an activity that we share with our ancestors, yet it is also something that can never be the same as what they experienced. "To put it more generally: what we count as 'reading' must inevitably be relative to particular cultural purposes, and depend on the contrasting modes of oral rendition which a particular culture may have institutionalized."[2] It is an illusionary pretense that we can step outside of time in order to make contact with authors who lived centuries ago. Even if their texts have come down to us unchanged—which they have not—our relation to those texts cannot be the same as that of readers in the past *because* reading has a history.

It is self-evident that concepts of reading and memory play formative roles in New Testament scholarship. By and large, these concepts are construed as corresponding to contemporary ideas. It is to that illusion of continuity I want to draw attention—the notion that New Testament scholarship can be practiced as *if there is no history of reading*. The conventional portrayal of those authors and readers is not a historical portrayal.

We must remind ourselves that the connection between education and literacy, which seems so natural to us, is simply a cultural convention of our own times. In Greco-Roman societies one could be educated without having

1. For the preceding paragraphs see Rosen, "Invention"; Trevor-Roper, *World*; Schottenloher, *Books and the Western World*; Burke, "Communication"; Darnton, "History of Reading"; Martin, *History and Power*; Small, *Wax Tablets*; Fischer, *History of Reading*, 11–43, 205–52.

2. Harris, *Origin*, 153–54.

the abilities to read or write. In fact, being literate (proficient with texts) was not even necessarily connected to writing and reading oneself. Concepts such as *illiterate*, or *literacy* are very much culture specific, historically determined.[3] "It is nevertheless that they [Greek and Roman elites] retained a strong element of orality in their lives . . . they relied on the spoken word for purposes which in some other cultures have been served by the written word. They frequently dictated letters instead of writing them for themselves; they listened to political news rather than reading it; they attended recitations and performances, or heard slaves reading without having to read literary texts for themselves; and so on."[4]

Ancient Reading

Reading in antiquity was not experienced as a silent scanning, mainly mental activity. It was a performative, vocal, oral–aural event.[5] The reader literally recited, with vocal and bodily gestures, the text that one usually memorized beforehand.

In antiquity reading was a physically demanding activity. Comfortable reading is something *we* are familiar with, and we need to visualize the very different way in which those people used their bodies when communicating by means of writing. There was a far more physical element in reading, and no one drew a clear distinction between the physical internalization and acquisition of knowledge. That is, when we consider the well-known fact that reading was done vocally as a *datum* to be interpreted, we realize that reading and memorizing were integrally connected. This brief chapter is an exploration of some evidence from antiquity to show just such aspects of the cultural embodiments of reading in antiquity.

In a cultural-anthropological sense, ancient reading practices indicate a whole range of cognitive and social effects and values particular to an oral

---

3. Street, *Literacy*, 8–11.

4. Harris, *Ancient Literacy*, 36.

5. Useful overviews of evidence, see Achtemeier, "*Omne verbum sonat*"; Fischer, *A History of Reading*, 45–97; Manguel, *A History of Reading*, 42–56; Marrou, "Education and Rhetoric," 196; McGuire, "Letters and Letter Carriers," 150; Saenger, "Separation of Words," 370–73. On the limitations of literacy in antiquity, see Carney, *Shape of the Past*, 110; Harris, "Literacy and Epigraphy"; Harris, *Ancient Literacy*; Lewis, *Life in Egypt*, 82; Youtie, "Ἀγράμματος"; Youtie, "Βραδέως Γράφων"; Youtie, "Because They"; Youtie, "Ὑπογρφεύς." The point being that even the literate facets of the culture must be understood within the context of first-century communication realities and historical-cultural continua.

and manuscript based communication technology.[6] It might seem super-fluous to emphasize these matters—especially in view of the technological changes separating our societies from theirs—but impreciseness and neglect of historical realities permeate discussions of the use of writing in antiquity.

Silent Reading?

Reading, as is well known, was often done aloud; it was mostly a vocal, re-sounding event.[7] Notice how Pliny, in his letter to Fuscus Salinator, describes how he spends a typical summer's day in Tuscany:

> After a short sleep and another walk I read a Greek or Latin speech aloud and with emphasis, not so much for the sake of my voice as my digestion, though both are strengthened by this . . . At dinner, if alone with my wife or with a few friends, I have a book read aloud; after the meal we listen to a comedy or lyre playing; then I walk again with the members of my household, among whom are educated individuals. Thus the evening passes in varied discus-sions, and even the longest day comes to a satisfying end.[8]

Antiquity did not recognize the separation of the visual and aural aspects of text in the same way or to the extent we do. Hence one of the Greekwords for "read" was ἀκούειν, which more commonly means "hear" or "listen."[9]

In fact, rather than noting something was read (ἀναγιγνώσκειν) when citing a source we mostly find ancient authors stating they *heard* some-one (long dead) *say* this or that. The reason why "the locution ἤκουσα 'X' λέγοντος could have become the regular Greek idiom derives from the fact

---

6. I am fully aware of the complexities involved with this statement. A good exposi-tion of the basic consequences would be the work of Olson, "Mind and Media"; Olson, *World on Paper*; Olson, "Literate Mentalities." See also Finnegan, *Literacy and Orality*; Goody, "Literacy and Achievement"; Lentz, *Orality and Literacy*; Thomas, *Oral Tradition*; Worthington, "Greek Oratory."

7. Harris writes, "The heavy reliance of the Roman upper class on readers is familiar, and even for them it is clear that listening, instead of reading for oneself, always seemed natural." See Harris, *Ancient Literacy*, 226.

8. See Pliny, *Ep.* 9.36.

9. Schenkeveld, "Prose Usage"; Johnson, "Oral Performance." Cassiodorus (490?–583 CE) remarks: "copying the precepts of the Lord . . . What happy application, what praiseworthy industry, to preach unto men by means of the hand, to untie the tongue by means of the fingers." See Cassiodorus, *Senatoris Institutiones* 1.30.1. Reference found in Metzger, *Text of the New Testament*, 18.

that in Antiquity reading aloud was the common way of reading" so that statements of this kind is simple indications that someone has read something in a book by X. This expression "is the proper Greek idiom for 'I have read in (e.g.) Plato that . . ', at least from the end of the Hellenistic period onwards."[10]

Reading aloud is an important feature of ancient reading—a crucial feature of written communication which must be understood, especially the role it played, in order to deal with texts from the first century. Of course, silent reading was not only possible but practiced as well.[11]

Recently Gavrilov questioned the scholarly consensus that the Greeks and Romans preferred to read aloud. He points to a range of reported incidents and references which, he contends, leaves only one conclusion: "silent reading was a quite ordinary practice for wide circles of the free population of classical Athens" and this was still the case "in the later Roman period."[12]

Here we find some obfuscation of issues involved. It begins with a historiographical principle, the difference between citing data as evidence and *analyzing* data to be interpreted as evidence. In other words, it is important to acknowledge that it is not just a case of evidence, but very much one of evidence *for what*. This "for what?" makes all the difference. The real key to Gavrilov's presentation is not the evidence quoted—a very useful list—but the final statement of his conclusion: "These ancient reflections help us to see that the phenomenon of reading itself is *fundamentally the same* in modern and in ancient culture. Cultural diversity does not exclude an underlying unity."[13]

A correct observation, but trivial and misleading. The fact that we all breathe does not mean that we think of air in the same way, or that we all

10 Schenkeveld, "Prose Usage," 129–30.

11. In his "Silent Reading" Knox criticizes the influential article by Balogh, "Voces Paginarum," for overestimating the extent of the practice of reading aloud. Balogh cites evidence mainly from medieval times, as pointed out by Knox. But Knox *assumes* that what ancient scholars did resembles what modern scholars do in libraries, therefore he scorns the proposal that ancient scholars read every book they consulted out loud. We first need to establish what reading techniques they practiced and consider that their way of study and research could have been quite strange to us. It is self-evident that if one can read one can read silently. Yet modern preferences reflect our times, our technology, our educational practices and our values. Also, note that the examples Knox gives has little to do with his thesis—namely that nothing shows that the silent reading of books was anything extraordinary—and actually shows *exceptions* to reading out loud. See also the note of Slusser's *Procatechesis* 14 on Cyril of Jerusalem.

12. Gavrilov, "Techniques of Reading," 68–69.

13. Ibid., 69, my italics.

hold breathing to be the same thing. Think of marriage: people marry to-day, as did people in antiquity; but consider the vast differences in values, perceptions, expectations, activities (at least when my context is set next to those of the Romans). To the point: even a highly trained scholar deals in a very different way with an ancient manuscript than with a modern printed text. A claim of cultural unity with ancient literacy is superficial and inconsequential.

With regard to understanding reading (and writing) activities, such supposed underlying cultural unity is proven a fallacy by the frequent *failure* of literacy programs. The long history of literacy programs[14] around the world reveals a narrative of considerable inadequacies and poor results.[15] Research on the complexities of implementing successful literacy shows that it is exactly the assumption of cultural unity which most often underlies such programs that is the problem. Cultural unity, it turns out, is often an attempt at integration of misplaced notions about a single "truth" in society. Literacy is not something neutral (or innocent), but a vast and immensely complex issue.[16] Its meanings and contextual roles are interwoven with political,

14. A useful starting point in this regard is the work of Graff who very effectively challenges current assumptions about the necessity and benefits of literacy. Western societies have misunderstood the nature of literacy and the role it plays (or can play) in the life of the individual and society. That misunderstanding, which can be explained historically, has determined the way in which "literacy crises" are conceptualized and how they are acted upon in various Western societies. See Graff, *Literacy Myth*; Graff, *Legacies*. Graff's *Labyrinths of Literacy* is a full-fledged history of the nature and spread of literacy from the earliest times to the present. The history of literacy in the West is one of contradictions and discontinuities rather than that of a progressive, uniform development. An over reliance on literacy as a solution to profound social problems has been at best misguided and at worst a disaster. A crucial point to take from Graff is to recognize literacy for the acquired technology that it is.

15. The literature is overwhelming. Regarding useful reviews of the complexities (and often negative results), see Bernardo, "On Defining"; Graff, *Labyrinths of Literacy*; Graff, *Legacies*; Hamilton and Barton, "International Adult Literacy"; Luke, "Literacy and the Other"; Olson, "Literacy"; Street, *Literacy in Theory*, 1–16, 183–228.

16. Amongst many possible references, see Akinnaso, "Consequences of Literacy"; Cook-Gumperz and Gumperz, "From Oral to Written"; Cook-Gumperz, "Introduction"; Hautecoeur, "Literacy in the Age"; Luke, "Genres of Power?"; Ogbu, "Minority Status"; Resnick and Resnick, "Nature of Literacy"; Resnick and Resnick, "Varieties of Literacy"; Stubbs, *Language and Literacy*. The *principle* at stake here is well put by Malina: "Literate people often take the process of reading for granted. Not a few readers innocent of what the reading process entails share the myth of the 'immaculate perception.' Because writing is presumed to be an object 'out there,' it can be observed and handled like other objects, such as rocks or trees . . . We call this misreading ethnocentrism, that is, imagining that all people everywhere and at all times think just like I do." See Malina, "Reading Theory Perspective," 7.

economical, technological and socio-cultural diversities. Understanding the phenomenon requires analysis of specific manifestations.

Manuscript Structure

There is a connection between forms of literacy and their textual structures, the material productions of literacy. The reason for emphasizing such connections is to suggest a different treatment of literacy: historical rather than formalistic (i.e., to understand writing and reading in context, rather than consider them as mere competencies). More specifically, the making of the written word—what texts look like and how they are created—also affect their use.

Darnton, in his analysis of *how* to research the history of reading, argues that such a history should include an "analysis . . . based on analytic bibliography. By studying books as physical objects, bibliographers have demonstrated that the typographical disposition of a text can to a considerable extent determine its meaning and the way it was read."[17] What this means is that an "artifact is not a simple aid. That is, you can't go out and find some cognitive artifact, and there you are, better at something."[18] Material specifics, technology and human activity interact to form a cognitive artifact. This must be taken into account when those artifacts are to be understood. Therefore, a good place to start one's ethnography of Greco-Roman communication is the characteristics of manuscripts. When considered from a linguistic point of view, the Greeks and Romans were capable of producing highly explicit texts, and have been doing that for several centuries by the time of the early Christians. Considering the manuscript as a functional tool, however, leads us to consider a rather unique concept of literacy.

The Scroll

A simple juxtaposition of a modern book and an ancient publication reveals overwhelming differences. The modern book is lightweight, small, easily manageable and *all* copies of the same publication are *exactly* alike.[19]

---

17. Darnton, "History of Reading," 159.

18. Norman, *Things that Make*, 78.

19. If you consult a copy of *Novum Testamentum Graece*[27] (NA[27]) Mark 7:17 will *always* be at the top of p. 112, with exactly the same notes positioned at precisely similar points on the page, for instance. Something not only almost impossible in antiquity, but probably also unimaginable.

Modern books have tables of contents, title pages, indexes, distinct and even margins, chapter divisions, pages, and page numbers: all make for effortless, comfortable use and access to the text itself. The ancient book is a cumbersome, unwieldy scroll, fairly readable while standing up and when the specific column of writing to be read does not matter, but physically demanding for reference and comparison.[20]

In fact, it takes a certain knack to read a scroll, keeping it open at the required place. The skills required, coiling and uncoiling a scroll (lit. "unfolding," ἀναπτύσσω, and "folding up," πτύσσω) are considerable feats.[21] Part of the expertise involved with being a reader at that time was to be dexterous with unwieldy objects.

The reader grasped the upper portion of the roll in the right hand, unscrolling it as one read, holding the already read part in the left hand. When finished, the scroll would be completely rolled up in the left hand. The easiest manner is simply to leave the unscrolled part draped over the left arm, but even this approach requires some dexterity. A number of complementary gestures and movements accompanied the reading process (of which quite a few can be deduced from figurative representations, as well as literary references). Sometimes a wooden reading stand was used to hold the scroll; the device could be resting on the lap of a seated reader or placed on a low supporting column.[22]

The noteworthy fact is that the technology, that is both the possibility and knowledge of alternatives for the scroll existed.[23] Large scale production of the codex started only in the seventh century CE. "From Homer in the eighth century B.C.E. to only parity and not total displacement of the roll took more than a millennium."[24]

Given that Greco-Roman writers and readers did not lack intelligence, the persistence with regard to the scroll can only be explained in terms of reading behavior. Unlike our needs and expectations with regard to texts,

20. For detail about "books" (i.e., scrolls, codices, tablets, etc.) in antiquity, I made use of Bischoff, *Latin Paleography*, 20–37; Kenyon, *Books and Readers*; Metzger, *Text of the New Testament*, 3–20; Turner, *Greek Manuscripts*.

21. Especially whilst reading the scroll. When finished, a practiced individual takes about two minutes to roll up a scroll while standing. See Skeat, "Two Notes on Papyrus."

22. Greeks and Romans did not use tables for writing or reading, though some made use of reading stands. The evidence for the use of tables for reading is slim and unconvincing; the evidence for chairs, however, is clear. Cf. Small, *Wax Tablets*, 160–67.

23. For instance, tying sheets of papyrus together as was done with wooden tablets. The linen codex was used by the Etruscans.

24. Small, *Wax Tablets*, 12.

ancient readers did not imagine their texts to be easily accessible and manageable, nor to be diverse sources of information. Most of those who read scrolls read "intensively." Typically they had access to only a few books and they read them over and over again, usually aloud and in groups, so that a narrow range of traditional literature became deeply impressed on their consciousness. (Today, in contrast, many readers of books read "extensively": all kinds of material, especially periodicals and newspapers, and read what is at hand only once, then move on to the next item, relying on technology to find and/or to return to information required).[25]

Formatting a Scroll

In the following I briefly review the format of the text on the ancient scroll, aspects such as paragraphs, punctuation, layout, the use of textual apparatus and word separation.

Consider the development and standardization of the paragraph as a means of marking off stages in an argument as a way of facilitating understanding. When teaching communication skills, and especially when writing is involved, we today emphasize the use of divisions, indentation, segmentation and other procedures because they contribute to the "rational" explicitness of the writing. When viewed from this perspective, Greco-Roman textual practices appear remarkably insufficient.

The Greco-Roman attitude toward the text is striking in its disregard of a rational order. Papyri from Hellenistic times and up until the end of the Roman Period show that texts were written continuously without paragraphs, chapters or division between words and sentences.[26] The papyri exhibit writing which is often jammed or cramped together producing coagulated blocks of text with no attention to rules governing the disposition of the written space or to the physical division within the text. Devices facilitating presentation and readability, such as page numbering, full punctuation and titles inserted at appropriate stages in an argument, did not form part of the textual system. Even scientific and philosophic treatises were written

25. The descriptive terms "intensive/extensive" reading come from Engelsing, "Die Perioden der Lesergeschichte," who is interested in demarcating the shift to "modern" reading towards the end of the eighteenth century. I use his hypothesis to illustrate a spectrum of reading styles: a slow, repeated, reverent manner on the one end and towards the other end a skimming, discarding style. Given the diversity of human individuality it is obvious that one should find all styles at various times, but the typology is useful for historical understanding in order to characterize reading practices.

26. Turner, *Greek Manuscripts*, 7–23; Kenyon, *Books and Readers*.

using arbitrary arrangements. Given these circumstances, the conventional papyrus roll was difficult to read with intelligence and almost impossible to use by way of reference to a given page or line.

In fact, basic text division was left to the readers in antiquity. For instance, Naevius's epic *Bellum Poenicum* was originally written in a single volume without a break, and was only divided into seven books *a century later* by Octavius Lampadio.[27]

The Greco-Roman text was constructed with almost no aids to the reader, whose task it was to divide the lines correctly into words and sentences. Finding one's place in complex prose argument without the aid of a system of reference or a scheme of division was an obvious source of difficulty and confusion. In any text of some length, and—most noteworthy—even in literary texts, readers were required to know the correct divisions *in advance.*

Many scholars have commented on the Greco-Roman practice of writing without separating words or sentences as well as the lack of textual expressions to expedite determining the sequence of what was written. Even the rather simple combination of lower and upper case letters greatly facilitates comprehension of a text—another feature that ancient authors ignored to a remarkable extent.

Consider the lack or very limited presence of punctuation in ancient texts. Punctuation functions as prosody or breathing, an aspect of speech; and as grammar. In antiquity prosody was emphasized, while the syntactical uses of punctuation do not appear until the Middle Ages. Morrison suggests that to the Greeks and Romans their texts were never more than a "variant of oral utterance due to the lack of procedures for transforming *writing* into text."[28] Only in the medieval period with the codex and its page format does "true" text appear. When the papyri are compared to later developments in the technique, design, and layout of texts, it is clear that the Greco-Roman attitude toward written language had not evolved beyond a variant of oral utterance due to the lack of procedures for transforming *writing* into text.

A brief digression is necessary to elaborate this point. We, nowadays, practice writing that employs a number of formulas reflecting a shift from oral to visual. In fact, formulas structuring writing are an essential characteristic of printed texts. This transition from "speaking in text" to "writing in text," however, can only be conceived of when a text is *seen* to include more than a succession of prose statements or sentences. It must be seen to

27. See Suetonius, *De Grammaticis*, 2.
28. Morrison, "Stabilizing the Text," 244.

include an apparatus which proposes a formal structure for a line of reasoning which makes explicit reference to the context created in the act of schematizing an extensive work. Formulas such as: "In this section we shall," "In the next paragraphs," "I suggested above," "Below, I reiterate," "In contrast," "for example," and others refer the reader to a class of textual statements that remains distinct or separate from the strictly linguistic or literary structure of a work. They establish the relative continuity of extended discourse that is written within the codes of the printed form. Statements of this class and type set coordinate the means by which the text refers to its relative order of material of which the distribution is accordingly structured into units of the text such as section, heading, paragraph, the page, and chapter: *writing* into text and not *speech*.

When we examine writings from antiquity, including copies of historical works (such as of Herodotus and Thucydides) among especially the papyri finds, we find ourselves very clearly within the realm of alphabetic literacy, but we do not find formal structures linking the accumulation of information to formulas making reference to the medium of the writing as such. There is an absence of a textual apparatus governing the movement from section to section. Statements linking narrative to the formal units of the text, such as the "book" or "chapter," are by and large absent and hamper the possibility of referring synoptically forward as in an accumulation of points, or backward in an appraisal of what has been said relative to section transitions.[29] The simple fact that requires contextualization is that these writings are *orally contrived texts*. The point I want to add to this fairly straightforward observation is the underlying implication of such composition and reading: the role of memory.

In contrast to the links which characterize a visually contrived textual work, Greco-Roman writings assume continuity from utterance to utterance on behalf of the reader; writings which are clearly assimilated to *hearers*, as in an oral culture. Contextual and structuring information is physically absent; there are very few if any such indications in the writing itself. Structuring was to be provided by the reader/audience—an assumption that reader/audience will "prepare" and "perform" the actual reading.

It is noteworthy that Quintilian, discussing the education of the orator, does not mention the unit of the sentence: "Then with these very syllables let [the student] begin to understand words and with these to construct a

---

29. A number of ancient writers note the serious difficulties in deciphering a manuscript: Arrian, *Discourses* 2.23; Aristotle, *Rhetoric* 1407b10–16; Aristotle, *Sophistical Refutations* 177b1–7, 177b35–178a3; Porphyry, *Life of Plotinus* 8; Strabo 13.1.54.

speech *[sermo]*."[30] Although limited forms of punctuation were used to mark the unit of the word for Latin in certain periods, the reader still had to read aloud in order to construe the words into phrases and then into sentences. So Quintilian recommends: "In . . . connection [with reading] there is much that can only be taught by practice, as for instance when the boy should take breath, at what point he should introduce a pause into a line, where the sense ends or begins, when the voice should be raised or lowered, what modulation should be given to each phrase . . . I will give but one golden rule: to do all these things, he must understand what he reads."[31]

Of course, as can be easily discovered by studying the material aspects of papyri, textual apparatus was not unknown, but its use in actual writings, even writings of length and of considerable importance, remained rudimentary. Punctuation occurs, but is unsystematic, and sometimes of a remarkably complex nature. Saenger maintains that the adoption of word separation began first in the British Isles, because the native readers learned Latin as a second language and needed the extra help of the spaces to parse Latin texts into words.[32] According to Gamble, because early Christian texts were often meant for reading aloud, by the fourth-century CE scribes began to arrange the text in visual chunks that matched "semantic units," though each unit still consisted of lines with no breaks for the words within them.[33]

Another datum that needs integration into an ethnography of ancient communication is the fact that they did not consider the concept of the written word as a visual unit to be important (although antiquity knew the concept of the word as a unit of speech). Contrast this with our textual aids, which depend, almost without exception, on the individual word. If you want to find something in a dictionary, thesaurus, encyclopedia, catalogue, indices or almost any reference, including the Web, you look it up by the unit of the word. Consider Dionysius of Halicarnassus's description of how children learn to read:

> When we are taught to read, first we learn by heart the names of the letters, then their shapes and their values, then, in the same way, the syllables and their effects, and finally words and their properties, by which I mean the ways they are lengthened, shortened, and scanned, and similar functions. And when we have acquired knowledge of these things, we begin to write and read,

---

30. Quintilian, *Orat* 1.1.31.

31. Ibid., 1.8.1–2.

32. Saenger, "Silent Reading," 377–79; Saenger, "Separation of Words," 205–7.

33. Gamble, *Books and Readers*, 229–230.

syllable by syllable and slowly at first. It is only when a considerable lapse of time has implanted firmly in our minds the forms of the words that we execute them with the utmost ease, and we read through any scroll that is given to us unfalteringly and with incredible confidence and speed.[34]

In the Greco-Roman curriculum, writing preceded reading and copying from a model was introduced at the beginning of the curriculum.[35]

What explanation can be offered to account for the lack of tolerance for the reader? Discussing the instability of classical Greek writing, Youtie notes that it "might well have created a preference for reading aloud [which] provided, contrary to modern expectation, a quicker route to intelligibility than mere visual inspection."[36]

Indeed, the most common way of reading was reading aloud, at all levels and for all functions. A text might be read directly or, (quite often) it was read by a reader intervening between the text and the listener or listeners. More than one reader could also be utilized and particularly the reading of literary texts usually involved multiple readers. These practices illustrate a writing style dominated by rhetoric, and its categories were adopted by all literary forms such as poetry, historiography, biography and philosophical and scientific treatises. Such texts (especially when read aloud before an audience) required a strong articulate reading style, in which the reader's tone of voice and cadences were adjusted to the nature of the writing and its stylistic effects.

Above I mentioned ἀκούω as a verb for reading; in Latin the verb used for poetic reading is often *cantare*[37]—the adjective *canore* indicating the voice interpreting poetry. Clearly a *different* bodily experience is involved here; a physical attitude that demanded a high level of technical skill and a broad culture. Even today, "inner speech increases when people are reading passages they find difficult."[38] Svenbro offers an interesting analogy: "Their [people in antiquity] relation to the written word might perhaps be compared to our relation to musical notation: not that it is impossible to read

---

34. Dionysius of Halicarnassus, *De Compositione Verborum* 25.

35. Cribiore, *Writing*, 242–49.

36. Youtie, *Textual Criticism*, 17 n. 6.

37. Quinn, "Poet," 155–58.

38. Ellis and Beattie, *Psychology of Language*, 227; Crowder and Wagner, *Psychology of Reading*, 161 (cf. 156–88).

music in silence, but the most common way of doing it is playing it on an instrument or singing it out aloud [sic] in order to know what it sounds like."[39]

In antiquity the default was oral reading, even if *sotto voce* when dealing with delicate communications.[40] Outside of reading public announcements, short letters or messages—which was facilitated by the repetition of certain formulas[41]—vocal articulation was a great help to understanding the meaning of a text. Literary works were "published" at collective ceremonies, *recitationes*. Such expressive forms of reading characterized reading practice; social gatherings associated with cementing patron-client relations, new social contacts, and perpetuating the habits of the cultured elite. *Recitationes* were held in places called *auditoria*, *stationes*, and *theatra*.

The relevant point—in terms of an ethnography of communication—is the recognition of the extensive role of memorizing and memory. Today we think of writing as an external store that substitutes for internal memory. Though the connection between writing and memory was apparent for writers and readers of the Roman period, reading was considered more a means of retrieval of what is inside of oneself.

Citing from and Referring to Manuscripts in Antiquity

It was not until after antiquity, especially from the Renaissance on, that readers felt a need for precise citation that never seemed to arise in our ancient forebears. When a classical writer cites another, he uses the same kind of vague reference as when making references within his own writings. The modern system of citation began in the thirteenth century.[42]

A concept of the page simply did not exist in antiquity. Pages could not be cited, not just because works were written on rolls, but because each roll was individually produced by hand and could vary tremendously in the amount written in any given width and column.[43] The codex was no better, since it too was subject to the same idiosyncrasies of individual, handwritten

39. Svenbro, "Phrasikleia," 236.

40. Schenkeveld, "Prose Usage"; Starr, "Reading Aloud."

41. Martin, *History and Power*, 71–72.

42. Rouse and Rouse, *Authentic Witnesses*, 221–55.

43. Kenyon and Roberts write, "The number of lines varies with the height of the column and the size of the writing; but numbers less than 25 or more than 45 are exceptional. Neither in the roll nor later in the codex, where reference was easy, as it could never have been with the roll, was the ancient scribe concerned to keep the same number of lines to a column. The number of letters to a line similarly varied," see Kenyon and Roberts, "Books," 173.

production. Fixed formats do not appear until print. Even something as self-evident (to us) as alphabetization was adopted remarkably late.[44] In fact, "the adoption of *alphabetic order* for the arrangement of concepts and the invention of techniques of reference required by the *subject index*, taken together constitute a major change in medieval society's perception of its relationship to the written heritage."[45] The practices of scholarship in the Roman period can be described as "rote familiarity with a finite body of authority, arranged according to rational principles and retained by memory."[46]

The table of contents does appear in writings from antiquity, but as a fairly rare occurrence. Pliny the Elder ends what we call the "Preface" to his *Naturalis historia*, but which is actually a covering letter to the emperor, with an explanation: "As it was my duty in the public interest to have consideration for the claims upon your [Titus's] time, I have appended to this letter a list of contents of the several books, and have taken very careful precautions to prevent your having to read them from cover to cover. By these means you will ensure that others do not need to peruse them either, but only look for whatever each of them wants, and will know in what place to find it."[47] What has been translated in English editions as "a table of contents" is rather misleading. Literally Pliny says, "I have attached to this letter what is contained in the individual books (*quid singulis continentur libris huic epistulae subiunxi . . .*)." Each section of the actual listing starts with a verb, *continentur* ("are contained"), and not a noun ("contents"). The list could not have been a table of contents because there was no means of referring to the precise locations where things were discussed. Pliny's list of contents takes up an entire ancient roll (in an English translation more than seventy pages of small type). Remember that the roll with the contents is not only long, but without divisions—none for paragraphs, sentences or words. Imagine the Emperor Titus with his new gift, Pliny's set of scrolls, and imagine the process of reading the more than one hundred columns of writing making up the list of contents to find the particular item one wants, then going to the roll that contains that item, and then reading through that until one reaches the item. Surely no speedy process! In fact, Pliny's list is practically useless as a reader's guide.

Why this complete lack of attention to possibilities for making things easier for the reader? These are intelligent men, and the technology for

44. Rouse and Rouse, *Authentic Witnesses*, 191–219.

45. Ibid., 7.

46. Ibid., 218.

47. Pliny, *Naturalis Historia* pref. 33.

indexing or page references was available (and familiar to them). I think it is because they perceived the role, function and responsibilities of the reader different from what we do. To them, reading entailed a good bit of memorizing.

Memorizing as Part of Ancient Reading

Quintilian's recommendation to murmur your text as you read forces one to focus directly on what one is reading, reducing the ability to notice distractions.[48] Baddeley has noted the importance of the "phonological loop" for short-term memory.[49] The phonological loop has two parts: the memory store that holds "speech-based information and articulatory control process based on inner speech." Generally, memory of speech fades rapidly (after about two seconds), but vocal rehearsal refreshes the memory store. Information from the articulatory control process returns it to the short-term memory store. Whether murmuring or reading aloud clearly not only aids the process of construing the *scriptio continua*, but also provides its own feedback and reinforcement.

It is also noteworthy that although Quintilian claims the superiority of the eye over the ear when it comes to memory, modern testing has conclusively proven the opposite. If only one sense, hearing or seeing is involved, one will remember better if the thing to be remembered is spoken than if one reads it.[50] Add to this the simple fact that punctuation was the responsibility of the *reader*. The use of *scriptio continua* forced the reader to punctuate the text but also aided the reader in memorizing, in making the text truly one's own.

Reading as an Interactive Activity

One evening at the end of the first century, Pliny the Younger left the house of a friend in Rome in a state of indignation. As soon as he reached his home, he wrote about that night's events to the lawyer Claudius Restitutus:

> and I feel I have to write to you at once, as there is no chance of telling the whole story in person. The work that was read was highly polished in every way, but two or three witty people, or so

48. See Quintilian, *Orat.* 11.2.33.
49. Baddeley, *Human Memory*, 72, cf. 71–95.
50. Ibid., 31–33.

they seemed to themselves, and a few others listened to it like deaf-mutes. They never opened their lips or moved a hand, or even rose to their feet to change from their seated postures. What's the point of all this sober demeanor and learning, or rather of this laziness and conceit, this lack of tact and good sense, which makes one spend an entire day giving offence and turning into an enemy the man one came to hear as one's dearest friend?[51]

A curious incident—and a remarkable example of the distance between modern and ancient reading of texts. "Publishing" was done by means of public readings which clearly were social ceremonies. As with any other ceremony, there was an established etiquette for both the listeners and the authors. This is nicely illustrated in a letter written by Pliny to Suetonius, asking advice about his poor reading skills:

> I am told that I read badly—I mean when I read verse, for I can manage speeches, though this seems to make my verse reading all the worse! So, as I am planning to give an informal reading to my personal friends, I am thinking of making use of one of my freedmen. This is certainly treating them informally, as the man I have chosen is not really a good reader, but I think he will do better than I can as long as he is not nervous . . . Now, I don't know what I am to do myself while he is reading, whether I am to sit still and silent like a mere spectator, or do as some people and accompany his words with lips, eye, and gesture.[52]

The listeners were expected to interact with the "performance," even provide critical response. These brief references have to suffice here, but the principle is evident: by and large reading in antiquity was a complex communal event. It is noteworthy that when Pliny Junior describes his uncle's reading habits there are *always* (at least) two people involved. Either Pliny (Senior) dictates the passages he wishes to excerpt to his secretary or the secretary reads to him and Pliny takes down the passage.[53] Reading and note-taking was a joint activity.[54]

---

51. Pliny, *Ep.* 6.17.
52. Ibid., 9.34.
53. Ibid., 3.5.10–15.
54. Bonner, *Education in Ancient Rome,* 127; Kenney, "Books and Readers," 16.

Composition and Memorized Reading

To understand reading, I have emphasized that we must understand something of the practices of writing: "There is a relationship between the physical form of an artifact and the function it is meant to serve."[55] In this section I want to explore another aspect of that relationship: what *composition* reveals about reading conventions. In the context of an orally oriented communication technology, composition and performance of writings are aspects of the same process, and the one cannot be understood without reference to the other. Essentially, I propose to apply an insight gained from the study by Mary Carruthers, *The Book of Memory*, to Greco-Roman reading culture.

The study by Carruthers is an impressive, wide-ranging account of the workings and functions of memory in medieval society. She points out that *memory* was the psychological faculty valued above all others from antiquity through to the Renaissance. "It is my contention that medieval culture was fundamentally memorial, to the same profound degree that modern culture in the West is documentary. This distinction . . . involves technologies— mnemotechnique and printing—but is not confined to them."[56]

She discusses medieval memory systems as a kind of artificial intelligence; the medieval assumption being that human learning is above all based in memorative processes. She shows how the written page was understood to be a memory device, how mnemonic techniques affected literary composition, and how reading itself was regarded as an activity of the memory. "*Memoria* refers not to how something is communicated, but to what happens once one has received it, to the interactive process of familiarizing—or textualizing—which occurs between oneself and others' words in memory."[57]

Such a comprehensive, interdisciplinary study of memory in the Roman world is unfortunately not yet available. It would be a very difficult undertaking in any case, if not impossible, for want of proper and representative evidence. Yet it should be clear that antiquity parallels medieval reading practices in many ways. Enough has already been referred to, to allow the claim that similar memory related strategies played a role in communication during Roman times. The incidental information that can be gleaned from ancient authors with regard to actual reading and composing activities and skills clearly reveals a world close to the one drawn by Carruthers.

55. Rouse and Rouse, *Authentic Witnesses*, 4.
56. Carruthers, *Book of Memory*, 8.
57. Ibid., 13.

It is well known that the Greek poets did not write anything down until the very last phase of composition. Without exception teachers of the Roman world emphasize *cogitatio*: mental preparation *before* writing. Premeditation was the key to writing.

Extensive memorization was the dominant characteristic of Greco-Roman education. It is in this context that Quintilian calls memory the treasure-chest of eloquence (*thesaurus eloquentiae*).[58] The equation of treasure directly to memory and only indirectly to writing relies on the fact that it is memory and not a superior filing technique that allows the Greco-Roman writer to retrieve the appropriate saying or narrative.

Structure in most ancient writings is clearly mnemotechnically oriented, based on a logic of recollection, which is associative and determined by individual habit. Ancient *tituli* and punctuation were meant to aid mnemonic division, deliberately inviting memorial *compositio*. Reading the written product assumes a re-collective process by means of which a particular reader engages a particular text on a particular occasion.

Above I referred to Pliny's letter to Fuscus Salinator. Pliny mentions how pleasing he finds it, early in the mornings, to lie in darkness, with his eyes not determining "the direction of my thinking" and to visualize his writing. "If I have anything on hand I work it out in my head, choosing and correcting the wording, and the amount I achieve depends on the ease or difficulty with which my thoughts can be marshaled and kept in my head. Then I call my secretary, the shutters are opened, and I dictate what I have put in to shape; he goes out, is recalled and again dismissed."[59] No scribbled outlines, frameworks, to-do lists. No consulting of summaries, index cards or keywords. Composition was a memory based activity. Plotinus, according to Porphyry, "worked out his train of thought from beginning to end in his own mind, and then, when he wrote it down, since he had set it all in order in his mind, he wrote as continuously as if he was copying from a book."[60]

A remarkable contemporary illustration of this way of "working" with sources and other material to compose in memory *before committing to writing* is the experiences of John Hull (New Testament and Religious Education scholar). As author and lecturer Hull had to adjust to writing lectures in his head when he went blind during his forties.

---

58. Quintilian, *Inst.* 9.2.1.

59. Pliny, *Ep.* 9.36.

60. Porphyry, *Vita Plotini* 8.

> I now seem to have developed a way of scanning ahead in my mind, to work out what I am going to say. Everybody does this in ordinary speech; otherwise we couldn't complete a sentence. Somehow or other, and without effort, I have developed a longer perspective, and now when I am speaking I can see paragraphs coming up from the recesses of my mind. It is a bit like reading them off a scanner. While I am speaking, another part of my mind is sorting out into paragraphs what I am going to be saying in the next few minutes, and a yet more remote part is selecting alternative lines of argument from a sort of bank of material. This seems to give my lecturing style a greater sense of order than I had before, and people seem to be able to follow me more easily.[61]

Keep in mind that Hull's lecture material is more complicated than typically dictated texts today (such as business letters). Compare this with Cicero's counsel: "I would not have the structure obtrude itself in such trivialities; but a practiced pen will nevertheless easily find the method of composition. For as the eye looks ahead in reading, so in speaking the mind will foresee what is to follow."[62]

Hull also describes how he organizes his material:

> A sighted author tends to paragraph his or her work retrospectively. You see the stuff unrolling on the typewriter or screen, and you think that it is about time you started a new paragraph. A person listening to books on cassettes, where the actual paragraphs in the printed page are not normally indicated, does his own paragraphing, and when composing tends to project this into the future of the composition. I think that this also helps me to organize my material in advance when I am speaking in public. A sighted lecturer reading from a typescript concentrates mainly upon what he has said, that is, the paragraphs slip away behind him as he 'swims' forward through his speech. A blind speaker has to concentrate entirely upon what he is about to say, or what he will be saying fifteen minutes from now, because otherwise he will lose direction.[63]

The way Hull uses his memory to understand something he hears from a tape is directly comparable to the way someone in antiquity would have heard a book being read. He says, "I have not put any particular effort into learning how to [remember structure in a written work read to me]. You

---

61. Hull, *Touching the Rock*, 123–24.

62. Cicero, *De oratore* 44.150.

63. Hull, *Touching the Rock*, 124

tend to make unconscious mental notes of the structure so that you can go back again if necessary."[64] The memorizing process works in both directions: it helps one compose in the mind and it helps one follow an oral "reading."

Rethinking Some "Common Wisdom"

A very necessary step for a responsible interpretation of ancient communication is to become aware of tacit assumptions. We must replace our misleading, modern view of ancient reading activities with a more nuanced view that takes into account their historical, religious, intellectual and psychological situation.

In his discussion of the religious views of the people in the Roman world, MacMullen notes how these "strike a modern reader as alien or outlandish."[65] This is partly the effect of how we simply overestimate and overrate textual evidence, because "[p]oints of contact and media of communication that we take for granted in our world simply did not exist in antiquity." However, those people were neither stupid nor "undeveloped." They did not just *lack* something, they made different use of things. The challenge is not to describe them by means of subtracting what we have, but to imaginatively *reconstruct* a fuller, more complex system of ancient communication.

Particularly useful is the critical concept employed by anthropologists: visualism. "The term is to connote a cultural, ideological bias towards vision as the 'noblest sense' and towards geometry qua graphic-spatial conceptualization as the most 'exact' way of communicating knowledge."[66] Not only are we "deaf" to the oral–aural worlds of other, less technologized communication systems, we reduce the symbolic forms of ancient people to "stuff," to disembodied things.[67]

Meaning and communication is about much more than delineating sources or labeling textual strategies. As an "object" of knowledge, the

---

64. Ibid., 124.

65. MacMullen, *Christianizing the Roman Empire*, 10–11, 21.

66. Fabian, *Time and the Other*, 106.

67. It is quite a challenge to think about reading and writing "without tacitly erecting our own standards of expectation concerning the correspondence between the written and the spoken word into cultural panchronic universals," see Harris, *Origin of Writing*, 154.

communicative event (experience) of an ancient author and his audiences are processed by us with visual-spatial tools and methods.[68]

Modern literary theories, when applied directly to ancient literature, have tended to obscure the very *foreignness* of that literature, its ancient *Romanness*, and to present those authors as crypto-moderns. Giving proper due to the fundamental role of memorizing and memory—with all the various aspects which that cultural modality involves—redresses imbalances in this regard.

The Synoptic Problem and Q

An immediate and very obvious implication of the argument presented here would be to the synoptic problem and the Q hypothesis.

Considered within the context of ancient reading practices, the *linear, literary* connections seen as a solution to the so-called synoptic problem become highly problematic. With the rejection of the "original form" concept,[69] most of the current reconstruction of pre-gospel traditions becomes dubious. If the gospel authors *listened* to Q and the other sayings traditions, one cannot possibly apply the concept of an original version in reconstructing them—to cite Kelber's own criticism.[70]

Taking into account the role memorizing played in reading and composition, we can place our understanding of the synoptic relationships on a more sound footing, at last achieving something of a historical understanding of the synoptic Gospels as first-century writings.

---

68. This is an adaptation of a description of Bauman. Bauman argues that study of oral literature should be done in an integrative spirit, with a performance-centered conception of these traditions as scholars operate within a frame of reference dominated by the canons of elite, modern literary perceptions. See Bauman, *Story, Performance, and Event*, 1–10, particularly 2.

69. Kelber, "Mark and Oral Tradition," 33.

70. With regard to the question of Q, note that Kelber's criticism of traditional *Traditionsgeschichte* undermines the methodological basis on which the identification of Q rests. In other words, if one accepts Kelber's criticism of "the dominant paradigm of linearity," one must realize that that is the exact paradigm underlying most of the research done on the synoptic traditions and specifically on Q. Further, if it is true that scholars have not really grasped what the oral foundations of the synoptic traditions entail, their reconstruction of it must be defective. Kelber, who wrote *Oral and the Written Gospel*, has developed his initial proposals considerably, see Kelber, "Sayings Collection"; Kelber, "Jesus and Tradition"; and Kelber, "The Two-Source Hypothesis." I still think that he tries to incorporate too much of traditional thinking about the history of the synoptic tradition into his approach (e.g., the Q hypothesis).

Imagine Luke (or Matthew) making a synopsis to guide access to his text, after completing the dictation (*à la* Pliny the Elder). Imagine Mark (or Luke) reading/preparing to read/present the Jesus story. Imagine Matthew (or Mark) "researching" scrolls to compose, in memory, his own writing.

What Horsley says about Q, contrasting his approach to conventional source criticism, I would like to extend to the gospels:

> In contrast with focusing on and attempting to establish (1) the transmission (2) of an individual saying (3) to another individual (4) who cognitively grasped the meaning of its words, this evolving approach to an oral-derived text focuses on and attempts to appreciate (1) the public performance (2) of a whole discourse or set of discourses focused on issues of common concern (3) to a community gathered for common purposes (4) who in the performance experience certain events verbally enacted and/or are affected by the performance. The transmission, individual sayings, individuals, and cognitive meaning would all have been included in the broader process of public performance of discourses addressed to communities who experienced events in verbal enactments, as can be seen in some brief elaboration.[71]

In a way this is to argue for the relative independence of the Gospels, against theories of literary dependence, by invoking a history as well as a theory of reader activity embedded in an ethnography of communication. What often happens in New Testament scholarship is that "oral tradition" gets smuggled into the discussion without a formal examination of that category, merely in order to cover up difficulties with a purely documentary solution. This paper attempts to counter that tendency.

Concluding Remarks

Historians of dress, costume, and ornamentation often criticize contemporary displays of period costume, including when actors wear period costumes, for emphasis on appearance. A realistic display demands that not only the outer, but also the inner garments must be accurate or the actors will not move in the right way. A similar situation faces anyone trying to interpret Greco-Roman antiquity. We have a pretty good idea of the surface—how things looked—but when we try to animate the scene, all the people walk with a modern stride. I have emphasized that well-known aspects of ancient literacy require more than description; they must also be interpreted. That is,

71. Horsley, *Whoever Hears*, 7–8.

the particular forms of display and retrieval of textual information in hand-written manuscripts are data for an ethnography of ancient communication.

Literacy is not merely the ability to write or to read. *How* one reads and writes matters. As students of the first-century Mediterranean world and early Christianity, our task with regard to understanding their literacy, their reading and writing, has barely been begun.

To conclude then, a paragraph from Mary Carruthers, perfectly apposite to my investigation:

> As I sought to understand the texts I was studying, they became stranger to me than I had thought them to be, yet their strangeness, I discovered, lay in my expectations. I had continually to adjust my preconceptions, not only about . . . [various periods], but about unexamined basics, such as the nature of "memory," "mind," "imitation," and "book." Many things I had believed could not be done, such as composing difficult works at length from memory, had to be entertained as possibilities—even as expected and much admired behavior.[72]

---

72. Carruthers, *Book of Memory*, 260.

6

Authorship in Historical Perspective

Authorship?

Author and *authorship* are very common concepts in New Testament scholarship. Remarkably, little attention is given to question as to what we mean by these terms.

> Luke is a *student* of the LXX. It is clear today that *the author* of the third Gospel *consciously intended* to cover his narrative in a 'sacred" mantle. Characteristic of Lk, in this sense, is the frequent use of the introductory formula καὶ ἐγένετο . . . which can create a certain sensation of *monotony*. Mk, . . . was *re-ordered* by Lk to *introduce* his own material into it, but *reinforcing* it to give the impression of a *coherent whole*. His *style is consciously simple*, taking account of the *level of his readers* and the tone of his sources. Luke exhibits a certain *awareness of style*.[1]

The italics are used to draw attention to how Piñero and Peláez (a randomly selected example) give contents to their use of the word "author" in the second sentence of the quotation: notice the number of concepts that are clearly open for anachronistic and modernizing construction. The typical way that "author" is used by NT scholars is probably along the lines of a thoughtful student working at a desk in a well-stocked study with texts and notes about discourses with other intellectuals lying about.

What we find is an underlying understanding of the "author" as a superior and solitary creative individual (if not genius), often implicitly understood as heroically striving for the "well-being" of *his* community; the

---

1. Piñero and Peláez, *Study of the New Testament*, 493, my italics.

sovereign author whose intention contains *the* meaning of the work and whose *biography* authorizes, directs and determines its writing.[2]

"Author" is a word easily used, but mostly without historical contextualization. In this chapter I offer a brief introduction to the problem, in order to contribute to developing a more adequate model of authorship.

Authorship is first and foremost a problem of culture, and it should be studied as a sociological problem in order to understand it historically. It is necessary to contextualize authorship because writing and reading are culturally embedded phenomena, similar to other social conventions. Furthermore, the historical constraints of ancient text production must be taken into account when we discuss the authors of Greco-Roman texts.

Authorship Has a History

One of the legacies of living with the conceptual construction called "Enlightenment" is the systematization of the history of ideas in terms of individual authors' biographies. Modern historiography organized itself, since its inception in the late nineteenth century, as a massive collective biography of writers. This "man and his work" biographical approach informs the problems, the understanding of sources, the methods and the outcomes of scholarship dealing with literary texts—including biblical scholarship.

However, we need to understand that "authorship" has a history. Consider the social, political and cultural contexts of authors: our modern, contemporary understanding of the concept is determined by the transformation and decline of European courts and aristocratic patronage, presupposes a large-scale commerce in print and other symbolic goods, and the development of specific, novel forms of associations and modern social institutions. Whereas authorship was, in earlier times, intimately part of patronage it has become, for us, something determined by printing, literary property, censorship, and income.

2. This concept of authorship, despite our tenacious belief in it, is not even realistic with regard to *modern* authors (cf. Borsche, "Wer Spricht?"). See, especially, analyses of the problems of defining and practicing copyright: Woodmansee, "Genius"; Jaszi, "Toward a Theory"; Price and Pollack, "Author in Copyright"; Rose, *Authors and Owners*, 1–8. In literary theory, Roland Barthes' "The Death of the Author," published in 1968 was a major influence: "The traditional, humanist concept of a single, human source of all meaning was discarded amid the clamour of disturbances and manifestations against authority all over Europe . . . With the jettisoning of the Author as the source and gauarantor of all meaning, the path was clear for the proliferation of questions about the process of reading. A revolution in thought had begun" (Biriotti, "Introduction," 1).

An array of sound scholarship undermines any continuity with regard to models of literacy and authorship between antiquity, the Middle Ages, and modern times by exposing the remarkable and important developments in practices of writing and practices of reading.[3]

A useful starting point for a theoretical reflection on these issues is a short essay by Michel Foucault.[4] Foucault asks the question, "What is an author?" against the background of how Western culture since the Enlightenment uses the concept *genius* to think about literary and intellectual creation. This emphasis on the singularity of particular individuals's creative knowledge should in itself alert us to the problems of anachronistic and ethnocentric thinking when conceptualizing authorship.

Foucault's interest in this particular essay is to set up "an introduction to the historical analysis of discourse."[5] He considers the "author as brilliant innovator" a Romanticist invention that had been projected onto history. To do a proper investigation he proposes a distinction between the "socio-historical analysis of the author's persona" ("biography") and the construction of an "author-function" as an attribute of a text. This author-function represents the social value a text is laden with (or given to) when it is designated as a work of literary creation: "the author is not an indefinite source of significations which fill a work; the author does not precede the works; he is a certain functional principle by which, in our culture, one limits, excludes, and chooses; in short, by which one impedes the free circulation, the free manipulation, the free composition, and recomposition of fiction."[6]

Thus, for Foucault, the Enlightenment produces a critical turning point in the history of authorship. Writing in this era took on a particular author-function; literature ceased to be understood as simply generally available knowledge and was seen more and more as a unique expression of a single consciousness in each instance.

---

3. For example, Jerome's and Augustine's fundamental restructuring of the theory of translation, see Copeland, *Rhetoric, Hermeneutics*, as well as Augustine's working out of a Christian theory of reading, Stock, *Augustine the Reader*. One can also consider the profound impact caused by changes in the function of punctuation which occurred in the fifth and sixth centuries (on which see Parkes, *Pause and Effect*) and the crucial intellectual changes associated with the development of word separation, Saenger, *Space between Words*. Elizabeth Eisenstein has written an assessment of the effects of printing on written records (hence on concepts of authorship) and on the shift from one kind of literate culture to another. See Eisenstein, *Printing Press*.

4. Foucault, "What Is an Author?"

5. Ibid., 117.

6. Ibid., 118–19.

Foucault also draws attention to another aspect of the systematic attribution of an author-function to texts in the eighteenth century: "penal appropriation."[7] He suggests the central aspect of Enlightenment authorship to have been censorship: the need for newly emergent states to control transgressive writings by punishing the authors of those writings. "Once a system of ownership for texts came into being, once strict rules concerning author's rights, author-publisher relations, rights of reproduction, and related matters were enacted . . . the possibility of transgression attached to the act of writing took on, more and more, the form of an imperative peculiar to literature."[8]

The process of autonomization for writers from the need for aristocratic protectors, and the period of professionalization by means of modern literary property regimes became a system in which writers found themselves isolated before and vulnerable to the monopoly on violence exercised by the modern state, according to Foucault.

The widespread assumption of what authorship constitutes, in terms of property and legislation, namely that it is connected to "genius", turns out to be a historically determined concept: a result of the limited opportunities for patronage for German-language authors in the eighteenth century who had to promote their texts on the print market.[9]

Chartier—in critical dialogue with Foucault—proposes that the major development in the history of authorship during the Enlightenment was that the writer's name, image, and often personality became publicly recognizable.[10] He draws attention to "the author" appearing for the first time in the late seventeenth century on title pages, frontispieces, and introductory biographies in, especially, editions of collected works. The appearance of these authorial representations suggests that the Enlightenment's new idea of an author was primarily to define a coherent body of work. This process began in the seventeenth century with playwrights, who more than any other type of writer mediated between court, market, and academic institutions. By the end of the eighteenth century the author's *name* became most important for the new genre of novels, as it specified a work's creativity and originality.

Be that as it may, the historical *principle* underlying Foucault's short essay is of major importance, namely that authorship is a *construction*, a historical, cultural, and contextual concept. That is, before a proper discussion

7. Ibid., 108.

8. Ibid.

9. Woodmansee, *Author.*

10. Chartier, "Figures of the Author."

of the authorship of a specific text can commence, we need a "lexicon of authorship." Much of this is still wanting with regard to the texts of early Christianity.

Towards a Historical Perspective

To discuss "authorship" in antiquity is complex and difficult, for a number of reasons. For instance, the term "author*ship*" did not exist in Greek or Latin. Of those who might today be considered "authors," few if any would have been described by their contemporaries with that rubric. Those who "wrote" also engaged in various other social and professional practices that were far more important as sources of status, power, and social identity.

The Latin term *auctoritas* (which would eventually evolve into "auteur") was used in medieval times to refer to the (few) ancient philosophers and their interpreters who could be cited in scholastic argumentation, but in "the Renaissance humanist vocabulary, auteur began to refer to writers in a different sense, that of creator, and late seventeenth-century dictionaries attributed a second etymology to auteur, of common derivation with artisan, meaning creator."[11]

Prior to the Enlightenment, the terminology for what we would think of as authors tended to distinguish according to genres, loosely related to different categories of knowledge or communication, such as poet, rhetorician, storyteller, reporter, and such. An entirely different set of terms described those who plied the craft of script and recordkeeping, including "writer," "clerk," "notary," and "calligrapher." It is only by the late seventeenth century that these terms, and the social institutions they describe, became increasingly distant from the world of literary works, and terms such as "writer" and "poet" began to describe creators of aesthetically valuable writing.[12]

Literary property emerged, as a concept and as a legal practice, during the Enlightenment.[13] Prior to the eighteenth century, a writer was typically

---

11. Brown, "Authorship."

12. Chartier, "Figures of the Author"; Hamesse, "Scholastic Model of Reading," 106–8. During the Enlightenment, the tendency was to consider an author to be one whose writing was presented before an audience, either orally or in print. It is against the background of the world of *gentlemen*—the world of dignified, autonomous displays of erudition, taste and intelligence—that we should picture the increasing use of "author." That is, claiming to be an author was to change register, to go out on a stage where the public (rather than other "gentlemen") is the judge of success or failure. See Brown, "Authorship."

13. *That the concept of literary property emerged during the Enlightenment has

identified with a patron or with the honorific office the writer enjoyed at the discretion of a patron. Since the eighteenth century writers began to establish identities independent from a particular patron (no small reason being the decreasing availability and sufficiency of such patronage). This autonomy claimed by writers could only be established through literary property. Prior to the Enlightenment, "authorial assertions of preeminent domain were all but unthinkable."[14]

Copyright, as Rose points out, "is not a transcendent moral idea, but a specifically modern formation produced by printing technology, marketplace economics, and the classical liberal culture of possessive individualism."[15] Certain shifts in worldview, and intellectual developments influenced by thinkers such as Locke, Smith, and Kant generated new, culturally specific ideas of property, labour, individuality, and the market. These interacted to justify writers demanding remuneration from and for their writings. Such is the setting for the development of the Continental and Anglo-American notions of copyright, that "charming notion that authors create something from nothing, that works owe their origin to the authors who produce them."[16]

Aspects of the Greco-Roman Setting for Authorship

In order to contextualize authorship in the first century we need historical information to "peer over the shoulders of ancient authors."[17] This is no mean task; in the following I *briefly* attend to *selected* aspects, as a preliminary exploration to contribute to a more comprehensive approach to our texts. These are: the practices of ancient authors, the publication and circulation of books in antiquity, and suggestions for investigating an "author-function" of a writing.

---

achieved widespread assent; exactly why and how to explain this appearance has generated considerable debate. See, among many possible references, Darnton, "Facts of Literary Life"; Hesse, "Enlightenment Epistemologies"; Chartier, "Man of Letters"; Rose, *Authors and Owners*; Woodmansee, *Author*; Brown, "After the Fall."

14. Loewenstein, "Script in the Marketplace," 102.

15. Rose, *Authors and Owners*, 142.

16. Litman, "Public Domain," 965.

17. Dorandi, "Den Autoren."

The Writing Phases and Methods of Ancient Authors

There are only a few reports about the work methods of ancient writers. They are mostly indirect and surprisingly difficult to interpret. The following is a cursory survey of some of the evidence.

A convenient starting point is Pliny the Younger's description of the work methods of his uncle, Pliny the Elder, in his letter to Baebius Macer, who asked for a complete list of Pliny Senior's books (*Ep.* 3.5). After listing his uncle's books, Pliny Junior explains "how such a busy man was able to complete so many volumes." Pliny describes an unusual "author," one who would even sometimes work halfway through the night—clearly a very exceptional practice which (in part) explains Pliny Senior's productivity. How much we can extrapolate from Pliny's description of his uncle's practices to other writers is therefore a question.

Research began by reading, but reading was done by a reader (*lector*). In summer Pliny Senior liked to lie in the sun while books were read to him and notes and extracts were made. Making use of every possible opportunity, Pliny had someone read to him during dinners and even at bath time ("while he was being rubbed down and dried"). If he was not being read to, he dictated (*audiebat aliquid aut dictabat*; *Ep.* 3.5.14). Possibly some notes were made by Pliny himself, but we know that he liked to keep at least one secretary at his side with book and notebook (*ad latus notarius cum libro et pugillaribus*; 3.5.15).

Lucian of Samosata, in his critique of the sudden rush of petty historians chronicling the Parthian War of 162–165 CE ("not only is everyone writing history, they are all Thucydideses, Herodotuses and Xenophons to us"—*Quomodo historia conscribenda sit* 2),[18] "offer a little advice" and warning: the writing of history requires effort and a great deal of thought (*Hist. conscr.* 5). Towards the end of his tractate, he offers us some ideas of how history writing should proceed:

> As to the contents (πράγματα αὐτά), he should not collect (συνακτέον) them at random, but only after much laborious and painstaking investigation (ἀνακρίναντα) . . . When he has assembled (ἀθροίσῃ) all or most of the facts let him first make them into a set of notes (ὑπόμνημα), a body of material as yet without charm and unorganised. Then, after arranging them into order (ἐπιθεὶς

---

18. οὐδεὶς ὅστις οὐχ ἱστορίαν συγγράφει· μᾶλλον δὲ Θουκυδίδαι καὶ Ἡρόδοτοι καὶ Ξενοφῶντες ἡμῖν ἄπαντες, *Hist. conscr.* 2.

τὴν τάξιν), let him give it beauty and enhance it with style (λέξις), structure (σχηματιζέτω), and rhythm. (*Hist. Conscr.* 47–48)

Despite the apparent familiarity of these activities we should be aware that we do not really know exactly what was meant by several words such as *adnoto* and *excerpta* (Pliny) or ὑπόμνημα. Or how should we picture these authors *collecting* material and managing their notes?[19]

However, on the basis of these (and some other references, such as Marcellinus, *Vita Thucydidis* 47e, and Plutarch's "I read parts of my notebooks"),[20] it is possible to gain some impressions of how Pliny the Elder (probably) and other ancient writers (possibly) carried out their work. Writing a book in antiquity began with a *lector reading a source book(s)*,[21] *of which notes were made, adnotationes*—possibly by means of marking the scroll itself, then excerpts were collected and dictated to a *notarius* (stenographer), who transferred them to *pugillares*, notebooks consisting of plates made from wood (and wax?) or scrolls of papyrus. From these a text was dictated for writing onto papyrus scrolls (later into a codex made from papyrus or parchment). Alternatively, a further intermediate step took place: an extended collection of notes was made (onto a scroll) from which a draft text was dictated.

Thus, a writer had his sources read to him, marking (*adnotare*) the places that seemed important for the preparation of his work. Collaborating with (an) assistant(s) he created excerpts and dictated them to a stenographer, who transferred them onto *pugillares*, or onto a scroll. The result was the first, incomplete version of the work.[22]

19. A fairly popular depiction, probably initiated by Prentice, "How Thucydides Wrote His History," 125, imagines authors making notes on single sheets or cards, which were "kept together in a bundle or in a box." This, to my mind, is a clear example of anachronistic projection. Dorandi points to the lack of evidence for such a practice; in fact, "man schrieb auf eine ganze Rolle, nicht etwa auf Einzelblätter," Dorandi, "Den Autoren," 12. Dorandi also refers to the informative study by Turner, "Sniffing Glue."

20. More precisely, "I read aloud (ἀνελεξάμην) from my note-books (ἐκ τῶν ὑπομνημάτων) the observations I have made for my own use" (Plutarch *De tranquillitate animi* 464e–465a).

21. In analogy to the ἀναγνώστης (slave trained to read, Nepos, *Atticus* 14.1) the *lector*—typically a slave—assumes the role that the author may claim for himself as *recitator* of his own works, or, if lacking confidence in his own elocution, which he may delegate (Pliny, *Ep.* 9.34; Suetonius, *Divus Claudius* 41.2: *recitavit per lectorem*).

22. An interesting possible confirmation of this process can be found in Herculaneum Papyrus 1021. This scroll contains a first version or scheme of the *Academicorum historia* by Philodemus of Gadara (philosopher of the Epicurean School, ± 110–40 BCE), i.e., the first, incomplete version of the work as described above (cf. Dorandi, "Den Autoren," 16–17.). Of course, P.Herc. 1021 can also be just a collection of pure excerpts.

We do not know in how many steps an author's work progressed or to what extent further readings and additional research and/or consultations resulted in actual reworkings of the text. We know that more material was noted in the margins of the previously collected parts or it could be added to the verso of the scroll. Various supplementary notes, and linguistic or stylistic improvements found their place either on the margins and on the empty places of the recto or on the verso, but these insertions and additions were not made by the author himself but instead were written down by a scribe or the professional διορθωτής (corrector).

It stands to reason that before the text was copied or dictated for the creation of a good copy in preparation for publication, the collected material could be reworked and rearranged—though how many times and how comprehensively obviously varied from author to author. What is clear is the labour intensiveness (the many hands involved) of "authoring," and given that, typically, one dealt frugally[23] with writing materials, extensive and repeated reworking of texts simply was not feasible. Final versions were distinguished from provisional, intermediate versions, though the difference often concerned form more than content. It is probable that the second phase could be avoided, or became an alternative (and not just an edited version) to the first. An author could organize the initial versions of his work either by compiling an unstructured conception or a detailed set of notes (ὑπόμνημα), either one of which was transferred into the final version (σύγγραμμα or σύνταγμα).[24]

Other words used for the preparatory stages of writing are succinct explanation (ἐξήγησις), preparatory draft (παρασκευή), or sketch, (ὑποτύπωσις).[25] Roughly, then, we can distinguish two phases of authoring an ancient work. The first phase was draft versions based on prior collections of excerpts that had possibly been written on small plates or *pugillares*. Such provisionary drafts could circulate for review or comments and could even

---

Several papyrus texts containing Philodemus' works were discovered at several locations within a villa in Herculaneum.

23. 'Sparsam' in the words of Blank *Das Buch*, 82. At issue is not so much the cost of papyrus, discussed in detail by Lewis in *Papyrus in Classical Antiquity*, 129–34, but availability. Writing materials simply was not in over-abundant supply to the extent we are familiar with.

24. Again, if we follow Dorandi, "Den Autoren," 26–29, something of this process can be substantiated from an analysis of the colophons of several papyri from Herculaneum (P.Hercul. 1427, 1506, and 1674), which contain books of rhetoric by Philodemus. Dorandi distinguishes between ὑπόμνημα and ὑπομνηματικόν, with the latter indicating a more preparatory and less definitive stage of the redaction of the text than the former.

25. Van den Hoek, "Techniques of Quotation," 238 n.15.

reappear under another name.[26] From these the final version or fair copy of the text (which was called either ὑπόμνημα *or* σύνταγμα) was prepared, which usually preceded the actual publication (ἔκδοσις).

Dictation played a dominant role during not just the compilation of the work but also when composing subsequent versions. Indeed, dictation determined all aspects of authoring, including the production of copies for distribution.[27] Dorandi refers to some indications that poets evidently preferred writing themselves, while the prose writers commonly used a system of dictation, perhaps even exclusively.[28] Generalizations are problematic as the evidence involves a wide arena and is tied to many different conditions, methods and personal or subjective circumstances.

Dictation, of course, facilitates an experience of writing as "a public performance, no matter how intimate the recording session and even physical absence of the audience."[29]

In the late Republican period and in the early Imperial period a few voices turned against the rampant use of dictation that occurred not only in scholarly works of prose but also in poetry (e.g., Quintilian, *Inst.* 1.1.20): dictation, it was felt, when composing, should be regarded with suspicion, as it requires the author's long and careful examination more than writing by one's own hand. Also, young and inexperienced authors may be tempted by dictation to publish careless and largely improvised works. Despite these protestations, dictation determined writing practices until medieval times.[30]

Depending on his skills and the needs of the author, the secretary recorded the dictation syllable-for-syllable or phrase-by-phrase (i.e. at the speed of writing) or by means of shorthand, at the speed of normal speech.[31] Often the secretary was entrusted with the responsibility of writing the text from incomplete notes. Authors left considerable scope to their secretaries; either on purpose, or due to rapid dictation, or because often only an outline or draft was provided. "The line between editing and co-authorship is impossible to draw. If one writer excerpts or copies portions of another's work,

---

26. Blank, *Das Buch*, 118.

27. Skeat, "Use of Dictation."

28. Dorandi, "Zwischen Autographie und Diktat."

29. Bauman, *Story*, 106.

30. Harris, *Ancient Literacy*, 36, 224 n. 247; Small, *Wax Tablets*, 171–74, 185.

31. Dictation *syllabitim* is self-evident. See, e.g. Seneca, *Ep.* 40.10. Dictation *viva voce* supposes shorthand systems and the use of a ταχυγράφος (cf. LSJ); see Seneca, *Ep.* 40.25; Suetonius, *Divus Titus* 3.2. It was possible for a secretary to record a speech in the Roman senate (Seneca, *Apocolocyntosis* 9.2). Cf. Sherwin-White, *Letters of Pliny*, 225.

but adds comments, supplements, appendices or insertions—or subtracts or epitomizes—then whether we regard the 'new' work thus produced as distinctively a different document in its own right, or as a 'new edition' or adaptation of the old, becomes a matter of degree only."[32]

Publication

The relationship between author, written language, and "reader/reading public" is not at all self-evident, especially where the concept of personal authorship had little association with property and individual, introspective identity. In antiquity books were often published without the name of the author or under another person's name. Works were collective, traditional, cultural enterprises.

Indeed, the very term "publication" is not quite appropriate to translate ἔκδοσις, which is (mostly) used to indicate the making public of a work by means of an oral presentation of the text.[33] It is self-evident that such an act included a wide range of activities.

Often, "publication" would be initiated by a dedication. The dedication of a literary work is the naming of a person with the intent of expressing an honour or gratitude to this person by association with the writing. Modern practice places the dedication as part of the so-called paratext (that is, on the title page, or on book covers, or in prefaces), but Greek and Latin dedications preserved from antiquity are part of the actual work.[34] The basic form of the dedication is an address at the opening of the text, as we find in Cicero when speaking of his literary plans in his letters to Atticus, or at some convenient point in the main part of the text.[35]

The use of dedications in Hellenistic and Roman literature is related to the patron-client system so characteristic of Greco-Roman times. The recipients of a dedication may be rulers (Ovid, *Fasti* 2.11–18 = to Caesar Augustus),[36] members of the ruling house (Ovid, *Fasti* 1.3–26 = Germanicus, son of Drusus, brother of Tiberius), politically powerful persons, known

32. Hall, "Hirtius and the *Bellum Alexandrinum*," 412–13.

33. Hadas, *Ancilla to Classical Reading*, 60–64; Harris, *Ancient Literacy*, 224–25.

34. Most often seen as parts of poetry volumes; examples: Lucretius, Virgil (*Georgics* 1), Catullus 1 (where the dedicatory poem introduces the body of the poetry book).

35. Janson, *Latin Prose Prefaces*, 105–6, 116–24.

36. Valerius Maximus *Factorum et dictorum memorabilium* praef. is a dedication to Tiberius. Valerius is the earliest extant prose author to invoke the emperor, see Wardle, *Valerius Maximus*, 68.

as patrons of poetry, such as Maecenas, Octavian's right hand man and patron of Virgil (*Georgics* 1.1–5); or Messala, patron of Tibullus (2.1.31–35).[37]
Often they are highly ranked friends (Statius, *Silvae* 1 praef.) It is evident
from statements in Cicero's letters that reciprocal dedications were an important means of group contact in literary circles. Plutarch dedicated several
of his treatises to friends, undoubtedly to maintain his associations. Often
the recipient is a protector or patron of the author.[38] An author also gained
prestige through dedication to high-ranking individuals.

A dedication copy is obviously presented or sent to the receiver, which
is (in a sense) a public ritual. How dedication and publication relate to each
other cannot be stated with certainty. Sometimes publication is made dependent on the recipient's approval. This obviously relates to the fairly common
practice of an author circulating his work among friends and requesting
criticism before publication. These circles of friends were also the primary
audience addressed by an author—only after discussions there would he
present his works to a wider audience in public readings or sometimes even
dramatic performances, thereby publishing them.[39] Authors sometimes
carefully planned the timing of making a work public. "As for the time when
he published (ἐξέδωκεν) his dialogues, this was not left to chance, but he
chose holy-days and festivals of the gods for his works to be offered up and
made known to the public (κηρύττωνται) . . . Thus he published (ἐξέδωκεν)
the *Timaeus* at the Bendidia . . . , the *Parmenides* at the Panathenaea, and
others at other festivals (*Anonyma prolegomena in Platonis philosophiam*
16.35)."[40]

The author could either promote his work himself or entrust it to a
publisher who arranged for copies, assuming the production costs (in some
cases with financial assistance from the author or his patron), and taking
care of the distribution. The most famous publisher in antiquity was probably Atticus, a friend of Cicero's. In his workshops, Atticus employed a
number of highly qualified scribes (*librarii*) and proof-readers (*anagnostae*),
whose service helped him to issue high-quality publications. In some cases,

---

37. About the aristocrat M. Valerius Messalla Corvinus, see Maltby, *Tibullus*, 41–42.

38. Baldwin, "Literature and Society"; Williams, "Phases in Political Patronage."

39. Cicero (*De oratore* 1.94), Arrian (ὑπομνήματα not intended for publication which
others got hold of without his will or knowledge, *Epicteti dissertationes* 1 dedicatio 2–4),
and Tertullian (*Adversus Marcionem* 1) all refer to this distinction between private/lim-
ited circulation and regular publication, and its attendant problems.

40. Westerink, *Anonymous Prolegomena*, 32, 33. The *Prolegomena* was a handbook
introducing Plato in the Alexandrian School. The point is not about Plato's methods, but
that this is how a teacher of Late Antiquity thought an important author operated.

the author himself or a scholar could examine the copies, a practice that often led to changes in content.

The "performative readings" of texts in the Roman era is crucial to understanding literary activity. The *recitatio* was, by and large, the medium through which an author's work came to be experienced by others. Pliny (*Ep.* 1.13) writes that in April one could hardly have a day go by without someone giving a public reading—he also praises "those whose interest in writing and reading aloud is not dampened by the idleness and conceit of their listeners."

The author could do the recitation himself, but often a *lector* was engaged. In a letter written to Suetonius, asking advice about his poor reading skills, Pliny explains:

> I am told that I read badly—I mean when I read verse, for I can manage speeches, though this seems to make my verse reading all the worse! So, as I am planning to give an informal reading to my personal friends, I am thinking of making use of one of my freedmen. This is certainly treating them informally, as the man I have chosen is not really a good reader, but I think he will do better than I can as long as he is not nervous . . . Now, I don't know what I am to do myself while he is reading, whether I am to sit still and silent like a mere spectator, or do as some people and accompany his words with lips, eye, and gesture. (*Ep.* 9.34)

The impact of this practice was extensive on how an author composed, structured and styled his work. Surely this must have been a contributing factor in the so-called increasing rhetoricization of Roman literature during the Empire.

Recitatio also helps to understand the relative lack of punctuation in texts from Greco-Roman antiquity. Prior to the fifth and sixth centuries texts had been written largely free of punctuation or word separation in keeping with the expectations of readers trained in the art of Roman rhetoric. "Writing, for them, was to be in the most neutral form possible, since it was the responsibility of the reader, declaiming aloud, to divine the rhythms of the *cursus* which signalled the formulaic *clausulae* marking the major divisions, or *cola* and *periodi*, of the discourse."[41]

Circulation of Books

After the book was copied the task of distribution was seen to by the publisher who sometimes was also the bookseller. However, given that publication

41. Briggs, "Literacy, Reading," 412–13.

in antiquity consisted of an oral presentation of the particular text, "the primary way of distributing books was not . . . by means of a trade of any kind, but through gifts and loans among friends."[42] The forces of social status that regulate such relationships must have been shaping forces for an author's work as well.[43] Most readers depended largely, if not exclusively, on privately made copies of texts, without the substantial intervention of any commercial system of distribution.[44] Bear in mind, that this was a world where one had no guarantee that a work was even by its putative author. In a world of copying, forgeries, and formula, the notions of originality and intellectual property were unknown.[45]

> At this point an important critical principle needs to be explicitly stated, for it is one that, used as we are to the printed word as a primary vehicle of communication, with its attendant apparatus of publishing houses and copyright law (and, in scrupulous scholarship, careful observance of distinctions between exact quotation, paraphrase and referential citation), we too easily overlook. Where all documentary communication is hand written, as for any ancient writer it was, the distinctions that appear clear to us between author and scribe, copyist and commentator, editor, secretary, "literary executor", and publisher, lose much of their significance.[46]

Book dealers were, in Starr's words, the owners of small shops that dealt in luxury items, apparently only handling current literature and not selling older works. It is important to keep in mind the underlying dynamics of ancient book circulation: literature was a symbol of social status (and conversely, a point of access to the upper class, a way of making contact with the elite), and remained the preserve of the aristocracy except in oratorical events and public performances.[47]

The viva vox as Author-Function

A discussion of possible author-functions of texts from the Roman Period will need to investigate how the emergence of the Principate affected the relationship between literature and politics, specifically the various positions

42. Harris, *Ancient Literacy*, 225.

43. Starr, "Circulation of Literary Texts," 213.

44. Ibid., 215–16.

45. Troll, "Illiterate Mode," 103.

46. Hall, "Hirtius and the *Bellum Alexandrinum*," 412.

47. Starr, "Circulation of Literary Texts," 220–23.

of an author within the Roman state with its increasingly monarchist structures. This would require detail as well as general trends, and must cover the entire range from panegyrics to fundamental opposition.

In addition to these socio-political aspects of writing several other salient aspects should also come into purview. For example, various works reveal authors' struggle to establish their identity or polemically dealing with their traditions in literary-historical self-reflection.[48]

Another challenge would be to understand the role of biographical information for the interpretation of texts *according to the ancients.* A number of indications make it quite clear that the biography of an author was considered important to ancient readers/exegetes: the *bios* of an author should be studied and known before one starts with his writings.[49] Despite this focus, the concept of an artistic oeuvre as an entity was unknown in antiquity; a publication "was not seen as the conclusion of a productive process, and thus third parties principally had no scruples interfering with an author's work—e.g. by interpolation or even to attribute other works to him in order to profit from the reputation of a famous name."[50] What is noteworthy is that the role of such biographical "information" was not historical as we would understand it. Often, it seems, the *bios* of the author—in the sense of the help it offers for understanding what he wrote — lies in its prescriptive implications, like the wise man striving to be useful even after his death (to adapt Seneca, *Epistulae morales* 102.30).

The self-statements by various authors can and should also be investigated. However, to conclude this list of possibilities I want to draw attention to the *viva vox.*

The Mediterranean world of Roman times is often described as "face-to-face" communities.[51] This "face-to-face" setting is the pre-condition for any attempts at formulating possible author-functions of ancient texts. Reading in antiquity was not experienced as a silent scanning, mainly mental activity. It was a performative, vocal, oral–aural event.[52] Reading aloud while others listened is a practice that cements sociability, adding distinct elements to the social functions of writing and publishing. It is printed matter that first, in the history of books, made it possible for an author to reach right into the heart of the single individual, and it is only the mass-produced printed book

48. See Schmitzer, *Die Macht.*
49. Mansfeld, *Prolegomena*, passim.
50. Ulrich Schmitzer, "Authors: Classical Antiquity."
51. Brown, *Making*, 3; Malina, *Social Gospel of Jesus*, 88–91.
52. Dorandi, "Zwischen Autographie und Diktat," 81.

that can be an object imbued with moments of private life, a memory or an emotion or some sign of identity.

The Greco-Roman emphasis on the living voice is well-known.[53] Yet, it is precisely this emphasis in *the context of writing* that—I propose—reveals something about textualized authors. A text, words written, the implied author, was meant to become a living voice.

Towards a Cultural-Historical Understanding of Authorship

To make some progress towards historically conceptualizing authorship and towards contextualizing the author-function in Roman times some imperatives seem appropriate.

Firstly, a distancing, self-critical move is necessary. Projecting the problematic nature of modern notions of authorship onto authors from antiquity is to underestimate the historical and cultural determinedness of communication. Writing is never merely writing; it is part of a communicative *event*, inscribed into a cultural pattern or system.[54] We need to be aware of the complexities of ancient literacy, orality, tradition and communication, and active steps towards this critical awareness should become part of our scholarship.

The "author" is a construct;[55] hence the requirement of a self-critical look at *our* understanding of authorship. Foucault has indicated the issues at stake when he observed that it would be worth examining "how the author became individualized in a culture like ours, what status [the author] has been given, at what moment studies of authenticity and attribution began, in what kind of system of valorization the author was involved, at what point we began to recount the lives of authors rather than of heroes, and how this fundamental category of 'the-man-and-his-work criticism' began."[56] Foucault's questions go to the heart of the problem that is the concern of this article; prompting us, when we study early Christian texts, to consider, "What are

---

53. See Alexander, "Living Voice," for a discussion of the use of this proverb, especially in the Hellenistic school setting.

54. Olson, "Mind and Media," 27.

55. This claim is, primarily, in terms of *discourse* and not *subjectivity*. The concern is with the *representation* of authorship and notions of property, originality, influence and authority. For a critique of treatments of authorship that are, in their words, "subject-centered" see Saunders and Hunter, "Lessons."

56. Foucault, "What Is an Author?" 101.

the modes of existence of this discourse? . . . Who can assume these various subject functions? . . . What difference does it make who is speaking?"[57]

Secondly, detailed consideration of the "substance" of authoring is imperative when discussing contexts of our texts. The material aspects and the communal interactivity of writing (and reading) in Roman times can no longer be neglected. An "author" was essentially a craftsman; basically he was master of a body of rules, preserved and handed down to him in rhetoric and poetics, for manipulating traditional materials in order to achieve the effects prescribed by the patron (and) or audience to which he owed both his livelihood and social status.

Thirdly, always to keep in mind that to practice his craft an author *required* a group effort. This wider circle of readers, assistants and secretaries determined the product, its dissemination and, *necessarily*, had various effects on loyalties in its creation. Research and reflection were by means of recitation and listening; composition by means of dictation. "Das Verfassen des Textes, das, wenn es autographisch war, von dem Geräusch der Stimme begleitet wurde, oder das Verfassen vermittels des Diktats oder auch die Probelektüre des Textes, die der Autor Freunden gab, waren zweckdienlich für eine Schrift, die in der Hauptsache zum Hören gedacht war."[58]

Given the "communal," interactive authorship of ancient documents, a number of typical exegetical interests of modern biblical scholarship require careful reconsideration. Authorship/author (as category of interpretation) is considered as central to our discipline not only in theory, but in practice: in the way single-figure studies dominate criticism; in the organization of texts in "editions"; in biographical studies; and above all, in the idea of "style," of a writing marked uniquely and characteristically, a style expressing a person's "mind" or "psyche" whose essential identity scrawls across a page and declares its supposed "ownership" of self-revealing and self-constituting discourse. Historicizing authorship must dramatically impact on this particular paradigm of scholarship.

Fourthly, a new appreciation for the importance of "micro-history," of the concretizing of social history seems relevant.[59]

---

57. Ibid., 120.

58. Guglielmo Cavallo, cited by Dorandi, "Zwischen Autographie und Diktat," 82: "The composition of the text, if autographical, was accompanied by the sound of a voice, or when the writer made use of dictation, or when giving a trial reading to friends, all served to make a writing mainly something intended for listening to" (my translation).

59. Magnússon, "Singularization of History."

Reading is a "way of taking meaning from texts." "Ways of taking" from books are "as much a part of learned behavior as are ways of eating, sitting, playing games and building houses."[60] Consequently the literacy events in which people participate and the meanings they "take" from them require a broad framework of socio-cultural analysis in order for ancient reading and writing to make sense.[61] It is in this sense that the importance of the history of the everyday becomes crucial.

To gain an understanding of the process of authoring and the writing of books in antiquity we clearly need the perspective of communication-as-performance theories, but they must be based on a history of everyday life, informed by the routines, habits, and phenomena associated with writing and reading in *those* times. To find ancient "author-functions" we need to reconsider everyday life as sites of cultural creativity. It is in the habits, rituals, routines, and traditions of daily life that meaningful communication was embedded, and writing and reading were pertinent occasions for and ways of associating with others, unique to the *poleis* and smaller communities of the Roman empire.

Fifthly, the role of patronage when construing ancient authorship can hardly be overestimated.

Concluding Remarks

In conclusion, the gist of the argument presented here, inviting further discussion and research.

Although socio-cultural history has become prominent in NT scholarship, crucial topics are still neglected. Many investigations of early Christian texts operate with a very inadequate model of authorship. We need to avoid anachronistic terminology and conceptualizations and uncritical ethnocentrism when it comes to authorship, literacy, tradition, writings, and other aspects of ancient communication. Romantic conceptions of authorship are inappropriate in discussing the cultural productions of antiquity. Authorship should be studied as a sociological and cultural problem, and analysed with the aid of cross-cultural models.

The history of the book is as relevant and as important to our disciplines as the history of the Roman empire. Much of biblical scholarship has been practised as if that history had no importance for the comprehension of works. It is precisely the history of the book that can inform us about

60. Heath, "What No Bedtime Story Means," 49.

61. See Heath, "What no Bedtime Story Means," 74.

the techniques, practices and expectations of those who produced the texts studied in NT scholarship.

Our practice and experience of authorship are determined by distinct values relating to literary property and censorship; authorship to us is inextricably linked to income, and due to the printing revolution our understanding thereof has become fundamentally *visual*. In earlier times, authorship was intimately part of patronage and mainly understood in aural, performative terms.

We should be conscious of the (vast) differences between the notions of the creative individual and intellectual property underlying contemporary notions of authorship, and the fact that most literary work in antiquity was corporate rather than individual. Furthermore, many of the written products of antiquity tend to be formulaic.

Questions about authorship are about the relationship between author, written language and "reader/reading public." The associations of personal author*ship* had unique meanings in antiquity. Books could be (and were) published without the name of the author or under another person's name. Literary works were collective undertakings. Individuals associated with texts related to *authority* (and not to origins). A lot about earliest Christianity, given current evidence, cannot be known. We should be willing critics committed to discrediting problematic claims and longstanding myths, even at the cost of an apparent reduction in historical knowledge.

Where all documentary communication is handwritten, as for any ancient writer it was, the distinctions that appear clear to us between author and scribe, copyist and commentator, editor, secretary, student, plagiarist and publisher, lose much of their significance.

The study of writing and authoring practices reveals not only an oral-aural communicative experience but also, and then vividly, the social inequalities and hierarchies determinative of the Greco-Roman world. The "living voice" played a major, if not the predominant role during the compilation of the work, in its production and its being made public, as well as in the exegesis and use of a work.

PART 2

Gospel Traditions

7

Transmitting the Jesus Traditions

The Importance of Conceptualizing the Tradition Process

Conceptualizing the various processes underlying the development of the Gospels is of considerable importance. Firstly, *every* historical Jesus study has a built-in concept of the synoptic problem and proceeds from certain assumptions concerning the methods and difficulties of the transmission of the gospel traditions. To understand our sources and how to use them responsibly for historical or religious purposes we need to know about their origins and the development of the traditions that constitute these writings.

Secondly, understanding the transmission of the Jesus traditions is also fundamental to understanding the Jesus movement, as form and redaction criticism have taught us. Thirdly, one's view of the history of the gospel traditions determines one's understanding of the Gospels themselves.

Study of this subject is important, not only because the Gospels shed light on the history of primitive Christianity, but also because light is shed back on the understanding of the very gospel writings. Indeed through a historical understanding of these writings, their process of formation in the history of primitive Christianity cannot be neglected.[1]

It is relevant to be reminded that the origins of the Jesus stories and how they were transmitted must be understood within the context of ancient communication, that is, within the setting of the particular forms and interplay of literacy and orality at the time.

In order to set the scene for the perspective proposed here, some aspects of the conventional approaches should be discussed. The focus will be mainly on the narrative material.

1. Simonsen, "Gospel Literature," 15.

Approaches to the Jesus Traditions

There has been a phenomenal upsurge in historical Jesus studies in recent times. Yet, as Boring rightly remarks, "What has been neglected in recent study is the period *between* Jesus and the Gospels. For this crucial period in the development of early Christianity and the formation of the Gospels, the appropriate starting point is still that of the classical form critics."[2] It is because the classic approaches are still so fundamental that it is worth our while to reflect on their underlying problems.

Form Criticism

Bultmann

Rudolf Bultmann saw the process (or history) of the gospel trditions as a dynamic one, the traditions being "open" and freely developing. To Bultman, "What the sources offer us is first of all the message of the early Christian community, which for the most part the church freely attributed to Jesus. This naturally gives no proof that all the words which are put into his mouth were actually spoken by him. As can be easily proved, many sayings originated in the church itself; others were modified by the church.[3] The process of transmission presupposed by Bultmann is clearly one of informal and uncontrolled oral tradition. The people involved in this retelling were not interested in either accurately preserving or controlling the tradition. "I do indeed think that we can now know almost nothing concerning the life and personality of Jesus, since the early Christian sources show no interest in either, are moreover fragmentary and often legendary; and other sources about Jesus do not exist."[4]

Bultmann was strongly criticized for his presuppositions.[5] Of particular relevance is the famous distinction between pre- and post-Easter traditions:

2. Boring, *Continuing Voice of Jesus*, 18.

3. Bultmann, *Jesus*, 13.

4. Ibid., 10.

5. Reicke, *Roots of the Synoptic Gospels*, 45–67. The discussion above is limited to a few *relevant* aspects. Other important issues, such as the supposed heuristic value of the categories of Palestinian versus Hellenistic (which is *very* problematic), will not be considered. Reference should also be made to the influential notion of the original form and its supposed compulsory development into progressively more complex and hybrid formations, to the thesis of an intrinsic gravitational or teleological pull toward the final gospel compositions, to the paradigm of linearity dominating source criticism, to the idea of anonymous collectivity as the shaping force both of oral materials and gospel

the belief in the Easter events as the watershed and real point of departure for the traditions of the synoptic gospels.[6]

However, the idea of a "rupture" in the history of the synoptic tradition cannot be maintained. In various ways and on many levels there must have been continuity between Jesus the teacher and the Jesus movement: "It is indisputable that this continuity existed on the personal level (the group of disciples from the period before Easter handed on the faith after Easter); it is also the case that the disciples continued their mode of life as travelling preachers. In this way they continued the activity of Jesus as wandering charismatic."[7] Reicke has developed an interesting argument that the basic structure of the synoptic gospels, the consistency of the self-contained pericopes and sequences of the triple tradition reflect the reminiscences of eyewitnesses and extensive continuity between Jesus and the oral tradition.[8]

It is interesting to note how influential the basic idea of some break or sharp change in the development of the gospels is in contemporary gospel criticism. This can be seen with particular clarity in the work of Kelber. Although Kelber criticizes the Bultmannian model of the pre-canonical synoptic transmission quite competently, he maintains that a radical change characterizes the history of the gospel traditions.[9] Kelber simply moves the point of rupture: he grants the continuity of the historical Jesus and the oral tradition, but sees a drastic change in the development of the gospel traditions at the point of their inscripturation.[10] With this radical separation of

---

textuality (which is a very romantic concept of storytelling), to the concept of "setting in life" as the sociological determinant of oral forms and to other invalid, inappropriate sociological conceptions based on a lack of understanding of orality and the dynamics of oral tradition (see Kelber, "Mark and Oral Tradition"; Ellis, *Prophecy and Hermeneutic*, 237–53; Ellis, "Gospel Criticism," 38–43).

6. To Bultmann (*Theology of the New Testament*, 33), "the essential thing to see" is the fact that "the proclaimer had become the proclaimed." "All that went before appears in a new light—new since the Easter faith in Jesus' resurrection and founded upon this faith" (ibid., 42–43). See also his famous theological discussion in response to the "new quest" (Bultmann, *History of the Synoptic Tradition*, esp. 27).

7. Theissen, *First Followers of Jesus*, 121.

8. However, I doubt Reicke's (*Roots of the Synoptic Gospels*, 16–24) general method in that he, despite a clear claim and intention to attend fully to the implications of oral tradition, still adheres to conventions underlying source critical theories. Problematic also is the assumption of preaching and teaching within sacramental communion as Sitz for the *whole* of the synoptic gospel traditions (see further below, 185–87).

9. Kelber, *Oral and the Written Gospel*, 2–8.

10. Ibid., 207 11.

oral and written tradition Kelber underestimates the role of orality in Greco-Roman society and romanticizes writing.[11]

Martin Dibelius

In distinct contrast, Dibelius saw the history of the synoptic gospels as a static, controlled process.

To Dibelius, it is obvious that there must have been some form of restraint inherent in the oral transmission of Jesus traditions: "At the period when eyewitnesses of Jesus were still alive, it was not possible to mar the picture of Jesus in the tradition."[12] We can see, in various ways, "that Jesus' sayings were handed down with great fidelity, thanks to the unencumbered memory of his unspoiled followers and to their reverence for their Master's word."[13]

Birger Gerhardsson

Probably the most famous exponent of the controlled tradition process is Birger Gerhardsson.[14] Whereas Bultmann and Dibelius both see the *Sitz im Leben* of the gospel traditions as early Christian worship, Gerhardsson sees the primary situation within the community for the transmission of Jesus tradition as tradition itself, that is, tradition as a conscious technical act of instruction. This perspective, therefore, has a distinct advantage over form criticism in that it is based on a historical analogy, rather than on a romantic notion of creative communities. The analogy is the transmission of the oral

---

11. Henderson ("*Didache* and Orality," 283) rightly refers to "ideological dichotomies," and argues, distinctly differently to Kelber, that "orality is . . . an exceptionally appropriate criterion for describing and comparing other early Christian texts—and not only for dissolving them into reconstructed oral traditions and social settings." I refer to some of my own work for further discussion and literature: Botha "Orality, Literacy and Worldview"; Botha, "Greco-Roman Literacy"; Botha, "Letter Writing and Oral Communication in Antiquity"; Botha, "Living Voice and Lifeless Letters" (chap. 2 above).

12. Dibelius, *From Tradition to Gospel*, 293.

13. Dibelius, *Jesus*, 23.

14. Gerhardsson, *Memory and Manuscript*. Useful (critical) discussions of Gerhardsson's work: Davies, "Reflections on a Scandinavian Approach to 'the Gospel Tradition'"; Smith, "A Comparison of Early Christian and Early Rabbinic Tradition"; Neusner, "Rabbinic Traditions about the Pharisees before 70 A.D."; Davids, "Gospels and Jewish Tradition"; Chilton, *Galilean Rabbi*, 36–38. Gerhardsson's recent work (*The Gospel Tradition*, "The Gospel Tradition") reflects a more sophisticated approach and contains much of considerable value.

Torah in rabbinic Judaism: the "ministry of the word" (ἡ διακονία τοῦ λόγου, Acts 6:4) exercised by the disciples of Jesus parallel the Jewish traditionists.[15]

Several problems with this perspective do remain. It is significant that Gerhardsson's argument depends more on Paul and Acts than on the gospels themselves. The theory does not explain our data, such as the significant differences between the Gospels.

Proposal

There seems to be two basic approaches to the development of the Gospels. On the one hand, we have a view of oral tradition that Bailey characterizes as *informal uncontrolled* tradition,[16] and Kelber as evolutionary progression.[17] On the other hand, we find a view that can be described as *formal controlled* tradition, or passive transmission. Much of the discussion surrounding the oral phase of the Jesus traditions focuses on which of these two approaches should be adopted.

There are, however, strengths in both positions. Clearly, the origins of the gospels lie with Jesus himself, and his disciples played a major role in the development of the gospels. But we also need to account for the obvious diversity and apparent unconcern with fidelity—that is, the general failure to preserve the *ipsissima verba* of Jesus—as regards the several strands of the Jesus traditions.[18]

Adding to the problems of these well-known approaches to the gospel traditions is the tendency to project (anachronistic) concepts onto the traditions themselves. "My chief objection to the form-critical scholars . . . is that their work is not sufficiently *historical*. They do not show sufficient energy in anchoring the question of the origin of the Gospel tradition within the framework of the question how holy, authoritative tradition was transmitted in the Jewish milieu of Palestine and elsewhere at the time of the New Testament. This must surely be the starting point if one wants to understand the origins of the early Christian tradition historically."[19] Gerhardsson himself

---

15. The basic idea of a formal, supervized process of transmission is also defended by Chilton, *Profiles of a Rabbi*, 160–67; Dungan, *Sayings of Jesus in the Churches of Paul*, 141–43; Riesner, "Jesus as Preacher and Teacher," 191 ("a teach-and-learn situation"); and Zimmermann, *Urchristliche Lehrer*, 23.

16. Bailey, "Informal Controlled Oral Tradition," 35.

17. Kelber, *Oral and the Written Gospel*, 7.

18. Smith, "Comparison of Early Christian and Early Rabbinic Tradition," 170–72; Abel, "Psychology of Memory and Rumor Transmission," 274.

19. Gerhardsson, *Origins of the Gospel Traditions*, 8–9.

assumes that all the Jesus traditions can be categorized as "holy, authoritative tradition." No doubt, parts, and eventually a great many of these stories, anecdotes and sayings of Jesus were considered holy and authoritative, but the description creates as many new problems as it solves. The point, however, that the transmission process should be pictured in a realistic, historical way remains valid.

The complexities of the origins, transmission and development of the Jesus traditions are well known. Various attempts have been made, and all have been criticized. There are, however, some areas of comparative research that have not been used extensively to understand (in the sense of interpretive, explanatory descriptions) aspects of the gospel traditions, and those are orality research and folklore scholarship.

Elsewhere I have suggested how we could apply the *idea* of a more formal, controlled model to the development of the Markan stories in a historically responsible manner, making use of orality research in a constructive manner.[20] Here I want to turn to the possibility of re-applying the concept of informal, evolutionary models in a social-scientifically responsible way to *parts* of the tradition process underlying some of the gospel traditions. This paper suggests that rumor research can meaningfully illuminate facets of the history of the gospel traditions.

The Study of Rumor

Although I am not the first to suggest that the study of rumor is relevant to gospel criticism,[21] it is noteworthy how little use has been made of available scholarship. Consequently, an argument utilizing rumor research for understanding the gospel tradition process must also include an explanation why this research has not been applied before.

---

20. Botha, "Mark's Story."

21. Abel ("Psychology of Memory and Rumor Transmission"), in a perceptive study, refers to scientific literature dealing with memory and rumour transmission. These studies "offer an opportunity to assess the validity of the conclusions of Form Criticism" (ibid., 273). Similarly, Gager ("Gospels and Jesus," 247–56) also utilizes the work of Vansina (*Oral Tradition*) and Allport and Postman (*Psychology of Rumor*) in his discussion of the oral tradition. Gager is doubtful of the validity of much of form-critical conclusions: "all previous attempts at the [historical Jesus] quest have proceeded on ill-founded and misleading assumptions about the oral tradition" (Gager, "Gospels and Jesus," 256).

Prejudice against Folklore Research

One need not document the fact that New Testament scholarship shares in the widespread prejudice against the study of folklore. For reasons difficult to fathom, folklore research is deemed to be frivolous stuff, and it is believed that little can be learned from it.[22] This prejudice springs from a lack of conceptual clarity with regard to early Christian history, in that interest is usually maintained in texts and theology. New Testament scholars often pay more attention to the texts than to the live *processes* by and through which those texts communicated and created meaning. The viewpoint adopted for this study is an attempt to provide a partial remedy for that situation by urging an attitude toward the gospel writings that stresses "the folk" and the dynamics of their conventional communicative activities and traditional expressions.

The possible relevance of rumor research is obscured by the attitude that such study would cast doubt on the historicity of the gospels. This (ideological) concern with regard to historical Jesus research proceeds from the starting point that rumor is *necessarily unreliable*. Consequently, the assumption seems to be that the only worthwhile information *must be* information that can be directly controlled: the only good communication is authoritative, approved (by whom?) communication. But is a rumor by definition a lie? Could we not understand the oral traditions better if we gained some insight into the origins and strengths of rumor?

Understanding Rumor

The idea of rumor is often ruled by a negative conception: rumors are taken to be necessarily false, fanciful, or irrational. Thus rumors—and anything smacking of rumor—are deplored, and treated like fleeting aberrations or momentary folly. In popular opinion—and sometimes also in scholarly circles—the word "rumor" connotes a mysterious, almost magical phenomenon. Their effect on people seems to be analogous to that of hypnosis: they fascinate, subjugate, seduce, and set them ablaze.[23]

This popular, but negative view is untenable. Rumor phenomena can be understood and explained. Far from being mysterious, rumors comply

---

22. Useful discussions of developments in folklore research in Ben-Amos, "Toward a Definition of Folklore in Context"; Bauman, "Verbal Art"; Bennett, "Traditions of Belief," 1 22.

23. See the overview in Koenig, *Rumor in the Marketplace*, 9–17.

with a logic of which the operation can be demonstrated. In fact, as we shall see, the importance of understanding rumor is immense. Underlying the logic of rumor lies the fundamental phenomenon of belief.

Rumors exist because people speak. A dogmatic prejudice and moralizing concern are the true sources of a negative attitude towards rumor phenomena. Indeed, if rumors were but incredible stories that circulate without any grounds whatsoever for their existence, their presence would be evidence of unreasonableness and a sign of madness. They must then be the sociological counterpart of hallucination. The association of rumors with affliction and even delusion appears logical but is misleading. "Far from being pathological, rumor is part and parcel of the efforts of [persons] to come to terms with the exigencies of life."[24] The sheer force of rumors, their "omnipresence," their immense sociological importance and the seriousness with which they are taken by *all* people belie the popular conception.[25]

Rumor and Truth

Rumors rarely arise out of "reality." If the relationship between rumors and evidence had been straightforward, rumor mongering would have been an insignificant and irrelevant activity of a few bored and unoccupied persons. They spring, rather, from raw, confused facts: a rumor's purpose is precisely that of explaining these raw facts, *to posit a reality*. Rumors do not take off from the truth but rather *seek out* the truth; "fuelled by a desire for meaning, a quest for clarification and closure."[26]

A first step towards a responsible understanding of the dynamics of rumors, therefore, is to realize that defining rumors as stories (or lies) circulating as "unverified" information ignores the fact that rumors generally present themselves with the pretensions of ideal verification. Rumors *always* reach us through a friend, colleague or relative (who is a friend of the first-hand witness).[27] Who is more believable than a first-hand witness? Or

---

24. Shibutani, *Improvised News*, 62.

25. Informative studies, on which my analysis is based, are Shibutani, *Improvised News*; Rosnow and Fine, *Rumor and Gossip*; Rosnow, "Psychology of Rumour Reconsidered,"; Rosnow, "Rumor as Communication"; Fine, "Rumors and Gossiping"; Kapferer, *Rumors*.

26. Rosnow and Fine, *Rumor and Gossip*, 4.

27. Fine, "Folklore diffusion through interactive social networks"; Koenig, *Rumor in the Marketplace*, 136. Kapferer (*Rumors*, 39, 131) provides an excellent discussion of the role of the "friend of a friend" phenomenon in exemplary stories. On the complexities of so-called "eyewitness testimony" see Buckhout, "Eyewitness Testimony."

someone that one has known intimately for a long time? What better proof can one expect? "Social life is based on confidence and on the delegation of the task of verification."[28]

A useful definition of rumors in terms of their dynamics is that of Shibutani: "Important, ambiguous events give rise to rumors. Rumors are improvised news resulting from a process of collective discussion entailing both an information-spreading procedure and a process of interpretation and commentary. In spreading and commenting upon presumed or ambiguous facts a group constructs one or two acceptable and valuable explanations. Changes in a rumor's content are not due to the failings of human memory, but rather to the development and contribution of commentaries made throughout the rumour's process."[29] "The reality to be studied, then, is not distortion in serial transmission but the social interaction of people caught in inadequately defined situations."[30]

This definition of rumor can be summarized in a simple model:

$$\text{Rumor} = \text{Importance} \times \text{Ambiguity.}^{31}$$

Where events carry no importance whatsoever or appear to be totally devoid of ambiguity, there would be no rumor. Generally speaking, all mysterious symbols / stories / events provide an ideal springboard for rumors: they are

28. Kapferer, *Rumors*, 5. The development of human knowledge is a social process. Or put differently, *all* knowledge is socially constructed (Berger and Luckmann, *Social Construction*, 33–61). Rumours, therefore, are not unlike any other information we come across in our lives: we believe or reject rumours at people's word. "So many people cannot be wrong: rumors acquire their credibility from our confidence in a mechanism of information-related *natural selection*. Were the rumor false, it wouldn't have gotten beyond the innumerable other people—like us but who came before us—who heard it" (Kapferer, *Rumors*, 103). To believe a rumour is to manifest one's allegiance to the group's voice, to identify with collective opinion.

29. Shibutani. *Improvised News*, 14–29. Reflecting on this exposition we discover another reason for reference to rumour research: many studies of the gospel traditions assume a similar process of distortion and the failure of memory in the history of the traditions. These assumptions should be measured against comparative research.

30. Shibutani, *Improvised News*, 17.

31. Underlying this model lies the identification of the essential conditions for a rumour by Allport and Postman. Allport and Postman (*Psychology of Rumor*, 33–4) attempted to formulate the elements of a rumour in a quantitative manner: $R \sim i \times a$. Their attempt has drawn criticism; the model suggested above is based on the considerable research that developed from their insights. See Shibutani, "Rumor," 577 ("the formula does specify the important variables"); Rosnow and Fine, *Rumor and Gossip*, 72; Kapferer, *Rumors*; Rosnow, "Psychology of Rumour Reconsidered" (who criticizes the supposed predictive power of the formula) for discussion.

ambiguous and thus fertile ground for speculation. Whenever a group of people endeavors to understand but receives no official answers, or they receive unbelievable ones, rumors arise. Rumor, in a manner of speaking, is like an informational black market.

Not all rumors relate to a concrete event which needs explanation. Rumors often arise due to faulty interpretations of messages. Misunderstandings relate to one person's report on what another person reported, and to a difference between what was transmitted and what was decoded; consequently certain rumors literally create events. Of this type of rumor, described as "exemplary stories" or "urban legends" by communication theorists and folklorists, we find stories that crop up without precipitating fact. These phenomena are related to the obscurity of the borderline between fantasy and reality. It is a well-documented fact that we find stories that, once convincingly told as if they were true, take on lives of their own.

All rumors are the product of both fact and imagination. Different types of rumors reflect the dominance of either realism or imagination and subjectivity in the production of a rumor's content. Some rumors dwell almost exclusively on the "social imagination," that is, the collective experience of symbols and myths and shared (myth related) motives. At the other end of the spectrum, we find rumors with a predominantly realistic slant (but even there one should not underestimate nor slight the role of subjectivity).

Societies are on-going things. The world is in a state of continuous flux, and as life conditions change, or are perceived to be endangered, knowledge and understanding must keep pace. Crisis situations arise whenever new events or information are incomprehensible in terms of established assumptions. New sensitivities must be created, and in order that they may continue to act in association with one another humans alter their orientations together. The emergence of hypotheses and explanations and their acceptance is a social process. It is in this process of transformation that rumor usually plays an important part. A rumor is a form of human behavior: it is a way of understanding and maintaining reality—a point that Kapferer emphasizes.[32]

Constructive Process

The first few investigations into rumor phenomena utilized the famous "telephone" simulation experiments, of which the classic study is Allport and Postman.[33] This approach assumed that rumor transmission is a system not

32. Kapferer, *Rumors*.

33. Allport and Postman, *Psychology of Rumor*.

unlike a message travelling along a telephone line: person A tells B who tells C and so forth. It was found that, in such a routine, right from the very first relays most of the details are omitted, the message being seriously reduced in length. Then it becomes stable in length and form, changing little in subsequent retellings. The counterpart of the reduction in length is the accentuating of certain details. As particular details survive they acquire considerable visibility and importance in the reduced message. The action involved, or numbers and sizes, the details are magnified: ten turns into a hundred, fast becomes very fast, a few women become five hundred brethren. As the message evolves, it tends to acquire a "good form": that of a well-constructed narrative respecting the stereotypes that are prevalent in the group in which the rumor circulates.

Despite the considerable value of these conclusions, several problems are built into this type of investigation as subsequent research has amply demonstrated.[34] Rumors do not necessarily become less accurate,[35] nor do they necessarily become shorter, or are details readily forgotten. In fact, details often accumulate. Underlying the problems of the conclusions by the simulation experiments is the concept of a linear, one-directional communication procedure.

In real life contexts the term "relay" is inappropriate with regard to the rumor process, as no information is passed on unidirectionally. Everyday communication, and thus exchange of rumors, is an interactional, reflective process and *not* like a linear relay line. Various concerned parties converse with each other, and the rumor is the final consensus of their collective deliberations seeking out a convincing, encompassing explanation. Rumors entail a subjective *construction* of reality.

In the following, this discussion of some of the elements of the origins of rumors and their transmission will be related to the history of the gospel tradition.

---

34. See Shibutani, *Improvised News*, 99–100; Fine, "Rumors and Gossiping," 227–28; Koenig, *Rumor in the Marketplace*, 105–20.

35. This is true particularly when the rumour content is highly important. Studies of informal communication among soldiers, for example, found that men involved in dangerous situations are not gullible (Shibutani, *Improvised News*, 63–94). In countries with strong news censorship rumour usually reflects truth more accurately than other news channels.

The Dynamics of Some Jesus Stories

It must be emphasized that I am not equating all the Jesus stories as we now know them with rumors, nor am I suggesting that we can know nothing about the historical Jesus. Rumor research provides us with useful instruments with which to conceptualize aspects of oral tradition—which by definition include hearsay. In fact, we can still discover traces of the origins of possible rumor processes within the synoptic gospels themselves, for example Mark 1:45 and 5:14. The Gospels are very complex documents. The aim is to understand some of the social dynamics underlying parts of the Gospels.

Early Christian Rumor Mongers

It seems as if rumors often fulfil a need for ritual, carrying almost ceremonial functions. Rumors are a form of transactional communication: they incite moral commentary, personal opinions and emotional reactions. Rumors and gossip marvellously fill up the empty spaces that must of necessity be part of communication with our in-group. Rumors are engaged when both ambiguity and importance correlate, and these social forces only become manifest where people interact.

Consequently, communal places and activities are the hubs of rumors. There people create or transmit a host of information, whether false or true, born of the need to arouse interest, converse, say something entertaining or to find intellectual "closure" with regard to something poorly understood. "To speak about a rumor with someone is to invite him to 'rumour' with oneself."[36]

Almost by definition rumor mongers are people at the crossroad of many communication networks. How does information spread? Via people most likely to play a bridging role, people who are allowed to move in different strata: slaves and craftworkers, or public officials such as scribes. That is, individuals whose occupations bring them into contact with a variety of social categories.

Of primary interest within our current investigation is, of course, the social characterisation of the disciples. Social information, though, is obvious for only four of them. Peter, Andrew, James, and John were fishermen,[37]

---

36. Kapferer, *Rumors*, 50.

37. Peter and Andrew appear to have been net casters (Mark 1:16–18), while James and John obviously fished from a boat (Mark 1:19). Literature dealing with fishing and

an occupation of which the social reputation was traditionally very low and sometimes even despised.

The increased demand for fish in the first century led to different systems of commercial ventures. Fish-salting seems to have been a prominent enterprise around the Sea of Galilee. Fishermen contracted with the wealthy for a specified amount of fish or they leased fishing rights from tax collectors (who acted as investment brokers) for a percentage of the catch (30–40%, assuming similarity of conditions between Egypt and Palestine[38]). Levied fishermen often worked with partners (μέτοχοι),[39] and the fishing done by the four may have been of this type as Mark specifies that James and John left their father with the hired hands.[40] In any case, the four disciples we can locate socially are clearly members of the lower class who also had extensive contact with other social and economic classes.

Even more relevant is to realize that they were people of liminal status. The very contact across social strata that they enjoyed probably contributed to limited acceptance on both sides of social barriers. These men were considered persons of dubious and indeterminate standing by most of the people who had dealings with them.

People in such a situation, described in social-psychological terms as "isolates" are often highly motivated to initiate the transmission of rumors.[41] Because communication is also a continuous process of proposing various relationships between those taking part in the conversation, rumors represent opportunities to transform or influence relationships.

It is possible to extend the group of people of undefined and problematic social status as relevant to the transmission of gospel stories. In a continuum from the lower echelons of the elite and ranging downward toward non-elite levels were those whom social scientists call *retainers*.[42] These included lower level military officers, educators, religious functionaries,

---

fishermen in first-century Mediterranean world: Rostovtzeff, *Social and Economic History*, 1177–80; Wuellner, "Fishermen (NT)"; Freyne, *Galilee from Alexander the Great to Hadrian*, 174. Applebaum ("Economic life in Palestine," 680–90) discusses the production and movement of goods in Palestine, noting the impact of taxes on the circulation and exchange of products. K. C. Hanson ("The Galilean Fishing Economy and the Jesus Tradition") creates a model of Galilean fishing, discussing the role of fishing and fishermen in the Jesus traditions.

38. Cf. Rostovtzeff, *Social and Economic History*, 1387 n.101.

39. Cf. Luke 5:7.

40. Mark 1:20.

41. Koenig, *Rumor in the Marketplace*, 114.

42. Saldarini, *Pharisees, Scribes and Sadducees*, 37–42.

scribes, and lower level aristocrats. In agrarian societies the "governing class and its retainers seldom exceeded 5 to 7% of the population."[43] Reference should also be made to the non-elite people of the cities which included merchants, artisans, day-laborers and service workers. Some among these accumulated considerable wealth, yet even they were not the bearers of much social influence.

We find a remarkable incidence of people from these circles depicted by the gospel (and early Christian) traditions as having contact with, or being involved with Jesus and his followers: servants (such as those from Jairus' house), Galilean and Judean priests, tax collectors, money changers and traders in the temple, doorkeepers, centurions and others. These persons worked primarily in the service of the elite and acted as mediators for both governmental and religious functions to the lower classes and to village areas, and were heavily dependent on their relationships with the urban elite.

Such functionaries possibly played key roles in the development of the gospel traditions. Significantly we find several people from this group who are followers of Jesus such as the people from Jairus' house, Levi, Judas Iscariot, tax collectors and several (or at least two) centurions. We even find among this group some Pharisees and scribes—who are in particular examples of persons caught "in between."

Pharisees (or proto-Pharisees) depended with the scribes on the wealthy upper classes for their livelihood while functioning as intermediaries between the populace and the upper echelons of society. They were most likely literate local village leaders.[44]

A scribe was more than a mere copyist and rather a middle level official, participating in a wide range of community activities.[45] "Their position gave them some power and influence, but they were subordinate to and dependent on the priests and leading families in Jerusalem and Herod Antipas in Galilee during the time of Jesus."[46]

Despite the general negativeness with which scribes are usually portrayed in the synoptic tradition we find some noteworthy exceptions, for example the scribe who is "not far from the kingdom" (Mark 12:34), Joseph of Arimithea (Mark 15:43), and Jairus (Mark 5:21–43). The first two are clearly urbanites, though the last is more likely to be part of some village leadership.

43. Ibid., 38.

44. Saldarini, "Social Class of the Pharisees in Mark," 71.

45. Saldarini, *Pharisees, Scribes and Sadducees*, 241–76; Orton, *Understanding Scribe*, 40–118.

46. Saldarini, ibid., 274.

Rumors that are introduced into a subsystem of interpersonal relations often exhibit the pattern of a network.[47] Interpersonal networks involve multiple interactions in which messages diffuse in numerous patterns. As a message is sent and received from several sources, various complicated patterns result, and several persons play prominent roles in the process.

People such as scribes probably played a significant role in early Christian rumors. The development and transmission of a rumor can be likened to a two-step process, in which the system is initiated by "isolates." The story is then transmitted by opinion-leaders to the prestigious members of a group. The acceptance or rejection of a story by perceived specialists contributes strongly to whether a story will be labelled as rumor or as useful information. Various studies have described this process in which the "influentials" with prestige and specialized "expertise" in certain areas of knowledge play an important part.[48]

Coping with Anxiety and Stress

Rumors can provide people throughout a society who feel frustrated, threatened and disturbed with answers or explanations in a wider sense. Stressful times can also bring about the frustration-aggression reaction mechanism, with hostile rumors being one of such possible aggressive responses. Stress contributes to a person's anxiety, and anxiety is a major factor in rumor activity.[49]

Rumor mongers, as several studies point out, have often found themselves in an adversarial position within a group or even within society, particularly concerning customs related to the role of religion. Such persons may feel under attack and threatened. Also, unemployment and economic depression seem to characterize regions that are the centres of the rumor activity.[50]

Rumors flourish when people have the feeling that they are not in control of their lives; when everything is perceived as being decided externally, without their own input. To cope with such anxiety-producing situations

47. Cf. Rosnow and Fine, *Rumor and Gossip*, 32, 132.

48. Cf. Jaeger, Anthony, and Rosnow, "Who Hears What from Whom and with What Effect"; Fine, "Folklore Diffusion through Interactive Social Networks," "Rumors and Gossiping," 232; Buckner, "A Theory of Rumor Transmission."

49. Anthony, "Anxiety and Rumour"; Rosnow, "Psychology of Rumour Reconsidered"; Rosnow, Esposito, and Gibney, "Factors Influencing Rumor Spreading," 30–31, 38–39.

50. Cf. Koenig, *Rumor in the Marketplace*, 62–69.

persons collectively define a distinct group identity. Anxiety is also reduced when fear can be objectified.[51]

In the following, three general factors that created stress and anxiety in first-century Palestine will be discussed, and the possible role of rumors related to Jesus traditions briefly indicated.

Health

Given the prominence of healing stories in the gospels, some mention should be made of general physical welfare in antiquity. The birth and death rates both approximated forty per thousand per year. Infant mortality rates have been estimated to average thirty percent in many peasant societies, and life expectancies were extremely short by contemporary, Western standards. Children in general suffered from disease, malnutrition and poverty and many never made it to adulthood before their parents were sick or dead. About sixty per cent of those who survived their first year of life were dead by age sixteen and in few families both parents would still be living when the youngest child reached puberty.[52] A child born among the lower classes during the first century had a life expectancy of little more than twenty years.[53]

Obviously disease and high death rates were not evenly spread across all elements of the population, but for most people who did make it to adulthood health would have been atrocious. "Infectious disease was undoubtedly the single greatest threat to life in antiquity, with epidemics killing half or more of the populations of the world's larger cities."[54] Parasites were also very common.[55] Most of the lower classes lived with the debilitating results of protein deficiency since childhood. Taking into account the paleopathological examination of skeletal remains from the Herodian period and infant mortality rates (by examining the ratio of children to adults in tombs), it is clear that particularly those of poorer socio-economic conditions suffered from malnutrition.[56]

---

51. Kapferer, *Rumors*, 172–73, 183–84.

52. Carney, *Shape of the Past*, 88.

53. Cf. Stark, "Antioch as the Social Situation for Matthew's Gospel," 195; Lenski, Lenski, and Nolan, *Human Societies*, 173.

54. Zias, "Death and Disease in Ancient Israel," 149.

55. Fifty percent of the hair combs from Qumran, Masada, and Murabbat were infected with lice and lice eggs, probably reflecting conditions elsewhere (ibid., 148).

56. Fiensy, *Social History of Palestine*, 97–98.

In summary, poor housing, non-existent sanitation, economically inaccessible medical care and bad diet—as much as one-fourth of a male Palestinian peasant's calorie intake came from alcohol[57]—all adds up to an experience of everyday life, by common people, as frightening and often incomprehensible. Given the belief in the activities of evil spiritual powers[58] and the widespread physical suffering prevalent within the context of ancient cosmology, one can readily detect the ubiquitous fear and anxiety characterizing the period.[59] That many situations, for instance the activities, news and reports of a powerful healer from Nazareth, could have given rise to experiences of ambiguity and enigmatic reports is highly plausible.

Violence and Conflict

Palestinian society, in the period 20–70 CE, was caught up in serious socio-economic and religio-political conflicts.

A variety of events created and/or contributed to stress, anxiety, and ambiguity: several military conquests, decades of legislation causing economic impoverishment, many acts of destruction, a whole series of violations of the traditional Jewish way of life, and a variety of incidents aimed at strict repressive control of people's lives under illegitimate/foreign rulers.[60]

Furthermore, fraud, robbery, forced imprisonment or labor, beatings, inheritance disputes and forceful removal of rent were all common events in village life. Oakman, in his study of the countryside in Luke, writes that violence "became a regular part of village experience and rural consciousness."[61] Life in the countryside of antiquity, and life among the peasants were characterized by violence; it approached "a state of endemic warfare, from which only a stout cudgel, a fast horse, or a well-built little fortress gave protection."[62]

---

57. Broshi, "Diet of Palestine in the Roman Period."

58. Cf. Pilch, "Sickness and Healing in Luke-Acts," 196–97.

59. Cf. also Dodds, *Pagan and Christian*.

60. Cf. Rhoads, *Israel in Revolution*; Horsley and Hanson, *Bandits, Prophets, and Messiahs*.

61. Oakman, "Countryside in Luke-Acts," 168.

62. MacMullen, *Roman Social Relations*, 4.

Taxes and Poverty

We read in Acts 2:46–47 that the earliest followers of Jesus enjoyed "the good will of all the people." Who were "all" these people? Predominantly, they would have been peasants, and that meant *poor* people. In any traditional agrarian society the peasantry composed seventy percent or more of the population and included all those living in towns or villages and engaged in working the soil or related activities, in contrast to the rulers, their retainers, supporting artisans, merchants, and so on, who lived in the cities.[63] Among the urban non-elite, poverty was also common. The peasants should be seen as "rural cultivators whose surpluses are transferred to a dominant group of rulers that uses the surpluses both to underwrite its own standard of living and to distribute the remainder to groups in society that do not farm but must be fed for their specific goods and services in turn."[64] Thus the high-priestly government and temple apparatus in Jerusalem, the extensive Herodian and Roman governmental structure, the elaborate development projects and the tribute taken by the Romans were all dependent on what was produced by the Palestinian peasantry.

Life was harsh for the peasants, with the day-laborers struggling even more. The demands for rents and taxes left most with a barely manageable, subsistence level of living.[65] Even Herod realized that his heavy demands on his subjects were becoming counterproductive and were simply killing off his producers.[66]

Due to aristocratic control of major portions of the arable land tenant farming was quite characteristic of Palestine. Rents for tenants could be as high as two-thirds of a crop, though in rabbinic sources the figures one-half, one-third, and one-fourth appear.[67] While all day-laborers were not necessarily without property, people who were without land were near the bottom of the social-economic scale. Commonly they were either peasants who had

63. See Garnsey and Saller, *Early Principate*, 28–34; Saldarini, *Pharisees, Scribes and Sadducees*, 35–39; Stambaugh and Balch, *New Testament in Its Social Environment*, 63–81. Note Josephus' description: "ours is not a maritime country; neither commerce nor the intercourse which it promotes with the outside world has any attraction for us. Our cities are built inland, remote from the sea; and we devote ourselves to the cultivation of the productive country with which we are blessed" (*Against Apion* 1.60). Cf. also *Jewish War* 3.41–50.

64. Wolf, *Peasants*, 3–4; cf. also Fiensy, *Social History of Palestine*, vi–vii.

65. Fiensy, *Social History of Palestine*, 105; Applebaum, "Economic life in Palestine," 664–67; "Judaea as a Roman Province," 365, 377.

66. Josephus, *Antiquities* 15.365.

67. Fiensy, *Social History of Palestine*, 81.

lost land through debt or non-inheriting sons whom small peasant plots could not support.[68]

The general tension between the Roman imperial rule and the Palestinian Jewish people was focused on the tribute that Rome demanded. This tension, I suggest, is the frame, the underlying condition for the story of Jesus' birth in Luke 2:1–20.

The inability to solve the supposed *historical* problems posed by the character and chronology of the census under Quirinius is well known.[69] These very difficulties prompt us to think in terms of social dynamics: ambiguity within a complex, stressful situation. The impact of Roman taxation on common people (such as Joseph and Mary, the fishermen, the narrators of Jesus stories) as well as what the birth of a "savior" may have meant to them in relation to that taxation, are problems which are probably very close to the intention of this story.

Far from being "a purely literary device"[70] to get Jesus born in Bethlehem, the story of the census probably reflects a response rumor: it responds to personal needs where there were distress, severe economic hardship, and hostility. Through interaction and communication, people making up a social group define for one another what is "real" and what "could have been."

Similarly, Matthew's story about the flight to Egypt by Mary and Joseph can also be seen to reflect the social relationships and political conditions that prevailed in Palestine under Roman (and earlier, Herodian) rule. To understand the story we need not search for the actual event. The story reflects rumors related to a historical situation in which, whether because of the steady impact of economic pressures or because of the direct effect of violence, often politically inspired, many people were forced to flee their homes in order to avoid being killed.

Ambiguity

"Rumour is a substitute for news; in fact, it *is* news that does not develop in institutional channels."[71] Ambiguity exists where there is an unsatisfied

68. Many such landless people migrated to urban areas which were in frequent need of new labour. The need for labour was created not because of economic opportunity but because of urban mortality due to the atrocious health conditions among the urban non-elite (Stark, "Antioch as the Social Situation for Matthew's Gospel," 194–95).

69. Brown, *Birth of the Messiah*, 395–96, 547–56; Fitzmyer, *Luke (I–IX)*, 392–94, 401–5.

70. Fitzmyer, ibid., 393.

71. Shibutani, *Improvised News*, 62.

demand for news; where there is a discrepancy between information needed to come to terms with a changing environment and what is provided by formal news channels (or available knowledge). Ambiguity arises when one is confronted with an unexpected event, an unexplained incident or incomplete report. When customary or commonplace activity is interrupted for want of more satisfying information, tension and frustration result. Rumor is the collective transaction through which humans try to fill the gap created by ambiguity.

One can readily imagine the widespread unsatisfied demand for news in antiquity by simply considering communication technology. In a community at a low level of technology most communications are private and person to person with information disseminating in irregular fashion. "If one were close to an important person, he would know far more of what was going on than would another man who was closer to the scene of the action but not well connected."[72]

An important source of ambiguity lies within the early Jesus movement itself. Many of the authoritative informants of the Jesus stories, such as Peter, were itinerant.[73] That is, they were present in a community for a limited period: a few days, maybe a few weeks at the most. The very way of spreading the Jesus stories contributed to considerable ambiguity—a problem not unknown to Paul either.[74]

In the following, four rumor "devices" for dealing with ambiguity will briefly be related to some gospel traditions.

Seeking out Truth

Rumors are not necessarily "false": they are, however, necessarily unofficial. Rumors constitute an alternative source of information, a source that is perforce uncontrolled.[75]

---

72. Carney, *Shape of the Past*, 111–12.

73. Theissen, *First Followers of Jesus*, 8–16; Botha, "Historical Setting of Mark's Gospel."

74. Cf. his problems with Christians in Thessalonica and Corinth.

75. Something that is often overlooked is the fact that informal oral tradition is usually more reliable than formal ones: "an official tradition is less trustworthy as a historical source . . . in so far as it is official, but more trustworthy in so far as it is much more carefully transmitted" (Vansina, *Oral Tradition*, 85). That is, formal oral tradition is more trustworthy as to care in transmission, less so as to historical reliability (ibid., 29–32, 107, 172, 190–93). This has implications for Gerhardsson's thesis.

An instance conducive to the development of rumors in search of truth that immediately comes to mind is the "final" events surrounding Pilate's career.[76] In 35 CE a Samaritan prophet promised to produce the sacred temple vessels (which, according to Samaritan beliefs had been buried on the Mount Gerizim since the time of Moses) if the people would assemble on that mountain. Great crowds of (armed) Samaritans flocked to Tirathana, ready to climb the mountain and watch the spectacle. Before they could carry out their intention, they were stopped by a detachment of cavalry and heavy-armed infantry in the village; some were killed, some put to flight, and still others were captured. Of these, Pilate executed the most respected and distinguished. After protests were made to Vitellius, the legate of Syria, Pilate was consequently sent to Rome to answer for his conduct.

The point is simple: we see these events through the lenses of Josephus, a historian's written works. The people involved, and others in Palestine were simply faced with *ambiguous, conflicting and exaggerated oral reports.* Bear in mind that it took Pilate about a year to arrive in Rome—and how long after that for reports to reach Palestine?—so that one can easily understand the rise of a variety of rumors concerning Pilate himself.[77] The whole series of events caused situations of extreme anxiety, and gave rise to the possible perception of highly ambiguous events: the appearance of a "messiah," the killing of innocents, etc.

It is not difficult to relate the origins of the story of the killing of the infants (Matt 2:16–18) to such a situation. It is against the background of Herod's, Pilate's, and other aristocratically inspired exploitation and tyranny that the pre-Matthean and Matthean story(-ies) of "the massacre of the innocents" and the stories depicting the birth of the newborn king of the Judeans originated and was cultivated. The activities of a variety of "kings" (or even powerful Roman officials) could have constituted the problem (from which liberation was sought), and the (historical) birth of Jesus combined with messianic and Davidic belief systems provided the ambiguity.

Another series of events can be related to the origins and development of the story about the visit of the Magi to the infant Jesus, namely the reminiscences associated with Tiridates.[78]

First we need more information about the "Magi." They were a priestly caste acting as political and religious advisers to the Persian courts and

76. Josephus, *Antiquities* 18.85–89.

77. Cf. Brandon, *Religion in Ancient History*, 254–67.

78. Dio Cassius, *Roman History* 63.1.1—63.7.2 (cf. 62.21.2—62.23.6); Suetonius, *Nero* 13; Pliny, *Nat. Hist.* 30.4.23—30.6.18.

were famous for their communication with and propitiation of the gods.[79] They were also instrumental in divine revelation as the interpreters of royal dreams or extraordinary natural phenomena. In this sense we sometimes find the term μάγος extended to magicians, astrologers and dream interpreters. In their official duties the Magi may well have been stationed in outlying administrative centres; at least, these centres were visited by them on various occasions. Because of their special stake in and attachment to the former Persian rule as *the* divinely ordained order and their wide dispersion under Hellenistic rule, the Magi are prime candidates to have been instigators or heralds of religiously inspired resistance against Roman imperial domination.[80]

The travels of Tiridates shed light on the role of, and the widespread fascination with (and consequently their contribution to the existence of equivocal and mystifying information), the Magi. In 66 CE Rome agreed to accept the Parthian candidate for king in Armenia if he would receive his crown from the hands of the Roman emperor. Thus the Armenian king Tiridates, accompanied by the sons of three neighboring Parthian rulers, made a nine month journey from the Euphrates to Naples to visit Nero. With an entourage of relatives, servants, three thousand horsemen and numerous Romans this triumphal procession was greeted with pomp and occasion in various cities along the route (picture the impact of such a group travelling through rural areas, confiscating supplies and commandeering assistance). The senior Pliny describes this Tiridates as a *Magus*,[81] and says that Tiridates brought Magi with him and initiated Nero into their banquets.

We have here prime circumstances for the development of rumors, particularly rumors that, while seeking the truth, attempt to express hoped-for liberation from foreign domination. Stories not unlike that which we find in Matt 2:1–12.

---

79. Bickerman and Tadmor, "Darius I," 250–59; Hengel and Merkel, "Die Magier," 142–46; Aus, "Magi," 110–13; all with many references to source material, of which Strabo 15.3.13–15 and Pliny, *Nat.Hist.* 24.102.160, 164–165; 25.5.13; 25.79.106 are particularly relevant.

80. Cicero (*On divination* 1.23.47) tells us that, "Everybody knows that on the same night that in which Olympias was delivered of Alexander the temple of Diana at Ephesus was burned, and that the Magi began to cry out as the day was breaking: 'Asia's deadly curse was born last night.'"

81. Pliny, *Nat. Hist.* 30.6.16.

Political Rumors

According to Kapferer political rumors amount to infinite variations on a small number of themes, such as the invisible hand, power or secret society that is controlling the flow of events, the revelation of the hidden or true meaning or agenda of things or persons, concern about morality and the movement of people.[82]

In this type of rumor stories we see a distinctive form of reality creation. When marginalized and perceived to be at times in the opposition, people challenge official reality by proposing other realities. In this sense we find that rumors are not substitutes; they constitute, rather, a complementary media—that of proposing an alternative reality.

These rumors aim at provocation. They attempt to create a more favorable psychological climate and thereby to put pressure on those in power. One can also find instances of wish fulfilment in political rumors.

A powerful stimulus for political rumors would be the configuration of eschatological myths, imperial propaganda, *adventus* coins and hearsay about Nero *Redivivus*.[83] A case related to the synoptic tradition that comes to mind is the prophecies of the destruction of the Temple by Jesus, and the related eschatological speech(es). The many source and tradition critical problems with these sayings of Jesus are well-known, and the hypothesis that there is an "apocalyptic flysheet" (ein apokalyptisches Flugblatt) underlying Mark 13 has found new support.[84]

A relevant example of an important (given a "Jewish" context and the concomitant social/religious values) yet ambiguous series of events is the sequence of negotiations between Gaius and Petronius, winter 39/40 until April 41 CE.

These events took place during the reign of Gaius Caligula (37–41 CE) about whom all rejoiced at first, the Jews included.[85] Though the first eighteen

---

82. Kapferer, *Rumors*, 215–25.

83. Cf. Kreitzer, "Hadrian and the Nero *redivivus* Myth," 95–99; Kreitzer, "Sibylline Oracles 8."

84. Particularly by Pesch, *Naherwartungen*, 207–23, who argues that Mark 13:6, 22, 7b, 8, 12, 13b, 14–20a(18?), and 24–27 reflect the original tract. Bultmann (*History of the Synoptic Tradition*, 125) considered Mark 13:5–27 to be "a Jewish Apocalypse with a Christian editing."

85. "When Gaius succeeded to the sovereignty, we were the first of the inhabitants of Syria to show our joy. Vitellius . . . during his stay in our city received the news, and it was from our city that the glad tidings (εὐαγγελιουμένη) spread. Our Temple was the first to accept sacrifices on behalf of Gaius's reign" (Philo, *Embassy to Gaius* 32.231–32). On the oath of loyalty: Josephus, *Antiquities* 18.124.

months—with regard to relationships with Jewish people—went peacefully, a bloody pogrom broke out in Alexandria, with considerable consequences for the relationship between Jews and imperial power.[86] Despite severe suffering and various efforts to appease matters, affairs remained unsettled until the death of Gaius Caligula, after which Claudius immediately restored the right to practice Jewish customs in Alexandria.

At the same time, in Palestine, a storm broke out at Jamnia (a town in the coastal plain inhabited mainly by Jews) when an altar dedicated to the emperor was destroyed. The procurator (or imperial tax collector) of the city,[87] Herennius Capito, reported this to the emperor. Gaius saw this as an act of audacious disloyalty and promptly ordered that a statue with his effigy be set up in the temple in Jerusalem.[88] The emperor knew perfectly well that there would be considerable resistance to the idea, and Publius Petronius, governor of Syria, was ordered to proceed with half the army stationed in Syria to Palestine to enforce compliance to Gaius' will. Petronius, apparently a capable and reasonable administrator, tried to deal with these commands as responsibly as possible (winter 39/40 CE).[89] While the statue was being prepared in Sidon, he sent for various Jewish leaders and tried to persuade them to accept the situation, without success.

The news of what was in store soon spread all over Palestine and people gathered in great masses at Ptolemais, where Petronius had his headquarters. "The multitude of Jews covered all Phoenicia like a cloud."[90]

A large deputation appeared before Petronius and he did his utmost to postpone the execution of the imperial orders through various means. When Caligula received Petronius' report (arguing for the postponement of the erection of the statue), he wrote Petronius a letter of acknowledgement congratulating him on his prudence but urging him to proceed as soon as possible. Petronius prolonged matters,[91] led his army back to Antioch (autumn 40) and wrote to Caligula arguing the prudence of revoking the edict, after extensive negotiations with Jewish leaders.

At that very moment Gaius sent a letter to Petronius informing him that nothing was to be changed in the Jerusalem Temple. Right after this

---

86. Balsdon, *Gaius (Caligula)*, 111–45.

87. Philo (*Embassy* 30.199) calls him the tax-collector (ἐκλογεὺς) for Judaea. Josephus (*Antiquities* 18.158) describes him as the procurator of Jamnia.

88. Philo, *Embassy* 30.230.

89. Ibid., 31.207–223; Josephus, *Antiquities* 18.261–268.

90. Philo, *Embassy* 32.226.

91. Philo says βραδὺς ἢ ἐγχειρητής, ibid., 31.213

letter, the emperor regretted and gave orders for a new statue to be made in Rome that would be taken by himself to Palestine. In January 41 Gaius received Petronius' petition and responded with an order that Petronius should commit suicide. On the 24th of January 41 Gaius was murdered. Petronius received the news of the emperor's death in March, and the command to commit suicide in April.[92]

In all this we have distinct evidence of the interplay of both importance and ambiguity: the impact of emperor worship, important cultural values[93] and little knowledge of and insight into official doings and arrangements (particularly without hindsight and written sources like we have) among the majority of people who felt affected by all this. The rise of apocalyptic rumors within the Jesus movement, based upon sayings understood to be relevant to these events are quite likely. Like other political rumors, Mark 13 has attention-getting and dramatic ingredients. It legitimates a cosmology for members of some strands of the early Jesus movement, justifies their fears and explains their anxieties.

Counter-rumor

Sometimes, rumors come into being with the aim of countering well-known and accepted hearsay, or of engaging disinformation. A possible example of such a reaction story could be the foundation for parts of the resurrection stories. Matthew 28:11–15 reflects an example of an "official" report and Matt 28:1–10, 16–20 the Christian response.

A form of counter-rumor that probably contributed to the development of the gospel traditions are hostile rumors. These are rumors that sow dissension in a larger group and are sometimes based on fear and anxiety that find an outlet in aggression directed at a scapegoat.

The New Testament is inundated with polemical and even defamatory traditions, and the role of "opponent" studies and anti-Jewish polemic is considered fundamental to reconstructing the "theologies" of the various early Christian authors. However, it is quite plausible that at least aspects of these polemical traditions could be related to the social dynamics of

92. For this see Josephus, *Jewish War* 2.184–203, *Antiquities* 18.298–18.309; Philo, *Embassy* 32.225–33.253. It is not easy to elucidate the sequence of events, as "the story has been much embroidered in the telling" (Balsdon, *Gaius (Caligula)*, 136).

93. Philo writes that "the Jews would willingly endure to die not once but a thousand times, if it were possible, rather than allow any of the prohibited actions to be committed. For all men guard their customs, but this is especially true of the Jewish nation" (*Embassy* 31.209–10).

groups attempting self-definition and responding to criticism (and slanderous rumors).[94] For a variety of reasons, many stories circulating in the Jesus movement targeted the (proto-)pharisaic rabbis—who, although they were a minority group pre-70, were probably often admired and/or feared and therefore perfect targets for rumors.

This type of information constitutes news: we expect negative people to commit negative acts. Negative acts are considered such because they are perceived to endanger the collectivity. A rumor of this kind feeds stereotypes: it justifies prejudices about the "other" ("them") and those who are not integrated into the community. It authorizes the open expression of aggressiveness in a safe way. Information in the form of hostile rumors has not only an alerting function, but also one of expressing and strengthening prejudices. A group becomes aware of its own existence and power as the rumor spreads farther and wider. A negative rumor is a powerful lever with which to reconstitute threatened social cohesion.

Numinous Places and Events

The confession of Peter and the transfiguration of Jesus[95] have defied all attempts at sorting out the synoptic relationships or possible sources and traditions. It is possible to suggest a scenario that could explain the extensive divergences in a tradition manifestly of great importance to early Christianity.

When one comes into contact with a powerful, charismatic person, or stays at a place perceived as numinous, one is easily confronted with ambiguity. Nickelsburg has pointed out that the immediate environment of Tel Dan in Upper Galilee has a long history as sacred territory. Mount Hermon, in particular, was considered to be a numinous area.[96]

Given the appearance of a powerful teacher/healer, reports of a messianic confession, the overlay of economic and religious tensions, all connected to a geographical region believed to be sacred, rumors about epiphanic commissioning would summarize all these elements convincingly.

94. Some early Christian groups tended to emphasize their separation and to reinforce their exclusiveness (to which Paul made no small contribution—e.g., 1 Corinthians 10). "They met in private houses, discreetly closed off from the street, and what went on in those meetings reinforced their sense that their true allegiance lay here rather than . . . outside" (Stambaugh and Balch, *New Testament*, 58–59). This style naturally encourages rumours, see Wilken, *Christians as the Romans Saw Them*, 1–62.

95. Mark 8:27—9:10; Matt 16:13—17:9, Luke 9:18–36.

96. Nickelsburg, "Enoch, Levi, and Peter," 582–83.

Some Implications and Concluding Remarks

The trajectories underlying the gospel traditions are of fundamental importance to understanding earliest Christianity. Despite several shortcomings, the informal, freely developing concept of tradition transmission still merits attention. This chapter presents an argument for analysing the transmission process with a social-scientific model developed from rumor research.

The elements of rumor are part of the social dynamics with which a group of people cope with changing circumstances, maintain or re-create reality and relieve anxiety. The proposed model was matched to aspects of the origins, background and evolution of parts of the synoptic gospel traditions, such as the birth narratives, healing and resurrection stories.

Besides the illustrative descriptive power generated by applying rumor research to the transmission of the Jesus stories, some general conclusions can also be drawn.

The first would obviously be with regard to the synoptic problem. A long time ago Westcott had argued for the relative independence of the Gospels, against theories of literary dependence, by referring to "the successive remoulding of the oral Gospel according to the peculiar requirements of different classes of hearers."[97] Right up to this day, many New Testament scholars still fail to engage the extensive body of knowledge with regard to orality and informal communication, in order to do better source and tradition criticism. What often happens is that "oral tradition" gets smuggled into the discussion without a formal examination of that category, merely in order to cover up difficulties with a purely documentary solution. The proposals in this chapter attempt to counter that tendency.

The context of an informal, evolutionary process also aids in explaining, in part at least, the anonymity of the Gospels. The anonymity of the Gospels makes it extremely difficult to say what the position of the gospel writer is in relation to the community tradition which he collects and edits[98]—a fact of severe implication for redaction criticism and narratological analyses of the Gospels. Utilizing relevant research about oral tradition (and also rumor research) shows how inappropriate many of the categories of established gospel criticism are.

Finally, the study of rumors confronts us with a question of vast epistemological—and consequently of theological—importance: why do we believe what we believe?

97. Westcott, *Introduction to the Study of the Gospels*, 214.

98. Simonsen, "Gospel Literature as a Source," 4.

A rumor process is, in the end, only a speeded up version of the comprehensive, imperceptible process through which we acquire all of our ideas, opinions, images and beliefs. Rumor research leads us once more to the realisation that reality is socially constructed. Certainty, in a final sense, is social: what the group to which we belong considers to be true *is* true. Truth is not something in itself: it is there, but always stands in relation to people.

Unfounded information can circulate in society as easily as established knowledge and has the same mobilizing effects.

A substantial percentage of our knowledge is, perhaps, unbeknownst to us, totally ungrounded. Rumors reconfirm something that is self-evident: we do not believe what we know because it is true, founded or proven. With all due measure we can affirm the opposite: it is true because we believe it.[99]

Therefore, understanding rumor leads us to religion. Like rumors, religion has its strength due to contagious beliefs. What matters to us is what someone we trust told us about. Truly, in the beginning was the word.

Knowledge is a fragile thing, and our vigilance and honesty are our only protection.

99. Kapferer, *Rumors*, 264.

8

Mark's Story as Oral Traditional Literature

The Origins of the Markan Gospel

To see the gospel of Mark as traditional material is certainly not a new observation. One can safely claim that it is almost standard practice, showing
that contrary to popular opinion, New Testament scholarship can reach consensus. However, what exactly is meant by claiming Mark to be traditional
elicits widely diverging answers.

Mark is usually seen as a "mixture" of tradition and redaction; tradition
referring to stories, sayings, words and short descriptions that the evangelist
(Mark) received from others. Most of these, either as such or at least their
essentials, are considered by scholars to be probably authentic. Redaction
then refers to the additions and interpretations of the author himself, changing—more or less—the received parts into a so-called gospel. How this
sort of activity should be pictured *historically* receives very little attention
in current research. Broadly speaking, two basic trends can be identified:
emphasizing continuity between tradition and redaction or alternatively
underscoring creative interpretation.

The work of Birger Gerhardsson can be used as a convenient illustration of the first trend, in that the picture he draws of the history of the
gospel traditions probably reflects many scholars' unspoken assumptions.
Gerhardsson emphasizes the fact that there "is certainly a complicated
development behind our synoptic Gospels,"[1] "a drawn-out and involved
process."[2] He argues for a balanced and extended perspective on the origin
and history of the synoptic tradition, stressing the interaction between the

1. Gerhardsson, *Origins*, 77.
2. Ibid., 76.

whole and the parts, "between the total view [of the Jesus traditions] and the concrete formation of the material."[3] However, he clearly sees the process as one of *linear development*: "private notes were probably made rather early. As time went on, blocks of tradition, large and small, have been put together, and eventually the time was ripe for the first Gospel in our sense of the word."[4] The development from the historical Jesus to gospel texts is, in Gerhardsson's view, the result of the disciples continuing what Jesus himself started. "Turning to Jesus' oral teaching, we must reckon with the fact that he used a method similar to that of Jewish—and Hellenistic—teachers: the scheme of text and interpretation, He must have made his disciples learn certain sayings off by heart: if he taught, he must have required his disciples to memorize."[5]

The Twelve, therefore, should be seen as a *collegium*, a "rabbinic academy" supervising ὁ λόγος τοῦ κυρίου, "i.e. the Holy Scriptures and the tradition from, and about, Christ"[6] during the decades following Jesus' crucifixion. "We must at all events take into account the fact that the actual transmission of such collections of traditions about Jesus was a distinct activity—a direct methodical delivery . . . The traditionist/teacher passed on the tractate, passage or saying to his pupil or pupils by means of continuous repetition; he taught the pupil to repeat it, after which he gave the required interpretation."[7]

Many scholars disagree with Gerhardsson on the extent of continuity between tradition and gospel text. In contrast, the unity of the text is posited and the all-encompassing input of the final redactor is stressed. Following the logic of this trend in gospel criticism, namely that the evangelists are authors, *interpreting* their received traditions, editorial activity can turn into active criticism of the tradition.[8]

However, Gerhardsson's criticism against the form-critical scholars, "that their work is not sufficiently *historical*,"[9] can also be extended to most discussions about Mark's creativity and/or literary activity. Those who understand the gospel of Mark as "narrative" or as "literature" tend to assume that these analytical concepts can be divorced from their historical

---

3. Ibid., 76.

4. Ibid., 76.

5. Gerhardsson, *Memory and Manuscript*, 328.

6. Ibid., 329–31

7. Ibid., 334.

8. E.g. Weeden, *Mark—Traditions in Conflict*; Kelber, "Apostolic Tradition."

9. Gerhardsson, *Origins*, 8.

communicative contexts. As little as one can speak of other social conventions as if unrelated to concrete historical and cultural phenomena, can one speak of "narrative" or "literature" without reference to text production, or outside social constructions such as authority, speaker, audiences, etc. It is in this sense that the questions about the transmission of (at least some) Jesus-traditions, the origins of the Markan gospel and the interpretation of the text as we have it, are involved with each other.

The major assumption underlying usual thinking about the origins of the gospels is that tradition and redaction are distinguishable and therefore separable from each other. The assumption is used to explain certain characteristics of the texts and this explanation is confirmed by thinking about tradition as *accruing* redaction. The traditional material is widely accepted as having been mainly oral material.

On the other hand, emphasizing the pervasive role of interpretation, that is, so-called radical redaction criticism, or consistent narratological approaches, raises the issue of continuity with tradition, or put more simply, of invention. But even this approach still assumes that tradition can somehow be "extracted," for otherwise it would not have been possible to recognize editorial activity.

Proving—or disproving—is of course strictly speaking impossible. Plausibility is, however, another matter. For instance, many studies have suggested that, seen within literary history, Mark's gospel stands quite close to popular, traditional texts.[10] The narrative lacks the consistency that one would expect from a sophisticated researcher—and although this is not a strong argument, it points away from Mack's picture of composition at a desk in a scholar's study lined with texts.[11] More importantly is that that sort of picture does not fit into a historical reconstruction of text-production in antiquity.[12]

The critical question—*how we should picture the transmission of the gospel tradition*—is inescapable in solving some questions about Mark's gospel. With this in mind it is of considerable importance to take into account the

---

10. Reiser, *Syntax und Stil*, 168; Votaw, *Gospels and Contemporary Biographies*, 1–2; Schmidt, *Die Stellung der Evangelien*, 127; Deissmann, *Light*, 247; Smith, *Comments*, 38 n.23; Hadas, *History*, 266; Bilezikian, *Liberated Gospel*, 19.

11. Mack, *Myth of Innocence*, 322–23.

12. Kenyon, *Books and Readers*, 66–85; Reynolds and Wilson, *Scribes and Scholars*; Künzl, "Die Entwicklung," 275–7; Eisenstein, *Printing Revolution*, 7; Boring, *Literacy in Ancient Sparta*, 62–3; Wiseman, "Practice and Theory," 384–87; Graham, *Beyond the Written Word*, 30–36; Saenger, "Silent Reading," 370–73.

various criticisms brought in against form criticism for not taking relevant sociological and linguistic research serious enough.[13]

Transmission and Composition of Tradition

Suppose we were to see the gospel of Mark as "oral traditional literature" it may be possible to approach the complexities of the story with a terminologically different discourse and have the advantage of multi-disciplinary research as "constraints."

When arguing for Mark to be approached as oral traditional literature, the use of the term "oral" reflects the generally accepted oral background of the Markan material as well as the historically given situation of a scribal culture, heavily oriented towards orality. The term "traditional" refers to the composition *technique* described by the oral formulaic theory. In other words, the proposal is that the narrative making up the gospel of Mark as "oral literature" was not transmitted verbatim through memorization, nor came into being as a creative reinterpretation, but was instead composed and recited with slight variations at various performances, and that *the text as we now have it* is but an instance, a reflection of one performance, of that traditional *process.*

The so-called "oral formulaic theory" or Parry-Lord theory is certainly one of the most widely used approaches to folklore and, more specifically, to traditions with a possible oral background.[14] Lord's study has been extended to materials composed in many different languages whose geography circles the entire globe.[15] To show the possible relevance of it to the analysis and interpretation of the gospel of Mark, it is necessary to discuss Lord's exposition in some detail.

Oral Formulaic Theory

In the introduction to *The Singer of Tales* Lord claims that "This is a book about Homer."[16] His purpose is more than simply arguing for possible orality with regard to the Homeric question; he aims at studying a specific type of

---

13. Sanders, *Tendencies*, 8–21; Brewer, "Gospels and the Laws of Folktale," 37; Güttgemanns, *Candid Questions*, 193–211; Abel, "Psychology of Memory"; Gager, "Gospels and Jesus"; Kelber, "Mark and Oral Tradition."

14. Foley, "Series Foreword," xii; Foley, "Oral Theory."

15. Renoir, "Oral-Formulaic Context," 418; Foley, "Introduction," 17–70.

16. Lord, *Singer of Tales*, iii.

oral communication and to make the results relevant to the interpretation of other texts.

Basic to Lord's approach is that the transmission of oral traditional material does not happen by rote memorization of fixed stories. Recounting traditions is done by dynamic, thriving and unique narrations by specific and talented individuals, not by nameless tradents. This is the opposite of the claims of *Formgeschichte*.[17] Traditional storytellers use phraseology and narrative themes provided by tradition and the particular story itself.

In *The Singer of Tales* Lord develops his argument in two parts: a theoretical part defining "oral epic song," which is then applied in the second part to Homer and other epic poetry. He bases his theory on the ideas of Milman Parry of utilizing empirical research done among existing "oral cultures" as comparative material and control in historical studies.[18] Parry and Lord completed extensive fieldwork in this regard among the folk singers and poets of the Balkan states during the thirties of the twentieth century, and also after the Second World War by Lord and his students. The theory is therefore based on comparative philology.

Lord himself applied some of his insights to the question of relationships among the Synoptic Gospels,[19] suggesting the relevance of his research for understanding the traditional nature of the gospels. Discussing the theory in this context is not to claim that the gospels in any sense resemble poetic or epic literature, but to develop a framework for understanding the traditional nature of the gospels. The suggestion is that utilizing and developing relevant theories from various disciplines can result in fruitful research as well as contribute to critical discussion of these theories.

Some Important Characteristics of Oral Traditional Composition according to Lord

Composition in Performance: The Tradent as Creative Carrier of Tradition

The oral poet/singer does not plan his song beforehand. Composition happens in the performance itself: the singer himself is the tradition in the moment of delivery. He is more than an expert of the tradition; he is organically

---

17. E.g., Schmidt, "Die Stellung der Evangelien," 166–74; Dibelius, *Formgeschichte*, 2–3.

18. Cf. A. Parry, "Introduction," xxxii–xli.

19. Lord, "Gospels as Oral."

part thereof: "not a mere carrier of the tradition but a creative artist making the tradition."[20] A performance is not a mechanical recital but something unique every time. Each performance is indeed a poem in its own right, stamped by "the signature of its poet singer."[21] The stories making up oral traditions are composed and "re-composed" each time that they are recited. A recording or transcription can never be *the* version of the song. The perfect or master version simply does not exist. In fact, the idea of an original version has, in this context and for this cultural phenomenon, little meaning.[22] Lord notes the "textual fluidity" of "oral traditional narrative."[23]

The Effect of the Audience

The interaction between listeners and singer has a powerful effect on the transmission of traditional material. A good singer must have considerable "dramatic ability and narrative skill," demanding "a marked degree of concentration"[24] in order to capture the attention of an audience with words only. The "setting" of oral composition demands both pace and flexibility. The specific techniques of oral composition enable the narrator/singer to keep the attention of his audience. These techniques consist of the use of formulas and themes. In this regard Rosenberg refers to the "aesthetics of form," "the various methods the artist employs to affect the traditional audience."[25] Style and diction are heavily influenced by the particular audience: the challenge of successfully performing before an audience creates a subtle interaction with the audience in which the epic story literally grows "into" the audience.

Formulas and Themes

The concrete situation of the narrator/singer forces him to the extensive use of formulas and themes. These formulas and themes become part of his repertoire via his experience—of this and other "stories" and songs—and his "training." "Each such narrator, using the phrases and devices picked up

---

20. Lord, *Singer of Tales*, 13.
21. Ibid., 4.
22. Ibid., 100.
23. Ibid., 37.
24. Ibid., 16.
25. Rosenberg, "Oral Sermons," 92.

from others, develops his or her own usage of lines and half-lines, clusters and passages, but always within the parameters of the tradition."[26]

Formulas refer to fixed verbal and metrical combinations making up sentences and lines. Themes are "repeated incidents and descriptive passages,"[27] a grouping of ideas,[28] stylistically constructed—something similar to what New Testament scholarship calls *formgeschichtliche* forms. Formulas can be described as "repetitions, stock epithets, stereo-typed phrases": "a group of words which is regularly employed under the same metrical conditions to express a given essential idea";[29] "the most stable formulas are those for the most common ideas of the poetry: names of actors and of places, and the time and description of actions."[30] Formulas can be very flexible. The true amount of formulas used by a narrator/singer can be surprisingly small, due to the fact that different formulations can be created in analogy to existing ones and almost endless possibilities can be employed by adaptation of current formulas.[31]

At issue is not the existence of formulas but the implications of their presence. The "formulaic style of expression" points to the composition of the story. The narrator/singer must create his phrases by adapting known words or by using existing formulas. It is this ability that makes it possible for the singer of tales to remember immense epic stories without a computer-like memory.[32]

An important characteristic of these compositional units is the so-called "adding style": detailed descriptions with interruptions, many repetitions and insertions, as well as a paratactic style.[33] With regard to themes, Lord notes: "Formulas and groups of formulas, both large and small, serve only one purpose. They provide a means for telling a story . . . [Reading any] collection of oral epic . . . the same basic incidents and descriptions are met with time and again . . . Following Parry, I have called the groups of ideas regularly used in telling a tale in the formulaic style of traditional song the 'themes' of the poetry."[34]

26. Lord, "Gospels as Oral," 37.
27. Lord, *Singer of Tales*, 4.
28. Ibid., 69.
29. Ibid., 30.
30. Ibid., 31–33.
31. Ibid., 36–37.
32. Ibid., 44–46.
33. Ibid., 54–55, 65.
34. Ibid., 68.

Obviously there will be both "minor" and "major" themes[35] and smaller themes are often inserted into each other (one is immediately reminded of Mark's "sandwich" structure). Lord also discovered that in "a traditional poem . . . there is a pull in two directions: one is toward the song being sung and the other is toward the previous uses of the same theme. The result is . . . an occasional inconsistency . . ."[36] The singer concentrates on the different episodes while seeing the whole in terms of his major themes; a tension creating at times some narrative inconsistencies.[37]

A subject that Lord deems relevant for understanding the gospels is what he calls "traditional pattern of the life of the hero," a subdivision of "mythic patterns."[38] Should one see the gospels as oral traditional material, they

> must belong to a tradition of oral life story or biography . . . From the Old Testament we can see a repeated pattern of life stories of significant figures . . . Because the stories are of the leaders of Israel, both priestly and secular, we can also assume that these stories were told by certain members of the priestly or ruling class to the Israelites for cultic purposes. The story of Jesus would fit into such a tradition, but it would, of course, be a life story of the leader of another religious group, albeit a splinter one, told to members of this group for cultic purposes.[39]

Lord sees myth as "sacred narrative in the full truth and efficaciousness of which people believe."[40] The historicity of a narrative in a gospel is something different from the question about the patterns in which a narrative is mould.

> Traditional narrators tend to tell what happened in terms of already existent patterns of story. Since the already existing patterns allow for many multi-forms and are the result of oft repeated human experience, including spiritual experience, it is not difficult to adjust another special case to the flexibly interpreted story patterns . . . That its essence was consonant with an element in a traditional mythic (i.e., sacred) pattern adds a dimension of spiritual weight

35. Ibid., 71, 81.
36. Ibid., 94.
37. Ibid., 95, 99.
38. Lord, "Gospels as Oral," 38–39.
39. Ibid., 38.
40. Lord follows Eliade; see ibid., 38.

to . . . [an] incident, but it does not deny (nor does it confirm, for that matter) the historicity of the incident.[41]

The Conservative Aspect of Traditional Transmission

Seen in the light of the narrator/singer's "training" and self-consciousness, oral tradition can be described as a conservative system. The narrator/singer sees himself as "defender of the historic truth of what is being sung."[42] He will not admit to the existence of any differences between various "editions" of his own version, or even between his version and what he originally heard from somebody else. The conviction is simply that he sings it "exactly" as he himself heard it, even when it can be proven beyond doubt (with recordings) that variations do exist. That various singers perform the same epic story differently is due to the art of reciting and not because of any conscious effort by the narrator/singer. Through these performances the essence of the story is preserved, and must be preserved.[43] The tradent "is not concerned with transmission of text, but with transmission a) of the art of composition and b) of the story itself."[44]

Although the tradition is carried by various persons and delivered at many occasions, it is *necessarily* conservative in nature, "for it is of the *necessary* nature of tradition that it seek and maintain stability, that it preserve itself. And this tenacity springs neither from perverseness, nor from an abstract principle of absolute art, but from a desperately compelling conviction that what the tradition is preserving is the very means of attaining life and happiness."[45] Although each performance is unique, there are certain "essential themes" making up the "stable skeleton of narrative"—the Song or Epic as such. So long as the recital maintains these essential themes the narrative remains consistent and stable. Variations between performances is usually due to: (i) expressing the same thing differently (adapting to situation), (ii) extensions or embellishments by adding detail, (iii) adaptations due to local features, (v) deletions, or (vi) replacement of themes.[46]

---

41. Ibid., 39.
42. Lord, *Singer of Tales*, 28.
43. Ibid., 28–29.
44. Lord, "Gospels as Oral," 37.
45. Lord, *Singer of Tales*, 220.
46. Ibid., 123.

Traditional transmission in this sense is therefore a strong conservative force in protecting the essential or central themes of a tradition. The multiformity of a tradition is *itself* a preservative factor as variations are formed by "forces" *within* the tradition.[47] Themes are of major importance: "There is a close relationship between hero and tale, but with some tales at least the *type* of hero is more important than the *specific* hero."[48]

Objections

The discussion points to some questions that need attention before we can meaningfully apply these theoretical insights to the gospels.

Oral Formulaic Theory in Context

It is neither my intent, nor is this the place to put the oral formulaic theory and the critical discussion generated by its applications in its full context. Not that it is possible: in 1976 Miletich already remarked that studies "relating in some degree to the oral theory . . . are legion and, to understate the case, have readily managed to defy bibliographical containment."[49] It is truly "impossible to concur or quarrel with the theory's many, often brilliant, advocates or critics."[50] But it is important, and true to the spirit of fair interdisciplinary research, to discuss some significant aspects to demonstrate the necessity of a comprehensive grasp of the theory's strengths and limitations.

A hypothesis designed to explain recurring verbal and narrative units (epithets, formulaic expressions, ballad commonplaces)—which is *usually* explained as the result of either borrowing or memorial transmission—the oral formulaic theory attempts to specify the conventions responsible for the process by which language becomes traditional discourse. It also encompasses the role of various conventions of this process in narrative meaning. "This focus on process, rather than the resultant text, or product, is the most important and innovative contribution of the theory, often overlooked by both adherents and detractors."[51] Lord has written that "the Serbo-Croatian tradition can show us the importance of formulas and themes as the

---

47. Ibid., 120.
48. Ibid.
49. Miletich, "Quest for the 'Formula,'" 111 n. 2.
50. Edwards, "Parry–Lord Theory," 162 n. 1.
51. Ibid., 152, italics mine.

pragmatic basic composition of oral story verse."[52] He views tradition as a unified system that generates a whole or subset of that tradition.[53]

Two aspects of the extensive critical discussion surrounding the oral formulaic theory need some elucidation. The first aspect concerns the fact that it designates, strictly speaking, two theories,[54] the primary facet being compositional technique and oral performance; the secondary facet concerns textual characteristics and origins of written texts. Formulaic-thematic composition is so fundamental to Lord's approach that the theory is used to determine the possible orality of texts. Consequently, an important context for the application of the Parry-Lord hypothesis has been the assessment of oral or non-oral qualities of certain texts and questions of poetics as they relate to authorial origins of traditional texts. This aspect of the theory, "quantitative analysis," has generated extensive critical debates.

It is feasible for Lord to claim the possibility of a "quantitative analysis" because, while each performance of a singer of an oral narrative song may be different, there is a fundamental continuity both in the composition and the story line which is preserved in spite of other variations. Such relative stability is due to the singer's use of formulas, formulaic expressions, and themes he has learned from his predecessors—from a tradition of composition which may extend over many generations. This process of composition is not one of approximate or word for word memorization. Based on his research he argues:

(1) "An oral text will yield a predominance of clearly demonstrable formulas."[55]

(2) The presence of certain stylistic features: "enjambment, the 'adding' style'";[56] specifically meter and/or rhythm.

(3) "While these elements of formula pattern and enjambment are vastly important for stylistic analysis in determining whether any text is oral or 'literary,' of greater significance for an understanding of the development of literary epic is the change that takes place in the ideas, in the themes presented in epic by a literate oral poet. The oral epic poet needs well-established themes for rapid composition."[57]

52. Lord, "Perspectives on Recent Work," 12.
53. Lord, *Singer of Tale*, 5. Cf. Edwards, "Parry-Lord Theory," 183.
54. Bäuml, "Medieval Texts and the Two Theories," 32.
55. Lord, *Singer of Tales*, 130.
56. Ibid., 131.
57. Ibid.

However: "As with any theory, there are times when its doctrine must be followed absolutely and times when specifics must be altered in order to preserve the principles which underlie them."[58] In our case it would be foolish to attempt a "quantitative formulaic analysis." The departure from Lord's metrical standard would for the purposes of statistical analysis be a wrong appropriation of the theory.[59]

The other aspect of the theory that has drawn extensive criticism is the theory's oral-improvisational foundation. Finnegan asserts that some oral materials are memorized, some fully improvised, and some fall somewhere in between.[60] Similarly, but with more nuanced variations also Opland argues for a range of possibilities.[61] Smith discusses some Indian epic traditions that, though variations during recitation do occur, and contain underlying memorized formulas, are non-improvisatory.[62]

However, the theory does not want to cover every possible instance of oral material. Clearly, each case must be argued carefully to determine the degree of improvisation or memorization involved. One should keep in mind that the singer of tales sings lengthy tales, as well as many tales on many occasions. There is no need to criticize the theory for not covering the Pabujis, or all African songs. Lord describes the typical given situation of the singers that was studied, and which influences the *extent* of the theory. The application of the theory should be related to: performing in an informal context, a concern with extended narratives, and performers with an extensive repertoire of songs/traditions. Lord's call for "a broader concept of oral tradition"[63] is simply that any one song or poem is part of many performances of many songs and poems by many performers with a broad geographic range.[64]

For the purpose of interpreting Mark, the theory is not primarily adopted to assess the text's orality. I doubt whether the theory can be used to indicate orality outside epic poetry, and the oral aspects of Mark can be substantiated with historical arguments. My interest is the compositional technique described by the theory: to discuss the possibility of seeing prominent characteristics of the gospel of Mark as textual symptoms of this type

---

58. Miletich, "Quest for the 'Formula,'" 114.

59. Cf. ibid., 115.

60. Finnegan, *What Is Oral Literature Anyway?*, 158–59.

61. Opland, *Anglo-Saxon Oral Poetry*, 75–79.

62. Smith, "Singer or the Song?"

63. Lord, "Perspectives on Recent Work," 8.

64. Cf. Foley, *Oral Traditional Literature*, 27.

of composition. It is, therefore, important to bear in mind that not the oral formulaic theory as such, but the *process of traditional transmission* is of concern here. That the theory does explain some Markan problems provides additional confirmation of the text's oral context, but only in a secondary sense. The discussion is mainly a springboard for further development.

Comparable Texts?

Lord researched ballads and epic stories: "narrative poetry"/"oral epic song" built up out of "metrical lines and half-lines by means of formulas and formulaic expressions and of the building of songs by the use of themes."[65] The gospels clearly are narratives, prose materials; much closer to "oral history" than "oral epic literature."[66] But: "The two categories are not always mutually exclusive, however. Oral history is sometimes incorporated into oral traditional literature. The telling of recent events by someone who is also an active narrator of the oral traditional literature of a culture tends to follow the patterns of traditional story . . . Thus oral history sometimes may be manifested in parts in oral traditional literature."[67]

The question is about the essence of the theory: the traditional *technique* of composition. It is therefore interesting to note that the oral formulaic theory has been applied to widely diverging types of traditions. Two factors influenced the wide dissemination of the original Parry-Lord hypothesis. On the one hand: "A sign of the times in many of the studies on the functions of narratives is a liberal concept of tradition: for today's folklorists narration is not always just folktales or stories handed down for hundreds of years, but any stories reported in speech."[68] This has been facilitated by the growing conviction that formulaic style is *the* linguistic characteristic of oral traditional communication.[69] On the other hand, the theory offers many possibilities for comparative research. It provides a useful and verifiable methodological approach for understanding traditional literature of which the original contexts are for all practical purposes lost.[70]

---

65. Lord, *Singer of Tales*, 4.

66. See the clear exposition of Lord, "Gospels as Oral," 33–34.

67. Ibid., 36–37.

68. Lehtipuro, "Folk-narrative Research," 16.

69. Wittig, "Theories of Formulaic Narrative," 66; Gray, "Repetition in Oral Literature," 289; Lord, "Perspectives on Recent Work," 16.

70. Foley, "Tradition-dependent and -independent Features," 262.

Naturally, the various developments affected aspects of the theory, for instance the perspective on oral traditional formula. Parry's original definition, "a group of words which is regularly employed under the same metrical conditions to express a given essential idea"[71] was aimed at the analysis of the composition of the Homeric texts. Lord used the same definition for various poetic epics—already a significant extension of the original concept. According to Foley, Nagy queried the one way relationship usually emphasized between meter and formula: the meter is generated by the formula rather than the other way round.[72]

Studies focusing on formulaic style tend to emphasize the lexical and syntactical elements rather than mere rhythm. The conclusion that (parts of) the Homeric texts are 90% "formulaic"[73] "is likely to be vacuously, and so uselessly, true."[74] Gray considers it a loss that oral formulaic theory did not originally note the high frequency of formulas in oral prose.[75] The research done by Dégh on folktales also leads to a description of composition in terms of the theory. According to her a traditional narrative comes into being because traditional material "[is] fashioned from stable formulas commonly known to the tellers who adjust them to a basic outline kept together by a frame."[76] She sees formulas as (i) motifs—narrative units reflecting typical persons, scenes or events, (ii) frame notices, (iii) "patterned figures of speech," (iv) repetitions structuring the narrative apart from (ii) and (iii).[77]

The Gospels as Oral Literature?

Talbert voices a general objection against the use of the oral formulaic theory for gospel criticism when he emphasizes that the gospels are "literary and interdependent."[78] "Since mythic patterns are not the exclusive property of oral traditional literature, Lord's argument that the presence of such patterns in the Synoptics is an indication of the oral traditional character of these gospels must be regarded as inconclusive."[79] Talbert concludes from the

71. Parry, *Making of Homeric Verse*, 272.

72. Foley, "Tradition-dependent and -independent Features," 263.

73. Lord, *Singer of Tales*, 142–44.

74. Hainsworth, "Structure and Content," 157.

75. Gray, "Repetition in Oral Literature," 301–2.

76. Dégh, "Folk Narrative," 60.

77. Ibid., 61–66.

78. Talbert, "Oral and Independent."

79. Ibid., 95.

"inconclusive" that it is impossible. However, Lord simply wanted to investigate options: "I have searched in the gospels for evidence of oral traditional narrative mythic patterns, to see whether such patterns might have played a role in the *formation* of the gospels."[80]

For Lord there can be little doubt that the gospels "vary from one another to such an extent as to rule out the possibility that, as a whole, one could have been copied from another."[81] The differences and similarities between the Synoptics can be understood as a reflection of their oral background.[82] Talbert argues that "the divergent wording is no obstacle to our viewing the Synoptic Problem as a literary one. Given the practices of the Hellenistic Age, it is exactly what one would expect."[83] He refers to Josephus' editing of biblical history in his *Antiquitates*. Talbert also claims that "Tyson has shown that the agreement in order among the Synoptics is so high that a literary explanation *is necessary*."[84] But what makes this explanation necessary? Neither Tyson[85] nor Talbert explains or substantiates this *necessity*. The implied assumption is apparently that verbal agreement and structural similarity make anything but literary dependency impossible.

Lord has shown in his many publications that oral traditions agree to a greater or lesser extent due to many factors. *Verbal agreement as such* is no argument against oral characteristics. It is problematic to compare a gospel such as Mark with Josephus (in contrast to Luke).[86] There are significant differences between the gospels, especially Mark, and other contemporary literature. But more fundamentally: one should in principle not approach the synoptic question with twentieth century ideas about textuality and literary activities. The possibilities of orality research for rethinking the synoptic problems are extensive.[87]

Talbert's statement: "In Mediterranean antiquity an author could select from several sources and alternate them in patches or blocks without any hesitation"[88] reflects *literate, typographic* assumptions about ancient authors. The sheer physical difficulties of having to cope with bulky *manuscripts*

---

80. Lord, "Gospels as Oral," 90, italics mine.
81. Ibid., 90.
82. Cf. Vansina, *Oral Tradition as History*, 159
83. Talbert, "Oral and Independent," 95.
84. Ibid., 96, italics mine.
85. Tyson, "Sequential Parallelism."
86. See Downing, "Common Ground"; Downing, "Redaction Criticism."
87. E.g. MacDonald, "From *Audita* to *Legenda*," 23–25, on miracle stories.
88. Talbert, "Oral and Independent," 99.

make Talbert's picture unlikely. The argument: "Christianity emerged in a Mediterranean culture that was not illiterate . . . Books were produced on a scale theretofore unknown. A large reading public . . . ,"[89] though formally true, has little impact. The educational attainment of the average person in the Greco-Roman world in terms of modern conceptions of literacy was negligible. Concepts such as *illiterate*, or *literacy* are very much culture specific, historically determined.[90] The experience of books in a world where children were taught to *recite* Homer instead of reading the text, is quite different to ours.

The Appropriateness of the Oral-Formulaic Theory

To conclude this section, the validity of applying the oral formulaic theory to solving some questions generated by Mark's gospel cannot be doubted.

It is possible to argue for prominent oral features of Mark's gospel on different grounds, especially historical ones, and the applicability of the oral formulaic theory lies in illuminating the traditional composition process. The extensive debate generated by the application of "quantitative formulaic analysis" warns one that it is something of a dead end. The true impact of the theory does not lie in testing for orality. The immense complexities of human communication exclude a straightforward statistical measure of syntactical patterns as proof of orality (assuming that "orality" is a useful, clear concept).

The search is for an answer to the question about the transmission and origins of the Gospel of Mark. The oral formulaic theory provides the means to picture a narrator composing his story with the aid of his internalized grammar of tradition.

Mark as Oral Traditional Composition

How the gospel of Mark came into being is a historical question and can only be answered by virtue of comparative criticism. So to pose the question is to ask whether the gospel reflects a formulaic style with thematic composition—in that case we are on the trail of Mark *the traditional storyteller*.

89. Ibid., 101–2.
90. Street, *Literacy in Theory and Practice*, 8–11.

Formulaic Style in Mark

The discussion about formulas within the application of the oral formulaic theory is wide ranging and comprehensive. On the one hand the very existence of formulas have been questioned—at least their possible appearance outside the Homeric and Slavic song-epics. Furthermore, should one redefine the essence of formulas, it may lead to the likelihood of becoming so abstract or general that all explanatory power is lost.

In this regard Rosenberg provides some valuable insights. He refers to the "chaotic situation regarding definitions of the formula: every man his own definition."[91] His research on popular sermons leads him "to question the usefulness of the very concepts of 'formula' and 'system.' These terms, given us by Parry, connote something precise, mechanical and above all, autonomous. No doubt such an attitude is a concomitant of the philosophy which was the legacy of the New Criticism . . ."[92] "With a fixed text in front of us we can define formulas as precisely or as liberally as we choose, but the singers are not thinking in terms of formulas and systems. One of the problems in defining these terms comes about because they are the scholar's attempts to impose a logical precision, a rationale, and a method where no such logical, rational method exists in the field—the singer's mind."[93] However, his conclusions are also highly relevant. Although the "oral sermons" studied by him are far removed from Homer and southern Yugoslavia in both time and geography, he found similar consistencies with regard to diction and style. His own words: the same theoretical assumptions were confirmed.[94]

Two developments are noteworthy in connection with the dissemination of the oral formulaic theory: emphasis on the wide range of fixedness and novelty with regard to lexical and syntactical repetitions; "familiar combinations of words, familiar syntactic patterns and so on,"[95] and the focus on matters of content, what Culley calls "stock episode, stock incident, or core plot . . . stringing together a series of standard elements."[96] Tannen notes, for example, that formulaic expressions, that is, "sayings, clichés, proverbs, and so on," "the repository of received wisdom," "function as wholes, as a

91. Rosenberg, "Oral Sermons," 96.
92. Ibid.
93. Ibid., 98.
94. Ibid., 76, 94.
95. Tannen, "Oral/Literate Continuum," 6.
96. Culley, "Oral Tradition," 9–10.

convenient way to signal knowledge that is already shared. In oral tradition, it is not assumed that the expressions contain meaning in themselves . . ."[97] When looking at possible formulaic style in Mark, preference should be given to phenomena typical of Mark's gospel, simply by reason of control: an expression could definitely have been said differently, or with greater variation. Since I am interested in proving that Mark's use of the compositional process implied by the oral formulaic theory can explain most of the prominent characteristics of the Markan gospel, it follows that I use the principle underlying the strict definition of formula.

Certain phrases in Mark can easily be identified as stylized expressions that may leap to the tongue, so to speak, when a new thought or saying needs to be formulated; as for example ἤρξατο διδάσκειν (4:1; 6:2; 6:34; 8:31). Mark provides us with several examples of regularly recurring, at times almost rhythmical, wording. So, for instance, the repeated use of the same verb in the same context (e.g., παρατιθέναι in 8:6–7; ἀκούειν in 6:20)[98] or of compound verbs with a repetition of the preposition (e.g., εἰς . . . εἰσέρχεσθαι 1:21, 45; 2:1, 26; 3:1, 27; 5:12, 13; 6:10; 7:17, 24; 9:25, 28, 45–47; 10:15, 23–25; εἰσπορεύεσθαι . . . εἰς 1:21; 6:56; 7:15, 18, 19; 11:2).

Initially, and in some applications of the oral formulaic theory the stylized use of epitaphs played an important part.[99] The use of a "noun-epithet formula" "suggests . . . habitual use or tradition."[100] We do not find in Mark such stylized use of epitaphs. Apparently that is particularly characteristic of oral poetries. However, there is in Mark an intriguing stereotyped use of names. For example:

- Πέτρος καὶ Ἰάκωβος καὶ Ἰωάννης (in this sequence)—5:37; 9:2; 14:33.

- Andrew is *always* named with Peter—1:16, 29; 3:8; 13:3.

- James is *always* named with John, and in this order—in addition to the texts cited above also 1:29, 10:35,41; compare 1:16–19; 3:16–18.

- Μαρία ἡ Μαγδαληνή and others and Σαλώμη: in this sequence only in Mark (15:40; 16:1).

97. Tannen, "Oral/Literate Continuum," 1–2.

98. Cf. Neirynck, *Duality in Mark*, 77–81.

99. Whallon, *Formula, Character, and Context*, 71–116; Parry, *Making of Homeric Verse*, 13–4.

100. Edwards, "Parry-Lord Theory," 160.

- οἱ ἀρχιερεῖς καὶ οἱ γραμματεῖς in this sequence—10:33; 11:18; 14:1; 15:31. Also note οἱ ἀρχιερεῖς καὶ οἱ γραμματεῖς καὶ οἱ πρεσβύτεροι: 8:31; 11:27; 14:43, 53; 15:1.

- The protagonist is tagged with various descriptive names: Χριστός (8x), but only once Jesus Christ (1:1); Ἰησοῦς (ὁ) Ναζαρηνός (12:4, 10:47, 14:67, 16:6); υἱός τοῦ θεοῦ (8x); υἱός τοῦ ἀνθρώπου (13x), and twice ὁ υἱός μου ὁ ἀγαπητός (1:11; 9:7); possibly 12:6.

- Other instances could be: οἱ δώδεκα—3:16; 4:10; 6:7; 9:35; 10:32; 11:11; 14:10, 17, 20, 43; Ἰωάννης ὁ βαπτίζων—1:4; 6:14, 24; and τὸ ὄρος τῶν ἐλαιῶν—11:1; 13:3; 14:26.

Certain phrases suggest an almost involuntary repetition used as introduction to narrative units or expressions. Examples are:

- καὶ ἔλεγεν αὐτοῖς (direct speech by Jesus)—2:27; 4:2, 11, 21, 24; 6:4, 10; 7:9; 8:21; 9:1, 31; 11:17. In 4:2; 9:31; and 11:17 the phrase is combined with ἐδίδασκεν. One can also point to καὶ λέγει αὐτοῖς and other variations (καὶ λέγει|-ουσιν and καὶ ἔλεγεν|-ον) of which instances abound in Mark.

- ἀποκριθεὶς . . . λέγει (+ dative) for direct speech—3:33; 8:29; 9:5, 19; 10:24; 11:22, 33; 15:2.

- προσκαλεσάμενος . . . λέγει | ἔλεγεν—3:23; 7:14; 8:1; 10:42.

- It is quite possible that Mark's use of εὐθύς (1:10, 12, 18, 20, 21, 23, 28 30, 42, 43; 2:8, 12; 3:6; 4:5, 15–17, 29; 5:2, 29, 30, 42; 6:25, 27, 45, 50, 54; 7:25; 8:10; 9:15, 20, 24; 10:52; 11:2, 3; 14:43, 45, 72; 15:1) and the predilection for ἄρχεσθαι with infinitive (1:45; 2:23; 4:1; 5:17, 20; 6:2, 7, 34, 55; 8:11, 31, 32; 10:28, 32, 41, 47; 11:15; 12:1; 13:5; 14:19, 33, 65, 69, 71; 15:8, 18) also reflects this aspect.

A prominent feature of Mark is a penchant for double expressions (e.g., 6:7; 14:19) and the habit of using series of threes.[101] Interesting is also the description of the crowd in 6:39–40: συμπόσια συμπόσια—πρασιαὶ πρασιαὶ—κατὰ ἑκατὸν καὶ κατὰ πεντήκοντα. There are many more instances of repeated phrases in Mark which can be seen (heard!) as refrains, with an almost cliché-like use.[102] Thus, we find lexical and syntactical characteristics that can be interpreted as reflecting oral traditional composition.

101. Neirynck, *Duality in Mark*, 110–12.

102. Botha, "Die Dissipels," 44–48; cf. the extensive lists of Markan "redactional"

Mark and Thematic Composition

The other essential aspect of oral composition identified by the Parry-Lord hypothesis is the performer's use of themes. That is the "passages" and "incidents" identified by Parry and named "themes" by Lord, "groups of ideas regularly used in telling a tale."[103] The repetition at stake here refers to *typical events*. Lord, for example, identifies the "theme of assembly" in the *Iliad*.[104] He also developed a typology of themes and analyzed their internal structure and contents, distinguishing between "composition theme" with a high degree of verbal agreement, and "type-scene" wherein one finds "a given set of repeated elements or details, not all of which are always present, nor always in the same order, but enough of which are present to make the scene a recognizable one."[105] Examples of both can be found in Mark.

Once again, it must be emphasized that for the purposes of this study the focus is on the *possibility* of thematic composition. The first association in this regard is the well-known forms identified by *Formgeschichte*, especially pronouncement stories and various miracle stories. These themes are not about social situation, but about the need of a narrator when learning or developing a story. Themes allow the narrator to use structure and "artistic imagination" in a situation of oral communication.[106]

Motifs

The role of motifs in Mark is noticeable in various ways. There are many instances of *general* motifs, shared with other narrative traditions of Mark's time, such as *proof of miracle* (1:31; 2:12; 5:13, 42; 10:52) or *command to secrecy* (1:44; 5:42; 7:36; 8:30; 9:9). This facet of Mark has been extensively discussed.[107]

---

characteristics compiled by Peabody, *Mark as Composer*, 35–113; Dschulnigg, *Sprache, Redaktion und Intention*, 84–226.

103. Lord, *Singer of Tales*, 68.

104. Ibid., 147.

105. Lord, "Perspectives on Recent Work," 21–23.

106. Lord, *Singer of Tales*, 80.

107. E.g., Theissen, *Urchristliche Wundergeschichten*, 57–89; Roth, *Hebrew Gospel*, 40–76; Robbins, *Jesus the Teacher*, passim; Bultmann, *Geschichte der synoptischen Tradition*, passim (e.g., 233–60 on miraculous and related motifs); Smith, " Good News is No News," 25; Botha, "Die Dissipels," 49.

Thematic Composition

Mark also combines motifs into complex themes. What is relevant here is the comparable identity that certain pericopes share with each other due to similar patterns or structures. Not only narrative elements but also narratives within the story influenced one another and could have—in terms of the oral formulaic theory—"created" one another. Some examples:

1. Confrontation with an unclean spirit: 1:23–26 / 3:11–12 / 9:25–26. Mark shows how historical knowledge "exists" through a traditional theme.[108]

2. Calling disciples: 1:16–18 / 1:19–20 / 2:13–14.

3. Healings: 5:21–24, 41–43 / 7:31–37 / 8:22–26.

4. Sea-miracles: 4:35–41 / 6:45–52. Not only verbal influence and similarity in "type-scene" but also corresponding underlying motifs such as *rescue, identity*[109] and *puzzlement* turn these stories into Markan thematic composition. This is an apt illustration of how a well-known, general motif (cf. Pss 88:9; 105:9; Job 9:8 (all LXX); Dio Chrysostom, *Or.* 3.30; Plutarch, *Caesar* 38.5–6; Aelius Aristides, *Or.* 42.10; 45.29–33; Lucian, *Philopseudes* 13) is adopted by the Jesus-traditions and becomes a specific instance of Mark, the storyteller's extensive internalized narrative grammar. The theme reflects, as "a subject unit, a group of ideas" not only this story but also the tradition as a whole[110]—an example of "that distinctive process in which oral learning, oral composition, and oral transmission almost merge; . . . facets of the same *process*."[111]

5. Bread miracles: 6:34–44 / 8:1–9.

6. Preparations: 11:1–7 / 14:12–16. The reciprocal relationship between both pericopes have often been discussed in the dispute about Markan redaction.[112] In terms of the oral formulaic theory this points to the *traditional* creativity of the storyteller: "the ability to compose

---

108. Regarding Jesus the exorcist, cf. Jeremias, *New Testament Theology*, 91–6, Vermes, *Jesus the Jew*, 65; Theissen, *Urchristliche Wundergeschichten*, 279.

109. Pesch, *Markusevangelium 1*, 358, describes 6:45–52 as *Epiphaniegeschichte*.

110. Cf. Foley, "Oral Theory in Context," 34.

111. Lord, *Singer of Tales*, 5.

112. E.g., Taylor, *Mark*, 536.

and recompose the phrases for the idea of the moment on the pattern established."[113]

7. Love command: 12:28–31, 32–34. Jesus' answer is a fusion of certain Old Testament motifs (Deut 6:4–5; Josh 22:5; Lev 19:18). The motif *generated* a Markan theme which was *transformed* in the scribe's response. Note the μείζων τούτων echoed in περισσότερόν ἐστιν πάντων (vv. 31 and 33).

8. Questioning: 14:60–64 / 15:2–5. The role of thematic composition can be illustrated by a comment of Taylor: "No disciple was present at the trial, and for his information the Evangelist was dependent upon hearsay."[114] With various motifs (such as the silence of faithful— Pss 38:13–16; 39:10; Isa 53:7–12—and the enemies who will see the victim again—Wis 5:1–2; 1 Enoch 62:3–5) the storyteller brings his knowledge of Jesus to life in front of his audience.

In these examples it is important to note the *verbal* repetitions and the structural similarities, thus by virtue of "both narrative sequence and verbal correspondence"[115] one can claim *thematic composition*. Particularly relevant is the relationships between the various elements of the individual themes, illustrating a whole that is transformed each time. A given "essential idea" is controlled by tradition both allowing *and* limiting variation. Although the expression of a theme is clearly in flux, no individual appropriation of a theme destroys the theme's continuity. Various applications of a theme are both autonomous and "vom selben Typus . . . und ist wohl als Variante beurteilen."[116]

The passion predictions can also be added (Mark 8:27–32; 9:30–32; 10:32–34), as well as the parable of the sower and its interpretation (4:2–9, 13–21). "The theme, even though it be verbal, is not any fixed set of words, but a grouping of ideas."[117] Some themes display a considerable diversity in verbal expression, as can be seen in the "sayings of Jesus" scenes (3:1–6; 3:20–30; 10:13–6; 11:15–9; 12:41–44; 14:43–52). Greater resemblance is reflected by the "epiphany" scenes (1:9–13; 9:2–10), the exorcisms, the various callings of disciples and the *Sammelberichte*, more correctly termed

113. Lord, *Singer of Tales*, 5.
114. Taylor, *Mark*, 563.
115. Foley, "Oral Theory," 79–91.
116. Bultmann, *Die Geschichte der Synoptischen Tradition*, 228.
117. Lord, *Singer of Tales*, 69.

typifying compositions. "Typisierend ist jedes erzählerische Arrangement, das Einzelmotive aus wenigen Erzählungen zum durchgehenden Zug der ganzen in der Rahmengattung beschriebenen Geschichte macht."[118] These typifying compositions (1:4–6, 14–15, 32–34; 2:13; 3:7–12; 6:30–34, 53–56; 10:1) reflect very similar verbal construction.[119]

Putting It All Together

Summary

The gospel of Mark clearly has a formulaic style, with a stereotyped diction, many stock phrases and a repetitive technique. Scholes and Kellogg remark that "Orally composed prose will necessarily be highly stylized,"[120] and I have argued that this is exactly what we have in Mark. A great part of Mark exists as thematic pericopes, "types of events" reflecting one another stylistically and structurally, more or less.

In the perspective of the "oral formulaic theory" the storyteller "Mark" had "at his disposal a great pool of narrative elements—plot motifs, verbal formulae (including stock descriptions, dialogue exchanges, opening and closing runs . . .)."[121] The "rules" according to which the elements combine with each other "are different, less restricted because prose tales have no set metrical framework, from the rules followed by the 'singer of tales.'"[122] So it is quite possible that the gospel of Mark is a casual transcription of what had been *performed* orally. The gospel probably reflects an improvisatory composition and re-composition within an informal context under the constraints of various traditions.

Tradition should not be seen as something permanent and unchanging. Nor does it refer to something older, more pure. Tradition is a dynamic process, intertwined with human self-interpretation and communication. Traditions are not things, moving by themselves. Human beings bring them to life and live through them. Taylor remarks: "If the Form Critics are right, the disciples must have been translated to heaven immediately after the Resurrection."[123] I use his comment for a different purpose, but it illustrates

---

118. Theissen, *Urchristliche Wundergeschichten*, 205.

119. Egger, *Frohbotschaft und Lehre*, 27–38.

120. Scholes and Kellogg, *Nature of Narrative*, 51.

121. Bruford, "Memory, Performance and Structure," 103.

122. Ibid., 103.

123. Taylor, *Formation*, 41; cf. 41–43, 107.

the issue. Who talked about Jesus? Who knew about him? Robinson showed in an interesting investigation the very "tiny group of friends and relatives from which it all began."[124] Short, anecdotal stories end up in a full-length story when someone *wants* to tell the story—and that need arose very shortly after Jesus' crucifixion. It is absurd to think that an extended narrative about Jesus became a reality outside the initial followers of Jesus and only after a long passage of time.

Jesus did not primarily establish local communities. He initiated a movement of itinerant radical prophets and teachers. The crucial figures in earliest Christianity were apostles, prophets, and disciples travelling and relying on sympathizers in various places,[125] such as Peter (Acts 8:14; 9:32; 10:20; Gal 2:11; 1 Cor 9:5). There are indications of other prophets such as Agabus (Acts 11:27; 21:10) moving between Antioch and Judea. Traveling prophets and teachers were still the important authorities by the time of the writing of the *Didache* (chaps. 11–13). The addressees of the Didache had to regard their own leaders as οἱ τετιμημένοι (honorees), similar to the regard given to travelling prophets and teachers (*Did.* 15.2).

Papias (according to Eusebius, *HE* 3.39.15) tells us that the important church leaders of his time considered Peter to be the authority behind the gospel of Mark. Rigg comments on this that "what Papias seems to say seems to go against what on nearly every other ground modern scholarship has come to conclude about Mark,"[126] an opinion widely shared today. However, thinking in terms of oral traditional composition it is not strange to picture Peter as travelling "teacher" entrusting his Jesus-story to a "disciple" at some stage. Although the connection with Peter was made to reinforce the authority and credibility of the Markan gospel[127]— at least, that is Eusebius' motive for citing Papias—the *picture* seems very plausible. And that remains so whether Peter was involved or not, and independent of the reliability of the Papias-notice. If our analysis of Mark is correct, oral traditional composition presupposes very much the situation envisaged by Papias. In fact, Kürzinger is quite possibly on the right track when he describes Mark as a composition of χρειά without τάξις.[128] The role of Peter in the origins of Mark appears to

124. Robinson, "How Small Was the Seed," 110; Gerhardsson, *Origins*, 59–65.

125. Riddle, "Early Christian Hospitality."

126. Rigg, "Papias on Mark," 161.

127. Niederwimmer, "Johannes Markus," 188; Körtner, "Markus der Mitarbeiter des Petrus."

128. Kürzinger, "Die Aussage des Papias," 252–58.

me quite acceptable. The lack of documentary data misleads one to underestimate the impact of Peter in the Jesus-movement.[129]

That we have a written copy today is probably due to the traditional narrator having dictated his story at some stage. In fact, almost *all* writing done at the time was by dictation.[130] Lord discusses some general theoretical aspects of formulaic poetic dictation.[131] It is quite possible that the storyteller himself wrote and/or used a μεμβράνα.[132] Dictation can have an effect on performance,[133] but seen historically, should not be overestimated in the first century Mediterranean situation. Dictating to oneself and public performing were overlapping phenomena; medieval texts, for example, carry "a heavy residue of primary orality."[134] Dictation done for the purpose of ensuring the continuing existence of the tradition can be experienced by the storyteller as "a public performance, no matter how intimate the recording session and even physical absence of the audience."[135] Lord found that the better singers among his informants produced their best performances in private situations; the recitations were more complete and complex.[136]

Towards a Better Understanding of the Markan Traditions

In a general sense it is clear that the whole topic of the *verbomotor* nature of antiquity,[137] their oral-aural determined culture, leads to an extensive rethinking of many issues surrounding the texts we study.[138] More specifically, I would like to submit that this has some very important implications for both gospel criticism and Markan research.

The immediate gain from the perspective of oral traditional composition is an alternative to the tradition/redaction cul-de-sac. The gospel

129. Cf. Dunn, *Unity and Diversity*, 385.

130. E.g., Dio Chrysostom, *Discourses* 18.18; cf. Skeat, "Use of Dictation"; Stambaugh and Balch, *New Testament in Its Social Environment*, 40.

131. Lord, *Singer of Tales*, 124–28; see also Whallon, *Formula, Character, and Context*, 208–10.

132. Roberts, "Books in the Graeco–Roman World," 53–54; Kennedy, "Classical and Christian,"148–54; Gerhardsson, *Origins*, 22–24.

133. Goody, *Interface*, 93–6.

134. Ong, "Orality," 3; Ong, *Orality and Literacy*, 95; Lord, "Merging of Two Worlds," 41.

135. Bauman, *Story, Performance and Event*, 106.

136. Lord, "Homer's Originality"; Lord, *Singer of Tales*, 124–28.

137. "Verbomotor": see Ong, *Orality and Literacy*, 68.

138. Ong, *Interfaces of the Word*; Ong, "Psychodynamics of Oral."

of Mark does not merely contain oral traditions, but *is* oral composition. Instead of approaching the gospel either as a merging of various chronological, geographically influenced and theological parts, identifiable by what is taken as narrative inconsistencies, linguistic usages and historical infelicities, or as a work of great literary merit with a perfect dramatic structure and consistent characterization, much like a modern topical author, the gospel appears to be part of a *traditional process*. The linguistic situation pertinent to oral traditional composition explains the effective narration through an ostensibly inept style.

Mark's gospel is neither a series of poorly integrated stages involving a mélange of contributions from various tradents, redactors, and interpolators, nor an individual act of poetic creation. Numerous elements of Mark take on new "meanings." The repetitions and thematic procedures have no overt theological or ideological basis. Many textual characteristics are simply involvement of oral mnemonics. The study of Dewey illustrates this principle very well.[139] The next step is to analyze Mark's generic traits. Should one argue that Mark's story is a hero tradition,[140] various elements of the story should be seen as having its definite position and function due to that particular narrative plot.[141] Jesus is then pictured as the powerful teacher, and all elements work towards that depiction. Along these lines it is possible to avoid discussing Mark's story a-historically in the sense of "Mark as literature" or "Mark as narrative."

It will be worthwhile to investigate the interwovenness of this story's religious aspects with a possible historical situation, such as radical, itinerant teachers. Similar to the famous κυνικοί (Cynics) who travelled all over the Roman Empire (especially during the second half of the first century) "with stick and knapsack, teaching and preaching," beggar teachers that propagated "the gospel of simplicity and independence, and comforted many in those troubled times by demonstrating that he who needs next to nothing, renounces all possessions, and keeps aloof from social entanglements, can live happily in the midst of war and disorder,"[142] the Markan storyteller(s) performed their traditional story in many places. The importance of a story (and storytelling as such) about a hero teaching the way of God in the cultural equipment of a socially marginal group is self-evident. Comparative

139. Dewey uses Havelock's "Oral Composition in the *Oedipus Tyrannus* of Sophocles"; see Dewey, "Oral Methods."

140. Cf. Botha, "Die Dissipels," 63–77.

141. Cf. Jason, "Content Analysis of Oral Literature," 275.

142. Von Fritz, "Cynics," 305.

studies can highlight the value and role of stories and story-activity in the lives of traveler-people and the difficulties they endure.

If it would have been possible to give Mark an electronic copy of his text stored on a computer diskette (or a flash drive) it is obvious that he would have had very little comprehension of what he would be holding in his hands. He would have lacked the conceptual framework and, obviously, the technological equipment and skills to "make" that object into a communicative event. Similarly, but in reverse, we lack many aspects of the conceptual framework and technical skills to really turn the object known as "manuscript Mark" into a communicative event. We must learn, at second hand, what it must have felt like to *hear* the gospel of Mark, to sense the evocative interplay of his "recreating" the traditions and feel the effect of his actualizing of powerful motifs.[143]

Some Questions

Insights from research done on orality and scribality obviously leads to a different conceptualization of the various strata of the Jesus traditions. "Perhaps the most basic and persistent problem confronted by students of oral literature is gauging the effect of the interplay of tradition and innovation, persistence and change, as manifested in the oral text."[144] We need to rethink the whole issue of creative innovation in early Christianity. In this regard Kellogg remarked: "As a cultural ideal, such blending of 'tradition' and 'individual talent' is more appropriately applied to the criticism of Romantic and post Romantic literature than to genuine oral literature, where . . . individual talent . . . is likely to be a function of our ignorance of the tradition."[145]

The limitations inherent in my study must also be noted. It is simply an exploratory starting point. This very analysis, is in a certain sense, still "constitutive of literate values and literate linguistic bias."[146] Therefore, one follow-up consequence must be a consistent approach of the text as *work*, bringing reception aesthetics to bear on the problem of a grammar of compositional units. Thus, moving away from phraseological formulas and the debates on what is or is not themes and motifs, addressing "the units of oral traditional narrative . . . not as objective entities in themselves but as necessarily incomplete cues to be contextualized by an audience's subjective

143. Cf. Foley, "Introduction," 14–17.
144. Bauman, *Story, Performance and Event*, 78.
145. Kellogg, "Oral Literature," 63.
146. Swearingen, "Oral Hermeneutics," 138.

participation in the tale-telling process."[147] The ideal is an informed involvement in which one strives to experience how "the story-pattern provides a map for construing the narrative as a whole, the theme forecasts further developments both immediate and long-range, and the noun-epithet formula reaches far beyond its metrical slot to the mythic identity of its phraseological designate." [148]

"The application of oral theory to problems of literary history, sociology, and criticism of the Middle Ages promises to yield results far beyond the areas I have attempted to outline here."[149] As a final remark I would like to endorse this observation for the texts of early Christianity.

147. Foley, *Oral Tradition in Literature*, 216.

148. Ibid., 217.

149. Haymes, "Oral Composition," 354.

PART 3

Paul's Letters

9

Letter Writing and Oral Communication: Galatians

Introduction

Stowers, after providing a longish list of things people could do with letters in antiquity, remarks:

> The study of early Christian letters has suffered because the letters have too often been forced into an interpretive mold formed by two questions: What theology does it contain, and what ideas was the author trying to defend or attack? The foregoing list suggests the vast multiplicity of things people did by means of letters. The list also illustrates that ancient letters will be difficult to understand on their own terms unless we also understand something about the contexts of Greco-Roman society in which the actions were performed and had their meanings.[1]

This equivocal attitude towards contextualizing can easily be illustrated by noting the influence of Deissmann's distinction between "epistles" (carefully composed literary productions for general publication) and "letters" (genuine correspondence addressed to specific persons and situations).[2] Though Deissmann's influence led to a valid recognition of the situational character of Paul's letters it, at the same time, drew attention away from questions about the form, structure and style of the letters. Deissmann himself saw a direct correlation between Paul's social situation and the form and style of his letters.[3] The effect of seeing Paul's letters as non-literary was that they were "conceived as salutation, thanksgiving, and closing, with virtually

1. Stowers, *Letter Writing*, 16.
2. Deismann, *Bible Studies*, 1–59; Deissmann, *Light*, 148–49, 230–45.
3. Deismann, *Light*, 240–41.

anything in any order in between."[4] But once the picture of Paul as a more sophisticated apologist took hold, the conviction grew that Paul composed his letters with self-conscious and subconscious concern with the conventions of Greco-Roman rhetoric and epistolography. Formal, structural and stylistic questions no longer seem inappropriate, and definitely not unimportant (witness the extensive range of literature dealing with these aspects of the Pauline letters). Yet, the context of ancient communication still remains peripheral to these studies.

Various scholars have pointed out the importance of attention to the overall function and structure of the letter as it existed in Paul's day; the necessity "to compare and contrast the Christian epistle with its Hellenistic counterpart."[5] This investigation has been aided by excellent surveys from scholars outside the New Testament guild[6] and has yielded some outstanding studies. A cautionary note or two is, however, in order. Despite the recent blossoming of interest, an immense amount of material has not yet been fully studied—and our ignorance remains, *nolens volens*, quite considerable. Furthermore, the tendency to study historical facets in isolation is amazingly strong. Valid interpretation is about relations, about context and contextualizing. The recent growth of interest in sociological and cultural-anthropological research with regard to early Christianity is a healthy development, and hopefully more than a mere fad.

This study is a modest contribution to contextualizing Paul's letter to the Galatians. It aims at explicating an often noted, but poorly developed, facet of Paul's letter writing. In literature discussing the letters of Paul, references to an oral context abound. So, for example, Malherbe, after pointing out that early Christian writings that have been preserved were not originally speeches, continues that, nevertheless, "they were dictated (cf. Rom 16:22) and intended to be read aloud to congregations (cf. 1 Thess 5:27; Rev 1:3), thus functioning like speeches or sermons, [meaning] that the writers were conscious of oral style."[7]

4. Funk, *Language*, 252.

5. Ibid., 254; Vielhauer, *Geschichte der Urchristlichen Literatur*, 58–70; Stirewalt, "Form and Function"; Bahr, "Paul and Letter Writing"; Bahr, "Subscriptions"; Bandstra, "Paul, the Letter Writer"; Doty, *Letters*; White, "Saint Paul and the Apostolic Letter Tradition"; White, "New Testament Epistolary Literature," in *Light from Ancient Letters*; Malherbe, "Ancient Epistolary Theorists"; Stowers, *Letter Writing*.

6. Ussher, "Letter Writing"; Koskenniemi, *Studien zur Idee Und Phraseologie*.

7. Malherbe, *Moral Exhortation*, 68. Examples can be multiplied; e.g., Lategan, "Is Paul Defending," 416; White, *Light*, 19; Vielhauer, *Geschichte*, 59; Doty, *Letters*, 75–76. In his monograph, *The Oral and the Written Gospel*, 140–77, Kelber has attempted to

Orality and Scribality in Paul's World

The very first step needed for a responsible interpretation of ancient com-munication is clearing our minds of tacit assumptions. We must replace our misleading, modern literate view of ancient writing activities with a more responsible view that takes into account their historical, religious, intellec-tual and psychological situation.

In modern society, people are considered literate if they can read and write with minimal skill. A person is considered educated when one is a particularly proficient reader/writer. In Greco-Roman societies one could be educated without having the ability to read and write. In fact, being literate (proficient with texts) was not even necessarily connected to writing and reading oneself. Modern literacy is measured by minimum and utilitarian standards; ancient literacy was measured by maximum and seemingly im-practical standards. Literacy was at the time a relatively limited social factor in the marketplace.

One would think these matters are obvious—especially in view of the technological changes separating our societies from theirs—but vagueness and neglect of historical realia mark references to ancient literacy. We are misled by our prejudice towards the (infinitesimal) elite section of antiquity. This, in part, is the natural result of our choice of witnesses:

> the ones most conveniently got at are those represented by their writings, or quoted or addressed in formal literature. They belong, then, to an elite who think in some respects like ourselves: Apu-leius, for example, or Plutarch. They are distinguished by at least some years of education beyond the ABCs, therefore they had possessed at some point money sufficient to free themselves from the necessity of full-time labor. It was not out of the question for a man (never a woman) to earn the necessary money and leisure out of a working-class background, or something not much better: Lucian did it and so did Saint Paul. But it was unusual to *want* to.[8]

---

interpret Paul's theology as orally constituted. Kelber misrepresents orality in Greco-Ro-man antiquity, underplays the complexities of oral-literacy interaction as anthropologi-cal phenomena, and consequently separates Paul's (oral) preaching from his (written) letters. It remains an important study, nevertheless. Earlier studies with valuable con-tributions to this discussion are Schniewind's *Die Begriffe Wort* and Funk's *Saying and Seeing*. One should add that many studies on Greco-Roman society also suffer from improper assumptions concerning literacy and education in antiquity.

8. MacMullen, *Christianizing the Roman Empire*, 10–11.

Lewis, in his study on Roman Egypt, refers to the "prevailing aura . . . of illiteracy: the cultured few lived surrounded by the illiterate many"; an observation certainly of importance to the rest of the Empire.[9] Consequently, a few remarks in this regard are necessary.

Orality

When discussing ancient communication we are in the uncomfortable situation where we must generalise about what cannot be disentangled from specific historical situations. Our fragmentary evidence on the one hand, and some misguided historical research on the other left us in the dark. When it comes to literacy in the Greco-Roman world, as to how, who and when people used written communications and how the inability to do so determined the character of Greco-Roman society, "much investigation is waiting to be done."[10] Furthermore, by not critically defining our concepts we can easily fall into the trap of facile oversimplification.

A favorite argument in this regard is reference to the so-called widespread influence of Hellenistic schools. But many statements on Greek elementary schools are vague, incomplete and without proper methodological concerns, making an argument against the pervasive presence of orality in Greco-Roman culture problematic. Two pointers must suffice. On the one hand, "the rarity of the records and the lack of any detailed descriptions . . . suggest that public interest in elementary education was not very widely diffused and nowhere intense: in the majority of cities the first stage of education was left to private enterprise and was not even subject to public control."[11] In fact, elementary teaching was an occupation with little prestige.[12] Greco-Roman society was quite the opposite from ours, with an interest and concern about παιδεία as a passport to certain kinds of careers for upper classes, and extremely little consideration for basic schooling in literature.

Secondly, for an average family to send a child to school meant not only paying fees but partly dispensing with the child's labour,[13] a not unimportant

---

9. Lewis, *Life in Egypt Under Roman Rule*, 82. See also the studies of Youtie, "Ἀγράμματος"; Youtie, "Because They Do not Know Letters"; Youtie, "Ὑπογραφεύς"; and the more general survey of Achtemeier, "*Omne Verbum Sonat.*"

10. Harris, "Literacy and Epigraphy," 87.

11. Jones, *Greek City*, 223.

12. Harris, "Literacy and Epigraphy," 98.

13. Ibid., 99.

consideration since "it took three to four years to learn to read, thanks to the mechanical technique."[14]

More theoretically, one must also ask, with regard to known research, what economic, social and cultural conditions create extensive literacy. In other words, we must apply the rules of historical probability. There is extensive historical scholarship showing that literacy never comes into being on a large scale except as a result of certain identifiable positive factors.[15] In his study on the growth of literacy in England, for instance, Stone examined various factors, such as education, the invention and use of printing, widespread urbanization, incipient industrialization, and religion, specifically Protestantism.[16] He notes that, despite the drive for popular education, the upper levels of education (skills beyond the first level of bare literacy) remained extraordinary elitist in scale and character.[17]

If we relate these insights to the Greco-Roman world, we must note not only the *absence* of modern communication technology, but the fact that they had a *manuscript* technology.[18] This situation can create an almost magical awe of books,[19] but does not facilitate reading and writing as natural communicative options. Also, the Roman Empire was a rural, agrarian, pre-industrial society.[20] Even more to the point is that those who controlled the labor force, whether slaves or free men, had limited needs for literate slaves or employees. Finally, with regard to possible impetus from religious activities, "there were no sacred texts which the population at large felt any obligation to read."[21]

Against this we need to balance the situation in Jewish circles, in which it is generally believed that education and literacy was higher than in Hellenistic circles. Aside from general and vague statements, I know of little

---

14. Marrou, "Education and Rhetoric," 188.

15. Cf. Street, *Literacy in Theory and Practice.*

16. Stone, "Literacy and Education," 70–98.

17. Ibid., 137.

18. Troll, "Illiterate Mode," 99–106; Metzger, *The Text of the New Testament,* 4–33; Chaytor, *From Script to Print.*

19. Cf. Clanchy, *From Memory,* 126–130, and the suspicion voiced by Doty, *Letters,* 44 n. 56.

20. Saldarini, *Pharisees,* 35–38; Stambaugh and Balch, *The New Testament in Its Social Environment,* 65–69.

21. Harris, "Literacy and Epigraphy," 92.

proper investigation.[22] The function of scrolls/manuscripts can be related to many others beside reading, especially in ancient societies.

MacMullen has noted that we should not overestimate the impact and influence of writings, even (or especially) when it comes to apologetic literature, apparently offered from within to an audience beyond the church, but in reality serving chiefly for internal consumption. "And there was little enough reading of any sort, anyway. Three-quarters or more of the population were illiterate. Points of contact and media of communication that we take for granted in our world simply did not exist in antiquity."[23] It is important to bear in mind that *even the literates were literate in an illiterate culture*. Orality (in a cultural-anthropological sense) and the social effects of illiteracy permeate even their 'literate' communication.

What I am after is not to claim exclusive validity for my viewpoint, but to convince you to think about ancient communication as *ancient* communication.[24] We are dealing with a different culture, a world that must be dealt with in its own right. MacMullen made a highly relevant remark (though in the context of ancient religiosity, but the point remains valid): "Here is a warning to anyone who attempts a historical reconstruction . . . The explicit record at important points fits badly with what are, to ourselves, entirely natural expectations."[25]

Scribes/Scribal Culture

An important aspect of the oral environment of Greco-Roman times is the role of scribes. To describe the Hellenistic age as an oral world does not mean that the people were not familiar with writing and did not employ writing during their lives. Clearly they did; but they did so through the use of *others'* writing skills.

Instead of assuming that the scribes valued writing because it expanded both their knowledge and their intellect, we now know that they valued writing as a craft and a form of income and status/power. If they read, what they read only reiterated what they heard; if they composed, they primarily

---

22. Some exploration: Botha, "Schools."

23. MacMullen, *Christianizing the Roman Empire*, 21.

24. Recall the case of Aurelius Ammonios, Christian lector (ἀναγνώστης) from the Egyptian village of Chysis in 304 who did not know how to write (*P.Oxy* 33.2673; on which see Clarke, "Illiterate Lector").

25. MacMullen, *Christianizing the Roman Empire*, 42.

wrote what they heard. Writing was a product and a commodity to be sold, not an intellectual process.[26] Lewis provides us with a handy description:

> The educational level of the scribes varied with the individual, but most leave the impression of being merely literate rather than highly educated. They wrote mostly in formulas and clichés, a fact which shows up in the various contracts they penned and most strikingly (to us) in the private letters, many of which are little more than the most impersonally worded collections of greetings and conventional good wishes.[27]

It is therefore valid to assume widespread orality, also in the Pauline communities. The dependence on orality was natural. Whatever we make of ancient letters, orality was part and parcel of the whole process.

Now, "In an age of computers and word processors, one easily forgets that conceiving and writing a text like Galatians or Romans was a long and wearisome procedure,"[28] and consequently we tend to underestimate the considerable effort that must have gone into the composition of Paul's letter. These letters were also written by rather sophisticated scribes (men like Timothy, Silas). The major point about Paul's letters does not lie in them having been written. The point to see is that they are texts that originated as and were designed for oral presentations.

Letter Writing and Letter Carriers

Co-authorship

Many students of the *corpus paulinium* operate with a very inadequate model of authorship. Betz quite appropriately states that "given the employment of an amanuensis and the common practices in letter writing in Paul's time, the problem of authorship may be more complicated than we have previously imagined."[29] Paul usually identifies not only himself but also some other persons as author(s) of his epistles. In fact, he writes in his own name only in Romans, Ephesians and the Pastoral Epistles. We have such a regard for Paul that we simply miss the salient fact that it is Paul *and* Sosthenes' letter to the Corinthians, or Paul *and* Timothy's follow-up letter to the Corinthians. Or

---

26. Cf. Troll, "Illiterate Mode," 115

27. Lewis, *Life in Egypt*, 82.

28. Hartman, "On Reading Others' Letters," 138.

29. Betz, *Galatians*, 313, 1.

that the letters to the Thessalonians are actually the Paul–Silvanus–Timothy corpus!

Paul is not unique in this,[30] though it seems as if explicit mention of co-authors is not common in the extant Greco-Roman letters. Galatians 1:1 refers only to unspecified authors, and there are no other indications. Galatians is a strongly personal statement, with copious use of the first person singular and there is the vaguest of hinting at "those" who preached in the Galatian area with Paul (Silas and Timothy if one can use Acts 16 in this regard). Prior surmises that it was Paul's personal authority that was at stake in the letter, and that is why all references to co-authors are suppressed.[31]

Concerning co-authorship various options present themselves. The authors may have considered the substance of the letter individually, and then gone over the general plan of what they were to compose, or perhaps suggested the style and expression which they had separately chosen while thinking about the message before collaborating towards an agreed content and form. The Younger Pliny, when he had enough leisure, liked to work out parts of his text in his head and then dictate the work in stages to his secretary.[32]

This is not to diminish Paul's contribution, but to put his communication in proper perspective.[33] What I am after is awareness that Paul's letter was not written by him as an individual, sitting at a desk and dropping a note to some friends. We must become aware of a much more complex event: some persons combined their efforts to deliberate and "perform" a letter; there was someone involved in the creation and transportation of it finally "recreating" for others a presentation/performance of the "message" intended for sharing.

Amanuenses

How strong our projection of individual values really is becomes clear with a perusal of research concerning Paul's use of amanuenses. That he did so

30. Bahr, "Paul and Letter Writing," 476; Prior, *Paul the Letter-Writer*, 38.

31. Prior, ibid., 41, 43.

32. Pliny, *Letters.* 9.36.

33. Schweizer has recently proposed that the joint authorship of Philemon, Philippians, 2 Corinthians and Colossians be taken seriously; and that Colossians be seen as neither simply Pauline nor post-Pauline. See Schweizer, *Der Brief an die Kolosser*, 25–26. Similarly Bruce in connection with Colossians. See Bruce, *Epistles to the Colossians*, 30. I still think that the true import of and context for this phenomenon seems to be missed by these scholars, however.

cannot be doubted.[34] But what to make of that fact still remains a problem for New Testament scholars. At all cost it is usually argued that the use of a secretary does not affect the inspiration of scripture, nor the authority of Paul and especially not the extent of Paul's contribution. The concern with Paul, as an individual leader/thinker/apostle, and his specific role is abundantly clear.

The true import of the issue about the use of an amanuensis is neither the authenticity of the epistle, nor the possible mixture of styles (nor even the orality involved). It is that communication was not experienced as a message from one mind to another. It was a communal event, much like a visit in our experience, a process, involving various persons and involving them all extensively.

An interesting side issue is the very strong probability that Paul was ἀγράμματος. Strictly speaking, Paul probably relied on scribes because he could not write Greek. A perusal of comments on Gal 6:11 bears out that though the similarity to the illiteracy formula is well known, no-one wants to accept the implication of this similarity![35]

Youtie has discussed the phenomenon of persons copying a model sentence or repeating it from memory in order to pass themselves off as literate.[36] Persons used a formula that they could write at the end of letters on their behalf as "an effective shield for barely literate writers."[37] Such a formula or subscription could be written in "upright capitals" or appear as "very clumsily" written;[38] "stiff, awkward, uneven, kept on the line with

---

34. See, among others, Longenecker, "Ancient Amanuenses."

35. In his *Die Brief an die Galasiërs*, 115, Lategan writes: "nie soseer op Paulus se onhandigheid of ongeoefendheid met die pen nie, maar meer waarskynlik op die belang van wat hy ten slotte weer wil onderstreep." Betz writes similarly in his *Galatians*, 314. Deissmann was of the opinion that Paul preferred to dictate his letters "no doubt because writing was not an easy thing to his workman's hand," in his *Light*, 166 n. 7. Paul's reference to his *large* letters was his way of making merry about this, "half jesting and half earnest" (ibid., 172). Typical of how Paul's "dictation" is handled can be seen in the approach of Stowers: discussing a letter from one Claudius Agathas Daimon to Sarapion he notes that the letter "was written by a secretary except for the closing prayer and farewell, which are in another hand, almost certainly that of Claudius himself. This practice was like adding a signature to a typed letter," continues that "Paul does the same at the close of some letters in order to provide a personal touch" (see Stowers, *Letter Writing*, 61).

36. Youtie, "Βραδέως Γράφων."

37. Ibid., 246.

38. Ibid.

obvious effort."[39] But illiteracy carried no stigma in itself.[40] Youtie's evidence and arguments concern primarily Greco-Roman Egypt, but his research is obviously pertinent to understanding Greco-Roman literacy in general.

Although it comes naturally, we must be cautious not to let our concepts intrude in our interpretation. Paul did not sign his letters (writing one's name like we do). As Bahr has shown, what Paul did was add a *subscription*: a summary that can be used as legal proof and to confirm authority.[41]

The possibility that Paul could not write himself should be seen within the context of Greco-Roman literacy. It is therefore neither demeaning nor reflecting on his intellectual skills. But it does warn us to beware of making his letter writing conform to our expectations.

Delivery of Letters

Getting private letters delivered was not easy, and was often extremely difficult, subject to many uncertainties, delays, and, at times, almost insuperable difficulties.[42] The imperial government maintained a postal service of some sorts, the *cursus publicus*, but made no provision whatever for the carrying of private letters. Of course, personal influence or friendships could make the transmission of private letters by public post possible (as with Ambrose and Basil in the fourth century). But, certainly not in the case of Paul. Private letters had to be sent by private means. Wealthy people had their own letter carriers (*tabellarii*), selected from household slaves. *Tabellarii* were usually briefed on the contents of the letters entrusted to them and often made supplementary reports on matters that were not set down in writing.

A good letter carrier had to be physically qualified as well as loyal and intelligent. The carelessness and untrustworthiness of casual or coincidental letter bearers became proverbial. Destinations far from the main roads created special problems, and during winter months, there usually was no letter carrying. None is immune to illness, and all letter carriers were vulnerable to the dangers of shipwreck and/or robbery on land. Disclosure of the contents and forgery were important realities, and various methods were used to cope with these problems.

---

39. Ibid., 240.

40. Cf. Youtie, "Ὑπογραφεύς," 200.

41. Bahr, "Subscriptions," 28–33.

42. Cf. McGuire, "Letters and Letter Carriers," 185, 199; White, *Light from Ancient Letters*, 214–15; Badian, "Postal Service."

Doty suggests that because of political intrigue and the vulnerability of the postal system, the letter writer was careful to entrust the *real* message of the letter to the carrier, not merely the text of the letter itself. He senses that "Paul, who made such a point of indicating his trust in those carriers (co-workers), did not think of his written letters as exhausting what he wished to communicate. He thought of his associates, especially those commissioned to carry his letter, as able to extend his own teachings."[43]

Therefore, in view of the *realia* of Greco-Roman epistolography, it is clear that the choice of a letter bearer was sometimes as crucial as the content of the letter. The confidential role played by letter carriers is illustrated by Pseudo-Demetrius' example of a typical letter of recommendation: "So-and-so, who is conveying this letter to you, has been tested by us and is loved on account of his trustworthiness. You will do well if you deem him worthy of hospitality both for my sake and his . . . For you will not be sorry if you entrust to him, in any manner you wish, either words or deeds of a confidential nature . . ."[44]

Though there is no explicit reference in Galatians to the letter bearer it would be foolish to think that he would have played no part in the communication. In view of typical practice, the fact that so much was invested in the letter, and the import attached to the letter, one *must* reckon with the letter as having been prepared for a careful performance, and that eventually the letter was delivered like a proper speech.

Receiving a letter meant hearing both a message conveyed on behalf of the sender and a written document. Letters were read aloud.[45] In the case of Paul's letter we have a fully briefed reader *with* the letter itself. "We gain a sense of the importance of his emissaries or letter carriers: they receive authority to convey the letters to expand upon them, and to continue Paul's work."[46]

It has often been remarked that letters bore a kinship with oral messages.[47] Considering the oral environment of antiquity, this insight must be taken seriously. Oral, in this sense refers to more than mere spoken language. Orality, as analytic concept, involves a mindset; a whole attitude towards reality and experience.

43. Doty, *Letters*, 289.

44. Malherbe, "Ancient Epistolary Theorists," 31.

45. McGuire, "Letters and Letter Carriers," 150; Marrou, "Education and Rhetoric," 196; Saenger, "Silent Reading," 370–73.

46. Doty, *Letters*, 37.

47. E.g., White, "New Testament Epistolary Literature," 1731.

"Reading" a Letter and Oral Performance

In an oral environment (culture) bodily incarnation of the word is of the utmost importance. Facial expressions, impressive rhetoric, convincing verbal art are essential to communication in orally based cultures.

All commentators refer to the "readers" of Paul's letter, identifying the Galatian Christians, the recipients of the letter. How should this be pictured historically? Not as a little book passing from member to member! Even reference to "reading in the assembly" or "in worship" is not spelt out. Was it read like a modern pastor engaging in scripture reading before the sermon, in an even, sonorous and respectful tone? There is abundant evidence that reading in antiquity was related to performance. Reading in antiquity, especially when it was not private reading, was similar to recitals or to oral delivery.

This is nicely illustrated in a charming little letter written by (*senator!*) Pliny to Suetonius, asking advice about his poor reading skills:

> I am told that I read badly—I mean when I read verse, for I can manage speeches, though this seems to make my verse reading all the worse! So, as I am planning to give an informal reading to my personal friends, I am thinking of making use of one of my freedmen. This is certainly treating them informally, as the man I have chosen is not really a good reader, but I think he will do better than I can as long as he is not nervous . . . Now, I don't know what I am to do myself while he is reading, whether I am to sit still and silent like a mere spectator, or do as some people and accompany his words with lips, eye, and gesture.[48]

For interpreting Paul's letters to the Galatians, I am thus, in effect, arguing for the exact opposite of what Betz claims the situation to have been: "Since it is simply a lifeless piece of paper, it eliminates one of the most important weapons of the rhetorician, the oral delivery. The actual delivery of speech includes a whole range of weapons relating to modulation of voice and to gestures, all of which a letter makes impossible. In his remarks Paul is fully aware of these disadvantages, as shown in 4:18–20."[49]

48. Pliny, *Letters* 9.34.

49. Betz, *Galatians*, 24.

Aesthetics of Performance

Both the importance and the essence of emphasizing ancient communication as performative communication (performed literature) can be seen once we become aware of how one-sided we think about rhetoric.

Aristotle understands the whole point of rhetoric (the τέλος of each kind of rhetoric) to be that the audience (ακροαταί) either as judge (κριτής) or as critic of the orator's ability (περὶ τῆς δυνάμεως ο θεωρός) should be enabled to arrive at a judgment.[50] They are viewed as nonspeaking partners actively engaged in the exchange taking place between speaker and auditor; passive listening would make speaking an exercise in the irrational. Consequently he spends a whole chapter (the second book of the *Rhetorica*) on *emotions*. The importance of the speaker and the auditors as persons, and the contribution each makes toward establishing communication is continually and explicitly recognised by ancient theorists. Demosthenes, in his *On the Embassy* (*De falsa legatione*), tells us that the ability of an orator can be paralysed by the recalcitrance of the audience.[51] Cicero calls the popular ear (*populi aures*) a kind of instrument for the orator.[52]

While many scholars have turned to Greco-Roman rhetoric for help in interpreting Paul's letter (with worthwhile results), the oral, *performative* aspect of ancient communication, and specifically ancient rhetoric have been neglected. Kennedy, in his (useful) introduction to rhetorical criticism states explicitly: "Discussion of memory and delivery is often omitted in the handbooks and will be omitted here, for they relate to oral presentation, about which we know little."[53] Yet he continues by noting that what was taught "applied both to oral speech and written composition." If it is worthwhile to use ancient rhetorical principles in order to understand New Testament documents better, at least we should use it as it was intended. Speech and rhetoric cannot be separated as Hellenistic culture basically was an oral culture. Their rhetorical principles aimed specifically at delivery of speech, at oral performance, and, consequently, *also* at creating successful communication through bodily presence.

---

50. Aristotle, *Rhetorica* 1.3.1–3

51. Demosthenes, *On the Embassy*, 339–40.

52. Cicero, *Brutus* 51.191–192; Cicero, *Orator* 8.24; Cicero, *De Inventione* 1.16.22; Cicero, *De Oratore* 2.79.321; Quintilian, *Institutio Oratoria* 11.1.1–11.3.184; Pseudo-Cicero, *Rhetorica ad Herennium* 1.4.7–8.

53. Kennedy, *New Testament Interpretation*, 14.

Quintilian, for instance, has many, many references to the role of the body whilst speaking. The face, and particularly the eyes would "reveal the passion of the mind (*animus eminet*)," even without movement.[54] To the audience, the performer's charm and good character must be obvious; "no man can be an orator unless he is a good man."[55] Quintilian insists on integration between voice and movement: "if gesture and the expression of the face is out of harmony with the speech . . . words will not only lack weight, but will fail to carry conviction."[56] Sound and movement are keys to the emotional and intellectual content of the presentation.

For example, the hands, "since they are almost as expressive as words," and speaking the universal language (*omnium hominum communis sermo*) are powerful instruments for the orator.[57] Gestures are discussed in detail; which are suitable for the *exordium* and the *statement of facts*, and which not;[58] what is appropriate to "continuous flowing passages" and how to express qualities of restraint and timidity, and so forth.

The orator studies in order to deliver an effective performance: to stimulate the audience by the animation of his presentation, and to kindle the imagination, not through ambitious imagery, but by bringing the audience into actual touch with the things themselves.[59] Quintilian focuses on forensic disputes, the perils of the *forum*,[60] but persuasive oratory so permeated Greco-Roman culture that Quintilian's discussions most certainly are relevant to understanding the public reading of texts. We gather a distinct sense of how thoroughly a reader must have been acquainted with his text, and must have worked to internalise its performative values.

Very much to the point is the role of memory and memorizing. Extensive memorisation, which was the dominant characteristic of Greco-Roman education, is fundamental to an oral-text oriented culture. It is well-known that the dissemination of texts in antiquity relied on recitals and oral performances. It is in this context that Quintilian calls memory the treasure-chest of eloquence (*thesaurus eloquentiae*).[61]

---

54. Quintilian, *Institutio Oratoria* 11.3.75–9.

55. Ibid., 12.1.1–3.

56. Ibid., 11.3.67.

57. Ibid., 11.3.85–87.

58. E.g., ibid., 11.3.92.

59. Cf. ibid., 10.1.16.

60. Ibid., 10.1.36.

61. Ibid., 9.2.1.

Although much too cursorily discussed, the point that the oral reader was the instrument for embodying the contents of the text being performed, has become clear. Through the skilful use of voice and gesture, the presentation of felt emotional values, and the thorough knowledge of the style and images of a given manuscript, the oral reciter in Greco-Roman culture was able to give powerful renditions of texts.

Paul's dictation of his letter was, in all probability, also a coaching of the letter carrier. The length, sophistication and style of Paul's letters, coupled with the very smallness of the group making up the core of the Pauline movement, show us that Paul's letters originated from a very small circle of friends; working together to communicate to their followers, with one (or more) of them transporting the letter and "delivering" it; putting up a special show of verbal rhetoric.

The Letter to the Galatians

Given that oral performance was intrinsic to the Greco-Roman world, I think the argument thus far is pressing us towards asking how "bodily presence" and "speech" are issues in Paul's "conflict" with the Galatians caught up in ἕτερον εὐαγγέλιον. Of course, we will never finally know what mode of communication with its various complexities was at stake here. But there are some things we *can* consider. We have a letter, we know some things about letter writing and exchange of meaning in antiquity, as well as something about presenting speeches, *and* we can make (careful) use of communication research, such as orality studies, performance studies and so forth, so that we can have an experiential understanding of what happens within the matrix of text, reciter and audience.

What were the criteria at stake which led to Paul being considered insufficient or unauthoritative (or ineffective as leader) in Galatia?

Authority and Verbal Presence

There is a widespread consensus that Paul's letters show evidence of what has come to be called apostolic parousia.[62] In the words of Kee, "Paul employs the letter as an instrument of his own apostolic authority. He cannot be in all his churches at once, but his spirit can be and, in his view, *is* there (1 Cor 5:4) . . . There is exact correspondence between his apostolic presence in the

---

62. Funk, "Apostolic Presence."

flesh and in his letters." [63] Reflection on this aspect must surely make one aware of the physical role of the reader of the letter, of his performance of the message.

In other words, the apostle's means of exercising power and influence in a community was dependent on his establishing *apostolic parousia* in that community. This "presence" refers to the apostle's social visibility and authority. When a personal visit was not possible (for whatever reasons), Paul would send someone to represent him to the particular group of early Christians. This chosen delegate (often) carried a letter from Paul which recommended that emissary as an authoritative "substitute" for the apostle.

Sending an emissary to read a letter aloud was probably one of the most effective ways of demonstrating parousia in distant communities. "The personal representative or messenger, the visitor or traveller, were almost the sole means of communication between . . . individuals."[64] In Paul's case the carrier would not only have been briefed on the contents of the letter; he (she?—possible; cf. Rom 16:2) would have been part of its creation.

The "Situation"

Besides theological content and doctrinal differences, if there was a conflict on the authority of Paul, it must have revolved (in part admittedly, but an important part) around the (oral) presentation of one's story/teaching/propaganda. In other words, the "opponents" were more successful in presenting their views. Logic, authority and persuasion are tightly connected to social and cultural conventions, and the performance of a story contributed extensively to the acceptability and credibility of an argument.

To understand the dilemma that the Galatians found themselves in, we should probably turn to the context of the apologetic or missionary movement of Diaspora Judaism. Schoeps has drawn attention to the success of the propaganda of Diaspora Judaism.[65] As this missionary activity had no central organisation, it must have been the synagogue and synagogue activities that created such "annexed bodies of Gentiles."[66] The new converts to the Jesus-movement clearly must have been in contact with the apologetic movement of the synagogue, or would now have become ideal targets for the synagogue movement. The central feature of religious events in the syna-

---

63. Kee, *Christian Origins*, 131–32.
64. McGuire, "Letters and Letter Carriers," 148.
65. Schoeps, *Paul*, 220–29.
66. Ibid., 225.

gogue was the oral reading and exegesis of scripture. Performance of sacred stories and oral interpretations of the traditions made the faith of Judaism accessible to outsiders and helped to assimilate them into the communities of worship.

In fact, the synagogue ceremony, with its focus on the oral reading and interpretation of scripture was the occasion for highly theatrical activity, quite possibly "the worship service was supposed to be a performance for an audience" in which "the immediacy of oral expression was probably preferred."[67] The so-called "Judaizers" that Paul did battle with can plausibly be related to the context of the synagogue apologetic movement, and probably even more specifically among the oral interpreters travelling about and offering performances in Jewish communities.

I would suggest that Paul was in danger of losing his following among and/or his status in the Galatian community to these other missionaries. They had made his ineffective speech and inadequate exposition of tradition cause for the Galatians' concern. Paul's problem was how to establish a presence in the Galatians' community that would recapture their attention and loyalty. This is where the recitation of Paul's letter plays a significant part in the "dialogue" and politics of the early church. In part, Paul needed to re-establish his authority with a performance that was more convincing than that of his opponents.

The challenge for the "faithful Paulinists" was exactly this: by means of an effective counter-performance, they must demonstrate their ability to be "present" in the same vigorous and authoritative way as Paul's opponents. This is a scenario quite to be expected in an orally based culture.

To situate such a scene historically one would like to be on more certain ground concerning the activities of early Christian house churches. "That scripture texts were read and homilies were based on them seems very credible indeed, but details are quite uncertain."[68] If we bring the exposition of scripture and telling and re-telling of Jesus stories amongst the Christians in relation to the very plausible picture of oral performances characterizing synagogue worship as drawn by Georgi,[69] we do have a probable setting for Paul's letter.

---

67. Georgi, *Opponents*, 113–14.

68. Meeks, *First Urban Christians*, 146.

69. Georgi, *Opponents*, 89–117.

Persuading the Galatians

The 'opponents' clearly had impressive claims to authority, and in view of the dynamics of an oral culture, could make their authority manifest in powerful speech. For Paul, and his loyal friends, to counteract this, a powerful attempt at persuading the Galatian Christians had to be made. So we have the reader of the letter frightening those whose preaching differed from Paul's (1:8–9). Then follows a narration, a story in which Paul is the hero (1:12—2:14), in order to have the listeners identify with Paul. Identifying with Paul forces one into choosing like Paul, imitating him, which is nothing but accepting his authority. Galatians 3 and 4 are characterised by rhetorical questions and emotional appeals: the letter makes the reproach that the audience would be acting foolishly and harming themselves if they change their behaviour (i.e. accept Jewish customs). The letter to the Galatians is quite like a *deliberative speech*,[70] and is putting honour and shame at stake. Paul reformulates the rules for shame: "there is no difference between Jews and Gentiles, between slaves and free men, between men and women; you are all one in Christ Jesus" (3:28).

The force (and efficacy) of these words, like the 'bewitchment' language of 3:1, the "hearing of faith/the law" (3:2, 5; 4:21) and the curses and blessings throughout the letter must be understood within the setting of the "magical power of words" characterizing orally based cultures.[71]

We think of Paul's exposition of scripture in terms of its doctrine, its theological content, whilst part of the issue is simply establishing authority by proving skill at the exposition of scripture. It is one of the ways of achieving honour and shaming others.

The letter provides abundant evidence of emotional considerations. Galatians 4:12–20 is an appeal to pity, imploring the audience in humble and submissive language to have mercy, to realise the extent of Paul's care and love for the audience (see especially 4:19–20). With Gal 5:7–12 the listeners are incited to hatred of the people provoking dissent (οἱ ἀναστατοῦντες).

Finally we have Paul writing a sentence learned by rote to authenticate the letter; and, with the help of others, or maybe clumsily copying himself from what someone else wrote for him, adding a reiteration of what the letter is about: a sharp antithesis between "those others" and Paul (6:11–18). Paul is the courageous one; they are cowards and half-hearted, fearing persecution. Paul advocates himself and his "way": that is how the greatest value,

70. This is noted by Kennedy, *New Testament Interpretation*, 145.
71. See Tambiah, *Culture*.

dignity and glory can be achieved. Heady stuff, but an effective means of recommending and dissuading.

What emerges in the performance of the letter is the presence of Paul: a potent and powerful voice which attempts to disrupt and subvert the social structure proposed and created by the oral presentations of Paul's opponents.

Summary

Various scholars have pointed out that there is an oral aspect to Paul's letter writing. This paper takes that insight as a starting point and attempts to situate Pauline epistolography within the context of ancient communicative practices.

To do this, attention is firstly directed to the *oral environment* of the Greco-Roman world. It is argued that, not only did limited literacy exist, but that the literacy of the time must be understood within the context of first-century historical reality: a scribal culture. Some implications for the writing and reading of letters are discussed: the issue of "multi"-authorship, the communal experience of letters, the oral, performative aspect of letter reading. These are briefly illustrated by means of Galatians. Paul, "writer" of letters, appears to be unlike a modern scholar, who is likely to be found turning his notes into a theological treatise. Rather, we discover a small group of early Christians struggling to maintain their identity and defending their views by means of oral presentations.

Though very introductory, and mostly exploratory (which must be emphasised), this chapter is about historical interpretation: to describe some of the activities, and something of the world, of those early Christians.

10

Paul and Gossip

Paul's career was marked by several conflicts. Communication (or lack of it) plays a major role in such misunderstandings and tense relationships. In this study my aim is to draw attention to the role of one form of communication, namely gossip, in some of the situations that Paul found himself in.

A number of South-African New Testament scholars, in various publications, prefer to emphasize the possible value of discourse analysis for proper understanding of the New Testament writings, although they acknowledge that other perspectives (such as narratology and sociology) can provide valuable insights.[1] Additionally, they also note the contribution of "context" to the interpretation of texts. In answer to this stress on the importance of *context*, on proper *historical understanding*,[2] I want to show the interconnection of several approaches to the New Testament writings, by highlighting aspects of the social dynamics in communicative contexts.

It is remarkable how little use has been made of available research on gossip, despite its obvious relevance to understanding the social tensions surrounding Paul. The possible benefits for understanding aspects of the Pauline correspondence from the perspective of gossip is obscured, I think, by the attitude that such study would cast doubt on the supposed *doctrinal* elements in the feuds and quarrels reflected in Paul's letters. The opinion seems to be that the only worthwhile information *must be* information that deals with "important ideas" (determined by whom?) and that the only good knowledge is that which is "authorized" and "approved" (by whom?).

---

1. E.g., Roberts, *Brief aan Filemon*, 2–5. For the impact of "discourse analysis" on South African NT scholarship, see Snyman, "Semiotic Discourse Perspective," 355.

2. Roberts, "Inleiding," 14–16.

Hannerz emphasizes that what gossip does must necessarily be tied to the social context in which it occurs.[3] Conversely, to describe a social context one must give attention to what gossip does in that community. By and large, New Testament scholarship describing "social context" perceives the "typical" social setting to have been one of big events, of major theological upheavals, great men interacting. But that is not what life is like at all. "Popular culture is so much a part of our daily existence that it is all but invisible. But, like other invisible forces, it loses none of its potence thereby . . . In large part it defines the texture if not the fabric of our environment."[4]

Conflict in the Pauline Communities

One of the key issues in the Pauline letters is conflict, and almost every investigation into either the letters or the addressees of Paul's letters deal with it—usually under the rubric of Paul's "opponents." The following viewpoint is very representative: "Die für das Verständnis der Paulusbriefe wichtigste Frage ist die nach den Gegnern, gegen die Paulus in mehreren Briefn kämpft; denn die Argumentation des Paulus wird durch die jeweilige Front entscheidend bestimmt, und nur das Verständnis dieser Front ermöglicht es, die Gedanken des Paulus voll zu begreifen."[5]

Considerable insight has been generated by the "quest" for Paul's opponents. The tendency is, however, to deal with the tensions and discord within the Pauline communities as about "true doctrine." Much of scholarship attempts to describe the conflicts in terms of a history of ideas. The assumption is that distinct groups, with a cohesive counter-theology opposed Paul's teachings. Consequently, the only worthwhile conception of Paul seems to be that of a man engaged solely in theological crisis and debate or in pious worship[6]. Such a perspective leaves far too much of *history* out of the picture.

That is, though everyone may agree that Paul's opponents "stand at the center of the issues involved,"[7] *how* they came to occupy that "centre" is left undiscussed. Precisely *how* the tension between them and Paul manifested and functioned—particularly with regard to social dynamics—is often left undiscussed.

---

3. Hannerz, "Gossip, Networks and Culture," 35.

4. Bigsby, "Preface," vii.

5. Kümmel, *Das Neue Testament im 20. Jahrhundert*, 56.

6. Cf. Hock, *Social Context*, 51.

7. Cf. King, "Paul and the Tannaim," 342.

Craffert reminds us "that the idea of a theological or doctrinal crisis is a scholarly creation based on a specific interpretive tradition. Since Paul neither identifies any opponents nor unequivocally mentions any . . . [in Galatians], all scholarly attempts to construct their identity presuppose a specific socio-historical setting and communication situation . . . In short, given the state of the evidence, it needs to be pointed out that the assumed nature of the conflict more often than not reflects a particular communicative context."[8] Whatever else that "communicative context" were, *informal communication*, daily talk, gossip, was undeniably part and parcel of it. This study suggests that some attention to the process of gossip could shed light on the conflicts and tensions reflected in the Pauline writings. In doing this, I want to urge an attitude toward early Christian writings that stresses "the folk" and the social dynamics of their everyday life.

It would obviously be unrealistic to argue that "doctrine" was the only disruptive force in early Christianity. In fact, as is well known, conflict and its causes in movements are quite complex,[9] and yet very few studies have attempted to utilize the social dynamics of gossip events to understand aspects of the disunity, quarrelling and unhappiness among the Pauline communities.

Gossip, for instance, can be a potent means of social control, a way of fine tuning social relationships.[10] Various studies refer to the control of morals through a gossip network.[11] The argument is not that gossip creates morality, but that it creates the *appearance* of morality. It motivates people to put up defenses, to hide vices and to keep up appearances.

Conversation, daily talk, is part of impression management with which people define identities; hence gossip plays a major part in factionalism, conflict and power struggles.[12]

Much like Theissen argues,[13] I want to emphasize the sociological and historical processes involved in theological and religious experiences. The point is not to reduce the phenomena we study but to *understand* them.

8. Craffert, "Social-scientific Key," 7.

9. Cf., e.g., ibid., 228–39; Craffert, "Herdefiniëring," 859–76; French, "Psycho-dynamics of Adversary Identity," 261–72; Kurtz, "Politics of Heresy," 1085–115; Malina and Neyrey, "Conflict in Luke-Acts."

10. Cf. Arno, "Fijian Gossip as Adjudication."

11. Gluckman, "Gossip and Scandal," 308, 312; Paine, "Informal Communication," 278; Bergmann, *Discreet Indiscretions*, 120–34.

12. Cf., e.g., Cox, "What is Hopi Gossip About?"; Layton, "Patterns of Informal Interaction"; Rasmussen, "Modes of Persuasion."

13. Theissen, *Social Setting*, 44–54.

A Most Gossipy World

General Comments

In antiquity, like today, gossip was mostly seen as a negative activity, something to be censured. In Jewish circles a number of scriptural sayings could be quoted. "Do not go about spreading slander among your father's kin (and do not take sides against your neighbor on a capital charge)" (Lev 19:16). Proverbs, in particular, has a number of things to say about gossip: "A tale-bearer gives away secrets, but a trustworthy person respects a confidence" (Prov 11:13); "Like a gold ring in a pig's snout is a beautiful woman without discretion" (Prov 11:22); or: "A gossip will betray secrets, so have nothing to do with a tale-bearer" (Prov 20:19).

Paul himself associates gossip with such serious transgressions as malice, envy, murder and deceit (Rom 1:29; 2 Cor 12:19). In 1 Timothy gossip is depicted as a feminine activity: the author of the letter dwells upon young widows who, besides their passions distracting them from supposed higher calling, also learn to "to be idle, indeed worse than idle, gossips and busybodies, speaking of things better left unspoken" when they go from house to house (1 Tim 5:13). The remedy for these sinful activities, according to the author of 1 Timothy, is to marry again and have children; in addition such actions will prevent themselves from becoming objects of gossip (5:14).

Plutarch writes in his treatise *Concerning Talkativeness*[14] that speech, "which is the most pleasant and human of social ties," is made inhuman and unsocial by those who use it badly and wantonly.[15] In many instances the "unspoken word" has done greater service than the "spoken word"; consequently, "I think, in speaking we have men as teachers, but in keeping silent we have gods . . ."[16]

Despite such sound insight, gossip permeated the communities of the ancient world. In courtyards, in the markets, in the gymnasia,[17] when meeting one another in the streets and, of course, in the barber shops, people gossiped. "It is not strange that barbers are a talkative clan, for the greatest chatterboxes stream in and sit in their chairs, so that they are themselves infected with the habit."[18]

14. Περι αδολεσχιας—*Moralia* 502–514.

15. Ibid., 504.6

16. Ibid., 505.8F

17. "The gymnasium was like a second public square, a place where anyone could go and where activity was not limited to gymnastics" (Veyne, "Roman Empire," 21).

18. Plutarch, *Moralia* 509A.

Paul suggests that gossip is characteristic of "gentile" behavior,[19] but the rabbis knew otherwise. In the Talmud we find the following despairing comments: "One who bears evil tales almost denies the foundation [of faith]"; or "Anyone who bears evil tales will be visited by the plague of leprosy"—discussing the "deceitful tongue" (*b. 'Arakhin* 15b). The remedy for the evil tongue is, of course, study of Torah.[20]

We must bear in mind that the first century Mediterranean world was, to adopt the words of Schein,[21] a "close" society—that is, a society in which people live not only "towards" each other, but close to each other. In the crowded cities of the Roman empire persons were never alone. Daily urban life in these cities was tantamount to being subject to constant surveillance—truly a "close" society.[22] The many who lived in the tiny apartments of ancient cities, typically "must have lived almost entirely outside [the] apartment, in the streets, shops, arcades, arenas and baths of the city. The average Roman domicile must have served only as a place to sleep and store possessions."[23] The counterpart of the many "little houses" which could not possibly fulfill any social functions, must have been the role of the "big houses," the houses belonging to the (wealthier) patrons and household-owners. In such houses, neither palaces nor yet mansions, were the only "general-purpose rooms" to which urban people of the first century Mediterranean world could have access to. And, to make use of Ariès' wonderfully evocative description of daily life in pre-industrial France, it is in these (few) rooms of the "big houses" that people "lived." "In the same room where they ate, people slept, danced, worked and received visitors."[24] In addition to the families occupying the house, their servants, employees, apprentices, teacher(s), secretary(-ies) and associates, must be added the friends, clients, relatives and protegés. Life in such houses in the world of antiquity, we must imagine, was one of a constant flow of visitors. "The latter apparently gave little thought to the hour

19. Rom 1:29. In his argument (Rom 1:18–32) Paul starts of by arguing for the ungodliness and unrighteousness of *human beings*, but from v. 21 further the point is very much an "explanation" and "illustration" of the wickedness of Gentile idolatry (see the discussion by Moo, *Romans*, 96–97). Paul is discussing "characteristically Gentile sins, all of which deserve death" (Countryman, *Dirt, Greed and Sex*, 110, cf. 110–23).

20. Other rabbinic comment on gossip: *b. Pesahim* 113a, 118a; *b. Mo'ed Qatan* 18b; *b. Sanhedrin* 8a; *b. 'Abodah Zarah* 3b; *m. Abot* 1.5; *b. Abot* 6.5.

21. Schein, "Used and Abused," 139.

22. Cf. MacMullen, *Roman Social Relations*, 62; Stowers, "Social Status," 81–82; Veyne, "Roman Empire," 72–75.

23. Packer, "Housing," 87; cf. Botha, "Houses in the World of Jesus," 54–57.

24. Ariès, *Centuries of Childhood*, 381.

and were never shown the door . . . In short, visits gave the impression of being a positive occupation, which governed the life of the household and even dictated its mealtimes. These visits were not simply friendly or social: they were also professional; but little or no distinction was made between these categories."[25]

In the world under discussion most information consisted of oral communication, face-to-face talk.[26] "These conditions fostered gossip, created a propensity to believe it (as there were no counter checks to information received through oral communication), and contributed to its power. Indeed, as in other "close" societies, gossip played a most powerful role."[27]

Attitudes to Gossip

Gossip was widely denounced. Clement of Rome, for instance, admonishes the Corinthian Christians: "Let us exercise mutual tolerance of one another's views, cultivating humility and self-restraint, avoiding all gossiping and backbiting, and be justified by deeds and not by words. For [Scripture] says, he who is full of words shall be answered in full measure. Does eloquence make righteous? A short life to any one born of woman is a blessing [since it provides less opportunity for talking too much]. Be weary of talking too much!"[28]

Further on in his letter Clement again urges that Christians should cast away from themselves "gossiping and evil-speaking."[29] Clement associates gossiping (ψιθυρισμός) and bad-mouthing or slander (καταλαλιά) with abominable passions, detestable adultery and, his "favorite" sin, pride. He

---

25. Ibid., 380.

26. "A community at a low level of technology has rather low levels of information circulating within it, whereas a society which is highly developed technologically is inundated by communicators' messages. Specifically, traditional societies rely on oral communications and have none of our mass media. Most of their populations are illiterate, whereas industrialization requires mass literacy. Most of their communications are private and person to person, whereas most of the communications circulating in industrialized society are mass-produced and impersonal . . . In the societies under review . . . communications percolate out in irregular fashion. If one were close to an important person, he would know far more of what was going on than would another man who was closer to the scene of the action but not well connected" (Carney, *Shape of the Past*, 111–12).

27. Schein, "Used and Abused," 139.

28. *1 Clem.* 30.3–5.

29. *1 Clem.* 35.5.

also lists gossiping among wickedness (in general?), covetousness, strife, malice, hatred of God, arrogance and inhospitality.

This negative attitude is well attested. In fact, very few people seek or willingly accept the designation of "gossiper." Usually, the moment we recognize gossip "morality" kicks in and we either avoid, correct or censure the gossiping. Despite such moralizing attitude, and the negative public image popularly ascribed to it, gossiping continues unabated.

Children, it seems, gossip practically from the time they learn to talk and to recognize other people.[30] Older people are widely considered to be notorious gossips. Through the ages, women have been accused of being natural gossips[31]—a false and dangerously misleading popular conception.[32] We all gossip, more or less, at one stage or another.[33]

30. Cf. Fine, "Social Components of Children's Gossip," 181–85; Goodwin, "He-said-she-said," 674–95; Schein, "Used and Abused," 143.

31. The Talmudic comment, "Ten measures of gossip descended to the world: nine were taken by women" (*b. Qiddushin* 49b), is quite typical of such stereotyping.

32. Men simply gossip about different things/persons than women; that is, the difference between the sexes lies in the subjects gossiped about, not in the general tendency to gossip (see Nevo, Nevo and Derech-Zehavi, "Tendency to Gossip," 180–89). Code ("Gossip, or in Praise of Chaos," 100–105) maintains that gossip is only as characteristic of communication among women as it is of other oppressed groups. Rysman ("How the 'Gossip' became a Woman," 176–80) shows how gossip functions in female solidarity, and because female solidarity is frowned upon in male dominant societies gossip is seen negatively (see further Jones, "Gossip: notes on women's oral culture," 193–98; Collins, "Gossip: a feminist defense," 106–15; Dorn, "Gender and Personhood," 295–301). Bergmann (*Discreet Indiscretions*, 62–67) shows how the organization of the division of labor contributes to the position of gossip producer.

33. All studies of gossip demonstrate its pervasive role in community life (cf., e.g., Gluckman, "Gossip and Scandal," 308; Goodman, "Introduction," 1; Bergmann, *Discreet Indiscretions*, 149). The maliciousness that is commonly attributed to gossip is an interesting social feature itself, and the popular moral bias with which gossip is commonly viewed limits proper understanding of the continuing and pervasive role of it. Indeed, if gossip were but slanderous stories that circulate without any grounds whatsoever for their existence, their presence would be evidence of unreasonableness and a sign of madness. They must then be the sociological counterpart of various pathologies (people would be universally malicious). The association of gossip with affliction and even destruction appears logical but is misleading—as is the association of gossip with lies. If gossip mainly conveyed false information, most people would not find it interesting. The sheer force of gossip, its ubiquitousness, its immense sociological importance and the seriousness with which it is taken by *all* people belie the popular conception. Ben-Ze'ev ("Vindication of Gossip") shows that gossip is an "intrinsically valuable activity" with, typically, a casual and nonconsequential nature. Spacks (*Gossip*) has written eloquently on the essential *humanness* of gossip (see, e.g. Spacks, *Gossip*, 23), its "positive energies" (ibid., 258). Though gossip provides fertile ground for the exercise of many vices, "such faults can no more be held against gossip in itself than they can be held against love,

Paul, who places gossip among such serious misdeeds as malice, murder and deceit, himself got involved with several gossip events that we know of. When certain reports reach Paul he is quick to evaluate and participate[34] in "news" about absent others—clearly a gossip event is occurring. "Discussions" of similar "reports"[35] too should probably be construed as gossip.

In fact, Paul himself could discuss an absent third party evaluatively.[36] In Gal 2:11–14 Paul gossips about Cephas, evaluating his inconsistent behavior in the controversy over gentile Christians living like Jews. Paul's complaint serves a number of functions, but is an especially clear example of how character evaluation plays a role in leadership issues and in competition for loyalty.

What Is Gossip?

Plutarch complains that gossips pass up nearly anything beautiful or worthwhile so they can "spend their time digging into other men's trifling communication, gluing their ears to their neighbor's walls, whispering with slaves and women of the streets, and often incurring danger, and always infamy."[37]

The implicit definition of gossip seems to be the repetition of hearsay with some moral connotation—supposedly the activity of an aberrant few. Yet gossip is among the most important social phenomena we can study. It is much more complex and far-reaching than is usually suspected, and can often be seen as a significant means of informal social formation and power. To understand the power and consequence of gossip one must recall the immense role of conversation in being human.[38]

The verb "gossip" refers to a diverse range of behaviors all of which have to a greater or lesser extent some things in common.[39] Two aspects in particular seem to characterize gossip. Gossip is personal, an "in-group" ac-

---

marriage, or commerce, all of which notoriously provide opportunities for the deployment of the very same vices [such as malice, envy, prevarication]" (De Sousa, "In Praise of Gossip," 26). A readable plea for "treating gossip seriously" is Sabini and Silver, *Moralities of Everyday Life*, 89–106.

34. 1 Cor 1:11.

35. E.g., 1 Corinthians 5–6.

36. Adopting Gilmore's ("Varieties of Gossip," 92) elucidation of gossip as "critical talk about absent third parties."

37. Plutarch, *De curiositate* 9; Plutarch, *Moralia* 6.519F

38. Emler, "Gossip, Reputation and Social Adaptation," 124–25.

39. Cf. Abrahams, "Performance-centred Approach," 290–91; see also Bergmann, *Discreet Indiscretions*, 26–44.

tivity: "To be able to gossip together, individuals must know one another."[40] Gossip is essentially information about known persons.[41]

The other aspect is that gossip is evaluative talk. It may be either positive or negative,[42] but it usually implies assessment, some moral characterization, of the subject under discussion.

For the purposes of this study, gossip can be defined as "spontaneous free ranging discussion between two or more persons about a third party external to the discussion group which centers on the party's personal characteristics, behavior, or associations and incorporates a critical element involving moral evaluation or judgment."[43] I emphasize that my interest is not in *defining* gossip[44] but in some of the *social dynamics* involved in certain forms of daily conversation.

Without denying or diminishing the possible adverse and harmful aspects of gossip, we need to move beyond the so-called commonsensical bias to understand this phenomenon. Gossip is not *necessarily* negative or malicious. It "was often motivated by a keen and healthy interest in one's neighbors or friends, in the affairs of one's prince or king, or by one's wish for a good time."[45] "Gossip can be a precious resource: people in businesses learn about their competitors; politicians require details about their rivals and supporters; citizens discover who are their friends and who their enemies, and so on . . . gossip can be useful: not only to uncover information, but also to promote, help, humiliate or criticize other people."[46]

Gossip is in a sense not different from simple word-of-mouth "news" about what is going on; it is information-sharing which develops into evaluative talk, a form of "information management." "In nonliterate societies, gossip is a method of storing and retrieving information about the social environment."[47] Gossip is a dynamic process intrinsic to human conversation

40. Yerkovich, "Gossiping as a Way of Speaking," 192; see also Bergmann, *Discreet Indiscretions*, 71–91.

41. Cf. Bergmann, *Discreet Indiscretions*, 54.

42. Cf. Rosnow and Fine, *Rumor and Gossip*, 87.

43. Allen and Guy, *Conversation Analysis*, 247.

44. Goldsmith, "Gossip from the Native's Point of View," 164–66 (see also Bergmann, *Discreet Indiscretions*; Sabini and Silver, *Moralities of Everyday Life*, 89–93).

45. Schein, "Used and Abused," 145.

46. Zinovieff, "Inside Out and Outside In," 124.

47. Levin and Arluke, *Gossip: Inside Scoop*, 22 (see also Cox, "What is Hopi Gossip About?"; Du Boulay, *Portrait of a Greek Mountain Village*, 201–29; Arno, "Fijian Gossip as Adjudication"; Paine, "Informal Communication," 172–88).

with a highly variable structure which searches for, exchanges and uses information about others.[48]

Carriers of Gossip

We often picture Paul's opponents to have been "strangers," the "other" in the community. We think of them as some concurrent group with "radically" different notions. But social conflicts most often erupt exactly between not only "equals" but especially among people close to one another. With regard to the family- and household-centered world of antiquity the following remark by Layton is particularly apt: "But if it is true that it is kin and neighbours who most often work together, it is also true that it is between these people that disputes most often develop: 'Quarrels usually occur within families.'"[49] "The prime competitor—the first enemy—is frequently the [person] nearest to you in rank . . . Those nearest are also those with whom you interact most frequently and, therefore, those with whom you are most likely to have a cause for contention."[50]

What Paul writes in admonishment to the Corinthians, namely that "perhaps there may be quarrelling, jealousy, anger, selfishness, slander, gossip, conceit and disorder"[51] should he arrive, is *exactly* what the general situation in many a household was.

Obviously, when we ask about who possible gossipers were, the list is endless. One significant role, not mentioned by Paul (and usually ignored by studies of early Christian social worlds) is that of children. Children must have been ever-present in the contexts in which Paul and his followers and interested associates moved. When we imagine children in ancient cities we should *not* project our modern, structured and public systems onto their situation.

In a community without mass-media communication channels, we should imagine, pre-adolescent children play a vital role in the dissemination of "news." Somewhat analogous to the following description:

> Children of this age group have full run of the community and enter any house without knocking. They are not as yet endowed with specific personalities by adults other than their own parents, and form more than anything else, simply a part of the

48. Yerkovich, "Gossiping as a Way of Speaking," 195.
49. Ibid., "Patterns of Informal Interaction," 98.
50. Bailey, "Gifts and Poison," 19.
51. 2 Cor 12:20.

> background—the setting. Either alone or in groups, boys or girls come in without a word and take a seat . . . They require no acknowledgement . . . On their return home, they will be asked where they have been and what is "new," whereupon they will relate all they have heard and witnessed with remarkable detail.[52]

The utility of children in the role of collecting "information" cannot be underestimated; women could often not leave the house or did not have access to certain groups and/or events.

Knowledge about others is, as Bergmann reminds us, unequally distributed in society.[53] The gossip producer is someone who is "well informed" about the affairs of another or about events. A gossiper is someone who "knows"—not as much as the person who knows everything about one's own affairs, but more than "typical" knowledge. It follows that certain "vocational groups" who *can* acquire information tend to be gossipers: people who, "because of their daily contacts at work and encounters with other members of their social network, . . . are very apt to be transmitters of information."[54]

One can readily imagine the role that trusted slaves, or servants such as doorkeepers and porters could play in this regard. Plutarch, incidentally, notes that doorkeepers became necessary so that the "busybody" (ὁ πολυπράγμων) might not discover a slave being punished or hear the maidservants screaming.[55] What is of relevance is to realize that servants in special positions were often caught between conflicting loyalties.

Bergmann argues that it is the inherently conflicting, indeed paradoxical loyalty structure of friendship and acquaintanceship that counts as the main source of energy for the communicative genre "gossip."[56] One is obligated to discretion towards one's friend. Yet, most people have to balance many loyalties; one is also obligated to inform, warn, consider and entertain—to trust—one's other friends. It is this contradictory situation that establishes and maintains gossip: "the social form of discreet indiscretion."[57]

This is a powerful social dynamic, and its workings cannot be predicted nor controlled. In an earlier study I draw attention to the importance of co-authors, secretaries and letter carriers in the production and dissemination

---

52. Faris, "Dynamics of Verbal Exchange," 239–40.

53. Bergmann, *Discreet Indiscretions*, 57.

54. Ibid., 66.

55. *Moralia* 6.516F—never mind the busybody, imagine the stories the doorkeeper could tell.

56. Bergmann, *Discreet Indiscretions*, 151.

57. Ibid., 150–52.

of Paul's letters. These very same people probably played an enormous role in the to-and-fro of information between Paul and the various communities in which he worked. We might like to think of these people as single-mindedly devoted to Paul with absolute and blind loyalty, but they were not. Clearly not, judging from the many misunderstandings evident from the Corinthian correspondence, Galatians, and 1 Thessalonians. It is realistic to imagine complex negotiations, difficult patrons, powerful skeptics, life-long friends, family bonds, and even survival strategies in the lives of these people: many discreet indiscretions.

The Subject Matter of Gossip

Obviously, the subject matters of gossip are most various and diverse. "Within their communities, people gossiped about the most usual and trivial events, as well as about the most extraordinary ones."[58] The arrival of travelers, for instance, surely drew interest. Paul travelled in groups.[59] Not only the appearance of (another) travelling teacher, but also his companions were occasions for interest and possibly suspicion.

The popular image of gossip is that of an overwhelming interest in scandal, specifically with regard to matters of love and marriage. Veyne notes that in the Roman empire rhetoric "became a society game" and the education of young men consequently became an expression of the Roman "taste for melodrama and sex."[60] In this sense gossip must have been (and probably still is, the world over) the most "rhetorical" of activities.

One might not easily imagine people talking about Paul within the context of love and sex, but surely his ideas that it was "good for a man not to touch a woman" (1 Cor 7:1), his celibacy and his not traveling with a wife as did other apostles (1 Cor 9:5) and his wish that "all were as I myself am" (1 Cor 7:7) provoked more than a neutral comment. Especially, one can imagine, when Paul *also* urged partners to engage in sex regularly (1 Cor 7:5) and was not above adopting patronesses: Phoebe, for instance (Rom 16:2)[61] or Lydia (Acts 16). Zealous persons always prompt evaluative discussion and

---

58. Schein, "Used and Abused," 146.

59. Mainly for reasons of safety: 2 Cor 11:25–27 (see Hock, *Social Context*, 28).

60. Veyne, "Roman Empire," 23.

61. In Rom 16:2 προστάτις should be understood in the sense of "patroness" (Sanders, *Paul*, 11; and especially Jewett, "Paul, Phoebe, and the Spanish Mission," 149–55). On the role of Phoebe in Paul's correspondence with the Romans see Vorster, "Rhetorical Situation of the Letter to the Romans," 204–5.

Paul was "a zealot fully and totally committed to the course which he felt called by God."[62]

Another topic of interest to people is that of origins: one's family, parents, genealogy. "Though we are quite indifferent and ignorant with regard to our own affairs, we pry into the pedigrees of others: our neighbour's grandfather was a Syrian and his grandmother a Thracian . . ."[63] At the time, perceptions of one's role, status and honor were influenced by one's roots, ancestry and genealogy—as shown by Malina and Neyrey.[64]

It is therefore to be expected that Paul would refer from time to time to his background: his origins and genealogy. What is remarkable, however, is that he does so to people who *already* know him, his followers (or converts). "Though, with Paul, overreaction is always possible, I still wish to argue that Paul's sensitivity, or oversensitivity, is explained, at least in part, by his opponents' sneering at his origins."[65]

The issue, I suggest, is not so much Paul being attacked by so-called opponents, but that some of the people who had dealings with Paul remained convinced—for whatever reasons—that not everything was being revealed. People who knew him believed that there was some doubts surrounding these issues; possibly some "secrets," which is exactly what generates gossip. It is also worth noting that Paul's response is not to refer to witnesses or evidence that can be checked, but to invoke God.[66] Paul's response is drastic: it forces one to the level of faith. Either one believes in God and hence Paul's version of his background or one challenges the "God and Father of the lord Jesus who is blessed forever."[67] In all probability Paul's "absolutizing" of the issue contributed to the suspicion of a difference between the image projected by Paul and the "real," private Paul.

North cites evidence to show that Paul's Cilician background was the issue: Cilicians are traditionally considered all to be liars, hence Paul's severe response.

Paul's conversion was construed as disloyalty and betrayal. His new attitudes towards ancestral institutions like circumcision and observance of the Law, as these related to Gentiles, only confirmed his fellow-Jews' judgment. His tortured relations with his new friends, e.g. at Corinth, were no

62. Sanders, *Paul*, 13, 108.
63. Plutarch, *Moralia* 6.516B.
64. Malina and Neyrey, *Portraits of Paul*, 158–61.
65. North, "Paul's Protest," 462.
66. Gal 1:20; 2 Cor 11:31.
67. Cf. 2 Cor 4:2, 5:10–11, 11:31.

better. Whether they were repeating what they knew the Jews were already saying or were proceeding independently with plenty of evidence of their own, the Corinthian Christians were ready to see in Paul's craft and guile, his taking advantage, robbing, wronging, and corrupting, simply the sort of thing one could expect to find in Cilicians. Like all men, but particularly so, they "were deceivers ever."[68]

The evidence adduced by North, though impressive, is not fully persuasive and it remains doubtful whether it was Paul's *Cilician* background that was the problem.[69] I do think that his basic insight is correct, however. Paul was a much discussed person, and his origins and genealogy did not really convince a number of people—probably exactly those whose opinions really mattered in many of the communities where he worked.

The Power of Gossip

Gossip can be a matter of life or death. People once gossiped about how adamantine the rule of Dionysius, tyrant of Syracuse, was. The barber, in whose shop the conversation took place, bragged: "Fancy your saying that about Dionysius, when I have my razor at his throat every few days or so." Needless to say, the barber was promptly crucified when Dionysius learned of the remark.[70]

Gossip can be a powerful social force in any society at any time, but to understand the potency of gossip in ancient society we must remember that in pre-industrial ages the chief source of vital information was oral narrative, a means of communication characterized more than any other by uncritical acceptance of what is said.[71] What Schein writes about medieval times is equally valid for antiquity: "Since oral communication was the main method of passing information from person to person, there was no way to distinguish precisely between 'gossip,' 'information,' or 'news.' They were often and sometimes even maliciously and intentionally confused."[72]

68. North, "Paul's Protest," 462.

69. The evidence is cited from a wide range of authors, covering several centuries, but are mostly incidental remarks. Undoubtedly antiquity was characterized by local cultures sneering at "others" (consider Titus 1:12, "Cretans are liars, evil beasts, lazy gluttons"), but "there is no evidence in Paul's letters and only a little early evidence elsewhere that it was explicitly Paul's Cilician origins that were ever the cause of criticism of him," as noted by North ("Paul's Protest," 462) himself.

70. Plutarch, *Moralia* 6.508F–509A.

71. Cf. Schein, "Used and Abused," 151.

72. Ibid., 144.

The power of gossip in first century Mediterranean urban society also arose from its social structure, which was highly hierarchic, with strict and well defined codes of behaviour for the social classes. Schein's summary is, once more, apt. "Together, these factors—the credibility of oral information, the strict codes of behavior, as well as immibility and closeness of the relatively small communities—gave gossip great potency. Gossip was often accepted as truth, and, given the strict codes of behavior, gossip could destroy people's reputation and their position in society. Gossip spread to all members of the small, close communities of the Middle Ages, and often a consensual 'group opinion' developed."[73] In a "close" and predominantly oral society, gossip can destroy one's honour, reputation, and even one's life—and it should be greatly feared. Nevertheless, and in spite of repeated warnings and admonitions against gossip in the various genres of ancient literature, people from all walks of life gossiped.

The Tentmaker Apostle

Although some possible controversies relating to Paul as a subject of gossip have already been introduced, two related aspects require further elaboration. The first is the household context of Paul's "ministry," the second is Paul's work as a tentmaker.

The Private House as Context for Paul's Teaching

A number of remarks already made in this study remind us of the importance of the household setting for understanding the Pauline movement. The large private house, I propose, due to its social structure and community functions, provided the favorable conditions for the structural possibility for the seriality of stories which makes gossip possible. It is in the "big houses" of the communities that Paul visited where we find the "communicative context that invites serial transmission of news and stories that have to be discreetly withheld within other contexts."[74]

To what extend did private houses provide the context for Paul's activities?[75] Despite popular opinion, Paul had limited options when he ar-

73. Ibid., 151.

74. Bergmann, *Discreet Indiscretions*, 136.

75. With regard to the so-called house churches: Blue, "Acts and the House Church," 119–222; Craffert, "Pauline Movement," 233–62; Malherbe, *Social Aspects of Early Christianity*, 61–65; Meeks, *First Urban Christians*, 29–30, 75–77, 142–50; Murphy-O'Connor,

rived in a city. He did not have the status, nor the reputation or recognized role which could enable him to be a public speaker: he was not invited by a "city" to come and "evangelize" them. Sometimes Paul used the synagogue;[76] when he did he (usually) encountered opposition. The synagogue must have been *a* locus for Paul to preach, where he by birth and heritage would have a recognized status (as a Jew). But being a Jewish *Christian* made him an ambiguous and controversial figure. But even Paul's synagogue activities would have been within specific households: "Synagogues were, in short, household based (Jewish) communities."[77]

In the case of a short stopover, lodging for Paul would be a minor concern. Either his travel companions would have assisted him or "elsewhere" would have sufficed. For instance, at Philippi Paul stayed somewhere else before moving to the house of Lydia.[78] Precisely where "elsewhere" was we do not know; it could have been an inn, but gymnasia, temples and synagogues accommodated travelers.[79] But when he intended to carry on missionary activity, as in the city of Corinth, Paul usually found long-term accommodation with someone sympathetic to his cause: Lydia's house in Philippi, Jason's house in Thessalonica for several months[80], Aquila and Priscilla's house in Corinth for a year and a half.[81]

The private home provided Paul with the setting where an audience could be obtained and taught without the problems of presenting oneself to be judged by the criteria of public speaking. Homes were an important centre of intellectual activity and the customary place for many types of speakers and teachers to do their work. Occasional lectures, declamations

---

St. Paul's Corinth, 153–61.

76. Though, clearly, not as often nor as consistently as Luke suggests in Acts. Luke has a special interest in portraying the Jesus movement as composed of pious Jews along with God-fearing Gentiles who are seeking the one God and that both groups can live alongside each other (see Stowers, "Social Status," 61–62). In this regard, Acts 20:20 is probably Luke's most reliable characterisation of Paul's activities: conversing and teaching in public and in houses (δημοσίᾳ καὶ κατ᾽ οἴκους)—"in public" here refers to ἐν τῇ σχολῇ Τυράννου (Acts 19:9). The gymnasium and synagogue were, in the words of Stowers (ibid., 82) "places of ambiguous status for Paul."

77. Craffert, "Pauline Movement," 249.

78. Acts 16:15.

79. Casson, *Travel in the Ancient World*, 209–18; Forbes, "Expanded Uses of the Greek Gymnasium," 35; Safrai, "Synagogue," 943; Stambaugh, "Functions of Roman temples," 585–91.

80. Acts 17:5–6.

81. Acts 18:3, 11.

and readings of various sorts of works often took place in homes.[82] Such sessions might be continued for several days—Pliny mentions two or three days.[83] These events were private affairs and audiences came by invitation. The point is that such homes were more than just a place to speak or an occasion for hospitality. The householder provided the speaker with an audience and social legitimation.

It is consequently no accident that patrons and households are so prominent in Paul's letters. The necessary invitations, sponsors, audiences and credentials to teach within a community could only become possible for Paul by means of patrons and (relatively) wealthy households.[84] When Paul says "I baptized the household of Stephanus" (1 Cor 1:16; 16:15–16), the implication is clearly that the "preaching" which led to these baptisms occurred in someone's house. In his letter to the Romans he mentions that Gaius is his patron; some Corinthian Christians met in Gaius' house (though Paul calls him host of the "whole congregation," Rom 16:23).

Within these houses Paul probably lectured—not unlike a travelling sophistic philosopher[85]—and established a temporary school. "If one imagines Paul as the central figure in teaching activity which involved the household of Gaius, believers from other households, Paul's travelling associates and fellow workers and invited outsiders, one has a situation which is in many ways remarkably like the school in the home of Plutarch in Chaeronea."[86]

What exactly went on, or was said, when the various Christian groups in Corinth "came together" in the respective houses (1 Cor 11:17–34), must have been oft asked questions. For the insider, meeting in a private house is a reminder of their distinctness. Not so for the outsider.

Furthermore, Paul probably had little appreciation for (or understanding of) the subtleties and complexities of household politics and organization. In the urban Mediterranean world familial love-patriarchalism placed a high value on hierarchy and on the obedience of women, children and slaves, frowning on any ethical radicalism.[87] Paul's teachings probably—in

82. Cf. Botha, "Community and Conviction in Luke-Acts," 150–51; Sherwin-White, *Letters of Pliny*, 116, 251. From many possible references I note the following: Epictetus, *Diss.* 3.23.23; Pliny, *Ep.* 3.18; 5.3,1–2, 11–12; 8.21.1–2; 9.34; Dio Chrysostom, *Or.* 77–78.34.

83. Pliny, *Ep.* 3.18.

84. Malherbe, *Social Aspects*, 45–59.

85. On which see Hatch, *Influence of Greek ideas on Christianity*, 91–92.

86. Stowers, "Social Status," 69. On Plutarch's house-school: Barrow, *Plutarch and His Time*, 18–19; Russell, *Plutarch*, 13–14.

87. Cf. Meeks, *First Urban Christians*, 76; Theissen, *Social Setting*, 37.

various ways—led to many misunderstandings, which surely set the tongues wagging.

Though the influential householder/patron provided Paul with an audience, that audience remained in a very real sense the audience *of the patron*. Given the harsh social and economic circumstances of ancient urban life, clients, friends, families, associates and servants had little choice but to support and promote the interests of their patron(s).

It is quite clear that Paul sometimes did not really join the households that provided him with teaching and lecturing opportunities (particularly in Corinth and Galatia). Immediately, one can surmise, loyalty and friendship must have been issues. "Friends have everything in common" was an important *topos*, and considered to be an essential feature of many a patron-client relationship.[88] It is quite understandable that some perceived in Paul's way of doing things a refusal of friendship. Yet, he unhesitatingly made use of the opportunities provided by these persons.

The complexities of (relatively short) participation in some households contributed to Paul's problems. "Absence, acquaintanceship, and privacy," writes Bergman,[89] are the "three constitutive features of the figure of gossip." Privacy should be understood as *distance or difference between projected life (by the gossipee) and perceived life (by the gossipers)*. And Paul provided many with ample ground for suspicion. At the personal level, Paul was unimpressive—yet he made bold and awesome statements. He was a poor speaker but wrote letters with strong presence. His letters came from afar, where like a coward he could remain out of direct confrontation and still lord it over others. To some, his morality was questionable. He could not make up his mind whether to visit Corinth or not; he had favorite groups and neglected the Corinthians. He was crafty, full of guile, dishonorable, played up to his audiences, worldly, an imposter. He took advantage, robbed, wronged and corrupted (2 Cor 12:16–18; 6:8; 7:2).

Tentmaking

In addition to lodging, Paul also had to find work in one of the local tentmaking shops. The earnings from Paul's tentmaking would have gone for necessities: food, clothing, perhaps part of his householder's rent. Sometimes, Paul was not able to make ends meet. Despite long hours in the workshop, he

88. Hock, *Social Context*, 56; O'Neill, "Plutarch on Friendship," 107–8.
89. Bergmann, *Discreet Indiscretions*, 54.

was in want at times.[90] Like any artisan Paul would have worked hard—day and night, amounting to exhausting toil (1 Thess 2:9). Being itinerant, Paul could not establish a reputation of being successful at his trade, or accumulate some (modest) affluence. Though his work allowed him the claim of being self-sufficient, his claim could only be made at the cost of considerable deprivations and poverty (Phil 4:12; 2 Cor 6:10; 11:9).

The greatest cost of his independence, however, was the hostility and contempt directed toward artisans in general (and Paul in particular) by representatives of the dominant ethos. In the social world of the cities of the Roman Mediterranean trades carried certain stigmas. Workshops employed virtually no one but slaves and artisans were poorly educated with little time for philanthropy and the pursuit of other virtues. "Stigmatized as slavish, uneducated, and often useless, artisans, to judge from scattered references, were frequently reviled or abused, often victimized, seldom if ever invited to dinner, never accorded status, and even excluded from one Stoic utopia . . . Making tents meant rising before dawn, toiling until sunset with leather, knives, and awls, and accepting the various social stigmas and humiliations that were part of the artisans' lot, not to mention the poverty—being cold, hungry, and poorly clothed."[91]

Paul's trade, and his continuing work, made his status problem more acute. "In other words, Paul's weak appearance was due in part to his plying a trade. In the social world of a city like Corinth, Paul would have been a weak figure, without power, prestige and privilege. We recall the shoemaker Micyllus, depicted by Lucian as penniless and powerless—poor, hungry, wearing an unsightly cloak, granted no status, and victimized. To those of wealth and power, the appearance (σχῆμα) of the artisan was that befitting a slave (δουλοπρεπές)."[92]

What complicates matters is that while Paul refused to forfeit his "independence," he also failed to win the unambiguous and full support of certain patrons (1 Cor 9:15–19; 2 Cor 2:17). Though Paul's choice may seem eminently sensible to us, it was not so considered by the Corinthians. Furthermore, Paul was also guilty of contradicting himself, accepting support from

90. Cf. 2 Cor 11:9; Phil 4:12. "We can appreciate Paul's self sufficiency when we note how dependent on their families were the students who had left home and had traveled to another city in order to study with a philosopher; they regularly received provisions, mostly foodstuffs, from home and even had a family slave along to help support them . . . It was clearly difficult to live away from home and from one's source of income and support" (Hock, *Social Context*, 81 n. 50).

91. Hock, *Social Context*, 36–37.

92. Ibid., 60.

the Macedonian Christians. No wonder his initial defense (in 1 Corinthians) did not convince the Corinthians.

Paul and Gossip

Gossip, as Emler notes, is a two-edged weapon.[93] It "offers scope to manipulate the reputations of others, but with risks to the self when such manipulation is too transparently self-serving or clumsy": "the audience wishes to evaluate the credibility of what they are being told (Is this all true? Does this person know what he or she is talking about? Is he/she attempting to manipulate or mislead me?)."[94]

In a way, that is precisely what Paul is attempting: to show or to convince that the "others" are self-serving, *they* are clumsy, *they* are bad news. He tries to show them up as *false confidants*. What is remarkable, is the way in which Paul is doing this.

What I am suggesting, in brief, is that sometimes (most of the time?) it was *not* a case of Paul being attacked by heretics propounding a serious counter-theology, but one of someone telling Paul, "they say that . . ." And Paul did not or could not deal with that simple "they say that . . ." He took it all very seriously, far too seriously, and interpreted such common, everyday talk in absolute terms: he theologized his own life and work. Because he saw himself as a divine instrument, as God's representative (e.g., Gal 1:6–9, 15–16; 2:20; 4:14; 5:10), Paul was convinced that he *had* to force the conversation onto the level of ultimate choices. His drastic attempts of dealing with the "others," those who "say that. . ." convinced some, but clearly not everyone.

The continued functioning, the strategic survival of a household, is of considerable importance to it its members. Gossip depends heavily on a shared history and common values among at least some part of every community.[95] Talk about the behavior of other people is the means by which a group's opinion on moral behavior emerges and then becomes a means for exploration and maintenance of group norms and expectations.[96] In fact, without hearsay and gossip the cohesiveness of groups of all kinds would probably be under pressure.

93. Emler, "Gossip, Reputation and Social Adaptation," 135.

94. Ibid., 136.

95. Abrahams, "Performance-centred Approach," 300; Bailey, "Gifts and Poison," 8–9; Du Boulay, *Portrait of a Greek Mountain Village*, 210–11.

96. Cf. Levin and Arluke, *Gossip: Inside Scoop*, 125–26.

The subjects discussed or gossiped about commonly deal with the proper maintenance of the household and the appropriate practice of interpersonal relationships within the family and among friends. Talk about such matters constantly serves to remind those involved of the importance of the norms of the community, but also rehearses the necessity of working within the decorum system by which household and friendship networks are maintained.[97]

An important function of gossip is to clarify group membership.[98] A gossip event involves at least three parties, and *usually* the first is implicitly seeking solidarity with the second against the (absent) third, thus re-affirming who is "in" and who is "out." Often, a critical step in gaining membership in any group is learning its gossip.[99]

The gossip circle thus marks a group off from all other groups which are not privy to its secrets. It does the same with individuals who are marked as outsiders because they are not given access to the group's gossip circle.[100] Insidership is characterized by the ability to gossip together: "gossip defines a community."[101]

Those who push the boundaries of acceptable behavior and "identity" of their social group too far are quickly penalized by the gossip network.[102] This is what happened to Paul. He had little time for (or appreciation of) the many daily conflicts of relationships. The very loyalty structure of a community which holds it together is also the source of energy for gossip.[103]

Gossip, as moral assessment, also differentiates *within* a group. Leaders are identified as those who embody (and can articulate) group norms.[104] Competition between leaders can take the form of gossip. As leaders talk about their rivals, and as followers pass along the gossip, factions owing allegiance to particular individuals begin to emerge.

97. Abrahams, "A Performance-centered Approach," 296–97.

98. Gluckman ("Gossip and Scandal ") is, in a way, the classic exponent of gossip as a mechanism of preserving social groups. His study is competently criticized by Bergmann (*Discreet Indiscretions*, 144–46). Though Gluckman's functionalist perspective may be his Achilles heel, his study contains many relevant insights.

99. Gluckman, "Gossip and Scandal," 314.

100. Ibid., 311–12.

101. Zinovieff, "Inside Out and Outside In," 123.

102. Cf. ibid., 122.

103. Bergmann, *Discreet Indiscretions*, 151.

104. Gluckman, "Gossip and Scandal," 307.

This "political" aspect of group interaction reveals that gossip partakes in "impression management."[105] Gossip is manipulative talk, highly selective in terms of both audience and content. A gossiper can control who knows what. Particularly in societies where the spread of information depends on word of mouth, information and impression management becomes critically important to those in power or those seeking power.

Conclusion

Levy writes about historiography which does not take anthropology and psychological history (and sociology, I would like to add) seriously as "a meditation of alien intellectuals on native intellectuals; a meditation on a world that never existed" and contrasts this with the anthropologists "who believe that their own dirty, imperfect, confused, field community is an infinitely better clue to what really was."[106] The reason why I consider gossip as an important facet of Paul's context is due to my conviction that our attempts at historical understanding should not be idealizations—nor should it distort *real* life. Too often we meet in studies of Paul and his world "a purified fantasy world." Our task is, among others, to "filter social life into history."[107]

It would be a serious neglect on our part to assume that the only speech genre related to power and context within early Christianity were Paul's letters.

In this study a basic exploration was made of a very common feature of community life: informal communication, specifically gossip. It is clear that a number of issues, hitherto considered as exclusively theological (doctrinal) in nature, can be *related* to common, everyday interaction of the persons interested in Paul's message.

Instead of imagining a process guided by a few (heretically inclined) men challenging the great apostle who was preparing the great texts for church and seminary, we should probably think about urban folk, groups of ordinary citizens, particularly women, who with news and reports and imaginative tales judged and problematized the provocative influence of the apostle to the heathen.

Most New Testament scholars have paid more attention to the texts than to the live processes by and through which those texts were produced.

---

105. Cox, "What is Hopi Gossip About?" 88, 95–97; Paine, "Informal Communication and Information-management"; Bergmann, *Discreet Indiscretions*, 147.

106. Levy, "Quest for Mind," 11.

107. Cf. ibid., 11.

One sometimes has an uncomfortable feeling that New Testament scholarship tends to "dehumanize" early Christianity. Since it is quite feasible and customary among New Testament scholars to separate their "reports" from the "folk" and to spend endless hours dissecting and studying the resultant texts, it is indeed possible for us to overlook, or to avoid intentionally, those very dynamic human elements that make the field an exciting one and worthwhile to study in the first place.

11

Aspects of the Verbal Art of the Pauline Letters

Communication is the activity that humans engage in to convey meanings, express attitudes and feelings, and to seek solutions to problems. *Rhetorical* communication creates a message with verbal and visual symbols/actions to influence an audience that has the ability to change its beliefs and behaviors as a consequence of experiencing the message (or at least, such is the perspective of the creator of the message). The format of these symbols and actions are determined by their socio-cultural context, and their effectiveness can only be described, and consequently understood within this context. This principle naturally also holds for ancient letters.[1] It has often been noted that there is an oral aspect to Paul's letters. Hester describes Paul's style "as much oral as it is written. It is as though Paul wrote speeches."[2] He continues: "If one accepts the notion that Paul's letters are rife with oral expression or

---

1. This is basically the same point made by Stowers. He writes, "Ancient letters will be difficult to understand on their own terms unless we also understand something about the contexts of Greco-Roman society in which the actions were performed and had their meanings." See Stowers, *Letter Writing*, 16.

2. See Hester, "Use and Influence," 387. Examples can be multiplied; e.g., Funk, *Language*, 245; Funk, "Saying and Seeing"; Lategan, "Is Paul Defending," 416; White, *Light*, 19; Vielhauer, *Geschichte*, 59; Doty, *Letters*, 75–76; Malherbe, *Moral Exhortation*, 68. Dahl draws attention to some of the implications of texts meant to be read aloud. He notes that Greek prose style was in general closer to oral speech than are modern literary products. See Dahl, *Studies in Paul*, 79. Kelber has attempted to interpret Paul's theology as orally constituted. Kelber tends to underplay the complexities of oral-literate interaction as anthropological phenomena. He separates Paul's (oral) preaching from his (written) letters. See Kelber, *Oral and the Written Gospel*, 140–77. It remains an important study, nevertheless. One should add that many studies on Greco-Roman society also suffer from improper assumptions concerning literacy and education in antiquity.

style . . . one had better begin to take seriously the possibility that Paul saw his letters as speeches."[3]

This study aims to do exactly that: to take the oral aspects of Paul's letters seriously. More than this, this study aspires to promote awareness of orality as a fundamental part of the context of ancient communication and therefore also of ancient rhetoric.

To see the significance of this when it comes to a proper historical understanding of Paul's letters, one need only ask how form, style and structure have been dealt with concerning these writings. *Any* discussion of style, form or rhetorical facets *always* presupposes a larger framework within which these "formal" aspects make sense. No one would deny that we find certain stylistic characteristics in any text. The problem is what to make of them. These characteristics do not explain themselves; they need to be interpreted, to be related to various communicative strategies, cultural conventions, historical and social phenomena before they make sense. Any claim that stylistic phenomena per se can guide one to valid interpretation is misleading. Structural phenomena, forms and "literary" characteristics all presuppose in some way a frame of reference from within which they can be identified for what they presumably are. They can only be interpreted once this larger frame is explicitly brought to bear on the issues. And, what must also be kept in mind is that in some way or another, *some* sense or idea of a larger framework is in any case at work when we read these ancient letters. The task is to identify the unhistorical and subjective parts of one's "preunderstanding," so to speak.

Literacy, Visualism, and Bias

The very first step needed for a responsible interpretation of ancient communication is to become aware of tacit assumptions. For instance, we must replace our misleading, modern literate view of ancient writing activities with a more responsible view that takes into account their historical, religious, intellectual and psychological situation.

Our literate bias is, however, part of a complex set of interrelated factors, and to understand how easily we can distort ancient rhetoric we need to make a short detour into the difficult terrain of language, culture, communication technology and cognition.

3. Hester, "Use and Influence," 389.

Method and Vision

Few New Testament scholars have considered the possibility that such simple and sensible methods or techniques like delineating a pericope, outlining the structure of a text, drawing syntactic diagrams, making tables, designing comparative charts, or even learning Greek might be biased towards a certain theory of knowledge of which the claims to validity are not beyond questioning.

Notice the way most of us go about the use of ancient languages, as becomes apparent in the metaphors we employ to indicate our methods and results. Most often, our knowledge of the language is pictured as a tool, as a means to elicit information. Somehow, what one seeks is thought to exist separately from language and the activity of speaking. We attempt to *extract*, or *discover*, or even *uncover* the meaning or the thought content. Greek is considered to be the vehicle (or receptacle) of Paul's intent or message. All these images reflect a manipulative use of language derived from visual and spatial conceptualisations.

Our studies abound in charts, diagrams, structural analyses and tables. These phenomena are manifestations of deeply ingrained empirical and positivistic convictions.[4] They rest on a corpuscular, atomic theory of knowledge and information, which is only possible with a prejudice towards visual and spatial conceptualisations. Such a theory encourages quantification and diagrammatic representation so that the ability to "visualize" someone's meaning (or intent) almost becomes synonymous with understanding it. Following Fabian, we can call this tendency *visualism*. "The term is to connote a cultural, ideological bias towards vision as the 'noblest sense' and towards geometry qua graphic-spatial conceptualization as the most "exact" way of communicating knowledge."[5] It is important to recognize a paradoxical consequence of visualism, namely that it leads to a (or maybe a symptom of) denigration of visual experience. Not only are we "deaf" to the oral-aural

---

4. These developments have a long history in Western philosophical tradition, going back to John Locke and David Hume. For the relation between the experience of the primacy of vision and the origins of modern science, see Lindberg and Steneck, "Sense of Vision." Though outside their scope of inquiry, we should add that visualism can be traced right back to Plato, *Phaedrus* 250d3. Greco-Roman culture is distinctly related to ours; at its closest, however, it is a (very much) younger forebear. On literate bias see McConnell, *Oral Cultures*; Botha, "Oral and Literate Traditions."

5. Fabian, *Time and the Other*, 106.

worlds of other, less technologized communication systems, we reduce the symbolic forms of ancient people to "stuff," to disembodied things.[6]

Another way visualism has a grasp on us is the variety of ways, often in the most simple and seemingly commonsensical recommendations, in which expeditiousness of procedure or notions of speed are involved or emphasized. For instance, notice what is usually *not* asked about Paul's activities: questions about the time Paul needed (wasted!) to get into the situation to deliver a message. Or about the skilful manipulation of social relations needed to have a letter presented in the first place.

There were no letter boxes in antiquity. A letter carrier did not simply deliver the letter. It had to be given to someone; the letter was probably discussed and it was physically handled by various people. Even if a letter was straightforwardly delivered, the receiver had to select the correct time to have it read. Since others were present, there must have been considerable interaction: getting together, waiting for each other; maybe some preparation of the audience. All this is simply ignored in our "reconstructions." With regard to the communicative *event*, the important aspects, those making lasting impression, could well have been everything but the letters inscribed on a piece of papyrus. As an "object" of knowledge, the communicative event (experience) of Paul and his audiences are processed by us with visual-spatial tools and methods.

> How does *method* deal with the hours of waiting, with maladroitness and gaffes due to confusion or bad timing? Where does it put the frustrations caused by diffidence and intransigence, where the joys of purposeless chatter and conviviality? Often this is written off as the "human side" of our scientific activity. Method is expected to yield objective knowledge by filtering out experiential "noise" thought to impinge on the quality of information. But what makes a (reported) sight more objective than a (reported) sound, smell or taste? Our bias for one and against the other is a matter of cultural choice rather than universal validity.[7]

How we read Paul's letters is in fact a reflection of our self-conception. We strive our very best to present visual knowledge: a neatly printed text, with

---

6. For an adaptation of a description of Bauman, see Bauman, *Story*, 2. Bauman argues that study of oral literature should be done in an integrative spirit, with a performance-centred conception of these traditions as scholars operate within a frame of reference dominated by the canons of elite, modern literary perceptions. See ibid., 1–10.

7. Fabian, *Time and the Other*, 108.

a clearly marked argument, well balanced paragraphs and properly support-ing notes. The intention is to present the perfect visual communication.

But what *Paul* did was to engage in dictation. He sent a hand-written, corrected but not without errors[8], ambiguous, damaged, travel worn manu-script with someone he trusted, to have that one, or someone else, present his intentions and symbols verbally and bodily to others. What we are looking for is the "objective argument," the "line of thought," the "flow of the argu-ment," which can be represented in spatial lines, diagrammatically, on paper. What we *should* be looking for is an emotional, subjective, playing-up-to-the-audience human being making meaning present and evoking authority.

Most of Paul's audience probably never even saw the text. The very source of their knowledge about Paul's message, or its content, was never imagined by them to be visible in a non-personal, static way. They did not experience it as knowledge that could be arranged, ordered and easily repre-sented in diagrammatic or tabular form.

This is exactly where the need for studying rhetoric comes to the fore. It is a very important way to discover our biases, and to cope with them. Rhetorical criticism leads us towards the fullness of language, making us attentive to context, symbols and semantics. Even more, it brings us back to language as an experience, not as a mere text.

In line with developments in the philosophy of science, we should rec-ognize that rhetoric belongs to the very essence of science.[9] Meaning and communication is about much more than delineating sources or labelling textual strategies.

Orality in Paul's World

Reading in antiquity was not experienced as a silently scanning, mainly mental activity. It was a performative, vocal, oral-aural happening. The read-er literally recited, with vocal and bodily gestures, the text which he (most probably he) usually memorized beforehand. It is to this aspect that refer-ence to the *oral environment* of the Greco-Roman world draws attention.[10]

8. Quite a few of our text-critical problems must have had their origin in the autogra-pha of Paul himself. An example is the famous ἔχομεν / ἔχωμεν of Rom 5:1.

9. The work of Kuhn is well known; see particularly Kuhn, *The Structure*, 48, 200–202. Feyerabend likens science to propaganda; within his argument he could as well have used the term rhetoric. See Feyerabend, *Against Method*, 123.

10. See Achtemeier, "*Omne Verbum Sonat.*" Ong describes the New Testament as "still exquisitely oral by comparison with texts coming out of latter-day . . . literacy." See Ong, "Maranatha," 433. Robbins helpfully distinguishes between oral, scribal, rhetorical

We must remind ourselves that the connection between education and literacy, which seems so natural to us, is simply a cultural convention of our own times. In Greco-Roman societies one could be educated without having the ability to read and write. In fact, being literate (proficient with texts) was not even necessarily connected to writing and reading oneself. Literacy was at the time *not* a social factor in the marketplace. Writing in antiquity was a technology employed by a small section of a pre-print society.

> It is nevertheless that they [Greek and Roman elites] retained a strong element of orality in their lives . . . they relied on the spoken word for purposes which in some other cultures have been served by the written word. They frequently dictated letters instead of writing them for themselves; they listened to political news rather than reading it; they attended recitations and performances, or heard slaves reading without having to read literary texts for themselves; and so on.[11]

Reading, as is well known, was done aloud; it was a vocal, resounding event. Notice the reason for Pliny's concern in his letter to Septicius Clarus:

> I had an easy journey, apart from the fact that some of my people were taken ill in the intense heat. Indeed, my reader Encolpius (the one who is our joy for work or play) found the dust so irritating to his throat that he spat blood, and it will be a sad blow to him and a great loss to me if this makes him unfit for his services to literature when they are his main recommendation. Who else will read and appreciate my efforts or hold my attention as he does?[12]

---

and print cultures, describing the environment of the New Testament as characterized by interaction among oral, scribal and rhetorical conditions. See Robbins, "Writing," 144–5. Not only did limited literacy exist in antiquity (see Carney, *Shape of the Past*, 110; Harris, "Literacy and Epigraphy"; Harris, *Ancient Literacy*; for the studies on Roman Egypt, see also Lewis, *Life in Egypt*, 82; Youtie, "Ἀγράμματος"; Youtie, "Βραδέως Γράφων"; Youtie, "Because They Do Not Know Letters"; Youtie, "Ὑπογραφεύς," with conclusions relevant to the rest of the Empire), but even the apparent literate facets of the culture must be understood within the context of first century historical reality: a cultural continuum different from our own. Furthermore, we should beware of ignorance of the complexities of the problems involved. For appraisals of the difficulties and literature see the references in note 13.

11. Harris, *Ancient Literacy*, 36.

12. Pliny, *Epistulae* 8.1. See Harris, *Ancient Literacy*, 225–26; McGuire, *Letters and Letter Carriers*, 150; Marrou, *Education and Rhetoric*, 196; Saenger, *Silent Reading*, 370–73; Achtemeier, "*Omne Verbum Sonat*," 15–7. Silent reading was possible, of course (Knox, "Silent Reading in Antiquity," who criticizes Balogh, "*Voces Paginarum*," for overestimating the extent of reading aloud), but not practiced. Harris writes, "The heavy reliance of the Roman upper class on readers is familiar, and even for them it is clear

The presence of orality in antiquity cannot be doubted. However, orality, it must be emphasized, is about much more than mere talk, or stylistic issues. In a cultural-anthropological sense, orality indicates a whole range of cognitive and social effects and values particular to an orally based communication technology.[13] It might seem superfluous to emphasize these matters—especially in view of the technological changes separating our societies from theirs—but impreciseness and neglect of historical realities permeate discussions of the use of writing in antiquity. This is, of course, partly the effect of our visualist bias; we simply overestimate and overrate textual evidence.[14]

While many scholars have turned to Greco-Roman rhetoric for help in interpreting Paul's letter (with worthwhile results), the oral, *performative* aspect of ancient communication, and specifically ancient rhetoric has been neglected. Speech and rhetoric cannot be separated in Hellenistic culture. Their rhetorical principles aimed specifically at the delivery of speech, at oral performance, and, consequently, *also* at creating successful communication through bodily presence.

Paul's Letters, Performance and Presence

Co-authors and Secretaries

It is generally accepted that Paul made use of a secretary when corresponding.[15] Yet, the impact of this fact seems to be consistently underestimated. As Betz notices, "the problem of authorship may be more complicated than we have previously imagined."[16] Paul usually identifies not only himself but also some other persons as author(s) of his epistles.[17]

---

that listening, instead of reading for oneself, always seemed natural." See Harris, *Ancient Literacy*, 226. It has often been remarked that letters bore a kinship to oral messages (e.g., White, *New Testament Epistolary*, 1/31).

13. Finnegan, *Literacy and Orality*; Zumthor, *Oral Poetry*; Olson, "Interpreting Texts"; Lentz, *Orality and Literacy in Hellenic Greece*. For an extensive bibliography concerning this and related issues see Botha, "Oral and Literate Traditions."

14. Cf. also MacMullen, *Christianizing*, 10–11, 21.

15. See Longenecker, "Ancient Amanuenses."

16. Betz, *Galatians*, 313, 1.

17. Gal 1:1; 1 Cor 1:1; 2 Cor 1:1; Phil 1:1; Col 1:1; Phlm 1; 1 Thess 1:1; 2 Thess 1:1. Regarding the position that Paul is not unique in this, see Roller, *Das Formular*, 153–64; Bahr, "Paul and Letter Writing," 476; Prior, *Paul the Letter-Writer*, 38. See also Schweizer, *Kolosser*, 25–6; Bruce, *Colossians*, 30. Relevant to understanding the role of co-author/editor/secretary is the phenomenon of scribes: cf. Troll, "Illiterate Mode," 115; Lewis, *Life*

It can be objected that there is a difference between a co-author and an *ammanuensis*. But how do we know the difference? Can we discover the difference between copying, editing and re-writing with regard to ancient letters? Depending on his skills and the needs of the author, the secretary recorded the dictation syllable-for-syllable or phrase-by-phrase (i.e. at the speed of writing) or by means of shorthand, at the speed of normal speech.[18] Or the secretary could be entrusted with the responsibility of writing the letter with incomplete notes. Either due to rapid dictation, or because often only an outline or draft was provided, authors left considerable scope to their secretaries. Invariably, letters contained editing by secretaries. The line between editing and co-authorship is impossible to draw. In fact, within one letter a secretary could play a variety of roles.[19]

Concerning co-authorship various options present themselves.[20] The authors may have considered the substance of the letter individually, and then gone over the general plan of what they were to compose, or perhaps suggested the style and expression which they had separately chosen while thinking about the message before collaborating towards an agreed content and form. Now, in "an age of computers and word processors, one easily forgets that conceiving and writing a text like Galatians or Romans was a long and wearisome procedure"[21] and consequently we tend to underestimate the considerable effort that must have gone into the composition of Paul's letters. These letters were also written by rather sophisticated scribes (men like Timothy, Silas). Yet notice how Sanders draws a quite probable picture of Paul "writing" to the Galatians: "To read the letter aright, one must read it as one half of a ferocious debate and imagine the harassed and distraught apostle pacing and dictating, sometimes pleading, sometimes grumbling, but often yelling . . ."[22]

Both suggestions, in the light of historical realities, can be correct. Paul's dictation of his letter was, in all probability, also a coaching of the letter carrier and eventual reader. The carrier of the letter would most likely

---

in Egypt, 82; Saldarini, *Pharisees*, 241–76.

18. Dictation *syllabitim* is self-evident. See, e.g., Seneca *Epistulae* 40.10; Bahr, "Paul and Letter Writing," 470–71. Dictation *viva voce* supposes shorthand systems and the use of a ταχυγράφος (cf. LSJ); see Seneca, *Epistulae* 40.25; Suetonius, *Divus Titus* 3.2. It was possible for a secretary to record a speech in the Roman senate (Seneca, *Apocolocyntosis* 9.2).

19. Cf. Roller, *Das Formular*, 16–23; Bahr, "Paul and Letter Writing," 470–76.

20. Prior, *Paul the Letter-writer*, 39–50.

21. Hartman, "On Reading," 138.

22. Sanders, *Paul*, 54.

have seen to it that it be read like Paul wanted it to be read. The implications of co-authorship for understanding Paul's letters are twofold. Firstly, written correspondence was essentially dependent on orality. Whether creating a letter or receiving it, oral-aural aspects were part and parcel of the whole process.

Secondly, we must realize that Paul's letters were not written by him as an individual. It was a complex communal event: some persons combined their efforts to deliberate and "perform" a letter; there was someone involved in the creation and transportation of it, that same person or someone else finally "recreated" for others a presentation/performance of the "message" intended for sharing. In the context of an orally oriented culture, composition and performance of "texts" are aspects of the same process, and the one cannot be understood without reference to the other.[23]

Receiving a Letter

In antiquity the letter carrier was, in a very real sense, the vital link between sender and recipients,[24] and the oral remarks from the carrier deemed essential to the communication and sometimes even preferred. Cicero often trusted the remarks of those "who travelled by this route" more than the news in the letters.[25] From Cicero we also learn that there were substantial interaction between letter writer and letter carriers.[26]

Receiving a letter meant more than acquiring a written document. Usually a message or news was also involved. To communicate effectively by letter in antiquity one faced several difficulties. Consider the problem of "how to convey information in an organized, understandable way apart from visible indications of such organization. One way . . . is to have someone deliver the writing who knows what it contains, and what the author intended with it, and have that person give such information. That in fact was frequently done with letters . . ."[27]

In the case of Paul's letters we should presume fully briefed readers carrying and presenting the letters. "We gain a sense of the importance of his emissaries or letter carriers: they receive authority to convey the letters to

23. This is the basic tenet of the oral formulaic theory. References in n. 54.

24. McGuire, "Letters and Letter Carriers," 148; Aune, *New Testament in Its Literary Environment*, 158.

25. Cicero, *Epistulae ad Familiares* 5.4.1; cf. 5.6.1.

26. Ibid., 15.17.1–2; Cicero, *Ad Quintum Fratrem*, 3.1.23; 3.7.1.

27. Achtemeier, *"Omne Verbum Sonat,"* 17.

expand upon them, and to continue Paul's work."[28] How should we picture the recipients of Paul's letters "reading" these writings?

> Technologized print cultures foster rapid reading, in which words are formed chiefly in the imagination and often sketchily . . . The case was different in the highly oral cultures in which the biblical texts came into being, where reading was less deeply interiorized, that is to say, where reading called for a more conscious effort, was considered a greater achievement, and was less a determinant of psychic structures and personality . . . In such highly oral cultures, it was not sufficient for the reader simply to imagine the sounds of the words being read. Books in such a culture do not "contain" something called "material." They speak or say words. The written words had to be mouthed aloud, in their full being, restored to and made to live in the oral cavities in which they came into existence.[29]

Reading in antiquity, especially when it was not private reading, was similar to recitals or to oral delivery.

Rhetoric and Oral Performance

The insight that we should perceive ancient communication as performative communication (performed literature) makes us aware of how one-sided we think about rhetoric. The great teachers of rhetoric in antiquity give extensive attention to the presentation (ὑπόκρισις, *actio*) of the rhetorical act. They do so, not simply because the delivery of a speech is important, but because the presentation is fundamentally the essence of rhetorical activity.

Cicero emphasizes that each emotion has its own natural expression in the *actio*.[30] Not only the voice, but the whole body is like a musical instrument, played by the emotions.[31] The full presentation is the "language of the body."[32] Cicero employs a range of citations from Latin plays to discuss the bodily depiction of sympathy, mourning, fear, power, joy or anger. The fact that he warns against becoming an actor, shows how powerful the impulse towards expressive representation in voice and body of the "meaning" of a

---

28. Doty, *Letters*, 7.
29. Ong, "Maranatha," 437.
30. Cicero, *De Oratore* 3.56.213—3.61.230.
31. Ibid., 3.57.216.
32. Cicero, ibid., 3.59.222: *sermo corporis.*

speech was at the time.[33] To Cicero, the face, which he calls an *imago animi*, is a very important part of the body when it comes to relevant gestures. Crucial is the voice, which can be varied endlessly.[34]

Quintilian spends a lengthy chapter on the art of using the voice and gesture[35], besides many asides scattered throughout his work. He even includes clothing (*cultus*) of the rhetor, which should be *splendidus et virilus*.[36] What is most noteworthy of Quintilian is his concern with appropriateness. The rhetor's activities, gestures, voice should be appropriate to the audience, to the content of the speech and fitting to the theme.[37] Quintilian is also very comprehensive: he touches upon every aspect of the rhetorical act, even those gestures preceding the actual speech itself.[38]

The point of highlighting this side of ancient rhetoric is to emphasize the performative, dynamic essence of ancient communication. The psychophysiology of gesture, that is, the connections between memory and bodily motions constituting the oral style[39] must be recognized if we want to understand orally constituted communication. We should not *look* at a text, scanning for visual clues or try to "see" the structure or "identify" the possible labels for parts of it. We should imagine the experience of participating in the *event* of performing that "text."

To reiterate a point made earlier: questions of meaning in orally based communicative events cannot be settled in terms of composition alone. The performance of a text, or its potential performance, must be kept in mind.

Paul's dictation of his letters was, in all probability, also a coaching of the letter carriers. The small group of "Paulinists" worked together to communicate to their followers. They took some care in preparing their letters, some of them transported these letters and delivered them. They probably also participated in the reading and performing of these writings.

Authority and Verbal Presence

Given that oral performance was intrinsic to the Greco-Roman world, and fundamentally part of communication by letter (particularly complex letters

33. Cicero, *De Oratore* 3.56.214, 220; cf. Quintilian, *Inst. Orat.* 11.3.57, 181–84.
34. Cicero, *De Oratore* 3.60.224.
35. Quintilian, *Inst. Orat.* 11.3.
36. Ibid., 11.3.137–49.
37. Ibid., 11.3.150–180.
38. E.g., ibid., 11.3.157.
39. Jousse, *Oral Style.*

such as the Pauline letters of exhortation and advice) the argument thus far is pressing us towards asking how "bodily presence" and "speech" are issues in early Christian letter writing. A performative text only takes on meaning by referring to the instance of its performance, and consequently, because the occasion has been lost, it is true that the intent of the utterance is destabilized. Although we will never be able to fully fathom the various complexities at stake here, we can and should make the attempt. We have considerable and substantial research on ancient letter writing and social values, *and* we can make careful use of anthropological and cultural research, such as orality studies, performance studies and so forth.

Paul's letters are, amongst other things, a means of exercising power and influence in various communities. This is dependent on the ability to establish presence and authority in a community, and related to the need to have social visibility and prestige. The fact that most of the addressees of Paul's letters would not have read the letters themselves, but would have *listened* to them leads us to the realisation that the presentation (the reading) of the letter itself must have been of concern to Paul and his co-authors.

When referring to the "contexts" or "audiences" of many early Christian writings we tend to underestimate the transpersonal identification of reciter and group, the manifestation of collective values that the performance of a "text" articulates.[40] The extent to which we have reduced the remains of Paul's communicative events to their (supposed) referential content is particularly clear in the strong scholarly tradition concerning Paul's opponents. In an astounding way, probably completely unrecognisable to Paul and his contemporaries, the identification and localisation of his enemies has become the interpretive key to his letters.[41]

But more relevant would be to relate Paul's highly polemical stance and biting denunciations to the oral-aural mindset. In an orally oriented mentality the "very structure of knowledge had been largely polemic, for the old oral–aural anxieties of a world polarized around persons had been institutionalized by the centering of formal education around dialectic and

---

40. Introductory discussions in Foley, "Traditional"; and Schechner, *Performance Theory*, 193–206.

41. Craffert shows how anachronistic and ethnocentric assumptions underlie most opponent hypotheses with regard to research on the letter to the Galatians. Adopting a social-scientific approach, he argues that this letter should not be read as a theological struggle but within a situation where Paul's authority and honor were at stake. Paul focused "on those aspects which, in the eyes of the Galatians, provided power and secured authority." See Craffert, *Social-Scientific Key*, 238.

rhetoric, both arts of verbal strife."[42] "Habits of auditory synthesis charged man's life-world with dynamism and threat . . . In such a view, polemic becomes a major constituent of actuality, an accepted element of existence of a magnitude no longer appealing to modern technological man."[43] Residual oralism reflects a reduction of irrelevant material to virtue-vice polarities. Even commonplace traditions were almost exclusively concerned with virtue and vice.[44] Virtue and vice polarities are deeply embedded in oral knowledge-storing systems.[45] Paul's caustic remarks and self-boosting claims do not necessarily point to the existence of theological schools. It might even be that Paul's controversy with the "Jew'" is simply an extension of this mentality "where individuals took for granted that their surroundings were swarming with active, enterprising foes."[46] The attempts at identification of the various opponents might be barking up the wrong tree. We might have attempts at in-group self-identification achieved and maintained by feeding on hostilities towards out-groups.[47]

Marshall has drawn attention to the importance of understanding Paul's invective and the issue of his "inconsistencies" in terms of Greek social and moral standards,[48] considering the social and cultural dimensions of these activities. He shows that invective had two objectives: disposing the hearers favorably to the speaker and to shame and humiliate the "enemy." "Using a wide range of rhetorical techniques, popular topics and physiognomic traditions, the speaker praised himself as a good person and censured his enemy as an unworthy person . . . Much of it [invective] was exaggerated or invented."[49]

Marshall is surely on the right track. But the argument presented in this paper pushes us beyond questions of reference and truth towards awareness and appreciation of the poetic, experiential function of language use. In performative communication—particularly within an orally based culture—the poetic operation, the breath of voice and the energy of the body, is, at the

42. Ong, *Presence*, 236.

43. Ibid., 200.

44. Cf. ibid., 202.

45. The considerable role that virtue-vice polarities and lists of virtues and vices play in Greco-Roman rhetoric (Marshall, *Enmity in Corinth*, 35–55) is probably due to the residual orality in Greco-Roman culture. Cicero explicitly defines memory as part of prudence. See Cicero, *De Inventione Rhetorica* 2.53.160.

46. Ong, *Presence*, 196.

47. Cf. ibid., 198.

48. Marshall, "Invective," 360.

49. Ibid., 362.

least, as crucial as the utterance's supposed abstraction. There is an "essence" to it which is more than an "act"; in Zumthor's graphic phrase, "a human being takes place, here."[50] This essence resides in the assumption of responsibility to an audience, and maintaining an audience through communicative skill as such. Enmity, invective, insults, disgrace, humiliation were ways of achieving, maintaining and defending honor and status which were the real values of antiquity and the very skill and power with which one displayed these activities determined their value, not the reference, truth, representability outside or unconnected to the speech event itself.

When Aristotle (*Rhetorica* 1.9.28) says that in praise and blame, qualities which closely resemble the real qualities are identical with them—the cautious man is cold and designing— surely, we should take him seriously. In these, and other rhetorical hints, we notice the use of words to affect certain experiences. At the least, we should recognize that these experiential aims are as important as their possible referents. Powerful speech and authority, given an oral environment, are basically the same thing.[51] "More: semantically, this society was still largely at the word-magic stage, with words 'representing' 'real' essences and involving a two-valued, antithetical logic. This makes for insensitivity to relativistic, multidimensional modes of thinking and problem-solving."[52]

In fact, orality studies provide us with an interpretive tool to build bridges across the cultural gap between us and the people of antiquity, where, for instance, mere blessings and curses clearly were events of grave magnitude.

Formulas in Paul's Letters

Very much to the point is the role of memory and memorising. Extensive memorisation, which was the dominant characteristic of Greco-Roman education, is fundamental to an oral-text oriented culture. The dissemination of texts in antiquity relied on recitals and oral performances. Ancient discussions of rhetoric emphasize that all effort concerning the preparation of a speech would be in vain if the speech could not be memorized properly.[53]

---

50. Zumthor, *Oral Poetry*, 229.

51. On the power of words and speech in orally based cultures, see Peek, "Power"; Tambiah, "Magical Power."

52. Carney, *Shape of the Past*, 110.

53. Cf. Leeman and Braet, *Klassieke Retorica*, 118–23.

It is possible to understand the functions of the many formulas and formulaic expressions in Paul's letters as effects of oral rhetoric. The role of formulaic phraseology in communication within an oral environment has been intensively studied[54] and the associative power of memory, and how to exploit this, was well-known in antiquity.[55]

Paul's reliance on formulaic language is not only limited to the conventional epistolary formulas and topoi[56] (which is in itself a manifestation of oral dynamics), but extends to a characteristic use of "summary phrases." Betz, in his study of Galatians, has listed a number of brief expressions, most of them prepositional phrases. "All of them are abbreviations of theological doctrines. Their origin is unknown, but they can be most likely explained as coming from the oral transmission of Paul's theology."[57] This phenomenon is not limited to the letter to the Galatians. The implication of this type of abbreviated expression is twofold.

They clearly are something like condensed reflexive statements. Tannen notes, "Formulaic expressions [= sayings, cliches, proverbs, and so on, familiar combinations of words, familiar syntactic patterns] function as wholes, as a convenient way to signal knowledge that is already shared. In oral tradition, it is not assumed that the expressions contain meaning in themselves . . . [but to be] the repository of received wisdom."[58]

They can also be mnemotechniques: the phrases can be pictured as *loci*, aiding Paul and his co-authors to keep track of an involved argument and to remember a complex speech. They could well have been clues (or opportunities) for the reader to expand and elaborate.

Concluding Remarks

This chapter takes the insight that orality is an essential aspect of pre-modern communication as a starting point and attempts to situate Pauline epistolography within the context of ancient communicative practices.

54. See, for instance, the immense literature on the oral-formulaic theory: Finnegan, *Literacy and Orality*, 70–78; Foley, *Theory*.

55. E.g., Quintilian, *Inst. Orat.* 11.2.18–22.

56. On the various types of stereotyped formulas in Paul's letters, see Roller, *Das Formular*; Mullins, "Petition"; Mullins, "Greeting"; Mullins, "Disclosure"; Mullins, "Formulas"; Mullins, "Ascription"; Mullins, "Topos"; White, "Introductory Formulae"; White, "Epistolary Formulas"; Lategan, "Formulas in the Language of Paul."

57. Betz, *Galatians*, 27–28.

58. Tannen, "Oral/Literate Continuum," 1–2, 6.

To do this attention is firstly directed to the importance of recognising (and compensating for) our *visualism*, which is related to modern, Western literate bias. On a historical plane, the *oral environment* of the Greco-Roman world is emphasized. It is argued that the (rather limited) literacy of the time must be understood within the context of first century historical reality namely that of a scribal culture.

Many references to Greco-Roman rhetoric in order to illuminate Pauline letter writing similarly mislead by neglecting the constraints of an orally based culture, and the performative side of classical rhetoric which cannot be separated from bodily presence. Some implications for the writing and reading of letters are discussed: the issue of 'multi'-authorship, the communal experience of letters, the oral, performative aspect of letter reading.

Brief discussions of authority and presence as manifested in polemic and formulaic language conclude the chapter. Paul, "writer" of letters, is not a modern scholar, writing theological treatises for modern, literate audiences. Seen within the communication activities of his times, we discover, instead, a small group of early Christians struggling to maintain their identity and defending their views by means of oral presentations.

Abbreviations

AJP	*American Journal of Philology*
ANRW	*Aufstieg und Niedergang der römischen Welt*
BETL	Bibliotheca Ephemeridum Theologicarum Lovaniensum
BTB	*Biblical Theology Bulletin*
CBQ	*Catholic Biblical Quarterly*
CQ	*Classical Quarterly*
GRBS	*Greek, Roman, and Byzantine Studies*
HTR	*Harvard Theological Review*
HvTSt	*Hervormde Teologiese Studies*
Int	*Interpretation*
JAF	*Journal of American Folklore*
JBL	*Journal of Biblical Literature*
JR	*Journal of Religion*
JSNT	*Journal for the Study of the New Testament*
JSNTSup	Journal for the Study of the New Testament Supplement Series
JTS	*Journal of Theological Studies*
LEC	Library of Early Christianity
LSJ	Liddell, Scott, Jones, *Greek-English Lexicon*
Neot	*Neotestamentica*
NLH	*New Literary History*
NovT	*Novum Testamentum*
NTS	*New Testament Studies*
OCD	*Oxford Classical Dictionary*, 2nd ed.
POxy	Oxyrynchus Papyrus

R&T	*Religion and Theology*
TAPA	*Transactions of the American Philological Association*
WUNT	Wissenschaftliche Untersuchungen zum Neuen Testament
ZNW	*Zeitschfrift für die neutestamentliche Wissenschaft und die Kunde der älteren Kirche*
ZPE	*Zeitschrift für Papyrologie und Epigraphik*

Note on Classical Authors

For Classical and early Christian authors I have consistently used the Loeb Classical Library volumes, however, often modifying the translation. Clement, *Stromata*, was consulted in *Die griechische christliche Schriftsteller der ersten Jahrhunderte*, edited by O. Stählin and L. Früchtel; Galen, *Claudii Galeni opera omnia*, vol. 12, edited by K. G. Kühn, reprinted, Hildesheim: Olms, 1965.

Bibliography

Abel, Ernest L. "The Psychology of Memory and Rumor Transmission and Their Bearing on Theories of Oral Transmission in Early Christianity." *JR* 51 (1971) 270–81.

Abrahams, Roger D. "A Performance-centred Approach to Gossip." *Man* 5 (1970) 290–301.

Achtemeier, Paul J. "*Omne verbum sonat*: The New Testament and the Oral Environment of Late Western Antiquity." *JBL* 109 (1990) 3–27.

Akinnaso, F. Niyi. "The Consequences of Literacy in Pragmatic and Theoretical Perspective." *Anthropology and Education Quarterly* 12 (1981) 163–200.

———. "On the Similarities between Spoken and Written Language." *Language and Speech* 28 (1985) 323–59.

Alexander, Loveday C. A. "The Living Voice: Scepticism Towards the Written Word in Early Christian and in Greco-Roman Texts." In *The Bible in Three Dimensions: Essays in Celebration of Forty Years of Biblical Studies in the University of Sheffield*, edited by David J. A Clines, Stephen E. Fowl, and Stanley E. Porter, 221–47. JSOTSup 87. Sheffield: Sheffield Academic, 1990.

Allen, Donald E., and Rebecca F. Guy. *Conversation Analysis: The Sociology of Talk*. The Hague: Mouton, 1974.

Allport, Gordon W., and, Leo Postman. *The Psychology of Rumor*. New York: Holt, 1947.

Anthony, S. "Anxiety and Rumour." *Journal of Social Psychology* 89 (1973) 91–98.

Applebaum, S. "Economic Life in Palestine." In *The Jewish people in the First Century: Historical Geography, Political History, Social, Cultural and Religious Life and Institutions*, edited by S. Safrai and M. Stern, 2:631–700. Philadelphia: Fortress, 1976.

———. "Judaea as a Roman Province: The Countryside as a Political and Economic Factor." In *ANRW* 2.8 (1977) 355–96.

Ariès, Philippe. *Centuries of Childhood*. London: Random House, 1996.

Arno, Andrew. "Fijian Gossip as Adjudication: A Communication Model of Informal Social Control." *Journal of Anthropological Research* 36 (1980) 343–60.

Aune, David E. *The New Testament in Its Literary Environment*. LEC 8. Philadelphia: Westminster, 1987.

———. *Revelation 17–22*. WBC 52C. Nashville: Nelson, 1998.

Aus, Roger David. "The Magi at the Birth of Cyrus, and the Magi at Jesus' Birth in Matt 2:1–12." In *New Perspectives on Judaism*. Vol. 2, *Religion, Literature, and Society in Ancient Israel, Formative Christianity and Judaism*, edited by J. Neusner et al., 99–114. Lanham, MD: University Press of America, 1987.

Baddeley, Alan. *Human Memory: Theory and Practice*. London: Erlbaum, 1990.

Badian, E. "Postal Service." In *OCD* (1970) 869.

Bagnall, Roger S. *Reading Papyri, Writing Ancient History*. London: Routledge, 1995.

Bibliography

Bahr, Gordon J. "Paul and Letter-Writing in the First Century." *CBQ* 28 (1966) 465–77.
——. "The Subscriptions in the Pauline Letters." *JBL* 87 (1968) 27–41.
Bailey, F. G. "Gifts and Poison." In *Gifts and Poison: The Politics of Reputation*, edited by F. G. Bailey, 1–25. Pavilion Series. Oxford: Blackwell, 1971.
Bailey, Kenneth E. "Informal Controlled Oral Tradition and the Synoptic Gospels." *Asia Journal of Theology* 5 (1991) 34–54.
Baldwin, Barry. "Literature and Society in the Later Roman Empire." In *Literary and Artistic Patronage in Ancient Rome*, edited by B. K. Gold, 67–83. Austin: University of Texas Press, 1982.
Balogh, J. "*Voces Paginarum*: Beiträge zur Geschichte des Lauten Lesens und Schreibens." *Philologus* 82 (1927) 84–109, 202–40.
Balsdon, J. P. V. D. *The Emperor Gaius (Caligula)*. Oxford: Clarendon, 1934.
Bandstra, Andrew J. "Paul, the Letter Writer." *Canadian Journal of Theology* 3 (1968) 176–88.
Barr, James. *The Bible in the Modern World*. London: SCM, 1973.
Barrow, R. H. *Plutarch and His Time*. London: Chatto & Windus, 1967.
Barton, David. "The Social Nature of Writing." In *Writing in the Community*, edited by David Barton and Roz Ivanič, 1–13. London: Sage, 1991.
Barton, John. "Reflections on Cultural Relativism." *Theology* 82 (1979) 103–13, 191–99.
Bauman, Richard. *Story, Performance, and Event: Contextual Studies of Oral Narrative*. Cambridge: Cambridge University Press, 1986.
——. "Verbal Art as Performance." *American Anthropologist* 77 (1975) 290–311.
Baumann, G. "Introduction." In *The Written Word: Literacy in Transition*, edited by G. Baumann, 1–22. Oxford: Clarendon, 1986.
Bäuml, Franz H. "Medieval Texts and the Two Theories of Oral-formulaic Composition: A Proposal for a Third Theory." *NLH* 16 (1984) 31–49.
——. "Varieties and Consequences of Medieval Literacy and Illiteracy." *Speculum* 55 (1980) 237–65.
Beare, W., and D. E. Eicholz. "Herodas." In *OCD* (1970) 507.
Beck, F. A. G. "Education." In *OCD* (1970) 369–73.
Ben-Amos, Dan. "Toward a Definition of Folklore in Context." *JAF* 34 (1971) 3–15.
Ben-Ze'ev, Aaron. "The Vindication of Gossip." In *Good Gossip*, edited by Robert F. Goodman and Aaron Ben-Ze'ev, 11–24. Lawrence: University Press of Kansas, 1994.
Bennett, Gillian. *Traditions of Belief: Women, Folklore and the Supernatural Today*. Harmondsworth, UK: Penguin, 1987.
Berger, Peter L., and Thomas Luckmann. *The Social Construction of Reality: A Treatise in the Sociology of Knowledge*. Harmondsworth, UK: Penguin, 1967.
Berger, Peter L., and Hansfried Kellner. *Sociology Reinterpreted: An Essay on Method and Vocation*. Harmondsworth, UK: Penguin, 1981.
Bergmann, Jörg R. *Discreet Indiscretions: The Social Organization of Gossip*. Translated by John Bednarz Jr. with Eva Kafka Barron. Communication and Social Order. New York: Aldine de Gruyter, 1993.
Bernardo, A. B. I. "On Defining and Developing Literacy across Communities." *International Review of Education* 46 (2000) 455–65.
Betz, Hans Dieter. *Galatians*. Hermeneia. Philadelphia: Fortress, 1979.
Bickerman, E. J. *The Jews in the Greek Age*. Cambridge: Harvard University Press, 1988.
Bickerman, E. J., and Hayim Tadmor. "Darius I, Pseudo-Smerdis, and the Magi." *Athenaeum* 56 (1978) 239–61.

Bigsby, C. W. E. "Preface." In *Approaches to Popular Culture*, edited by C. W. E. Bigsby, vii–viii. Bowling Green: Bowling Green University Popular Press, 1976.

Bilezikian, Gilbert G. *The Liberated Gospel: A Comparison of the Gospel of Mark and Greek Traedy*. Grand Rapids: Baker, 1977.

Biriotti, Maurice. "Introduction: Authorship, Authority, Authorisation." In *What Is an Author?*, edited by Maurice Biriotti and Nicola Miller, 1–16. Manchester: Manchester Uni-versity Press, 1993.

Bischoff, Bernhard. *Latin Paleography: Antiquity and the Middle Ages*. Translated by Daibhi O. Cróinín and David Ganz. Cambridge: Cambridge University Press, 1990.

Blank, Horst. *Das Buch in der Antike*. Munich: Beck, 1992.

Bloomer, W. Martin. "Schooling in Persona: Imagination and Subordination in Roman Education." *Classical Antiquity* 16 (1997) 57–78.

Blue, Bradley. "Acts and the House Church." In *The Book of Acts in Its First Century Setting*, vol 2: *The Book of Acts in Its Graeco-Roman Setting*, edited by D. W. J. Gill and C. Gempf, 119–222. Grand Rapids: Eerdmans, 1994.

Bonner, Stanley F. *Education in Ancient Rome: From the Elder Cato to the Younger Pliny*. London: Methuen, 1977.

———. "The Street-teacher: An Educational Scene in Horace." *AJP* 93 (1972) 509–28.

Boomershine, Thomas E. "Peter's Denial as Polemic or Confession: The Implications of Media Criticism for Biblical Hermeneutics." *Semeia* 39 (1987) 48–68.

Booth, Alan D. "Elementary and Secondary Education in the Roman Empire." *Florilegium* 1 (1979) 1–14.

———. "The Schooling of Slaves in First-Century Rome." *TAPA* 109 (1979) 11–19.

Boring, M. Eugene. *The Continuing Voice of Jesus: Christian Prophecy and the Gospel Tradition*. Louisville: Westminster, 1991.

Boring, Terrence A. *Literacy in Ancient Sparta*. Mnemosyne Supplements 54. Leiden: Brill, 1979.

Borsche, Tilman. "Wer Spricht, Wenn Wir Sprechen? Überlegungen zum Problem der Autorschaft." *Allgemeine Zeitschrift für Philosophie* 13.3 (1988) 37–50.

Botha, Pieter J. J. "Community and Conviction in Luke-Acts." *Neot* 29 (1995) 145–65.

———. "Cultural Anthropological History and the Jesus Traditions." *Theologia Viatorum* 32 (2008) 92–141.

———. "Die Dissipels in die Markusevangelie." PhD thesis. Pretoria: University of Pretoria, 1989.

———. "The Historical Setting of Mark's Gospel: Problems and Possibilities." *JSNT* 51 (1993) 27–55.

———. "Houses in the World of Jesus." *Neot* 32 (1998) 37–74.

———. "Oral and Literate Traditions." *Koers* 57.3 (1992) 3–22.

———. "Orality, Literacy and Worldview: Exploring the Interaction." *Communicatio* 17.2 (1991) 2–15.

———. "Schools in the World of Jesus: Analysing the Evidence." *Neot* 33 (1999) 225–60.

———. "Die Teks van die Nuwe Testament: Steeds 'n vraagstuk in die Nuwe Testamentiese Wetenskap." *Theologia Evangelica* 25.2. (1992) 2–28.

Bourguignon, Erika. *Psychological Anthropology: An Introduction to Human Nature and Cultural Differences*. New York: Holt, Rinehart & Winston, 1979.

Brandon, S. G. F. *Religion in Ancient History: Studies in Ideas, Men and Events*. New York: Scribner, 1969.

255

Bradley, Keith R. *Slavery and Society at Rome.* Cambridge: Cambridge University Press, 1994.

Brewer, Derek. "The Gospels and the Laws of Folktale." *Folklore* 90 (1979) 37–52.

Briggs, Charles F. "Literacy, Reading and Writing in the Medieval West." *Journal of Medieval History* 26 (2000) 397–420.

Bright, William. "Literature: Written and Oral." In *Analyzing Discourse: Text and Talk,* edited by Deborah Tannen, 271–83. Washington, DC: Georgetown University Press, 1982.

Broshi, Magen. "The Diet of Palestine in the Roman Period—Introductory Notes." *Israel Museum Journal* 5 (1986) 41–56.

Brown, G. S. "After the Fall: The *'Chute'* of a Play, *'Droits d'Auteur',* and Literary Property in the Old Regime." *French Historical Studies* 22 (1999) 465–91.

———. "Authorship." In *Encyclopedia of the Enlightenment,* edited by A. C. Kors. Oxford: Oxford University Press, 2003. Online: http://www.oxfordreference.com.

Brown, J. S., T. L. Brown, T. H. Carr, and J. L. McDonald. "Adapting to Processing Demands in Discourse Production: The Case of Handwriting." *Journal of Experimental Psychology: Learning, Memory, and Cognition* 14.1 (1988) 45–59.

Brown, Peter. *The Making of Late Antiquity.* Cambridge: Harvard University Press, 1978.

Brown, Raymond E. *The Birth of the Messiah: A Commentary on the Infancy Narratives in Matthew and Luke.* London: Chapman, 1977.

Bruce, F. F. *The Epistles to the Colossians, to Philemon, and to the Ephesians.* New International Commentary on the New Testament. Grand Rapids: Eerdmans, 1984.

Bruford, Alan. "Memory, Performance and Structure in Traditional Tales." *Arv: Nordic Yearbook of Folklore* 37 (1983) 103–9.

Buckhout, Robert. "Eyewitness Testimony." *Scientific American* 231.6 (1974) 23–31.

Buckner, H. T. "A Theory of Rumor Transmission." *Public Opinion Quarterly* 29 (1965) 54–70.

Bultmann, Rudolf. *Die Geschichte der synoptischen Tradition.* 3rd ed. Göttingen: Vandenhoeck & Ruprecht, 1957.

———. *The History of the Synoptic Tradition.* Translated by John Marsh. Oxford: Blackwell, 1968.

———. *Jesus.* 1926. Reprinted, Gütersloh: Mohn, 1977.

———. *Theology of the New Testament.* Vol. 1. London: SCM, 1952.

Burke, J. "Communication in the Middle Ages." In *Communication in History: Technology, Culture, Society,* edited by David Crowley and Paul Heyer, 67–76. New York: Longman, 1991.

Carney, T. F. *The Shape of the Past: Models and Antiquity.* Lawrence, KS: Coronado, 1975.

Carothers, John C. "Culture, Psychiatry, and the Written Word." *Psychiatry* 22 (1959) 307–20.

Carruthers, Mary J. *The Book of Memory: A Study of Memory in Medieval Culture.* Cambridge Studies in Medieval Literature 10. Cambridge: Cambridge University Press, 1990.

Casson, Lionel. *Travel in the Ancient World.* London: Allen & Unwin, 1974.

Černý, J. *Paper & Books in Ancient Egypt.* London: University College, 1952.

Chartier, Roger. "Figures of the Author." In *The Order of Books: Readers, Authors and Libraries in Europe Between the Fourteenth and Eighteenth Centuries,* 25–60. Oxford: Polity, 1994.

———. "The Man of Letters." In *Enlightenment Portraits*, edited by M. Vovelle, translated by L. G. Cochrane. 1992, 142–89. Chicago: University of Chicago Press, 1997.

Chaytor, H. J. *From Script to Print: An Introduction to Medieval Vernacular Literature.* Cambridge: Heffer, 1950.

Chilton, Bruce. *A Galilean Rabbi and his Bible: Jesus' Own Interpretation of Isaiah.* London: SPCK, 1984.

———. *Profiles of a Rabbi: Synoptic Opportunities in Reading about Jesus.* Brown Judaic Studies 177. Atlanta: Scholars, 1989.

Clanchy, M. T. *From Memory to Written Record: England 1066–1307.* London: Arnold, 1979.

Clarke, G. W. "An Illiterate Lector?" *ZPE* 57 (1984) 103–4.

Code, Lorraine. "Gossip, or in Praise of Chaos." In *Good Gossip*, edited by Robert F. Goodman and Aaron Ben-Ze'ev, 100–105. Lawrence: University Press of Kansas, 1994.

Cole, Michael, and Jennifer Cole. "Rethinking the Goody Myth." In *Technology, Literacy, and the Evolution of Society: Implications of the Work of Jack Goody*, edited by David R. Olson and Michael Cole, 305–24. Mahwah, NJ: Erlbaum, 2006.

Cole, Michael, and Sylvia Scribner. *Culture and Thought: A Psychological Introduction.* New York: Wiley, 1974.

Collins, Louise. "Gossip: A Feminist Defense." In *Good Gossip*, edited by Robert F. Goodman and Aaron Ben-Ze'ev, 106–15. Lawrence: University Press of Kansas, 1994.

Collinson, P. "The Significance of Signatures." *Times Literary Supplement*, Jan. 9, 1981, 31.

Combrink, H. J. B. "Readings, Readers and Authors: An Introduction." *Neot* 22 (1988) 189–203.

———. "The Role of the Reader and Other Literary Categories in Philippians." *Scriptura* 20 (1987) 33–40.

Cook, C., R. Burgess-Limerick, and S. Papalia. "The Effect of Upper Extremity Support on Upper Extremity Posture and Muscle Activity during Keyboard Use." *Applied Ergonomics* 35 (2004) 285–92.

Cook-Gumperz, Jenny. "Introduction: The Social Construction of Literacy." In *The Social Construction of Literacy*, edited by J. Cook-Gumperz, 1–15. Cambridge: Cambridge University Press, 1986.

Cook-Gumperz, Jenny, and John J. Gumperz. "From Oral to Written Culture: The Transition to Literacy." In *Writing: The Nature, Development, and Teaching of Written Communication 1. Variation in Writing: Functional and Linguistic-Cultural Differences*, edited by Marcia Farr Whiteman, 89–109. Hillsdale, NJ: Erlbaum, 1981.

Copeland, Rita. *Rhetoric, Hermeneutics and Translation in the Middle Ages: Academic Traditions and Vernacular Texts.* Cambridge: Cambridge University Press, 1991.

Corbett, E. P. J. "An Historical View of the Relationship Between Reading and Writing." In *Oral and Written Communication: Historical Approaches*, edited by Richard Leo Enos, 32–45. Newbury Park, CA: Sage, 1990.

Corbett, John. "The Pharisaic Revolution and Jesus As Embodied Torah." *Studies in Religion* 15 (1986) 375–91.

Corbier, M. "Coinage, Society and Economy." In *The Cambridge Ancient History*, vol. 12.2: *The Crisis of Empire, A.D. 193–337*, edited by A. K. Bowman et al., 397–439. Cambridge: Cambridge University Press, 2005.

Couch, Carl J. "Oral Technologies: A Cornerstone of Ancient Civilizations?" *Sociological Quarterly* 30 (1989) 587–602.

Countryman, L. William. *Dirt, Greed and Sex: Sexual Ethics in the New Testament and Their Implications for Today.* Philadelphia: Fortress, 1988.

Courtney, E. *A Commentary on the Satires of Juvenal.* London: Athlone, 1980.

Cox, B. A. "What Is Hopi Gossip About? Information Management and Hopi Factions." *Man* 5 (1970) 88–98.

Craffert, Pieter F. "'n Herdefiniëring van Paulus se konflik in Galasië: die Brief aan die Galasiërs deur die Bril van die Sosiale Wetenskappe." *HvTSt* 50 (1994) 859–76.

———. "Historical-Anthropological Jesus Research: The Status of Authentic Pictures beyond Authentic Material." *HvTSt* 58 (2002) 440–71.

———. "Jesus and the Shamanic Complex: First Steps in Utilising a Social Type Model." *Neot* 33 (1999) 321–42.

———. *The Life of a Galilean Shaman: Jesus of Nazareth in Anthropological-Historical Perspective.* Matrix 3. Eugene, OR: Cascade Books, 2008.

———. "Multiple Realities and Historiography: Rethinking Historical Jesus Research." In *The New Testament Interpreted: Essays in Honour of Bernard C. Lategan*, edited by Cilliers Breytenbach, Johan C. Thom, and Jeremy Punt, 87–116. Novum Testamentum Supplements 124. Leiden: Brill, 2006.

———. "On New Testament Interpretation and Ethnocentrism." In *Ethnicity and the Bible*, edited by Mark G. Brett, 449–68. Biblical Interpretation Series 19. Leiden: Brill, 1996.

———. "Opposing World-Views: The Border Guards between Traditional and Biomedical Health Care Practices." *S.A. Jnl Ethnol* 20.1 (1997) 1–9.

———. "The Pauline Movement and First-Century Judaism: A Framework for Transforming the Issues." *Neot* 27 (1993) 233–62.

———. "'Seeing' a Body into Being: Reflections on Scholarly Interpretations of the Nature and Reality of Jesus' Resurrected Body." *R&T* 9 (2002) 89–107.

———. "A Social-Scientific Key to Paul's Letter to the Galatians: An Alternative to Opponent Hypotheses as a Cypher Key." Ph.D. diss., University of South Africa, 1992.

———. "The Stuff World-Views Are Made Of." *Scriptura* 61 (1997) 193–212.

———. "Wie sê jy is Jesus? Die Dialektiek tussen Christus Vandag en Jesus van ouds." *R&T* 2 (1995) 298–312.

Cribiore, Raffaella. *Gymnastics of the Mind: Greek Education in Hellenistic and Roman Egypt.* Princeton: Princeton University Press, 2001.

———. *Writing, Teachers, and Students in Graeco-Roman Egypt.* American Studies in Papyrology 36. Atlanta: Scholars, 1996.

Cross, Frank Moore. "The Invention and Development of the Alphabet." In *The Origins of Writing*, edited by W. M. Senner, 77–90. Lincoln: University of Nebraska Press, 1989.

Crowder, Robert G., and Richard K. Wagner. *The Psychology of Reading: An Introduction.* 2nd ed. Oxford: Oxford University Press, 1992.

Culley, Robert C. "Oral Tradition and the OT: Some Recent Discussion." *Semeia* 5 (1976) 1–33.

D'Andrade, R. G. "Cultural Meaning Systems." In *Culture Theory: Essays on Mind, Self, and Emotion*, edited by R. A. Shweder and R. A. LeVine, 88–119. Cambridge: Cambridge University Press, 1984.

Dahl, Nils Alstrup. *Studies in Paul: Theology for the Early Christian Mission.* Minneapolis: Augsburg, 1977.

Daniels, John William. "Gossip in John's Gospel and the Social Processing of Jesus's Identity." *Journal of Early Christian History (Acta Patristica)* 1 (2011).

Darnton, Robert. "The Facts of Literary Life in Pre-Revolutionary France." In *The Political Culture of the Old Regime*, edited by Keith Michael Baker, 261–91. Oxford: Oxford University Press, 1989.

———. "History of Reading." In *New Perspectives on Historical Writing*, edited by Peter Burke, 140–67. University Park: University of Pennsylvania Press, 1991.

Davids, P. H. "The Gospels and Jewish Tradition: Twenty Years after Gerhardsson." In *Gospel Perspectives: Studies of History and Tradition in the Four Gospels*, vol. 1, edited by R. T. France and D. Wenham, 75–99. Sheffield: JSOT Press, 1980.

Davies, W. D. "Reflections on a Scandinavian Approach to 'the Gospel Tradition.'" In *Neotestamentica et Patristica*, edited by W. C. Van Unnik, 14–34. Leiden: Brill, 1962.

De Castell, Suzanne, Allan Luke, and Kieran Egan, editors. *Literacy, Society, and Schooling: A Reader*. Cambridge: Cambridge University Press, 1986.

De Castell, Suzanne, Allan Luke, and D. MacLennan. "On Defining Literacy." In *Literacy, Society, and Schooling: A Reader*, edited by Suzanne De Castell, Allan Luke, and Kieran Egan, 3–14. Cambridge: Cambridge University Press, 1986.

De Sousa, R. "In Praise of Gossip: Indiscretion as a Saintly Virtue." In *Good Gossip*, edited by Robert F. Goodman and Aaaron Ben-Ze'ev, 25–33. Lawrence: University Press of Kansas, 1994.

DeConick, April D. "Human Memory and the Sayings of Jesus: Contemporary Experimental Exercises in the Transmission of Jesus Traditions." In *Jesus, the Voice, and the Text: Beyond the Oral and the Written Gospel*, edited by Tom Thatcher, 135–80. Waco, TX: Baylor University Press, 2008.

Dégh, Linda. "Folk Narrative." In *Folklore and Folklife: An Introduction*, edited by Richard M. Dorson, 53–83. Chicago: University of Chicago Press, 1972.

Deissmann, Adolf. *Bible Studies: Contributions Chiefly from Papyri and Inscriptions to the History of the Language and the Religion of Hellenistic Judaism and Primitive Christianity*. 2nd ed. 1909. Reprinted, Eugene, OR: Wipf & Stock, 2004.

———. *Light from the Ancient East: The New Testament Illustrated by Recently Discovered Texts of the Greco-Roman World*. 1927. Reprinted, Eugene, OR: Wipf & Stock, 2004.

Dewey, Joanna. "Oral Methods of Structuring in Mark." *Int* 43 (1989) 32–44.

Dibelius, Martin. *Die Formgeschichte des Evangeliums*. 3rd ed. Tübingen: Mohr, 1959.

———. *From Tradition to Gospel*. Translated by Bertram Lee Woolf. 1934. Reprinted, Greenwood, SC: Attic, 1982.

———. *Jesus*. 1939. London: SCM, 1963.

Dionisotti, A. C. "From Ausonius' Schooldays? A Schoolbook and Its Relatives." *Journal of Roman Studies* 72 (1982) 83–125.

Dixon, R. A., et al. "Handwriting Performance in Younger and Older Adults: Age, Familiarity, and Practice Effects." *Psychology and Aging* 8 (1993) 360–70.

Dodds, E. R. *Pagan and Christian in an Age of Anxiety: Some Aspects of Religious Experience from Marcus Aurelius to Constantine*. Cambridge: Cambridge University Press, 1965.

Dorandi, Tiziano. "Den Autoren über die Schulter Geschaut: Arbeitsweise und Autographie bei den Antiken Schriftstellern." *ZPE* 87 (1991) 11–33.

———. "Zwischen Autographie und Diktat: Momente der Textualität in der Antiken Welt." In *Vermittlung und Tradierung von Wissen in der Griechischen Kultur*, edited by Wolfgang Kullmann and Jochen Althoff, 71–83. ScriptOralia 61. Tübingen: Narr, 1993.

Dorn, Paméla J. "Gender and Personhood: Turkish Jewish Proverbs and the Politics of Reputation." *Women's Studies International Forum* 9.3 (1986) 295–301.

Doty, William G. *Letters in Primitive Christianity.* Guides to Biblical Scholarship. Philadelphia: Fortress, 1973.

Downing, F. Gerald. "Common Ground with Paganism in Luke and in Josephus." *NTS* 28 (1980) 546–59.

———. "Interpretation and the 'Culture Gap.'" *Scottish Journal of Theology* 40 (1987) 161–71.

———. "Our Access to Other Cultures: Past and Present." *Modern Churchman* 21 (1977) 28–42.

———. "Redaction Criticism: Josephus' *Antiquities* and the Synoptic Gospels." *JSNT* 9 (1982) 29–48.

Drexhage, H. J. *Preise, Mieten/Pachten, Kosten und Löhne im römischen Ägypten bis zum Regierungsantritt Diokletians.* St. Katharinen: Scripta Mercaturae, 1991.

Drinkwater, J. "Maximinus to Diocletian and the 'Crisis.'" In *Cambridge Ancient History,* vol. 12.2: *The Crisis of Empire, A.D. 193–337,* edited by A. K. Bowman et al., 28–66. Cambridge: Cambridge University Press, 2005.

Dschulnigg, Peter. *Sprache, Redaktion und Intention des Markus-Evangeliums: Eigentümlichkeiten der Sprache des Markus-Evangeliums und Ihre Bedeutung für die Redaktionskritik.* Stuttgarter biblische Beiträge 11. Stuttgart: Katholisches Bibelwerk, 1984.

Du Boulay, Juliet. *Portrait of a Greek Mountain Village.* Oxford Monographs on Social Anthropology. Oxford: Clarendon, 1974.

Duncan-Jones, Richard. "Age-rounding, Illiteracy and Social Differentiation." *Chiron* 7 (1977) 333–53.

———. *Money and Government in the Roman Empire.* Cambridge: Cambridge University Press, 1994.

Dungan, David L. *The Sayings of Jesus in the Churches of Paul: The Uses of the Synoptic Tradition in the Regulation of Early Church Life.* Philadelphia: Fortress, 1971.

Dunn, James D. G. *Unity and Diversity in the New Testament: An Inquiry into the Character of Earliest Christianity.* London: SCM, 1977.

Dupont, Florence. *The Invention of Literature: From Greek Intoxication to the Latin Book.* Translated by Janet Lloyd. 1994. Baltimore: Johns Hopkins University Press, 1999.

Easterling, P. E. "Books and Readers in the Greek World 2: The Hellenistic and Imperial Periods." In *The Cambridge History of Classical Literature 1: Greek Literature,* edited by P. E. Easterling and B. M. W. Knox, 16–41. Cambridge: Cambridge University Press, 1985.

Edwards, C. L. "The Parry–Lord Theory Meets Operational Structuralism." *JAF* 96 (1983) 151–69.

Egger, Wilhelm. *Frohbotschaft und Lehre: Die Sammelberichte des Wirkens Jesu im Markusevangelium.* Frankfurter theologische Studien 19. Frankfurt: Knecht, 1976.

Eisenstein, Elizabeth L. "Some Conjectures about the Impact of Printing on Western Society and Thought: A Preliminary Report." In *Literacy and Social Development in the West: A Reader,* edited by Harvey J. Graff, 53–68. Cambridge Studies in Oral and Literate Culture 3. Cambridge: Cambridge University Press, 1981.

———. *The Printing Revolution in Early Modern Europe.* Cambridge: Cambridge University Press, 1983.

Ellis, Andrew, and Geoffrey Beattie. *The Psychology of Language and Communication.* London: Weidenfeld & Nicolson, 1986.

Ellis, E. Earle. *Prophecy and Hermeneutic in Early Christianity: New Testament Essays.* WUNT 18. Tübingen: Mohr/Siebeck, 1978.

———. "Gospel Criticism: A Perspective on the State of the Art." In *Das Evangelium und die Evangelien: Vorträge vom Tübinger Symposium 1982*, edited by Peter Stuhlmacher, 27–54. WUNT 28. Tübingen: Mohr/Siebeck, 1983.

Emler, Nicholas. "Gossip, Reputation and Social Adaptation." In *Good Gossip*, edited by Robert F. Goodman and Aaron Ben-Ze'ev, 117–38. Lawrence: University Press of Kansas, 1994.

Engelsing, R. "Die Perioden der Lesergeschichte in der Neuzeit." *Archiv für Geschichte des Buchwesens* 10 (1970) 945–1002.

Fabian, Johannes. *Time and the Other: How Anthropology Makes it Object.* New York: Columbia University Press, 1983.

Faris, J. C. "The Dynamics of Verbal Exchange: a Newfoundland example." *Anthropologica* 8 (1966) 235–48.

Ferguson, John. *Clement of Alexandria.* Twayne's World Authors Series 289. New York: Twayne, 1974.

Feyerabend, Paul. *Against Method.* 2nd ed. London: Verso, 1988.

Fiensy, David A. *The Social History of Palestine in the Herodian Period: The Land is Mine.* Studies in the Bible and Early Christianity 20. Lewiston, NY: Mellen, 1991.

Fine, Gary Alan. "Social Components of Children's Gossip." *Journal of Communication* 27 (1977) 181–85.

———. "Folklore Diffusion through Interactive Social Networks: Conduits in a Preadolescent Community." *New York Folklore* 5 (1979) 99–125.

Finley, M. I. *Ancient History: Evidence and Models.* London: Chatto & Windus, 1985.

———. "Rumors and Gossiping." In *Discourse and Dialogue.* Vol. 3 of *Handbook of Discourse Analysis*, edited by T. A. Van Dijk, 223–37. London: Academic, 1985.

Finnegan, Ruth. "What Is Oral Literature Anyway? Comments in the Light of Some African and Other Comparative Material." In *Oral Literature and the Formula*, edited by Benjamin A. Stolz and Richard S. Shannon III, 127–66. Ann Arbor: University of Michigan, 1976.

———. *Oral Poetry: Its Nature, Significance and Social Context.* Cambridge: Cambridge University Press, 1977.

———. *Literacy and Orality: Studies in the Technology of Communication.* Oxford: Blackwell, 1988.

Fischer, Steven Roger. *A History of Reading.* London: Reaktion, 2003.

Fishman, Andrea R. "Because This Is Who We Are: Writing in the Amish Community." In *Writing in the Community*, edited by David Barton and Roz Ivanič, 14–37. Written Communication Annual 6. London: Sage, 1991.

Fitzgerald, William. *Slavery and the Roman Literary Imagination.* Roman Literature and Its Contents. Cambridge: Cambridge University Press, 2000.

Fitzmyer, Joseph A. *The Gospel according to Luke (I–IX).* Anchor Bible 28. Garden City, NY: Doubleday, 1981.

Foley, John Miles. "Introduction." In *Oral-formulaic Theory and Research: An Introduction and Annotated Bibliography*, edited by John Miles Foley, 3–77. New York: Garland, 1985.

———. "Introduction." In *Oral Tradition in Literature: Interpretation in Context*, edited by John Miles Foley, 1–18. Columbia: University of Missouri Press, 1986.

———. "Oral Literature: Premises and Problems." *Choice* 18 (1980) 187–96.

————. "The Oral Theory in Context." In *Oral Traditional Literature: A Festschrift for Albert Bates Lord*, edited by John Miles Foley, 27–122. Columbus, OH: Slavica, 1981.

————, editor. *Oral Tradition in Literature: Interpretation in Context*. Columbia: University of Missouri Press, 1986.

————. *Oral Traditional Literature: A Festschrift for Albert Bates Lord*. Columbus, OH: Slavica, 1981.

————. "Series Foreword." In *Oral Tradition in Judaism: The Case of the Mishnah*, edited by Jacob Neusner, xiii–xv. New York: Garland, 1987.

————. *The Theory of Oral Composition: History and Methodology*. Folkloristics. Bloomington: Indiana University Press, 1988.

————. "Tradition and the Collective Talent: Oral Epic, Textual Meaning, and Receptionalist Theory." *Cultural Anthropology* 1 (1986) 203–22.

————. "Tradition-Dependent and -Independent Features in Oral Literature: A Comparative View of the Formula." In *Oral Traditional Literature: A Festschrift for Albert Bates Lord*, edited by John Miles Foley, 262–81. Columbus, OH: Slavica, 1981.

————. "The Traditional Oral Audience." *Balkan Studies* 18.1 (1977) 145–53.

Forbes, C. A. "The Education and Training of Slaves in Antiquity." *Transactions and Proceedings of the American Philological Association* 86 (1955) 321–60.

————. "Expanded Uses of the Greek Gymnasium." *Classical Philology* 40 (1945) 32–42.

Foucault, Michel. "What Is an Author?" In *The Foucault Reader*, edited by Paul Rabinow, 101–20. London: Penguin, 1984.

Fouquet-Plümacher, Doris. "Buch/Buchwesen 3: Die Entwicklung von der Antike bis zur Neuzeit." In *Theologische Realenzyklopädie* 7 (1981) 275–290.

Fowler, Robert M. "Who Is 'the Reader' in Reader Response Criticism?" *Semeia* 31 (1985) 5–23.

Fox, Robin Lane. 1994. "Literacy and Power in Early Christianity." In *Literacy and Power in the Ancient World*, edited by Alan K. Bowman and Greg Woolf, 126–48. Cambridge: Cambridge University Press.

French, Hal W. "The Psycho-dynamics of Adversary Identity." *Studies in Religion* 18 (1989) 261–72.

Freyne, Sean. *Galilee from Alexander the Great to Hadrian 323 B.C.E. to 135 C.E.: A Study of Second Temple Judaism*. Wilmington, DE: Glazier, 1980.

Funk, Robert W. "The Apostolic Presence: Paul." In *Parables and Presence: Forms of the New Testament Tradition*, 81–102. Philadelphia: Fortress, 1982.

————. *Language, Hermeneutic, and Word of God: The Problem of Language in the New Testament and Contemporary Theology*. New York: Harper & Row, 1966.

————. "Saying and Seeing: Phenomenology of Language and the New Testament." *Journal of Bible and Religion* 34 (1966) 197–213.

Gager, John. "The Gospels and Jesus: Some Doubts about Method." *JR* 54 (1974) 244–72.

Gamble, Harry Y. *Books and Readers in the Early Church: A History of Early Christian Texts*. New Haven: Yale University Press, 1995.

Garnsey, Peter, and Richard Saller. *The Early Principate: Augustus to Trajan*. Oxford: Clarendon, 1982.

Gavrilov, A. K. "Techniques of Reading in Classical Antiquity." *CQ* 47 (1997) 56–73.

Gee, James Paul. "The Legacies of Literacy: From Plato to Freire through Harvey Graff." *Harvard Educational Review* 58 (1988) 195–213.

Geertz, Clifford. *Local Knowledge: Further Essays in Interpretive Anthropology*. New York: Basic Books, 1983.

Georgi, Dieter. *The Opponents of Paul in Second Corinthians: A Study of Religious Propaganda in Late Antiquity.* Philadelphia: Fortress, 1986.

Gerhardsson, Birger. "The Gospel Tradition." In *The Interrelations of the Gospels,* edited by David L. Dungan, 497–545. BETL 95. Leuven: Leuven University Press, 1990.

———. *The Gospel Tradition.* Coniectanea Biblica: New Testament Series 15. Lund: Gleerup, 1986.

———. *Memory and Manuscript: Oral Tradition and Written Transmission in Rabbinic Judaism and Early Christianity.* Translated by Eric J. Sharpe. Acta Seminarii Neotestamentici Upsaliensis 22. Lund: Gleerup, 1961.

———. *The Origins of the Gospel Traditions.* Translated by Gene J. Lund. Philadelphia: Fortress, 1979.

Gilmore, David D. "Varieties of Gossip in a Spanish Rural Community." *Ethnology* 17 (1978) 89–99.

Giovè Marchioli, Nicoletta, and G. Menci. "Tachygraphie." In *Der Neue Pauly: Enzyklopädie der Antike, Altertum,* edited by H. Cancik and H. Schneider, 11:1205–8. Stuttgart: Metzler, 1998.

Gluckman, Max. "Gossip and Scandal." *Current Anthropology* 4 (1963) 307–16.

Goldsmith, Daena. "Gossip from the Native's Point of View: A Comparative Analysis." *Research on Language and Social Interaction* 23 (1989) 163–94.

Goodman, Robert F. "Introduction." In *Good Gossip,* edited by Robert F. Goodman and Aaron Ben-Ze'ev, 1–10. Lawrence: University Press of Kansas, 1994.

Goodwin, Marjorie H. "'He-said-she-said': Formal Cultural Procedures for the Construction of a Gossip Dispute Activity." *American Ethnologist* 7 (1980) 674–95.

Goody, Jack. *The Domestication of the Savage Mind.* Themes in the Social Sciences. Cambridge: Cambridge University Press, 1977.

———. *The Interface between the Written and the Oral.* Studies in Literacy, Family, Culture, and the State. Cambridge: Cambridge University Press, 1987.

———. "Introduction." In *Literacy in Traditional Societies,* edited by Jack Goody, 1–26. Cambridge: Cambridge University Press, 1968.

———. "Literacy and Achievement in the Ancient World." In *Writing in Focus,* edited by Florian Coulmas and Konrad Ehlich, 83–97. Trends in Linguistics: Studies and Monographs 24. Berlin: Mouton, 1983.

———. "Literacy, Criticism and the Growth of Knowledge." In *Culture and Its Creators: Essays in Honor of Edward Shils,* edited by Joseph Ben–David and Terry Nichols Clark, 226–43. Chicago: University of Chicago Press, 1977.

———. *The Logic of Writing and the Organization of Society.* Studies in Literacy, Family, Culture, and the State. Cambridge: Cambridge University Press, 1986.

Gould, John D., and Stephen J. Boies. "Writing, Dictating, and Speaking Letters." *Science* 201/4361 (22 Sept 1978) 1145–47.

Graff, Harvey J. *The Labyrinths of Literacy: Reflections on Literacy Past and Present.* London: Falmer, 1987.

———. *The Legacies of Literacy: Continuities and Contradictions in Western Culture and Society.* Bloomington: Indiana University Press, 1987.

———. "The Legacies of Literacy: Continuities and Contradictions in Western Society and Culture." In *Literacy, Society, and Schooling: A Reader,* edited by Suzanne De Castell, Allan Luke, and Kieran Egan, 61–86. Cambridge: Cambridge University Press, 1986.

———. "Literacy." In *The Social Science Encyclopedia*, edited by Adam Kuper and Jessica Kuper, 469–71. London: Routledge & Kegan Paul, 1985.

———, editor. *Literacy and Social Development in the West: A Reader*. Cambridge Studies in Oral and Literate Culture 3. Cambridge: Cambridge University Press, 1981.

———. *The Literacy Myth: Literacy and Social Structure in the Nineteenth-Century City*. Studies in Social Discontinuity. New York: Academic, 1979.

Graham, William A. *Beyond the Written Word: Oral Aspects of Scripture in the History of Religion*. Cambridge: Cambridge University Press, 1987.

Grant, Michael. *History of Rome*. London: Faber, 1979.

Graser, E. R. "The Edict of Diocletian on Maximum Prices." In *An Economic Survey of Ancient Rome*. Vol. 5, *Rome and Italy of the Empire*, edited by Tenney Frank, 305–421. Baltimore: Johns Hopkins Press, 1940.

Gray, Bennison. "Repetition in Oral Literature." *JAF* 84 (1971) 289–303.

Gulletta, Maria Ida, and Valentin Kockel. "Pompeii." In *Brill's New Pauly: Encyclopaedia of the Ancient World*, edited by Hubert Cancik and Helmuth Schneider, 7:546–54. Leiden: Brill, 2007.

Güttgemanns, Erhardt. *Candid Questions Concerning Gospel Form Criticism: A Methodological Sketch of the Fundamental Problematics of Form and Redaction Criticism*. 2nd ed. Translated by William G. Doty. Pittsburgh Theological Monograph Series 26. Pittsburgh: Pickwick, 1979.

Hadas, Moses. *Ancilla to Classical Reading*. New York: Colombia University Press, 1954.

———. *A History of Greek Literature*. New York: Colombia University Press, 1950.

Haines-Eitzen, Kim. "'Girls Trained in Beautiful Writing': Female Scribes in Roman Antiquity and Early Christianity." *Journal of Early Christian Studies* 6 (1998) 629–46.

———. *Guardians of Letters: Literacy, Power, and the Transmission of Early Christian Literature*. Oxford: Oxford University Press, 2002.

Hainsworth, J. B. "Structure and Content in Epic Formulae: The Question of the Unique Expression." *CQ* 14 (1964) 155–64.

Hall, L. G. H. "Hirtius and the *Bellum Alexandrinum*." *CQ* 46 (1996) 411–15.

Hamesse, J. "The Scholastic Model of Reading." In *A History of Reading in the West*, edited by Guglielmo Cavallo and Roger Chartier, 103–19. Translated by Lydia G. Cochrane. Oxford: Polity, 1999.

Hamilton, Mary, and David Barton. "The International Adult Literacy Survey: What Does It Really Measure?" *International Review of Education* 46.5 (2000) 377–89.

Hannerz, Ulf. "Gossip, Networks and Culture in a Black American Ghetto." *Ethnos* 32 (1967) 35–60.

Hanson, A. E. "Ancient Illiteracy." In *Literacy in the Roman World*, edited by Mary Beard et al., 159–98. Journal of Roman Archaeology Supplementary Series 3. Ann Arbor: University of Michigan, 1991.

Hanson, K. C. "The Galilean Fishing Economy and the Jesus Tradition." *BTB* 27 (1997) 99–111.

Harris, J. R. "Stichometry." *AJP* 4 (1883) 133–57.

———. "Stichometry. Part II." *AJP* 4 (1883) 309–31.

Harris, Roy. *The Origin of Writing*. London: Duckworth, 1986.

———. *Rethinking Writing*. London: Athlone, 2000.

Harris, William V. "Literacy and Epigraphy." *ZPE* 52 (1983) 87–111.

———. *Ancient Literacy*. Cambridge: Harvard University Press, 1989.

Hartman, Lars. "On Reading Others' Letters." *HTR* 79 (1986) 137–46.

Harvey, A. "Review of M. D. Goulder, *Midrash and Lection in Matthew*." *JTS* 27 (1976) 188–95.

Hatch, Edwin. *The Influence of Greek Ideas on Christianity*. New York: Harper Torchbooks, 1957.

Hautecoeur, Jean-Paul. "Literacy in the Age of Information: Knowledge, Power or Domination?" *International Review of Education* 46.5 (2000) 357–65.

Havelock, Eric A. *The Literate Revolution in Greece and Its Cultural Consequences*. Princeton: University Press, 1982.

———. *The Muse Learns to Write: Reflections on Orality and Literacy from Antiquity to the Present*. New Haven: Yale University Press, 1986.

———. "Oral Composition in the *Oedipus Tyrannus* of Sophocles." *NLH* 16 (1984) 175–97.

———. *Origins of Western Literacy*. Toronto: Ontario Institute for Studies in Education, 1976.

———. *Preface to Plato*. Cambridge, MA: Belknap, 1963.

Haymes, E. R. "Oral Composition in Middle High German Epic Poetry." In *Oral Traditional Literature: A Festschrift for Albert Bates Lord*, edited by John Miles Foley, 341–46. Columbus, OH: Slavica, 1981.

Heath, S. B. "The Functions and Uses of Literacy." In *Literacy, Society and Schooling: A Reader*, edited by Suzanne de Castell, Allan Luke, and Kieran Egan, 15–26. Cambridge: Cambridge University Press, 1986.

———. "What No Bedtime Story Means: Narrative Skills at Home and School." *Language in Society* 11 (1982) 49–76.

Hedrick, Charles W. Jr. *Ancient History: Monuments and Documents*. Oxford: Wiley-Blackwell, 2005.

Henderson, Ian H. "*Didache* and Orality in Synoptic Comparison." *JBL* 111 (1992) 283–306.

Hengel, Martin, and Helmut Merkel. "Die Magier aus dem Osten und die Flucht nach Ägypten (Mt 2) im Rahmen der antiken Religionsgeschiche und der Theologie des Matthäus." In *Orientierung an Jesus: Zur Theologie der Synoptiker*, edited by Paul Hoffmann, 139–69. Freiburg: Herder, 1973.

Hesse, Carla. "Enlightenment Epistemologies and the Laws of Authorship in Revolutionary France, 1777–1793." *Representations* 30 (1990) 114–16.

Hester, James D. "The Use and Influence of Rhetoric in Galatians." *Theologische Zeitschrift* 42 (1986) 386–408.

Hezser, Catherine. *Jewish Literacy in Roman Palestine*. Texts and Studies in Ancient Judaism 81. Tübingen: Mohr/Siebeck, 2001.

Hock, Ronald F. *The Social Context of Paul's Ministry: Tentmaking and Apostleship*. Philadelphia: Fortress, 1980.

Hollenbach, Paul. "Defining Rich and Poor Using Social Sciences." In *SBL 1984 Seminar Papers*, edited by Kent H. Richards, 50–63. Atlanta: Scholars, 1987.

Hopkins, Keith. "Economic Growth and Towns in Classical Antiquity." In *Towns in Societies: Essays in Economic History and Historical Sociology*, edited by Philip Abrams and E. A. Wrigley, 35–77. Past and Present Publications. Cambridge: Cambridge University Press, 1978.

Horsfall, Nicholas. "Statistics or States of Mind?" In *Literacy in the Roman World*, 59–76. Journal of Roman Archaeology Supplementary Series 3. Ann Arbor: University of Michigan, 1991.

Horsley, Richard A., in collaboration with Jonathan A. Draper. *Whoever Hears You Hears Me: Prophets, Performance, and Tradition in Q*. Harrisburg, PA: Trinity, 1999.

Horsley, Richard A., and John S. Hanson. *Bandits, Prophets, and Messiahs: Popular Movements at the Time of Jesus*. Minneapolis: Winston, 1985.

Hull, John M. *Touching the Rock: An Experience of Blindness*. New York: Pantheon, 1990.

Isaac, E. "1 (Ethiopic Apocalypse of) Enoch." In *The Old Testament Pseudepigrapha*, edited by James H. Charlesworth, 1:5–90. Garden City, NY: Doubleday, 1983.

Jackson, David R. "Education and Entertainment: Some Aspects of Life in New Testament Times." *Vox Evangelica* 6 (1969) 4–30.

Jaeger, Marianne E., Susan Anthony, and Ralph L. Rosnow. "Who Hears What from Whom and with What Effect: A Study of Rumor." *Personality and Social Psychology Bulletin* 6 (1980) 473–78.

Janko, Richard. "The Homeric Poems as Oral Dictated Texts." *CQ* 48 (1998) 1–13.

Janson, Tore. *Latin Prose Prefaces: Studies in Literary Convention*. Studia Latina Stockholmiensia 13. Stockholm: Almqvist & Wiksell, 1964.

Jason, Heda. "Content Analysis of Oral Literature: A Discussion." In *Patterns in Oral Literature*, edited by Heda Jason and Dimitri Segal, 298–310. The Hague: Mouton, 1977.

Jaszi, Peter. "Toward a Theory of Copyright: The Metamorphoses of 'Authorship.'" *Duke Law Journal* 1991/2 (1991) 455–502.

Jeremias, Joachim. *New Testament Theology: The Proclamation of Jesus*. Translated by John Bowden. London: SCM, 1971.

Jewett, Robert. "Paul, Phoebe, and the Spanish Mission." In *The Social World of Formative Christianity and Judaism: Essays in Tribute to Howard Clark Kee*, edited by Jacob Neusner et al., 142–61. Philadelphia: Fortress, 1988.

Johnson, William A. *Bookrolls and Scribes in Oxyrhynchus*. Studies in Book and Print Culture. Toronto: University of Toronto Press, 2004.

———. "Oral Performance and the Composition of Herodotus' *Histories*." *GRBS* 35 (1994) 229–54.

Jones, A. H. M. *The Greek City from Alexander to Justinian*. Oxford: Clarendon, 1966.

Jones, Deborah. "Gossip: Notes on Women's Oral Culture." *Women's Studies International Quarterly* 3 (1980) 193–98.

Joshel, Sandra R. "Work, Identity and Legal Status at Rome." In *Roman Sexualities*, edited by Judith P. Hallett and Marilyn B. Skinner. Norman: University of Oklahoma Press, 1992.

Jousse, Marcel. *The Oral Style*. Translated by Edgard Sienaert and Richard Whitaker. Garland Reference Library of the Humanities 1352. New York: Garland, 1990.

Kaimio, Jorma. *The Romans and the Greek Language*. Commentationes Humanarum Litterarum 64. Helsinki: Societas Scientiarum Fennica, 1979.

Kapferer, Jean-Noël. *Rumors: Uses, Interpretations, and Images*. New Brunswick: Transaction, 1990.

Kartzow, Marianne Bjelland. "Female Gossipers and Their Reputation in the Pastoral Epistles." *Neot* 39 (2005) 255–72.

———. *Gossip and Gender: Othering of Speech in the Pastoral Epistles*. Beihefte zur Zeitschrift für die neutestamentliche Wissenschaft 164. Berlin: de Gruyter, 2009.

Kaster, Robert A. "Notes on 'Primary' and 'Secondary' Schools in Late Antiquity." *TAPA* 113 (1983) 323–46.

Kee, Howard Clark. *Christian Origins in Sociological Perspective*. Philadelphia: Westminster, 1980.

Kelber, Werner H. "Apostolic Tradition and the Form of the Gospel." In *Discipleship in the New Testament*, edited by Fernando F. Segovia, 24–46. Philadelphia: Fortress, 1985.

———. "Jesus and Tradition: Words in Time, Words in Space." *Semeia* 65 (1994) 139–67.

———. "Mark and Oral Tradition." *Semeia* 16 (1980) 7–55.

———. *The Oral and the Written Gospel: The Hermeneutics of Speaking and Writing in the Synoptic Tradition, Mark, Paul and Q*. Philadelphia: Fortress, 1983.

———. "The Oral-Scribal-Memorial Arts of Communication in Early Christianity." In *Jesus, the Voice, and the Text: Beyond the Oral and the Written Gospel*, edited by Tom Thatcher, 234–62. Waco, TX: Baylor University Press, 2008.

———. "Sayings Collection and Sayings Gospel: A Study in the Clustering Management of Knowledge." *Language & Communication* 9 (1989) 213–24.

———. "The Two-Source Hypothesis: Oral Tradition, the Poetics of Gospel Narrativity, and Memorial Arbitration." Paper presented at the SNTS 2002 meeting, Durham, UK.

Kellogg, Robert L. "Oral Literature." *NLH* 5 (1973) 55–66.

Kennedy, George A. *New Testament Interpretation through Rhetorical Criticism*. Chapel Hill: University of North Carolina Press, 1984.

Kenney, E. J. "Books and Readers in the Roman World." In *Cambridge History of Classical Literature*, vol. 2: *Latin Literature*, edited by E. J. Kenney and W. V. Clausen, 3–32. Cambridge: Cambridge University Press, 1982.

———. "Small Writing and Less Reading." *Classical Review* 41 (1991) 168–69.

Kenyon, Frederic G. *Books and Readers in Ancient Greece and Rome*. 2nd ed. Oxford: Clarendon, 1951.

———. *The Palaeography of Greek Papyri*. Oxford: Clarendon, 1989.

Kenyon, Frederic G, and C. H. Roberts. "Books, Greek and Latin." In *OCD* (1970) 172–75.

King, Daniel H. "Paul and the Tannaim: A Study in Galatians." *Westminster Theological Journal* 45 (1983) 340–70.

Kitzinger, Rachel. "Alphabets and Writing." In *Civilization of the Ancient Mediterranean: Greece and Rome*, edited by Michael Grant and Rachel Kitzinger, 1:397–419. New York: Scribner, 1988.

Knox, B. M. W. "Silent Reading in Antiquity." *GRBS* 9 (1968) 421–35.

Koenig, Fredrick. *Rumor in the Marketplace: The Social Psychology of Commercial Hearsay*. Dover, NY: Auburn, 1985.

Körtner, Ulrich. H. J. "Markus der Mitarbeiter des Petrus." *ZNW* 71 (1980) 160–73.

Koskenniemi, Heikki. *Studien zur Idee Und Phraseologie des Griechischen Briefes bis 400 n.Chr*. Suomalaisen Tiedeakatemian Toimituksia B/102.2. Helsinki: Suomalaisen Kirjallisuuden Seura, 1956.

Kreitzer, L. Joseph. "Hadrian and the Nero *Redivivus* Myth." *ZNW* 79 (1988) 92–115.

———. "Sibylline Oracles 8, the Roman Imperial *Adventus* Coinage of Hadrian and the Apocalypse of John." *Journal for the Study of the Pseudepigrapha* 4 (1989) 69–84.

Kuhn, Thomas S. *The Structure of Scientific Revolutions*. 2nd ed. Chicago: University Press, 1970.

Kurtz, Lester R. "The Politics of Heresy." *American Journal of Sociology* 88 (1983) 1085–115.

Kümmel, Werner Georg. *Das Neue Testament im 20. Jahrhundert: Ein Forschungsbericht*. Stuttgart: Katholisches Bibelwerk, 1970.

Künzl, Hannalore. "Buch/Buchwesen III. Die Entwicklung von der Antike bis zur Neuzeit." In *Theologische Realenzyklopädie* 7 (1981) 275–304.

Kürzinger, Josef. "Die Aussage des Papias von Hierapolis zur Literarischen Form des Markusevangeliums." *Biblische Zeitschrift* 21 (1977) 245–64.

Laino Entralgo, Pedro. *The Therapy of the Word in Classical Antiquity*. Edited and translated by L. J. Rather and John M. Sharp. New Haven: Yale University Press, 1970.

Lategan, Bernard C. *Die Brief aan die Galasiërs*. Kaapstad: Kerk, 1986.

———. "Is Paul Defending His Apostleship in Galatians? The Function of Galatians 1.11–12 and 2.19–20 in the Development of Paul's Argument." *NTS* 34 (1988) 411–30.

———. "Formulas in the Language of Paul: A Study of Prepositional Phrases in Galatians." *Neot* 25 (1991) 75–87.

Layton, Robert. "Patterns of Informal Interaction in Pellaport." In *Gifts and Poison: The Politics of Reputation*, edited by F. G. Bailey, 97–118. Pavillion Series: Social Anthropology. Oxford: Blackwell, 1971.

Leeman, A. D., and A. C. Braet. *Klassieke Retorica: Haar Inhoud, Functie en Betekenis*. Groningen: Wolters-Noordhoff, 1987.

Lehtipuro, Outi. "Folk-narrative Research." *Arv: Nordic Yearbook of Folklore* 36 (1980) 3–23.

Lenski, Gerhard, Jean Lenski, and Patrick Nolan. *Human Societies: An Introduction to Macrosociology*. 6th ed. New York: McGraw-Hill, 1991.

Lentz, Tony M. *Orality and Literacy in Hellenic Greece*. Carbondale: Southern Illinois University Press, 1989.

Lévi-Strauss, Claude. *Tristes Tropiques*. Translated by John Weightman and Doreen Weightman. New York: Atheneum, 1974.

Levin, Jack, and Arnold Arluke. *Gossip: The Inside Scoop*. New York: Plenum, 1987.

Levy, R. I. "The Quest for Mind in Different Times and Different Places." In *Social History and Issues in Human Consciousness: Some Interdisciplinary Connections*, edited by A. E. Barnes and P. N. Stearns, 3–40. New York: New York University Press, 1989.

Lewis, Naphtali. *Life in Egypt under Roman rule*. Oxford: Clarendon, 1983.

———. *Papyrus in Classical Antiquity*. Oxford: Clarendon, 1974.

Lieberman, Saul. *Hellenism in Jewish Palestine: Studies in the Literary Transmission of Beliefs and Manners of Palestine in the I Century B.C.E.—IV Century C.E.* 2nd ed. New York: Jewish Theological Seminary of America, 1962.

Lindberg, D. C., and N. H. Steneck. "The Sense of Vision and the Origins of Modern Science." In *Science, Medicine and Society in the Renaissance*, 1:29–45, edited by A. G. Debus. New York: Science History Publications, 1972.

Litman, J. "The Public Domain." *Emory Law Journal* 39 (1990) 965–1023.

Lockridge, K. "Literacy in Early America 1650–1800." In *Literacy and Social Development in the West: A Reader*, edited by Harvey J. Graff, 183–200. Cambridge Studies in Oral and Literate Culture 3. Cambridge: Cambridge University Press, 1981.

Loewenstein, Joseph. "The Script in the Marketplace." *Representations* 12 (1985) 101–14.

Lohr, Charles H. "Oral Techniques in the Gospel of Matthew." *CBQ* 23 (1961) 403–35.

Longenecker, Richard N. "Ancient Amanuenses and the Pauline Epistles." In *New Dimensions in New Testament Study*, edited by Richard N. Longenecker and Merrill C. Tenney, 281–97. Grand Rapids: Zondervan, 1974.

Lord, A. B. "Formula and Non-narrative Theme in South Slavic Oral Epic and the OT." *Semeia* 5 (1976) 93–105.

———. "The Gospels As Oral Traditional Literature." In *The Relationship among the Gospels: An Interdisciplinary Dialogue*, edited by W. O. Walker, 33–91. San Antonio: Trinity University Press, 1978.

———. "Homer's Originality: Dictated Texts." *Transactions and Proceedings of the American Philological Association* 84 (1953) 124–34.

———. "The Merging of Two Worlds: Oral and Written Poetries As Carriers of Ancient Values." In *Oral Tradition in Literature: Interpretation in Context*, edited by John Miles Foley, 19–64. Columbia: University of Missouri Press, 1986b.

———. "Perspectives on Recent Work on Oral Literature." In *Oral Literature*, edited by J. J. Duggan, 1–24. Edinburgh: Scottish Academic Press, 1975.

———. *The Singer of Tales.* Cambridge: Harvard University Press, 1960.

———. "The Traditional Song." In *Oral Literature and the Formula*, edited by B. A. Stolz and R. S. Shannon, 1–15. Ann Arbor: Center for the Coördination of Ancient and Modern Studies, University of Michigan, 1976.

Luke, Allan. "Genres of Power? Literacy Education and the Production of Capital." In *Literacy in Society*, edited by Ruqaiya Hasan and Geoffrey Williams, 308–38. Applied Linguistics and Language Study. London: Longman, 1996.

———. "Literacy and the Other: A Sociological Approach to Literacy Research and Policy in Multilingual Societies." *Reading Research Quarterly* 38.1 (2003) 132–41.

Macdonald, Dennis R. "From Audita to Legenda: Oral and Written Miracle Stories." *Foundations and Facets Forum* 2.4 (1986) 15–26.

Mack, Burton L. *A Myth of Innocence: Mark and Christian Origins.* Philadelphia: Fortress, 1988.

MacMullen, Ramsay. *Changes in the Roman Empire: Essays in the Ordinary.* Princeton: University Press, 1990.

———. *Christianizing the Roman Empire (A.D. 100–400).* New Haven: Yale University Press, 1984.

———. "The Epigraphic Habit in the Roman Empire." *AJP* 103 (1982) 233–46.

———. *Paganism in the Roman Empire.* New Haven: Yale University Press, 1981.

———. *Roman Social Relations: 50 B.C. to A.D. 284.* New Haven: Yale University Press, 1974.

Magnússon, S. G. "The Singularization of History: Social and Microhistory Within the Postmodern State of Knowledge." *Journal of Social History* 36 (2003) 701–35.

Malherbe, Abraham J. "Ancient Epistolary Theorists." *Ohio Journal of Religious Studies* 5.2 (1977) 3–77.

———. *Moral Exhortation: A Greco-Roman Sourcebook.* Library of Early Christianity 4. Philadelphia: Westminster, 1986.

———. *Social Aspects of Early Christianity.* 2nd ed. Philadelphia: Fortress, 1983.

Malina, Bruce J. "Reading Theory Perspective: Reading Luke-Acts." In *The Social World of Luke-Acts: Models for Interpretation*, edited by Jerome H. Neyrey, 3–24. Peabody: Hendrickson, 1991.

———. "Rhetorical Criticism and Social-Scientific Criticism: Why Won't Romanticism Leave Us Alone?" In *Rhetoric, Scripture and Theology: Essays from the 1994 Pretoria Conference*, edited by Stanley E. Porter and Thomas H. Olbricht, 72–101. JSNTSup 131. Sheffield: Sheffield Academic, 1996.

———. *The Social Gospel of Jesus: The Kingdom of God in Mediterranean Perspective.* Minneapolis: Fortress, 2001.

———. "Wealth and Poverty in the New Testament and Its World." *Int* 41 (1987) 354–67.

Malina, Bruce J., and Jerome H. Neyrey. "Conflict in Luke-Acts: Labelling and Deviance Theory." In *The Social World of Luke-Acts: Models for Interpretation*, edited by Jerome H. Neyrey, 97–122. Peabody: Hendrickson, 1991.

———. *Portraits of Paul: An Archaeology of Ancient Personality*. Louisville: Westminster John Knox, 1996.

Maltby, Robert. *Tibullus: Elegies*. ARCA 41. Cambridge: Cairns, 2002.

Manguel, Alberto. *A History of Reading*. New York: Viking, 1996.

Mansfeld, Jaap. *Prolegomena: Questions to Be Settled before the Study of an Author, or a Text*. Philosophia Antiqua 61. Leiden: Brill, 1994.

Marcus, Michelle, et al. "A Prospective Study of Computer Users, II: Postural Risk Factors for Musculoskeletal Symptoms and Disorders." *American Journal of Industrial Medicine* 41 (2002) 236–49.

Marrou, H. I. "Education and Rhetoric." In *The Legacy of Greece*, edited by M. I. Finley, 185–201. Oxford: Oxford University Press, 1984.

———. *A History of Education in Antiquity*. Translated by George Lamb. New York: Sheed & Ward, 1956.

Marshall, Peter. *Enmity in Corinth:Social Conventions in Paul's Relations with the Corinthians*. WUNT 2/23. Tübingen: Mohr/Siebeck, 1987.

———. "Invective: Paul and His Enemies in Corinth." In *Perspectives on Language and Text: Essays and Poems in Honor of Francis I. Anderson*, edited by Edgar W. Conrad and Edward G. Newing, 359–73. Winona Lake, IN: Eisenbrauns, 1987.

Martin, Henri-Jean. *The History and Power of Writing*. Translated by Lydia G. Cochrane. 1988. Reprinted, Chicago: University of Chicago Press, 1994.

Martin, Richard P. "Telemachus and the Last Hero Song." *Colby Quarterly* 29 (1993) 222–40.

Marzillo, P. "Performing an Academic Talk: Proclus on Hesiod's *Work and Days*." In *Orality, Literacy and Performance in the Ancient World*, edited by Elizabeth Minchin, 183–200. Mnemosyne Supplements 335. Leiden: Brill, 2012.

McConnell, Taylor. "Oral Cultures and Literate Research." *Religious Education* 81 (1986) 341–55.

McDermott, W. C. "M Cicero and M Tiro." *Historia* 21 (1972) 259–86.

McGuire, M. R. P. "Letters and Letter Carriers in Christian Antiquity." *Classical World* 53.5–6 (1960) 148–53, 184–200.

Meeks, Wayne A. *The First Urban Christians: The Social World of the Apostle Paul*. New Haven: Yale University Press, 1983.

Meissner, Burkhard. "Über Zweck und Anlass von Diokletians Preisedikts." *Historia* 49 (2000) 79–100.

Metzger, Bruce M. *The Canon of the New Testament: Its Origin, Development, and Significance*. Oxford: Clarendon, 1987.

———. *Manuscripts of the Greek Bible: An Introduction to Greek Palaeography*. Oxford: Oxford University Press, 1981.

———. *The Text of the New Testament: Its Transmission, Corruption and Restoration*. 3rd ed. Oxford: Oxford University Press, 1992.

———. "When Did Scribes Begin to Use Writing Desks?" In *Historical and Literary Studies: Pagan, Jewish, and Christian*, 123–38. New Testament Tools and Studies 8. Leiden: Brill, 1968.

Miletich, John S. "The Quest for the 'Formula': A Comparative Reappraisal." *Modern Philology* 74 (1976) 111–23.

Millar, Fergus. *The Emperor in the Roman World.* London: Duckworth, 1977.

———. "Epigraphy." In *Sources for Ancient history,* edited by Michael Crawford, 80–136. Sources of History: Studies in the Uses of Historical Evidence. Cambridge: Cambridge University Press, 1983.

Milne, H. J. M. *Greek Shorthand Manuals: Syllabary and Commentary.* Graeco-Roman Memoirs 24. London: Egypt Exploration Society, 1934.

Mohler, S. L. "Slave Education in the Roman Empire." *Transactions and Proceedings of the American Philological Association* 71 (1940) 262–280.

Moo, Douglas J. *The Epistle to the Romans.* New International Commentary on the New Testament. Grand Rapids: Eerdmans, 1996.

Morgan, Teresa. *Literate Education in the Hellenistic and Roman Worlds.* Cambridge Classical Studies. Cambridge: Cambridge University Press, 1998.

Morrison, Ken. "Stabilizing the Text: The Institutionalization of Knowledge in Historical and Philosophical Forms of Argument." *Canadian Journal of Sociology* 12 (1987) 242–74.

Mullins, Terence Y. "Ascription As a Literary Form." *NTS* 19 (1973) 194–205.

———. "Disclosure: a Literary Form in the New Testament." *NovT* 7 (1972) 44–50.

———. "Formulas in New Testament Epistles." *JBL* 91 (1972) 380–90.

———. "Greeting As a New Testament Form." *JBL* 87 (1968) 418–26.

———. "Petition As a Literary Form." *NovT* 5 (1962) 46–54.

———. "Topos As a New Testament Form." *JBL* 90 (1980) 541–47.

Murphy–O'Connor, Jerome. *Paul: His Story.* Oxford: Clarendon, 2004.

———. *Paul the Letter-writer: His World, His Options, His Skills.* Collegeville: Liturgical, 1995.

———. *St. Paul's Corinth: Texts and Archaeology.* Good News Studies 6. Wilmington, DE: Glazier, 1983.

Nagy, Gregory. "Homeric questions." *TAPA* 122 (1992) 17–60.

———. *Poetry as Performance: Homer and Beyond.* Cambridge: Cambridge University Press, 1996.

Neirynck, Frans. *Duality in Mark: Contributions to the Study of the Markan Redaction.* BETL 31. Leuven: Leuven University Press, 1972.

Nelson, William "From 'Listen, Lordings' to 'Dear Reader.'" *University of Toronto Quarterly* 46.2 (1976) 110–24.

Neusner, Jacob. "The Rabbinic Traditions About the Pharisees Before 70 A.D.: The Problem of Oral Tradition." *Kairos* 14 (1972) 57–70.

Nevo, Ofra, Baruch Nevo, and Anat Derech-Zehavi. "The Tendency to Gossip as a Psychological Disposition: Constructing a Measure and Validating It." In *Good Gossip,* edited by Robert F. Goodman and Aaron Ben-Ze'ev, 180–89. Lawrence: University Press of Kansas, 1994.

Nickelsburg, George W. E. "Enoch, Levi and Peter: Recipients of Revelation in Upper Galilee." *JBL* 100 (1981) 575–600.

Nineham, Dennis. *The Use and Abuse of the Bible: A Study of the Bible in an Age of Rapid Cultural Change.* Library of Philosophy and Religion. New York: Barnes & Noble, 1976.

Niederwimmer, Kurt. "Johannes Markus und die Frage nach dem Verfasser des zweiten Evangeliums." *ZNW* 58 (1967) 172–88.

Norman, Donald A. *Things That Make Us Smart: Defending Human Attributes in the Age of the Machine.* Reading, MA: Addison-Wesley, 1993.

North, J. Lionel. "Paul's Protest that He Does not Lie in the Light of His Cilician Origin." *JTS* 47 (1996) 439–63.

O'Neill, Edward N. "Plutarch on Friendship." In *Greco-Roman Perspectives on Friendship*, edited by John T. Fitzgerald, 105–22. Resources for Biblical Study 34. Atlanta: Scholars, 1997.

O'Sullivan, Peter et al. "Lumbopelvic Kinematics and Trunk Muscle Activity during Sitting on Stable and Unstable Surfaces." *Journal of Orthopaedic and Sports Physical Therapy* 36 (2006) 19–25.

Oakman, Douglas E. "The Countryside in Luke-Acts." In *The Social World of Luke-Acts: Models for Interpretation*, edited by Jerome H. Neyrey, 151–79. Peabody: Hendrickson, 1991.

Ogbu, John U. "Minority Status and Literacy in Comparative Perspective." *Daedalus* 119.2 (1990) 141–68.

Ohly, Kurt. *Stichometrische Untersuchungen.* Beiheft zum Zentralblatt für Bibliothekswesen 61. Leipzig: Harassowitz, 1928.

Olson, David R. "Interpreting Texts and Interpreting Nature: The Effects of Literacy on Hermeneutics and Epistemology." In *The Written World: Studies in Literate Thought and Action*, edited by R. Säljö, 123–38. Berlin: Springer, 1988.

———. "Literacy." In *The MIT Encyclopedia of the Cognitive Sciences*, edited by Robert A. Wilson and Frank C. Keil, 481–82. Cambridge: MIT Press, 1999.

———. "Literate Mentalities: Literacy, Consciousness of Language, and Modes of Thought." In *Modes of Thought: Explorations in Culture and Cognition*, edited by David R. Olson and Nancy Torrance, 141–51. Cambridge: Cambridge University Press, 1996.

———. "Mind and Media: The Epistemic Functions of Literacy." *Journal of Communication* 38.3 (1988) 27–36.

———. *The World on Paper: The Conceptual and Cognitive Implications of Writing and Reading.* Cambridge: Cambridge University Press, 1994.

Ong, Walter J. "Before Textuality: Orality and Interpretation." *Oral Tradition* 3 (1988) 259–69.

———. *Interfaces of the Word: Studies in the Evolution of Consciousness and Culture.* Ithaca, NY: Cornell University Press, 1977.

———. "*Maranatha*: Death and Life in the Text of the Book." *Journal of the American Academy of Religion* 45 (1977) 419–49.

———. *Orality and Literacy: The Technologizing of the Word.* London: Methuen, 1982.

———. "Orality, Literacy and Medieval Textualization." *NLH* 16 (1984) 12.

———. *The Presence of the Word: Some Prolegomena for Cultural and Religious History.* New Haven: Yale University Press, 1967.

———. "The Psychodynamics of Oral Memory and Narrative: Some Implications for Biblical Studies." In *The Pedagogy of God's Image. Essays on Symbol and the Religious Imagination*, edited by Robert Masson, 55–73. Annual Publication of the College Theology Society 1981. Chico, CA: Scholars, 1981.

———. "Text As Interpretation: Mark and after." In *Oral Tradition in Literature: Interpretation in Context*, edited by John Miles Foley, 147–69. Columbia: University of Missouri Press, 1986.

———. "The Writer's Audience is Always a Fiction." *Publications of the Modern Language Association* 90 (1975) 9–21.

————. "Writing is a Technology that Restructures Thought." In *The Written Word: Literacy in Transition*, edited by Gerd Baumann, 23–48. Wolfson College Lectures 1985. Oxford: Clarendon, 1986.

Opland, Jeff. *Anglo-Saxon Oral Poetry: A Study of the Traditions*. New Haven: Yale University Press, 1980.

Orton, David E. *The Understanding Scribe: Matthew and the Apocalyptic Ideal*. JSNTSup 25. Sheffield: Sheffield Academic, 1989.

Osborn, E. F. "Teaching and Writing in the First Chapter of the *Stromateis* of Clement of Alexandria." *JTS* 10 (1959) 335–43.

Oster, R. "Numismatic Windows in the Social World of Early Christianity: A Methodological Enquiry." *JBL* 101 (1982) 195–223.

Packer, J. E. "Housing and Population in Imperial Ostia and Rome." *Journal of Roman Studies* 57 (1967) 80–95.

Paine, R. "Informal Communication and Information-Management." *Canadian Review of Social Anthropology* 7 (1970) 172–88.

Parássoglou, George M. "Δεξιὰ Χεὶρ καὶ Γόνου: Some Thoughts on the Postures of the Ancient Greeks and Romans When Writing on Papyrus Rolls." *Scrittura e Civiltà* 3 (1979) 5–21.

————. "A Roll upon His Knees." *Yale Classical Studies* 28 (1985) 273–76.

Parkes, M. B. *Pause and Effect: An Introduction to the History of Punctuation in the West*. Berkeley: University of California Press, 1993.

Parry, Adam. "Introduction." In *The Making of Homeric Verse: The Collected Papers of Milman Parry*, edited by Adam Parry, ix–lxii. Oxford: Clarendon, 1971.

Parry, Milman. *The Making of Homeric Verse: The Collected Papers of Milman Parry*. Edited by Adam Parry. Oxford: Clarendon, 1971.

Pattison, Robert. *On Literacy: The Politics of the Word from Homer to the Age of Rock*. New York: Oxford University Press, 1982.

Peabody, David Barrett. *Mark as Composer*. New Gospel Studies 1. Macon, GA: Mercer University Press, 1987.

Pease, A. S. "Sibylla." In *OCD* (1970) 984.

Peek, Philip M. "The Power of Words in African Verbal Art." *JAF* 94 (1981) 19–43.

Pesch, Rudolf. *Naherwartungen: Tradition und Redaktion in Mk 13*. Kommentare und Beiträge zum Alten und Neuen Testament. Düsseldorf: Patmos, 1968.

————. *Das Markusevangelium. 1. Teil: Einleitung und Kommentar zu Kap. 1,1–8,26*. Herders theologischer Kommentar zum Neuen Testament 2. Freiburg: Herder, 1976.

Petersen, Norman R. "The Reader in the Gospel." *Neot* 18 (1984) 38–51.

Pfeiffer, Rudolf. *History of Classical Scholarship: From the Beginnings to the End of the Hellenistic Age*. Oxford: Clarendon, 1968.

Piaget, Jean. *The Language and Thought of the Child*. 3rd ed. London: Routledge, 1959.

Pilch, John J. "Sickness and Healing in Luke-Acts." In *The Social World of Luke-Acts: Models for Interpretation*, edited by Jerome H. Neyrey, 181–209. Peabody, MA: Hendrickson, 1991.

Piñero, Antonio, and Jesús Peláez. *The Study of the New Testament: A Comprehensive Introduction*. Translated by David E. Orton and Paul Ellingworth. Tools for Biblical Study Series 3. Leiden: Deo, 2003.

Popper, Karl R. *Objective Knowledge: An Evolutionary Approach*. Oxford: Clarendon, 1972.

Prentice, W. K. "How Thucydides Wrote His History." *Classical Philology* 25 (1930) 117–27.

Price, M. E., and M. Pollack. "The Author in Copyright: Notes for the Literary Critic." *Cardozo Arts and Entertainment Law Journal* 10 (1992) 703–20.

Prior, Michael. *Paul the Letter-writer: The Second Letter to Timothy.* JSNTSup 23. Sheffield: Sheffield Academic, 1989.

Quinn, K. "The Poet and his Audience in the Augustan Age." In *ANRW* 2.30.1 (1982) 75–180.

Rasmussen, Susan J. "Modes of Persuasion: Gossip, Song, and Divination in Tuareg Conflict Resolution." *Anthropological Quarterly* 64 (1991) 30–46.

Rea, J. R. "Declaration of Church Property." In *The Oxyrhynchus Papyri* vol. 33, edited by P. Parsons et al., 105–8. London: Egypt Exploration Society, 1968.

Reicke, Bo. *The Roots of the Synoptic Gospels.* Philadelphia: Fortress, 1986.

Reiser, Marius. *Syntax und Stil des Markusevangeliums im Licht der Hellenistischen Volksliteratur.* WUNT 2/11. Tübingen: Mohr/Siebeck, 1984.

Rempel, D. M., et al. "A Randomised Controlled Trial Evaluating the Effects of Two Workstation Interventions on Upper Body Pain and Incident Musculoskeletal Disorders among Computer Operators." *Occupational Environmental Medicine* 63 (2006) 300–306.

Renoir, Alain. "Oral-formulaic Context: Implications for the Comparative Criticism of Medieval Texts." In *Oral Traditional Literature: A Festschrift for Albert Bates Lord*, edited by John Miles Foley, 416–39. Columbus, OH: Slavica, 1981.

Resnick, D. P., and L.B. Resnick. "Varieties of Literacy." In *Social History and Issues in Human Consciousness: Some Interdisciplinary Connections*, edited by Andrew E. Barnes and Peter N. Stearns, 171–96. New York: New York University Press, 1989.

———. "The Nature of Literacy: An Historical Exploration." *Harvard Educational Review* 47 (1977) 370–85.

Reynolds, L. D., and N. G. Wilson. *Scribes and Scholars: A Guide to the Transmission of Greek and Latin Literature.* 2nd ed. Oxford: Clarendon, 1974.

Rhoads, David M. *Israel in Revolution: 6–74 C.E. A Political History Based on the Writings of Josephus.* Philadelphia: Fortress, 1976.

———. "Performance Criticism: An Emerging Methodology in Second Testament Studies—Part I." *BTB* 36. 4 (2006) 118–33.

———. "Performance Criticism: An Emerging Methodology in Second Testament Studies—Part II." *BTB* 36 (2006) 164–84.

———. "Performance Events in Early Christianity: New Testament Writings in an Oral Context." In *The Interface of Orality and Writing*, edited by Annette Weissenrieder and Robert B. Coote. WUNT 1/260. Tübingen: Mohr/Siebeck, 2010.

Richards, E. Randolph. *The Secretary in the Letters of Paul.* WUNT 2/42. Tübingen: Mohr, 1991.

Riddle, Donald Wayne. "Early Christian Hospitality: A Factor in the Gospel Transmission." *JBL* 57 (1938) 141–54.

Riesner, Rainer. "Jesus as Preacher and Teacher." In *Jesus and the Oral Gospel Tradition*, edited by Henry Wansbrough, 185–210. JSNTSup 64. Sheffield: Sheffield Academic, 1991.

Rigg, H. A. "Papias on Mark." *NovT* 1 (1956) 161–74.

Robbins, Vernon K. *Jesus the Teacher: A Socio-rhetorical Interpretation of Mark.* Philadelphia: Fortress, 1984.

———."Writing As a Rhetorical Act in Plutarch and the Gospels." In *Persuasive Artistry: Studies in New Testament Rhetoric in Honor of George A. Kennedy*, edited by Duane F. Watson, 142–68. JSNTSup 50. Sheffield: JSOT Press, 1991.

Roberts, C. H. "Books in the Graeco-Roman World and in the New Testament." In *The Cambridge History of the Bible*. Vol. 1, *From the Beginnings to Jerome*, edited by G. W. H Lampe, 48–66. Cambridge: Cambridge University Press, 1970.

Roberts, J. H. *Die Brief aan Filemon*. Kaapstad: Lux Verbi, 1992.

———. "Inleiding tot die Studie van die Nuwe Testament — Prinsipiële Gesigspunte en Terreinverkenning." In *Handleiding by die Nuwe Testament, 1*, edited by A. B. Du Toit, 3–84. Pretoria: N. G. Kerkboekhandel, 1978.

Robinson, J. A. T. "How Small Was the Seed of the Church?" In *Twelve More New Testament Studies*, 95–111. London: SCM, 1984.

Roller, Otto. *Das Formular der Paulinischen Briefe: Ein Beitrag zur Lehre vom Antiken Briefe*. Beiträge zur Wissenschaft vom Alten und Neuen Testament 58. Stuttgart: Kohlhammer, 1933.

Rose, Mark. *Authors and Owners: The Invention of Copyright*. Cambridge: Harvard University Press, 1993.

Rosen, Edward. "The Invention of Eyeglasses." *Journal of the History of Medicine and Allied Sciences* 11 (1956) 13–46, 183–218.

Rosenberg, B. A. "Oral Sermons and Oral Narrative." In *Folklore: Performance and Communication*, edited by Dan Ben-Amos and Kenneth S. Goldstein, 75–101. Approaches to Semiotics 40. The Hague: Mouton, 1975.

Rosenberg, B. A. "The Complexities of Oral Tradition." *Oral Tradition* 2 (1987) 73–90.

Rosnow, Ralph L. "Psychology of Rumor Reconsidered." *Psychological Bulletin* 87 (1980) 578–91.

———. "Rumor as Communication: A Contextualist Approach." *Journal of Communication* 38.1 (1988) 12–28.

Rosnow, Ralph L., John L. Esposito, and Leo Gibney. "Factors Influencing Rumor Spreading: Replication and Extension." *Language & Communication* 8.1 (1988) 29–42.

Rosnow, Ralph L., and Gary Alan Fine. *Rumor and Gossip: The Social Psychology of Hearsay*. New York: Elsevier, 1976.

Rostovtzeff, M. *The Social and Economic History of the Hellenistic World*. Vol 2. Oxford: Clarendon, 1953.

———. *The Social and Economic History of the Hellenistic World*. Vol 3. Oxford: Clarendon, 1953.

Roth, Wolfgang. *Hebrew Gospel: Cracking the Code of Mark*. Yorktown Heights, NY: Meyer-Stone, 1988.

Rouse, Mary A., and Richard H. Rouse. *Authentic Witnesses: Approaches to Medieval Texts and Manuscripts*. Notre Dame: University of Notre Dame Press, 1991.

Russell, D. A. *Plutarch*. Classical Life and Letters. New York: Scribner, 1973.

Rysman, A. R. "How the 'Gossip' Became a Woman." *Journal of Communication* 27.1 (1977) 176–80.

Sabini, John, and Maury Silver. *Moralities of Everyday Life*. Oxford: Oxford University Press, 1982.

Saenger, Paul. "Silent Reading: Its Impact on Late Medieval Script and Society." *Viator* 13 (1982) 367–414.

———. "The Separation of Words and the Physiology of Reading." In *Literacy and Orality*, edited by David R. Olson and Nancy Torrance, 198–214. Cambridge: Cambridge University Press, 1991.

———. *Space Between Words: The Origins of Silent Reading*. Figurae. Stanford: Stanford University Press, 1997.

Safrai, S. "The Synagogue." In *The Jewish People in the First Century: Historical Geography, Political History, Social, Cultural and Religious Life and Institutions*. Vol 2, edited by S. Safrai and M. Stern, 908–44. Philadelphia: Fortress, 1976.

Saldarini, Anthony J. "The Social Class of the Pharisees in Mark." In *The Social World of Formative Chrisitanity and Judaism: Essays in Tribute to Howard Clark Kee*, edited by Jacob Neusner et al., 69–77. Philadelphia: Fortress, 1988.

———. *Pharisees, Scribes and Sadducees in Palestinian Society*. Wilmington, DE: Glazier, 1988.

Sanders, E. P. *The Tendencies of the Synoptic Tradition*. Cambridge: Cambridge University Press, 1969.

———. *Paul*. Past Masters. Oxford: University Press, 1991.

Sapir, Edward. "The Status of Linguistics as a Science." *Language* 5 (1929) 207–14.

Saunders, D., and I. Hunter. "Lessons from the 'Literatory': How to Historicise Authorship." *Critical Inquiry* 17 (1991) 479–509.

Sbordone, F. "Preambolo per l'edizione critica delle tavolette cerate di Pompei." *Rendiconti dell' Accademia di Archeologia, Lettere e Belle Arti* 51 (1976) 145–68.

Schein, Sylvia. "Used and Abused: Gossip in Medieval Society." In *Good Gossip*, edited by Robert F. Goodman and Aaron Ben-Ze'ev, 139–53. Lawrence: University Press of Kansas, 1994.

Schenkeveld, Dirk M. "Prose Usage of ἀκούειν 'to read.'" *CQ* 42 (1992) 129–41.

Schmidt, Karl Ludwig. "Die Stellung der Evangelien in der Allgemeinen Literaturgeschichte." In *Zur Formgeschichte des Evangeliums*, edited by Ferdinand Hahn, 126–228. Wege der Forschung 81. Darmstadt: Wissenschaftliche Buchgesellschaft, [1923] 1985.

Schmitzer, Ulrich. "Die Macht über die Imagination: Literatur und Politik unter den Bedingungen des Frühen Prinzipats." *Rheinisches Museum für Philologie* 145 (2002) 113–35.

———. "Authors: Classical Antiquity." In *Brill's New Pauly: Encyclopaedia of the Ancient World: Antiquity*, edited by Hubert Cancik and Helmuth Schneider, vol. 2. Leiden: Brill, 2002.

Schniewind, Julius. *Die Begriffe Wort und Evangelium bei Paulus*. Bonn: Georgi, 1910.

Schoedel, William R. *The Apostolic Fathers: A New Translation and Commentary* 5. *Polycarp, Martyrdom of Polycarp, Fragments of Papias*. London: Nelson, 1967.

Schoeps, Hans Joachim. *Paul: The Theology of the Apostle in the Light of Jewish Religious History*. Philadelphia: Westminster, 1961.

Scholes, Robert, and Robert Kellogg. *The Nature of Narrative*. New York: Oxford Univesity Press, 1966.

Schottenloher, Karl. *Books and the Western World: A Cultural History*. Translated by William D. Boyd and Irmgard H. Wolfe. Jefferson: McFarland, 1989 (Original work pub-lished 1968).

Schweizer, Eduard. *Der Brief an die Kolosser*. Zürich: Benziger, 1976.

Scribner, Sylvia, and Michael Cole. *The Psychology of Literacy*. Cambridge: Harvard University Press, 1981.

Senner, Wayne M. "Theories and Myths on the Origins of Writing: A Historical Overview." In *The Origins of Writing,* edited by Wayne M. Senner, 1–26. Lincoln: University of Nebraska Press, 1989.

Sherwin-White, A. N. *The Letters of Pliny: a Historical and Social Commentary.* Oxford: Clarendon, 1966.

Shibutani, Tamotsu. *Improvised News: A Sociological Study of Rumor.* An Advanced Study in Sociology. Indianapolis: Bobbs-Merrill, 1966.

———. "Rumor." In *International Encyclopedia of Sociology* 13 (1968) 570–85.

"The Shorthand Congress." *Science* 10.246 (21 October 1887) 194–95.

Simonsen, Hejne. "The Gospel Literature as a Source for the History of Primitive Christianity." *Studia Theologica* 37 (1983) 3–16.

Skeat, T. C. "The Length of the Standard Papyrus Roll and the Cost-advantage of the Codex." In *The Collected Biblical Writings of T. C. Skeat,* edited by J. K. Elliott, 65–70. Leiden: Brill, 2004. (Original essay published 1982.)

———. "Two Notes on Papyrus." In *Scritti in onore di Orsolina Mentevecchi,* edited by E. Bresciani, 373–78. Bologna: Editrice Clueb, 1981.

———. "The Use of Dictation in Ancient Book-production." *Proceedings of the British Academy* 42 (1956) 179–208.

———. "Was Papyrus Regarded as "Cheap" or "Expensive" in the Ancient World?" *Aegyptus* 75 (1995) 75–93.

Small, Jocelyn Penny. "Visual Copies and Memory." In *Orality, Literacy, Memory in the Ancient Greek and Roman World,* edited by E. Anne Mackay, 227–52. Mnemosyne Supplements 298 Leiden: Brill, 2008.

———. *Wax Tablets of the Mind: Cognitive Studies of Memory and Literacy in Classical Antiquity.* London: Routledge, 1997.

Smith, A. "On Audio Visual Technologies: A Future for the Printed World." In *The Written Word: Literacy in Transition,* edited by G. Baumann, 171–92. Oxford: Clarendon, 1986.

Smith, J. D. "The Singer or the Song? A Reassessment of Lord's 'Oral Theory.'" *Man* 12 (1977) 141–53.

Smith, Jonathan Z. "Good News Is No News: Aretalogy and Gospel." In *Christianity, Judaism and Other Greco-Roman Cults.* Vol. 1, edited by Jacob Neusner, 21–38. Leiden: Brill, 1975.

Smith, Morton. "Comments on Taylor's Commentary on Mark." *HTR* 48 (1955) 21–64.

———. "A Comparison of Early Christian and Early Rabbinic Tradition." *JBL* 82 (1963) 169–76.

Snyman, Andries H. "Hebrews 6.4–6 from a Semiotic Discourse Perspective." In *Discourse Analysis and the New Testament: Approaches and Results,* edited by Stanley E. Porter and Jeffrey T. Reed, 354–65. JSNTSup 170. Sheffield: Sheffield Academic, 1999.

Spacks, Patricia Meyer. *Gossip.* Chicago: University of Chicago Press, 1985.

Stambaugh, John E. "The Functions of Roman Temples." In *ANRW* 2.16.1 (1978) 554–608.

Stambaugh, John E., and David L. Balch. *The New Testament in Its Social Environment.* LEC 2. Philadelphia: Westminster, 1986.

Stange, E. "Diktierpausen in den Paulusbriefen." *ZNW* 18 (1918) 109–17.

Stark, Rodney. "Antioch as the Social Situation for Matthew's Gospel." In *Social History of the Matthean Community: Cross-Disciplinary Approaches,* edited by David L. Balch, 189–210. Minneapolis: Fortress, 1991.

Starr, Raymond J. "The Circulation of Literary Texts in the Roman World." *CQ* 37 (1987) 213–23.

———. "Reading Aloud: Lectores and Roman reading." *Classical Journal* 86 (1991) 337–43.

———. "The Used-book Trade in the Roman World." *Phoenix* 44 (1990) 148–57.

Stirewalt, M. Luther. "The Form and Function of the Greek Letter-essay." In *The Romans Debate*, edited by Karl P. Donfried, 175–206. Minneapolis: Augsburg, 1977.

Stock, Brian. *Augustine the Reader: Meditation, Self-Knowledge, and the Ethics of Interpretation.* Cambridge: Harvard University Press, 1996.

Stone, Lawrence. "Literacy and Education in England, 1640–1900." *Past & Present* 42 (1969) 69–139.

Stowers, Stanley K. *Letter Writing in Greco-Roman Antiquity.* LEC 5. Philadelphia: Westminster, 1986.

———. "Social Status, Public Speaking and Private Teaching: The Circumstances of Paul's Preaching Activity." *NovT* 26 (1984) 59–82.

Street, Brian V. *Literacy in Theory and Practice.* Cambridge Studies in Oral and Literate Culture 9. Cambridge: Cambridge University Press, 1984.

———. "Literacy Practices and Literacy Myths." In *The Written World: Studies in Literate Thought and Action*, edited by Roger Säljö, 59–72. Springer Series in Language and Communication 23. Berlin: Springer, 1988.

Stubbs, Michael. *Language and Literacy: The Sociolinguistics of Reading and Writing.* Routledge Education Books. London: Routledge, 1980.

Sutherland, C. H. V. "The Intelligibility of Roman Imperial Coin Types." *Journal of Roman Studies* 49 (1959) 46–55.

Svenbro, Jesper. "Phrasikleia—An Archaic Greek Theory of Writing." In *Literacy and Society*, edited by Karen Schousboe and Mogens Trolle Larsen, 229–46. Copenhagen: Akademisk, 1989.

Swearingen, C. Jan. "Oral Hermeneutics during the Transition to Literacy: The Contemporary Debate." *Cultural Anthropology* 1 (1986) 138–56.

Szaivert, Wolfgang, and Reinhard Wolters. *Löhne, Preise, Werte: Quellen zur Römischen Geldwirtschaft.* Darmstadt: Wissenschaftliche Buchgesellschaft, 2005.

Talbert, Charles H. "Oral and Independent or Literary and Interdependent? A Response to Albert B. Lord." In *The Relationships among the Gospels: An Interdisciplinary Dialogue*, edited by William O. Walker Jr., 93–102. Trinity University Monograph Series in Religion 5. San Antonio: Trinity University Press, 1978.

Tambiah, Stanley Jeyaraja. *Culture, Thought, and Social Action: An Anthropological Perspective.* Cambridge: Harvard University Press, 1985.

Tannen, Deborah. "The Myth of Orality and Literacy." In *Linguistics and Literacy*, edited by William Frawley, 37–50. Topics in Language and Linguistics. New York: Plenum, 1982.

———. "The Oral/Literate Continuum in Discourse." In *Spoken and Written Language: Exploring Orality and Literacy*, edited by Deborah Tannen, 1–16. Norwood, NJ: Ablex, 1982.

Tarn, W., and G. T. Griffith. *Hellenistic Civilization.* 3rd ed. London: Arnold, 1952.

Taylor, Vincent. *The Formation of the Gospel Tradition: Eight Lectures.* London: Macmillan, 1933.

———. *The Gospel according to St. Mark.* 2nd ed. London: Macmillan, 1966.

Teitler, H. C. *Notarii and Exceptores: An Inquiry into Role and Significance of Shorthand Writers in the Imperial and Ecclesiastical Bureaucracy of the Roman Empire (from the Early Principate to c. 450 A.D.).* Amsterdam: Gieben, 1985.

Theissen, Gerd. *The First Followers of Jesus: A Sociological Analysis of the Earliest Christianity.* Translated by John Bowden. London: SCM, 1978.

———. *The Social Setting of Pauline Christianity.* Edited and translated by John H. Schütz. Philadelphia: Fortress, 1982.

———. *Urchristliche Wundergeschichten. Ein Beitrag zur formgeschichtlichen Erforschung der synoptischen Evangelien.* Studien zum Neuen Testament 8. Gütersloh: Mohn, 1974.

Thomas, Rosalind. *Oral Tradition and Written Record in Classical Athens.* Cambridge Studies in Oral and Literate Culture 18. Cambridge: Cambridge University Press, 1989.

Tilley, John J. "The Problem for Normative Cultural Relativism." *Ratio Juris* 11 (1998) 272–90.

Treggiari, Susan. *Roman Freedmen during the Late Republic.* Oxford: Oxford University Press, 1969.

Trevor-Roper, Patrick. *The World through Blunted Sight: An Inquiry into the Influence of Defective Vision on Art and Character.* Rev. ed. London: Lane, 1988.

Troll, Denise A. "The Illiterate Mode of Written Communication: The Work of the Medieval Scribe." In *Oral and Written Communication: Historical Approaches,* edited by Richard Leo Enos, 96–125. Written Communication Annual 4. Newbury Park, CA: Sage, 1990.

Turner, E. G. *The Papyrologist at Work.* Greek, Roman and Byzantine Monographs 6. Durham: Duke University Press, 1973.

———. "Sniffing Glue." *Cronache Ercolanesi* 13 (1983) 7–14.

Turner, E. G., and P. J. Parsons. *Greek Manuscripts of the Ancient World.* 2nd ed. Oxford: Clarendon, 1987.

Tyson, Joseph B. "Sequential Parallelism in the Synoptic Gospels." *NTS* 22 (1976) 276–308.

Ussher, Robert G. "Letter Writing." In *Civilization of the Ancient Mediterranean: Greece and Rome,* edited by Michael Grant and Rachel Kitizinger, 3:1573–82. New York: Scribner, 1988.

Van den Hoek, Annewies. "Techniques of Quotation in Clement of Alexandria: A View of Ancient Literary Working Methods." *Vigiliae Christianae* 50 (1996) 223–43.

Van Galen, Gerard P. "Handwriting: Issues for a Psychomotor Theory." *Human Movement Science* 10 (1991) 165–91.

Vansina, Jan. *Oral Tradition: A Study in Historical Methodology.* Translated by H. M. Wright. 1961. Harmondsworth, UK: Penguin, 1965.

———. *Oral Tradition as History.* London: Currey, 1985.

Vermes, Geza. *Jesus the Jew: A Historian's Reading of the Gospels.* London: Collins, 1973.

Veyne, Paul. "The Roman Empire." In *A History of Private Life.* Vol. 1, *From Pagan Rome to Byzantium,* edited by Paul Veyne, 5–233. Cambridge, MA: Belknap, 1987.

Vielhauer, Philipp. *Geschichte der Urchristlichen Literatur: Einleitung in das Neue Testament, die Apokryphen und die Apostolischen Väter.* De Gruyter Lehrbuch. Berlin: de Gruyter, 1975.

Von Fritz, K. "Cynics." In *OCD* (1970) 305.

Vorster, J. N. "The Rhetorical Situation of the Letter to the Romans—An Interactional Approach." Ph.D. diss. Pretoria: University of Pretoria, 1991.

Votaw, Clyde Votaw. *The Gospels and Contemporary Biographies in the Greco-Roman World*. Philadelphia: Fortress, 1970. (Originally in *American Journal of Theology* 14 (1915) 45–73, 217–49).

Wainschenker, R., J. Doorn, and M. Castro. "Quantitative Values for Perceptual Notion of Speech Speed." *Medical Engineering & Physics* 24 (2002) 479–83.

Wardle, D. *Valerius Maximus* Memorable Deeds and Sayings, *Book 1: Translated with Introduction and Commentary*. Oxford: Clarendon, 1998.

Webb, R. "The Progymnasmata As Practice." In *Education in Greek and Roman Antiquity*, edited by Yun Lee Too, 289–316. Leiden: Brill, 2001.

Weeden, Theodore J. *Mark—Traditions in Conflict*. Philadelphia: Fortress, 1971.

Westcott, B. F. *Introduction to the Study of the Gospels*. London: Macmillan, 1896.

Westerink, L. G. *Anonymous Prolegomena to Platonic Philosophy: Introduction, Text, Translation and Indices*. Amsterdam: North-Holland, 1962.

Whallon, William. *Formula, Character, and Context: Studies in Homeric, Old English, and Old Testament Poetry*. Washington, DC: Center for Hellenic Studies, 1969.

White, John L. Epistolary Formulas and Cliches in Greek Papyrus Letters." In *SBL Seminar Papers* (1978) 289–319.

———. "Introductory Formulae in the Body of the Pauline Letter." *JBL* 90 (1971) 91–97.

———. *Light from Ancient Letters*. Foundations and Facets. Philadelphia: Fortress, 1986.

———. "New Testament Epistolary Literature in the Framework of Ancient Epistolography." In *ANRW* 2.25.2 (1984) 1730–56.

———. "Saint Paul and the Apostolic Letter Tradition." *CBQ* 45 (1983) 433–44.

Wilken, Robert L. *The Christians as the Romans Saw Them*. New Haven: Yale University Press, 1984.

Williams, Gordon. "Phases in Political Patronage of Literature in Rome." In *Literary and Artistic Patronage in Ancient Rome*, edited by Barbara K. Gold, 3–27. Austin: University of Texas Press, 1982.

Wincor, Richard. *From Ritual to Royalties: An Anatomy of Literary Property*. New York: Walker, 1962.

Wire, Antoinette C. *The Case for Mark Composed in Performance*. Biblical Performance Criticism Series 3. Eugene, OR: Cascade Books, 2011.

Wiseman, T. P. "Practice and Theory in Roman Historiography." *History* 66 (1981) 374–93.

Wittig, Susan. "Theories of Formulaic Narrative." *Semeia* 5 (1976) 65–91.

Wolf, Eric R. *Peasants*. Foundations of Modern Anthropology Series. Englewood Cliffs, NJ: Prentice-Hall, 1966.

Wood, Ellen Meiksins, and Neal Wood. *Class Ideology and Ancient Political Theory: Socrates, Plato and Aristotle in Social Context*. Blackwell's Classical Studies. Oxford: Blackwell, 1978.

Woodmansee, Martha. *The Author, Art, and the Market: Rereading the History of Aesthetics*. Social Foundations of Aesthetic Forms Series. New York: Columbia University Press, 1994.

———. "The Genius and the Copyright: Economic and Legal Conditions of the Emergence of the 'Author.'" *Eighteenth-Century Studies* 17 (1984) 425–48.

Woolf, G. 2000. "Literacy" In *The Cambridge Ancient History*. Vol. 11, part 2: *The High Empire, A.D. 70–192*, edited by A. K. Bowman, P. Garnsey, and D. Rathbone, 875–97. Cambridge: Cambridge University Press, 2000.

Worthington, Ian. "Greek Oratory and the Oral/Literate Division." In *Voice into Text: Orality and Literacy in Ancient Greece*, edited by Ian Worthington, 165–77. Mnemosyne Supplements 157. Leiden: Brill, 1996.

Wuellner, Wilhelm. "Fishermen." In *Interpreter's Dictionary of the Bible Supplementary Volume*, edited by Keith R. Crim, 338–39. Nashville: Abingdon, 1976.

Yates, Francis A. *The Art of Memory*. London: Routledge & Kegan Paul, 1966.

Yerkovich, S. "Gossiping as a Way of Speaking." *Journal of Communication* 27.1 (1977) 192–97.

Youtie, Herbert C. "Ἀγράμματος: An Aspect of Greek Society in Egypt." *Harvard Studies in Classical Philology* 75 (1971) 161–76.

———. "Because They Do Not Know Letters." *ZPE* 19 (1975), 101–8.

———. "Βραδέως Γράφων: Between Literacy and Illiteracy." *GRBS* 12 (1971) 239–61.

———. *The Textual Criticism of Documentary Papryi: Prolegomena*. 2nd ed. London: Institute of Classical Studies, University of London, 1974.

———. "Ὑπογραφεύς: The Social Impact of Illiteracy in Greco-Roman Egypt." *ZPE* 17 (1975), 201–21.

———. "P.Mich.inv.855: Letter from Herakleides to Nemesion." *ZPE* 27 (1977) 147–50.

Zias, Joseph. "Death and Disease in Ancient Israel." *Biblical Archaeologist* 54 (1991) 147–59.

Zimmerman, Alfred F. *Die urchristliche Lehrer: Studien zur Traditionskreis der Didaskaloi im frühen Urchristentum*. WUNT 2/12. Tübingen: Mohr/Siebeck, 1984.

Zinovieff, Sofka. "Inside Out and Outside In: Gossip, Hospitality and the Greek Character." *Journal of Mediterranean Studies* 1.1 (1991) 120–34.

Zumthor, Paul. "The Impossible Closure of the Oral Text." *Yale French Studies* 67 (1984) 25–42.

———. *Oral Poetry: An Introduction*. Theory and History of Literature 70. Minneapolis: University of Minnesota Press, 1990.

Index of Modern Authors

Index of Subjects

Index of Ancient Documents

∽

Greek and Latin Works

〜

Papyri

Herculaneum Papyri

Made in the USA
Middletown, DE
06 January 2017